Higher Education, Good Governance and Development

About the Editor

Anisur Rahman is currently Professor and Director, UGC-Human Resource Development Centre, Jamia Millia Islamia, New Delhi. He holds Masters degree in two disciplines–Economics (AMU) and Sociology, M. Phil and Ph. D (JNU). Before joining Jamia, he worked at the Institute of Applied Manpower Research, Planning Commission, and Government of India. His area of interest includes Migration and Diaspora, Gulf Social Demography, Issues of Higher Education and Minorities. He has published 4 books and over 23 Research Papers in Reputed Journals in India and Abroad. He has also contributed 28 chapters in edited books. Dr Rahman has presented over 60 Research Papers in several Conferences/ Seminar/ Workshops in India and Abroad. He has also visited France under Indo-French Social Scientist Exchange Programme thrice for research in 2010, 2013, and 2015. He has delivered over 100 invited talks at different institutions of higher learning in India and abroad. He is also a member of several academic bodies and editorial boards.

He may be contacted at arahman@jmi.ac.in, anis_1964@yahoo.co.uk

Higher Education, Good Governance and Development

Issues, Challenges and Prospects

Edited by
Anisur Rahman

CONCEPT PUBLISHING COMPANY PVT. LTD.
NEW DELHI-110059

ISBN-13: 978-93-88937-65-8

First Published 2020

Published and Printed by

Concept Since 1974

Concept Publishing Company Pvt. Ltd.
A/15-16, Commercial Block, Mohan Garden,
New Delhi-110059 (INDIA)
T : 91 11 25351460, 91 11 25351794
E : publishing@conceptpub.com; *W* : www.conceptpub.com

Cataloging in Publication Data--Courtesy: D.K. Agencies (P) Ltd. <docinfo@dkagencies.com>

Higher education, good governance and development : issues, challenges and prospects / edited by Anisur Rahman.
pages cm
Contributed articles.
Includes bibliographical references and index.
ISBN 9789388937658

1. Education, Higher—India. 2. India—Politics and government. 3. Human rights—India. 4. Sustainable development—India. I. Rahman, Anisur, 1964- editor.

LCC HC440.E5H54 2020 | DDC 338.954 23

Foreword

Education is the bedrock of development and growth in any society. It is the best tool to tap the human resource potential, and secure an input in development achievements from diverse fields like health, agriculture, engineering, environment, efficient public administration and private sector growth. It is an established fact that investment and innovations in higher education help social, economic and political advancements in any country. As the awareness levels of the youth increases, it can be chanellized to ensure a vibrant social dialogue, political debate and an empowered human resource that would help the country in raising its economic potential.

India too has been focussing on developing the human potential of students who are ready to take the next step into the world. With this in mind, our governments have been formulating education policies that will promote higher education institutions and their students to get an access to the best knowledge bases in the world. It will strengthen their foundations and also help them in identifying fields where they can innovate.

Our governments have been ably assisted in the task by academics and educators who have been giving their inputs in the fields of education in their own unique ways. Whether it is by pedagogy research methodology facilitating muti-disciplinary studies or by detailing new teachniques of teaching, inputs by our educators serve as an important guide for policy makers, teachers and students alike. Under the initiative of the Ministry of Human Resource Development, the UGC-HRDC of Jamia Millia Islamia has been trying to work on ways to collate information regarding various fields of studies, trans-disciplinary approaches of research methods that can be applied to various disciplines and new methods of learning.

Edited by Prof. Anisur Rehman, Director, UGC-HRDC, the book consists of valuable essays on science, social science and education. I hope inputs on subjects as diverse as environment and development of pedagogy, communications and higher education, of experienced teachers and researchers would be of great help to policy-makers and the teaching community. The book has been designed keeping in mind faculty members who come to UGC-HRDC at Jamia for development programmes. The book as the potential to expose the readers to modern approaches to teaching, development, governance, understanding globalization, human rights and uses of media.

I would like to wish the editor and contributors the very best in their effort to reach out to educationists, policy-makers and readers interested in the subject.

New Delhi
27-9-2019

Prof. Najma Akhtar
Vice Chancellor,
Jamia Millia Islamia

Acknowledgements

The idea of this book has a genesis. After wide discussions, over a period of time, with different resource persons and teacher participants attending Orientation and Refresher courses in UGC-Human Resource Developement Centre of Jamia Millia Islamia it was felt that no good book covering the syllabi of these UGC courses is available in India. With an objective to fill this vacuum the present book was conceived. All the resource persons who were contacted readily agreed to contribute their articles; their collective efforts and cooperation gave birth to this academic venture.

I extend my thanks to all scholars who contributed their papers to this volume. Some of the contributers did not show their anger on receiving reminders for delay in receiving their essays. Infact they responded via Email with a smile with an attachment of their article.The book is a collaborative exercise of all its contributers. I also extend my special thanks to Prof. Abdulrahim Vijapur of Aligarh Muslim University who rendered different kind of help from conception of the book till its publication.

My sincere thanks and gratitude are due to Prof Najma Akhtar, Vice Chancellor, Jamia Millia Islamia, New Delhi for having created academic friendly environment in the Campus of Jamia. She was kind enough to spare her valuable time to write the Foreword of the book.

I am thankful to HRDC Staff Members who helped me a lot in bringing out this volume. Ms. Shahla Tarannum and Mr. Faisal Farooqui deserve speical appreciation who provided all support whenever required. Mr. Waseem Ahmad and Ms. Naziya Ph.D. scholars, West Asian Studies, JMI, deserve special thanks and acknowledgement for their unstained support and cooperation throughout.

I would like to extend my heart-felt thanks to my colleagues, friends and well-wishers whose names have not been mentioned here but they helped me in this academic endeavour. I am really indebted to my family members—Nargis (wife), Tabish (son) and Tooba (daughter) who were indeed the sources of great strength to me. I will fail in my duty if I don't mention the name of Dr. Rushda Siddiqui who went through this entire manuscript and detected several errors and unfailing cooperation during the compilation of the volume.

Finally, Concept Publishing Company Pvt. Ltd.,, New Delhi, deserves appreciation for brining out the book for the benefit of all stockholders expecially, all scholars.

Anisur Rahman

Contents

List of Contributors

Aarti Shrivastava is Associate Professor, Department of Higher and Professional Education at the National University of Educational Planning and Administration, Ministry of Human Resource Development, New Delhi. She may be contacted at aartijnu@gmail.com

Abdulrahim P. Vijapur is Professor, Department of Political Science, AMU, Aligarh and Director, Centre for Nehru Studies. He may be contacted at arvijapur@gmail.com

Amna Mirza is currently Assistant Professor of Political Studies at SPM College, University of Delhi. She may be contacted at amna.mirza786@gmail.com

Anil Dutta Mishra is a distinguished Gandhian scholar and writer. He started his career as Assistant Professor in the Department of Nonviolence and Peace Studies, Jain Vishva Bharati University, Ladnun, Rajasthan. He may be contacted at anilduttamishra@gmail.com

Anisur Rahman is Professor and Director of UGC-HRDC Jamia Millia Islamia, New Delhi. He may be contacted at arahman@jmi.ac.in

Aslam Mahmood retired as professor from Jawharlal Nehru University, New Delhi. He may be contacted at aslammahmood@gmail.com

Atiqur Rahman is a Professor of Geography at Dept. of Geography, Jamia Millia Islamia, New Delhi, India. He may be contacted at ateeqgeog@yahoo.co.in

D.K. Giri is currently a visiting professor of International Politics at Jamia Millia Islamia, New Delhi. He may be contacted at dr.dkgiri@gmail.com

Fauzia Khan is Professor in Department of Teacher Training and Non Formal Education, Faculty of Education, Jamia Millia Islamia, New Delhi. fauziakhanjmi@yahoo.co.in

Ghulam Yazdani is presently working as an Associate Professor, Faculty of Law, Jamia Millia Islamia, New Delhi. He may be contacted at gyazdani@jmi.ac.in

Jasim Ahmad is Professor at IASE, Faculty of Education, Jamia Millia Islamia, New Delhi. He may be contacted at jahmad@jmi.ac.in

K. Srinivas is Professor of ICT at National University of Educational Planning and Administration (NUEPA), a Government of India, Ministry of Human Resource Development (MHRD) Institution in New Delhi. He may be contacted at drksvasu@gmail.com

L.C Singh. Professor of NCERT, New Delhi. He may be contacted at lcsinghphd@gmail.com

Md. Kalimuddin Ahmad Professor, Department of Mathematics, AMU, Aligarh, UP. He may be contacted at ahmad_kalimuddin@yahoo.co.in

Md. Zafar Mahfooz Nomani, Professor, Faculty of Law, AMU, Aligarh, UP.

Monowar Alam Khalid retired as Professor from Jawharlal Nehru University New Delhi in 2009. He may be contacted at makhalid2007@gmail.com

Mujibur Rehman is Assistant Professor in the K.R. Narayan Centre for Dalit and Minority Studies, Jamia Millia Islamia, New Delhi. He may be contacted at mujibrehman1971@gmail.com

Niharika Tiwari is Assistant Professor, Government P.G. College, Saidabad, Pryagraj, U.P. She did M. Phil and Ph. D., Jawaharlal Nehru University (JNU), New Delhi. She may be contacted at niharikatiwari15@gmail.com

S. Prabhakar is a Joint Director in Parliament of India (Lok Sabha), New Delhi. He may be contacted at sprabhakar_2000@yahoo.com

Prabodh Saxena, is a career civil servant from the Indian Administrative Service, is currently Principal Secretary Finance, Government of Himachal Pradesh. He may be contacted at pjhingan@hotmail.com

Sabiha Hussain is working as Professor and Director at Sarojini Naidu Centre for Women's Studies, Jamia Millia Islamia , New Delhi. She may be contacted at sabihajaz@gmail.com

Sadhna Shanker is an officer of the 1987 Batch of the Indian Revenue Service, currently posted as Principal Commissioner, Income Tax, Delhi. She may be contacted at sadhna99@hotmail.com

Sana Beg is an Assistant Professor in the Department of Management, School of Management and Business Studies, Jamia Hamdard, where she has been faculty since 2000. She may be contacted at sbeg@jamiahamdard.ac.in

Sanjay Kumar Tiwari Associate Professor & Dy. Director, UGC-ASC (HRDC) and Adjunct Faculty, Deptt. of Geology, Institute of Science, Banaras Hindu University, Varanasi. He may be contacted at sktiwari.bhu@gmail.com

Shabina Nishat Omar is Professor and Head, Department of English in Milli Al-Ameen College (for girls) affiliated to University of Calcutta in West Bengal for the last seventeen years. She may be contacted at shabinaomar@gmail.com

Sheetal Kapoor is a global face in the field of Consumer Affairs. Presently she is working as an Associate Professor in the Department of Commerce at Kamala Nehru College, University of Delhi, Delhi. She may be contacted at sheetal_kpr@hotmail.com

Shikha Kapur is an Associate Professor at the Department of Adult and Continuing Education & Extension (DACEE), Jamia Millia Islamia, New Delhi. She may be contacted at skapoor@jmi.ac.in

Soumini Ghosh is currently working as a Project Junior Consultant at the National Institute of Educational Planning and Administration.

Suresh Prasad Singh is presently Director of Cambridge Institute of Technology, Tatisilwai, Ranchi, Jharkhand. He may be contacted at sureshprasad_singh@yahoo.co.in

Syeda Afshana is a Senior Assistant Professor at Media Education Research Centre, University of Kashmir. She may be contacted at afshana@kashmiruniversity.ac.in

Tabasum Firdous is Associate Professor in Centre of Central Asian Studies, Kashmir University. She may be contacted at tfdm2@yahoo.com

Introduction

As India undergoes tremendous political, economic and social changes, the editor of this volume felt that it was time to organize a book to reflect some of the challenges faced, as well as highlight subjects and themes of relevance to social science researchers. It is an attempt to integrate thinkers, philosophy and the manner in which they would address the socio-political challenges of our times. The developments of modernization have percolated geography, ecology, economics and most importantly the constitutional development of the country. There is not a single aspect of our life that has not been affected by the changes in perception of history, or human rights or climate change, among many other subjects. This book is an attempt to introduce researchers and teachers from different fields about new developments in other areas. All chapters, in their own way emphasize the need for the readers to know about developments in various subjects, the manner whereby the government tries to meet the challenges of constant change through its policy making process and the areas that need more nuanced approaches by policy makers. Most importantly, it is a study in research methodology. Whether it is understanding how policies are drafted and implemented, or how programmes are designed and run, or how subjects are studied in various paradigms, the book aims to cover a wide gamut of research methodologies. Some chapters, like E-Content Development, detail the manner in which new policies regarding a subject (here it is education) have been dealt with by the government. It spells out the objective of the project, the rationale behind its aim and implementation, how the project would function in real time environment.

As most of the authors are educationists and teachers, they have contributed chapters on the issue of communication with students and how best to educated students at various levels. They have dealt with the theories of education, communication and experimentation to educate. A major component of the chapters, include use of advanced technology to effectively bring about changes in the methods of teaching and learning. They have elaborated on the efforts of both the government policy makers as well as teachers on the inclusion of technology in the methodology of communication and teaching.

The book has been divided into five sections based on the relevance of the subjects. The emphasis in the classification is on the author's understanding of the subject that has been analyzed using different paradigms of research, diverse research methodologies and perspectives. The selection of hypothesis and arguments validating or rebutting have been done by authors using unique methods of logic. There are subjects that are universal in their impact, but have been included to allow the readers to formulate local solutions using global understanding and precedents.

The First Section of the book deals with the issue of education. It seeks to highlight the fact that education cannot be limited to class-room learning. Every individual learns through various media. The process of education could be as banal as lectures in class by teachers, to innovative advertisement campaigns by governments and civil society organizations that seek to inform people about changes, policies, lacunae in policies and create awareness about changes that are affecting the every individual. The authors have attempted to highlight the need to innovate and constantly work towards new techniques of education keeping in mind the changing socio-political dynamics as well as innovations in technology. Basic understanding of education as a process of transforming the personality of learners through various approaches and methods of teaching and learning has been developed throughout the book. Different approaches to education have been analyzed and evaluated, leaving it to the readers to choose their approaches and method of teaching. Authors, while being partial towards an integrated approach to teaching, have been detailed and unbiased in explaining comparative approaches.

L.C. Singh, in the chapter Scientific Approach of Teaching, studies the various approaches of teaching and learning. It is argued that if there is a satisfactory theory of learning and the teacher can act upon this theory without developing a separate theory of teaching, then teaching can be understood in terms of learning. Psychologists, scientists, social scientists, all have attempted to formulate and articulate theories of teaching. Though teaching and learning are specific processes yet they are highly associated with each other. However, teaching however, needs to be studied separately. While learning theories of learning were formulated by conducting experiments on animals, teaching theories of teaching however, have been developed by dealing with human's subjects in normal situations. So a teacher needs to understand the process of both teaching and learning to successfully educate the students.

Jasim Ahmed has authored the chapter on Pedagogical Understanding of Teaching and Learning. He argues that no society is static, so is the child's and individual's interest and needs are also dynamic. Therefore, teachers also require making them up-to-date in terms of the knowledge explosion, methodology of teaching, learners' psychology and other factors that affect teaching and learning process. Active participation in the process of learning makes learners understand concepts deeply and develop the ability of application and higher order thinking skills which are essentials of healthy and successful life in the present day competitive and innovative society.

K. Srinivas has written the chapter, Adoption of e-Resources and Learning Management Systems for innovative Teaching & Learning and Effective Class room Interaction. Here he discusses the role of Information and Communication Technology as a major driving force in contemporary education system. UGC has been utilizing the resources of its IUCs, specially CEC and INFLIBNET in providing ICT educational support for education and research, both in colleges and university sector. While technology is extremely useful in research and education, it carries with itself challenges of space and time.

Shikha Kapur, in the chapter Communication Skills for Effective Teaching, has studied various means and methods of communication that are used as teaching tools. She elaborates how the use of appropriate Communication skills is the key to effectiveness in the teaching and learning process between the teachers and the students. For effective teaching teachers have to develop appropriate communication skills. They have to be both expressive as well as receptive. They have to be skilled in explaining concepts simply and clearly and also be skilled at listening.

Shabina N. Omar has authored the chapter, Inclusive Education as an Equitable Option for Disabled Children, where she deals with the important but grossly neglected subject of education of the differently abled children. Disabled children are often denied education as they are excluded, ostracised, marginalised and neglected. Even if they attend school, they are more likely to drop out early. The level of schooling they receive is usually inferior to that of their peers. The children with disabilities often do not go to school because of inadequate infrastructure and facilities suitable to their special needs.

S.K. Tiwari in the chapter titled: E-Content Development: A New Paradigm Shift in Higher Education in India looks at policy initiative of the MHRD, under its National Mission on Education through ICT (NMEICT) launched in 2009. The policy is ambitious with a potential to reach out to students, researchers and teachers across the country. It meets the challenge of education outreach using technology. ICT provides new opportunities for capturing, storing, disseminating and communicating a wide variety of information. The availability of variety and rapid expansion of databases has made inclusion and integration of ICT in teaching and learning inevitable.

Fauzia Khan in the chapter Some Issues and Challenges in Higher Education discusses the challenges faced in the field of education. Problems arise in the field of higher education as a result of an increasing population and lack of resources to invest in infrastructure for providing the right education to the youth. As a result there is a mismatch between employability of the students and demands of the industry. A faulty education system is largely responsible for the socio-economic problems faced by the country today.

Arti Srivastava & Soumini Ghosh combined to write the chapter, Higher Education in India: Policy Contestations, where they have evaluated the only two Education Policies formulated at the national level since independence. In their analysis, they conclude that the two education policies were very idealistic in nature but left much to be desired in reality. There have been serious gaps between the vision of the policies and their implementation. The disconnect between political will to bring about qualitative and quantitative changes and the idealism of the policy makers has taken a toll on education.

The **Second section** of the book deals with the changing dimensions of Democracy, Globalization and Development.

S. Prabhakar's chapter, Evolution of Parliamentary Democracy in India Today, is one of the most important chapters of the book. It discusses the history and more importantly, uses the empirical research methodology to detail the functioning of one of the largest democracies in the world. Yes, there are problems in formulating laws and policy making, but understanding the procedures and precedents are a good way of beginning to look for a solution.

Anil Dutt Mishra, author of the chapter Debating Gandhi, has argued that the ideology formulated by the Mahatma needs to be studied and understood as it may be the best way to providing a solution to today's socio-political dilemmas. Gandhian principles are capable of mitigate the greatest challenge of the modern age. Gandhi was a thinker and as a phenomenon need to be understood and analysed. In order to come out of the present malaise and dilemma, the only remedy lies is in adopting Gandhian path to resolve conflicts.

D.K. Giri's chapter, The Quest for Real Independence, deals with the complex subject of pluralism using theoretical concepts articulated by various political theorists and activists. An important topic for any social scientist is the concept of pluralism. In the Indian context, Dr. Giri evaluates how the subject has been understood by different political leaders and civil society movements. Pluralism is the bedrock of a multi-cultural society and polity. While it gives a rich diversity to the demographic profile, it also poses a challenge to a polity that is trying to fit in the mould of a nation-state.

Mujibur Rehman's chapter, rearticulating the Notion of Communalism in Post- 2014 India, is important for its contemporariness. He argues that the manner in which the intolerance debate has unfolded, it appears as if the notion of "intolerance" has a greater explanatory power than communalism. The "notion of intolerance", is only one of the many tendencies of communalism. He has analyzed the many dimensions of communalism and its impact on the socio-political fabric of the country and its implications for Muslims.

Amna Mirza's chapter, Issues of Globalization, has dealt with the globalization as a vehicle for change. She explains its integrative and transnational character and its impact on society, economy and technology. While it leads to development on one hand that is visible in the development of various goods and services, it also has the impact of destroying ecology, human relations and economic equations. On one hand, that is integrating economy, culture and governance but at the other hand, it is fragmenting societies.

Tabasum Firdous's chapter, India's Neighborhood Policy, uses the foreign policy of India to explain the problems that a democracy faces. She lists the evolution of India's neighbourhood policy under the Prime Ministers from the time of Independence. What is important in this approach is to remember that though the country is a democracy, the role of the PM is instrumental in shaping the course of history. Policies are framed and designed keeping the priorities of the current PM in mind.

The **Third section** of the book deals with media and communication. In this day and age we tend to take the media for granted forgetting its diversity and the impact that each form of media has on different sections of the population. From the formal print and audio-visual media that has come under the ambit of government control and regulation, to the spurt of social media that uses various platforms like the internet and telephones, the outreach and impact of the different forms have been discussed in the various chapters. The media is a powerful tool to educate the literate and the illiterate and a means to communicate. Used differently, communication is a teaching tool. It can be used as a social change campaign or as a mechanism for teaching various subjects to children. The role of communication in bringing about change cannot be underestimated. The section takes a look at different concerns that the country is facing in different fields. It deals with issues that range from re-interpreting leaders, to understanding the problems of women in relation to religion, to communalism and shifts in the formulation of foreign policy.

Abdulrahim P. Vijapur's chapter, Understanding the Concept of Human Rights: Meaning and Evolution of Rights, discusses the evolution of the terms rights and human rights. He concludes that as man is a social being and cannot live outside society (as he/she is not self-sufficient for one's needs), the problem of rights arose involving man's relations with other individuals in a society, and his relations with State/ government. Through these relationships men evolved certain norms of social behaviour, which got crystallized, over centuries' struggles, into what we call today as human rights. These rights have evolved through various struggles in history and need to be understood if we want to safeguard the human rights of every man, woman and child in the world.

Prabodh Saxena's chapter, Status of Right to Information in India, discusses one of the most important tools for accountability in a democracy, particularly India, The Right to Information. Going from the evolution of the concept of accountability, he traces the origin of the RTI Act and the manner in which it has grown in strength. He carefully studies the problems of the mechanism, and the possible pitfalls it can fall into, despite the fact that it is supposed to be an act that empowers the weakest of the weak.

Sheetal Kapoor in the chapter, Protection of Consumer Rights in India, highlights how we tend to see consumer rights as something that is secondary and not a part of our daily rights. The author addresses this lack of education regarding the rights of consumers, particularly in an economy that is part capitalist. Our government, along with global agencies have addressed the issue and formulated laws for safeguarding the interests of every consumer. The most important take from the chapter is the process of understanding an issue and formulating policies or laws regarding it. Each policy or law has to be futuristic in its outlook, encompass every citizen and is a measure to protect every individual.

Syeda Afshana's chapter Role of Media in Society, analyses the various theories regarding the social impact of various media. There is a strong link between the media, the government and various forces of change. The media informs and explains the effect of decisions taken by the government. But this is just one facet of media and because media is such an integral part of our lives, it generates a great deal of debate about the workings, role and impact of media itself. We need to look both media and society from a sociological perspective which allows us to consider the role of media in our individual lives but in context of broader social forces like economy, politics and technological developments, thereby allowing us to understand the dynamics of media and society from a multi-pronged approach.

Sabiha Hussain, in the chapter titled Gender and Sexuality in Islam: An interface of Patriarchy, Religion and Customary Practices, has dealt with the complex co-relation between gender, religion and their evolution with time. In light of the issues regarding the welfare and well-being of Muslim women, we felt it was important for the readers to read about the issues regarding patriarchy and sexuality in the community. The chapter is important for multiple reasons, primarily as a social science research methodology example of using a case study with primary and secondary sources to validate hypotheses in the field of gender studies. The author has attempted to analyze gender equations within the framework of religion, interpretation of religious texts, political and social influencers. This is how social history, stigmas and traditions are created and perpetuated.

Dr. Ghulam Yazdani in his article highlights the Cyber Crime issues in India. He argues that women in our society are subject to be a soft target by individuals or inmates through computers and modern tools of communications. Although many laws have been adopted by rule of the law but still there are many lacuna which pushes our younger generation to commit and bear the burn. Indian women in the age of information technology are not safe either on computer or by using various social sites. Therefore he tries to cover up cyber crime issues in India and its implications for upcoming young generation.

The **Fourth section** of the book deals with the issues of Growth, Governance and Development. In this scenario, Suresh Prasad Singh's chapter, Inclusive Growth and Sustainable Development, uses the concept of Inclusiveness in elaborating the variables that constitute sustainable development. He emphasizes that quality of the variables are more important in ensuring that every citizen of the country benefits from a policy of development. From education and environmental development to economic policies, it is important for them to be structured in a manner that they include all citizens. The chapter takes into consideration factors and forces that have shaped international laws. It covers the dilemma of development at the cost of ecological degradation, fallout of which is violation of human rights.

Anisur Rehman, in the chapter, Indian Diaspora: A factor for Development and Social Change, explores the potential of Diasporas to influence socio-political change in both the home and adopted country. There is a specific pattern that has been established with time, used by the Diasporas to influence politics, economy and society.

Niharika Tiwari in her chapter, Good Governance and Human Development: A Conceptual Analysis has discussed the definitions of the concepts as well as the co-relations between the two. The words 'Governance', 'Good-governance', and 'Government' are related to same realm but have different meanings. All the terms and actors are inter-connected in a symbiotic relationship that impacts every citizen of the world. All three are the keys ensuring positive human development.

Sana Beg gives an extremely important contribution, particularly in the field of research methodology. In the chapter, Introducing Islamic Banking in India for Economic Growth and Social Welfare, she takes the framework of Islamic Banking, complete with its spirit and details, and checks for its feasibility as an economic principle in Indian economics.

Sadhna Shankar uses the case study of the Pulse Polio Campaign in the chapter, Development Communication: case study of the pulse polio campaign, to show how various communication tools can be used to educate masses outside of a classroom. Creating awareness about a subject and responsibly educating a large population is a challenge. The outreach has to be widespread, while the message needs to be crisp, short and effective.

The **Last section** of the book deals with some of the many challenges to human development. The subjects vary from climate change to sustainable development and various variables that can provide a solution to challenges.

Atiqur Rahman, author of the chapter, addressing some of the Issues and Concern of Climate Change and Its Impact at the Global Level, meticulously gives proof of the changes that the global ecological exploitation has been having on the world, since 1900. He argues that climate change is not a myth. Global carbon emissions from fossil fuels have significantly increased resulting in patterns of change in temperature, water levels and land mass. The chapter has meticulously documented the implications climate change will have on humans as a population by 2100. If we take the case of India, the ongoing climate change impact of climate changê, it is expected that there will be more frequent droughts in some region, particularly in north-western part of like, Jharkhand, Orissa and Chhattisgarh. Also there will be unexpected and substantial fall in yield of crop because of extreme rise in atmospheric temperature by 2040s due to climate change.

Monowar Alam Khalid, in the chapter Biodiversity Conservation—Key for Sustenance of Lifc, discusses the problem of an endangered bio-diversity and the critical need for preserving the ecological cover of the planet is important for the survival of the human race. He reiterates that we may have decline in species populations, lesser ecosystem services, increased droughts and floods, outbreak of diseases due to increased pests, if we are not careful about preserving our ecology.

Zafar Naomani's chapter on Environment and Sustainable Development Law: Theoretical and Juridical Framework deals with the issues of definition of sustainable development and policy making. The recognition of environmental problems is inseparable from those of human welfare and the process of economic development. An important component of virtually all definitions of sustainable development is to foster equity encompassing economic, human, environmental, and technological dimensions. One of the challenges that society faces today is framing laws that balance all the variables and deliver human welfare.

Aslam Mahmood's chapter Population and Sustainable Development in The Third World: A case study of India, discusses the issue of population as a deterrent factor in development, particularly in India, a developing country with an increasing population. He discusses different theories of dealing an expanding population. While Malthus looked at the causal issues, Marx and later social scientists have been dealing with the management of the rising demographic. The author concludes that the phenomenal success of India on food production and literacy etc., suggests that if similar efforts are made in social sectors also, population control will not be an unachievable target.

Md. Kalimuddin Ahmad in his chapter starts by highlighting the use of science and technology in day to day life during Greeks and Roman periods. He further points out how Indian and Chines lerned the technological advancement from various other civilizations. More precisely he discusses the effectiveness and use of technology in present time. He inspires youth by remembering the contribution of our great scientists such as late Dr. A.P.J. Abdul Kalam and his remarkable achievements in the fields of science and technology. Indeed new inventions and innovative ideas are needed to inculcate among Indian upcoming generations.

Prof. Anisur Rahman
Editor

SECTION-I

Pedagogy, Communications and Higher Education

1

Scientific Approach of Teaching

L.C. Singh

Introduction

Better understanding of the scientific method is a common component of pleas for increased literacy. It is argued that if there is a satisfactory theory of learning and the teacher can act upon this theory without developing a separate theory of teaching, then teaching can be understood in terms of learning. As a result teaching had been seen as a mirror image of learning. There is, however, much learning without formal teaching. Individuals learn through maturation, observation and life experience. A theory of teaching answers three questions: how do teachers behave, why do they behave as they perform and with what effect.

Classroom learning is an outcome of teaching. All teaching does not result in learning and all learning cannot be attributed to teacher. During the last century, rapid advances in Psychology took place that dominated the neglect of Pedagogy or the theories of learning influenced the concept of teaching. Pedagogy is the science and art of education, specifically instructional theory. An instructor develops conceptual knowledge and manages the content of learning activities in pedagogical settings. It involves being able to convey knowledge and skills in ways that students can understand, remember and apply.

It applies for all teachers, students and situations where teaching occurs. It considers the teacher-behaviour as the cause and student's learning effect. It explains, predicts and controls ways a teacher's behaviour affects learning of students. A theory of teaching must answer questions of teaching for effective learning, and also has following advantages:

- Theories of teaching explain the relationship between teaching and learning and indentifies common factors.
- Theories of teaching give knowledge about the assumptions of teaching activities that provide guidelines for organizing teaching.
- Designs for instruction can be developed with the help of Theories of teaching.
- Theories of teaching provides a scientific basis for planning, organizing, leading and evaluation of the teaching.
- Classroom problems may be studied scientifically through Theories of teaching.
- Pupil-teachers can develop teaching skills and competency by employing knowledge from theory of teaching.
- Teaching objectives may be successfully achieved by using Theories of teaching.
- Teachers are able to get better results by using Theories of teaching.
- N.L. Gage suggests that theories of teaching may be used to increase the understanding, prediction and control of teaching.

The theories of teaching and learning have some common relationships. They do not mirror each other but are closely related. Any theory of learning is broader than a theory of teaching, and the behaviour of a teacher is only one factor in education. There are many different theories regarding the way people learn. For example, Behaviourism assumes a learner is essentially passive, and will be shaped through positive or negative reinforcement; Cognitivism focuses on what happens in the mind such as thinking and problem-solving; Constructivism is about learning being an active, contextualized process of constructing knowledge rather than acquiring it; Experiential learning is about the learner experiencing things for themselves and learning from them. There are a lot of theories that help educators understand how best their students can learn. Learning needs to be understood as a more embracing experience than teaching.

Teaching is an Activity

According to N.L. Gage, teaching is an activity of one person intended to facilitate learning by another. The activity generally involves language, rational thinking and intellectual process, but it is not always so.

Teaching proceeds by many different ways and methods — old and new. These can be grouped according to number of students being taught as given below:

One student at a time	- Tutoring, seat work, CAI.
2 to 20 students at a time	- discussion, role playing, simulation and gaming
20-50 students at a time	- Classroom Teaching
50 students and above	- Lecture, film, T.V., radio, teleconferencing

Classroom teaching incorporates many other methods. like personalized teaching, lectures in classrooms, discussion for large groups, and many more that care commonly called as Teaching Styles. Teaching styles are set of different teacher-pupil behaviour patterns within a class.

Art of Teaching

What is Art? It is dedicated to creation of beauty and it is for evocation of aesthetic pleasure. It is a process that calls for intuition, creativity, improvisation and expressiveness. Now let us examine how teaching can be a form of Art. Teaching can be a practical and useful art but definitely not creation of beauty or aesthetic pleasure. Watching impressionable minds turn on to new ideas is what truly represents the real art of teaching. Educators face a constantly changing environment, one that is shaped by emerging trends, fiscal challenges and organizational pressures. And yet through it all they adapt, they improvise and they overcome — all in an effort to teach.

The concept of teaching is a departure from rules, principles, formulae, method. It shows that in teaching there is a need for artistry. No one can prescribe twists and turns taken by a lecturer. A classroom teacher uses judgment, insight, sensitivity and agility to promote learning. Use of motivational devices, examples and pace of teaching are based on a teachers' intuition and judgment. In face to face situations too, interaction provides opportunity for ARTISTRY.

In art, we study holistic qualities rather than analytically derived quantities. The viewpoint regarding the use of "inside" rather than an objective external view, has been developed for criticism of literature, visual arts and music. As an illustration, while judging human face as beautiful or ugly, quantitative scheme of physical measurement has not yet succeeded in specifying what makes a face beautiful or plain. We use our ability to perceive integrated pattern of features to appreciate, describe and judge faces. The ability to look at a student (young or old) see where he/she is currently and bring some inspiration to them to learn something is an ART form. Learning might be a science, but teaching is an art.

Science of Teaching

When a chemist uses available knowledge, he practices science and not art, to obtain almost completely predictable results. Specific elements and compounds are brought together under certain conditions. However, when scientists research by using judgment, intuition and insight in handling the unpredicted, it becomes a work of art like painting or a poem.

In order to be an educator, and a good educator, one needs to know the formula for education. It takes knowledge of curriculum, behaviour, philosophy, psychology and other areas to successfully become an educator. A scientist working in a lab (inside or outside) needs to consistently factor several variables and constants when doing experiments to successfully reach the desired outcomes. In education, these outcomes are called "learning." The aim of every educator is to ensure that the students want to learn.

Need for Scientific Basis of Teaching as Humanistic Art

In teaching when artistic elements are unavoidable, a scientific base can also be developed. Teaching is not a science by itself but using science to achieve practical ends requires artistry and knowledge comprising laws that require scientific basis.

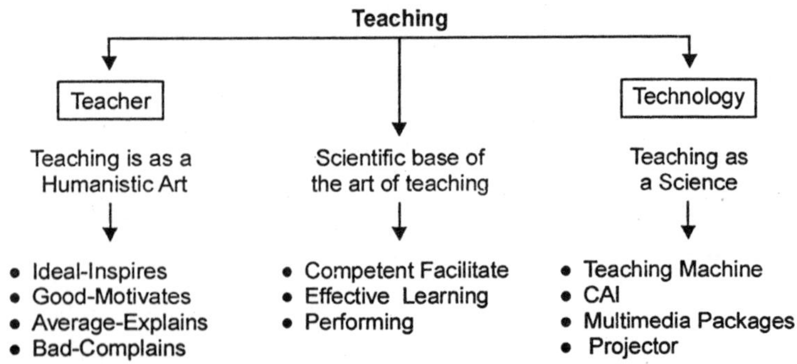

Landmarks in Search of Scientific Basis of the State of Art of Teaching

I. Teaching as a Communication Process

Communication is a process of sharing or exchanging experiences, information, ideas, opinions, sentiments, thoughts and feelings etc. between the source of communication and the receiver through some mutually agreeable or known media (verbal or non-verbal). Communication is a two-way process. There is a sender and a receiver. Effective communication refers to getting message across to the receiver. It is the sender's responsibility to make sure that the receiver gets the message and that the message received is the one sent. Based on Morse Key Communication Model, teaching is considered as the communication process.

The various components of communication paradigm of teaching are shown below:

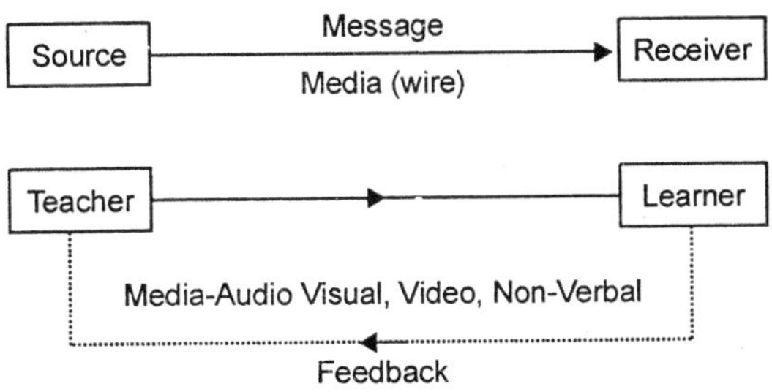

The process of communication starts by identifying a source. In teaching-learning process, the teacher is regarded as the source of communication, imparting knowledge to students, or the contents of communication with the help of verbal and non-verbal media. For transmission, a teacher organizes communication material in the proper shape then searches for an appropriate media, verbal (spoken or written words) or non-verbal (gestures, sign language, body language etc.).

For conveying information and ideas by verbal or non-verbal means, one has to make use of a transfer mechanism known as encoding. For transmitting response or feedback receiver takes help of encoding his response in verbal or non-verbal symbols. The quality and effectiveness of the process of communication is affected by the presence of intervening variables between the source of communication and receiver.

In order to develop communication skills in relation with the teaching process we must identify the future needs. Interaction between teachers and students can contribute to effective communication in the classroom or may be the source of problematic situations. When communication is effective, both the student and the teacher benefit. Communication makes learning easier, helps students achieve goals, increases opportunities for expanded learning, strengthens the connection between student and teacher, and creates an overall positive experience.

II. Teaching According to System's Approach

The second landmark in the scientific approach to teaching is System Approach that deals with systematic planning, designing, construction and evaluation of education system. It helps develop, implement and evaluate the education system, curriculum and designing of lesson. System approach advocates making continuous comparisons of different roles played by man, machine and media in the system of Education.

System is a process incorporating all aspects and parts, namely pupils, teachers, curriculum, content, instructional strategies, physical environment and the evaluation of instructional objectives. The system provides a framework for visualizing internal and external environmental factors as an integrated whole. It is a way of thinking that helps us recognize the nature of complex problems and provides insights enabling us to operate within the perceived environment.

System approach is a way of identifying goals of any system and scientifically working out different steps to move towards goals. The approach in general includes the following steps:

- Analyse the existing situation.
- Set goal for the desired situation.
- Define mechanism to evaluate the achievement of goals.
- Create alternative situation.
- Select most appropriate solution through cost benefit analysis.
- Work out layout of the system.
- Design monitory mechanisms for the system.
- Plan introducing new solution.

Instructional System and its Components

In education planned, organized use of all available learning resources, including audio-visual media, to achieve the desirable learning objectives by the most efficient means is possible.

The system approach focuses first upon learner and the performance required of him, and then take decisions regarding course content, learning experiences and the most effective media and instructional strategies for realizing the objectives.

The Instructional System employs the following steps:

- Defining instructional objectives in behavioural terms or measuring terms.
- Determining functions created to the achievement of the objectives by appropriate multi-media approach.
- Defining learner's characteristics or entering behaviour.
- Selecting appropriate instructional strategies for effective learning.
- Selecting suitable learning experiences for available alternatives.
- Choosing appropriate instructional aides, resources to facilitate student learning.
- Defining and assigning appropriate personal roles: teachers of team teaching members and supporting personal students.
- Implementing the programme — try out with a small group of pupils in appropriate condition.
- Evaluating the pupils learning outcome in terms of learning objectives.
- Revising if necessary to improve the efficiency of the system to improve student learning.

The system approach takes education as a system having a set of *input* which are subjected to a process, designed to produce certain *outputs* which are intended to meet the stipulated *objectives* of a system. Application of this type takes the system of education as a whole and views it in the context of the specific objectives and functioning of its interrelated parts and the whole system under the existing constraints. If the system meets the objectives, it is maintained else it is modified. As a result various alternative strategies and tactics are explored, designed and implemented and the most appropriate and feasible one is retained.

The system approach applied to educational situations includes: input, process, output and feedback. These are interlinked and interdependent and can be described as:

(a) Planned input and processes involving learning materials and strategies suitably organized to cater to the needs of a particular group of students,
(b) Explicitly stated standard of outcome performances, including sequence behavioural objectives,
(c) Monitoring output that is used to revise, improve and evaluate the instructional system, providing feedback to the learner and teacher, and
(d) A degree of in-built flexibility to adjust to individual situations.

System approach can be applied for the development of educational administration, organization, examination system, system of instruction, models of teacher-education, models of curriculum and educational and vocational guidance system. These three approaches can be applied simultaneously for education and training.

System Approach to Instructional System

Robb (1974) analysed an instruction system and suggested that an instructional system can be employed into three phases: Planning, Execution and Evaluation. These phases involve seven steps and indicate the development of instructional system.

Phase 1. — Planning instructional system. (INPUT)

Step (1) Defining objectives
Step (2) Pre-assessment or determining entering behaviour.
Step (3) Specifying appropriate strategies.

Phase 2. — Execution of instruction. (PROCESS)

Step (4) Defining and assigning personnel roles.
Step (5) Synthesizing and implementing the system of instruction.

Phase 3.—Evaluation of Instruction. (OUTPUT)

Step (6) Evaluation and outcome.
Step (7) Analysing results and modifying the system.

The paradigm based on system approach is given below:

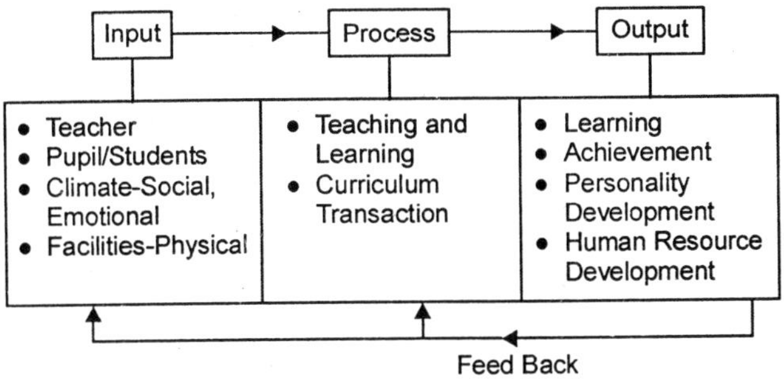

III. Gage Model of Teaching Effectiveness

The Father of the field of research on Teaching, N.L. Gage, designed a model that is a modified framework of the systems approach as applied to teaching. The variables of this paradigm are presented below.

- **Teacher Characteristics:** Age, Sex, Social Status, Training, Experience

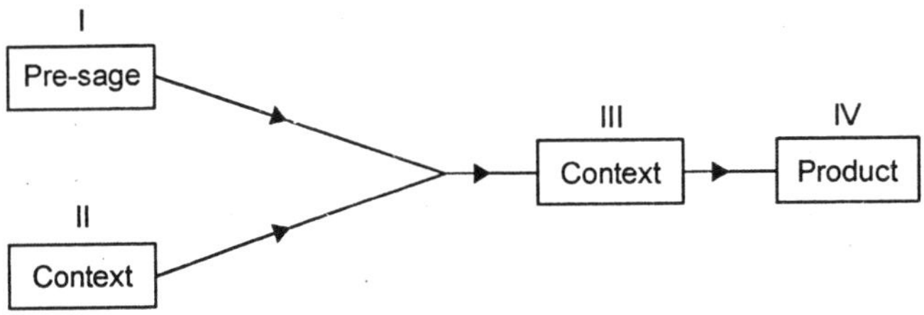

- **Student Characteristics:** Age, Sex, Social Status, Previous Knowledge
    - grade, level
    - class size
    - subject
    - environment in which teaching and learning take place
    - physical conditions
    - Curriculum Transactions
    - Realm of method and style of teaching
    - Learning objectives
    - Content
      - Knowledge
      - Understanding
      - skills
    - Learning
    - Achievement
    - Personality Development
    - Human Resource Development

Presage variables deal with characteristics of teachers that affect their teaching effectiveness. Teacher's characteristics include variables such as age, sex, social status, pre-service training and experience of a teacher. Training experiences include events and experiences attending college or university. These events include the undergraduate courses taken, post-graduate education, teaching practice experience, in-service and all evidences that have the possibilities of shaping their beliefs in the teaching profession.

Context variables consist of the characteristics of pupils and the physical or instructional situation/setting where the educational process takes place. Characteristics include age, sex, social status, prior knowledge, goals and beliefs they bring into class with them, have a great impact on their learning.

A student's social status and family background can determine classroom interaction. It is favourable if teachers could observe and identify the nature of their students, their background and disposition they bring into class to reciprocate with teaching methods suitable for them to attain maximum learning.

Process Variables include curriculum and its transaction using teaching strategies and methods for effective learning of the subject matter.

Finally, achievement level, personality development and learning by the students are product of all previous variables.

IV. Teaching as a Socially Interactive Form

Interaction in social sense between two persons means initiative by one and related response by the second person.

Flander's Interaction Analysis Category System

Interaction analysis refers to a technique that consists of objective and systematic observation of classroom events to study the teacher's behaviour and the process of interaction. It helps bring desirable modifications in their behaviour and improve interaction with pupils for making teaching more effective.

This method by Flander is specially used for verbal classroom communication. Flander believed that the verbal behaviour of the class reflects upon the general class behaviour. Analysis of Verbal behaviour involves categorization of all the sets of possible verbal behaviour of a teacher in the classroom while interacting with students.

Flanders' Interaction Analysis Category System (FIACS) is a classification of social interaction in classroom teaching. This method of interaction analysis is a type of category system:

Teacher Talk: Consists of seven categories where the first three categories belong to direct and the later four belongs to indirect influence. The category of indirect influence covers verbal behaviour of the teacher that gives students greater opportunity to respond or maximize their freedom of action.

Direct influence, on the other hand, exhibits verbal behaviour of the teacher that tends to restrict or minimize a student's freedom of action.

Pupil Talk: Consists of two categories in which pupil role is dominated by initiating and/or responding in the classroom.

Silence or Confusion: The third section related to silence or confusion in the classroom includes all behaviours are not covered in the first and second sections. It may prevail for some time.

Teacher Talk	Response Direct influence	1. Accepts feeling 2. Praises or encourages 3. Accepts or uses ideas of pupils
	Initiation Indirect influence	4. Asks questions 5. Lecturing 6. Giving directions 7. Criticising or justifying authority
Pupil Talk	Response	8. Pupil-Talk response
	Initiation	9. Pupil-Talk initiation
Silence		10. Silence or confusion

All the categories are mutually exclusive yet together they are totally inclusive of all interaction occurring in the classroom. Flander believed that the ten category system exhausts all possible teaching behaviour and hence with this system, we can study the teacher behaviour or classroom interaction in minute details.

V. Teaching as a Complex Skill

An important landmark in the scientific approach of teaching, found on the basis of empirical studies in USA, asserts that teaching is a complex skill comprising of simpler sub-skills (a set of teacher behaviours called a teaching skill). These are observable, trainable, measurable and transferable. Primary, secondary, senior secondary and university stage of education require specific teaching skills.

Some teaching skills are subject specific. Language, science, mathematics and art subjects require specific skills. Skill of demonstrating an experiment is specific to science teaching, whereas skill of recitation and narration are essential for teaching a language. However, there are common teaching skills, common to both levels/stages and subjects. These are termed as 'Core teaching Skills'.

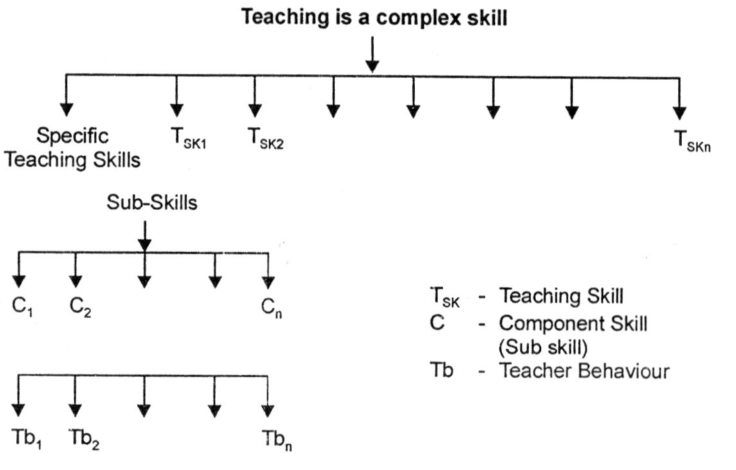

Characteristics of Teaching Skills

- Observable
- Trainable
- Measurable
- Transferable

Classification of Teaching Skills

- Stage specific
- Subject specific
- Core Teaching Skills (Common)

Each of the core teaching skills has specific objective as given below:

Core Teaching Skill	*Objective of the Skill*
1. Questioning	Initiation of thinking process
2. Explaining	Developing understanding of new concepts
3. Illustrating with examples	Further clarifying for better and easy understanding
4. Reinforcement	Strengthening of socially desirable behaviours and weakening of undesirable behaviours
5. Regulating students' attending behaviour (Stimulus Variation)	Securing and sustaining pupils' attention in the class

Certainly, in choosing teaching skills, we are working from a proposition of considerable ignorance of what behaviour comprises effective teaching, hence reference to their hypothesized effects on pupil learning. Till recently, research has concentrated on finding how best they can be imparted to teachers, their assuming relevance and value in the classroom. Exploratory research is also needed in individualizing technical skill training.

VI. Emergence of Models of Teaching

The latest landmark in the scientific approach of teaching is known as 'Models of Teaching'. Attempts have been made by researchers to match the different approaches, strategies or styles of teaching with the objectives of instruction and pupils. Dunn and Dunn (1979), Fischer and Fischcr (1979), Ellis (1979), Joyce and Weil (1980) also believed that strength in education resides in the intelligent use of powerful variety of approaches—matching them to different goals and adapting them to the students' styles and characterstics. Competence in teaching stems from the capacity to reach out to different children and create a rich and multidimensional environment for them. Models of teaching emerged out of the search by Joyce and Weil (1972) to find a variety of approaches or strategies of teaching to match the various learning styles. They present a solution to the dilemma of differing learning styles.

The word 'model' is used by people in different ways in different contexts. Engineers and architects use the word 'model' for dams, projects, building, machines etc. They also carry out the construction work according to the plan or pattern envisaged in the model. Thus a model of a bridge does not guide an engineer to construct a building. It is meant for a particular purpose. In the teaching-learning process, models have the same interpretation as they have in the case of construction of dams, buildings. etc. Thus, models of teaching, like plans, patterns or blueprints, present the steps necessary to bring about a desired outcome. According to Joyce and Weil (1972), a teaching model is a pattern or plan which can be used to shape curriculum or course to design instructional materials and to guide a teacher's actions. A model of teaching can be used to design face-to-face teaching in classrooms or tutorial settings to shape instructional materials, including books, films, tapes, computer-mediated programmes, and curricula and long-term courses of study (Joyce, Weil and Showers, 1992). Apart from these, it creates the necessary environment which facilitates the teaching-learning process. The core of the process of teaching is therefore an arrangement of environment within which the student can interact (Dewey, 1916).

A model of teaching consists of guidelines for designing educational activities and environments. It specifies ways of teaching and learning that are intended to achieve certain kinds of goals (Joyce and Weil, 1978). It is a step-by-step procedure that leads to specific learning outcomes (Gunter, Estes and Schwab, 1990). Models are prescriptive teaching strategies, designed to accomplish particular instructional goals (Eggen Pal, D. *et al.*, 1979). A model of teaching is designed to achieve a particular set of objectives. It is not a substitute to any teaching skill, rather, it creates the conducive teaching-learning environment by making the teaching act more systematic and efficient. The significant characteristics of models of teaching can be stated as below:

(i) Sort of plans or guidelines or patterns or strategies of teaching.
(ii) Are not a haphazard combination of facts but systematic procedures to modify the behaviour of the learners.
(iii) Specify the learning outcomes or instructional objectives in terms of observable and measurable performance of students.
(iv) Specify in definite terms the environmental condition under which a student's response should be observed.
(v) Specify the criteria of acceptable performance expected from students.

Models of teaching are based on assumptions given by Joyce and Weil (1980) are as follows:

(i) Alternative approaches to teaching: Many of these are practical and can be implemented in schools and classrooms where students and teachers have skills and will.
(ii) Methods make a difference in what is learned as well as how it is learned.
(iii) Students react differently to any given different teaching method. Combinations of personality, aptitudes, interpersonal skills, and previous achievement, contribute to configurations of learning styles of that so that no two people react in exactly the same way to anyone model of teaching.

Components of Teaching

Three major components involved in the act of teaching the teacher, the student and the curriculum imply the existence of the strategies, commonly known as methods of teaching. While the teacher and the student are human components, the curriculum/content constitutes material component. Methods of teaching are skill-based. The success of any teaching act depends on the interplay among the components of teaching. The teacher performs a significant role in planning, organising, leading and controlling teaching with a view to facilitating learning. -

In a classroom the student is made to act according to the planning and organisation of teaching activities by the teacher. The curriculum and methods of teaching are intervening components which mediate between the teacher and the student and help their interaction. All these components together create a teaching-learning environment which is geared to achieve instructional objectives.

Methods of Teaching—Historical Perspective

History of methods of teaching can traced to methods of literary education followed in ancient Greece and China. The most long-lived and widespread set of teaching methods are those associated with the study of language and literature (Singh and Jaimini, 1989). Memorisation and analogical reasoning were used as methods of teaching and in ancient Greece, the Socratic technique of teaching, i.e., the method of skilful inquiry was very popular.

Scientific approach to teaching methods began with the emergence of Comenius, Pestalozzi, Froebel and Herbart. Comenius (1592-1670) stressed on five major elements for scientific teaching method: (a) a world of sense and experience and not the work of a teacher or a book should be used as a starting point; (b) 'nature' as a phenomenon of biological and physical world can contribute significantly to the educational method; (c) content to be taught should be what the pupils are ready to take according to their mental age and strength (spiral curriculum); (d) learning should proceed from activity which should be interesting, pleasant and relevant; and (e) teachers should encourage pupils to discover and learn by their own efforts.

A similar approach was also propounded by J.H. Pestalozzi (1746-1827) who emphasised that teaching methods should be in accordance with the developmental pattern of children's growth. Froebel (1782-1852) followed the same line and stressed the self-activity of child, taking into account the emotional as well as intellectual development of the child. J.F. Herbert (1776-1841) propounded five instructional activities associated with teaching methods: (a) preparation, (b) presentation, (c) association, (d) assimilation, and (e) application.

Apart from efforts made by above-mentioned thinkers to perceive methods of teaching, these were also influenced by behaviouristic, humanistic and cognitive psychological orientations. The behaviouristic approach to instruction believes in the influence of environment on the learning behaviour of the learner. Among the behaviourialists, the most important contribution to methods of teaching has been made by Skinner who stresses on a stimulus-response-reinforcement chain as the basic of any kind of learning. This has led to the birth of the famous programmed instruction. Humanistic approach to instruction puts stress on the uniqueness of individual learners and the methods of teaching depend on the quality of the interpersonal relationship that exists between learners and teacher. According to cognitive psychologists however, mental processes such as thinking, reasoning and problem-solving form the basis of teaching methods.

With the introduction of the mass media and other technological interventions in teaching-learning process, methods of teaching are now well oriented to educational technology. In this context, a look at the major developments in pedagogy identified by Elton (1977) is necessary. These developments are mass communication instructions, individualised instructions, and group learning. Mass communication gains relevance with the introduction of electronics hardware into teaching-learning process. For example, the closed-circuit television is used to teach classes with a large number of students and also to different classes.

The second development in the field of pedagogy is individualised instruction. Significantly programmed learning/instruction was developed by Skinner. The personalised system of instruction, another form of individualised instruction, was developed by Fred S. Kellar (1963). Computer-Assisted Instruction (CAI), the most recent form of individualised instruction is an extension of programmed instruction and the porsonalised system of instruction. The third development has been in group-learning methods. These methods became popular due to the failure of individualised instruction to develop interpersonal skills. Group-learning methods are oriented to develop more humanistic skills.

Conclusion

The write-up has clarified that teaching and learning are specific processes yet associated with each other. Teaching however, needs to be studied separately. The work on developing a separate theory of teaching started since fifties of the twentieth century. There are six major landmarks in the journey of search for scientific approach of teaching which are presented in detail for deeper understanding of the concept, nature and practice of teaching. It also presents in detail the historical development of teaching methods.

"The available literature reveals that so far there is no well established theory of teaching. There are conceptualisation or several models or paradigms of teaching. Teachers and pupils are the major variables of a theory of teaching. While theories of learning were formulated by conducting experiments on animals, theories of teaching however, have been developed by dealing with humans in normal situations. Its main concern must be with learning and development of pupils as far as teacher's effects are concerned."

References

Bloom, B.S. (1956). "Taxonomy of Educational Objectives", *Handbook I: Cognitive Domain*, David Mc Kay Co., New York.

DeCecco, J.P. (1977). *The Psychology of Learning and Instruction*, Prentice Hall of India, New Delhi.

Eggen Paul, D., *et al.*, (1979). *Strategies for Teachers — Information Processing Model in the Classroom*, Prentice Hall Inc., New Jersey.

Flander, N.A. (1970). *Analyzing Teacher Behaviour*. Addison Wesley, Reading.

Gage, N.L.(1964). *Theories of Teaching and Theories of Learning and Instruction*, National Society for the Study of Education, University of Chicago Press, Chicago.

Gage, N.L. (Ed) (1963). *Handbook of Research on Teaching*. Rand McNally, Chicago.

Gunter, M.A.; Estes, L.H. and Schwab, J.H. (1990). *Instruction: A Models Approach*, Boston, Allyn and Bacon.

Jangira, N.K., and Singh, Ajit (1984). *Core Teaching Skills—Microteaching Approach*, NCERT, New Delhi.

Joyce, B. and Weil, M. (1972). *Models of Teaching*, Prentice Hall, Inc., New Jersey.

Joyce, B. and Weil, M. (1980). *Models of Teaching*. Prentice Hall, Inc., New Jersey.

Myers, David G. (2008). *Exploring Psychology*, New York.

Ormrod, Jeanne (2012). *Human Learning* (6th Ed.). Boston: Pearson.

Passi, B.K. Singh, L.C. Singh, Sansanwal, D.N. (1991). *Models of Teaching: Report of Three Phase Study of ITM and CAM*, NCERT, New Delhi.

Singh L.C. (2005). *Microteaching—Theory Research and Practice*. National Psychological Corporation, Agra.

Singh, L.C. (1995). *Multiple Models of Teaching for Educators*. Vikas Publishing House, New Delhi.

Singh, L.C. (1995). *Teacher Education and the Teacher*. Vikas Publishing House, New Delhi.

Singh, L.C. (Ed.) (1992). *Teacher Education India — A Resource Book*, NCERT, New Delhi.

Singh, L.C. and Sharma, R.D. (1987). *Microteaching — Theory and Practice*. National Psychological Corporation, Agra.

2
Pedagogical Understanding of Teaching and Learning

Jasim Ahmad

Introduction

The word 'Education' is derived from Latin 'Educatum' that means: to train, act of teaching or training, and 'Educare' that means: to lead out, to draw out, to bring up, to raise, or to educate. Education is a process of development through which an individual's physical, mental, emotional and social development takes place. Education makes an individual adaptable to changing nature of society. Education instills in an individual all those competencies through which he or she can occupy a suitable position in the society. Education is a tripolar process, as it contains three poles, namely: (i) Teacher, (ii) Learner, and (iii) Parent (Fig. 2.1) that revolves round the society and the social norms. All three stakeholders actively interact in the efficient and successful working of the educational process. The more efficient and cooperative interaction among these three

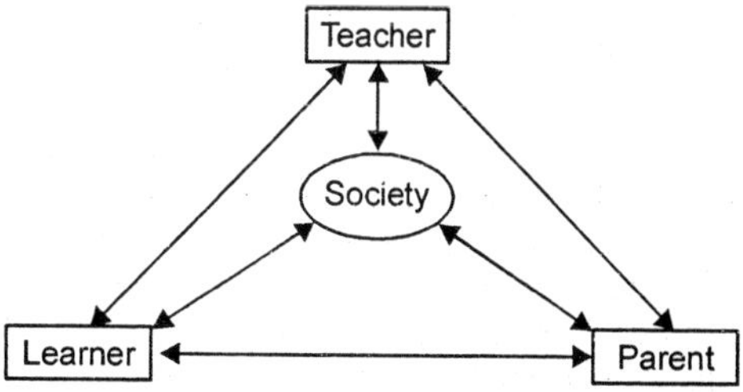

Fig. 2.1: Education as a Tripolar Process.

poles, the better and effective education of the learner will be and the child will be developing his personality suitable to the needs of the present society. As we know, no society is static, so is the child's and individual's interest and needs are also dynamic. Therefore, teachers also require making them up-to-date in terms of the knowledge explosion, methodology of teaching, learners' psychology and other factors that affect teaching and learning process.

Prof. Drever defines education as, "a process in which and by which knowledge, character and behaviour of the young are shaped and molded." For M.K. Gandhi, education meant the all-round drawing out the best in child and man-body, mind and soul. T.P. Nun defined education as the complete development of individuality of the child, so that he can make his original contribution to human life according to his best capacity. According to Kant, "education is the development in the individual of all the perfection of which he is capable."

Meaning of Teaching and Learning

Teaching is a complex process. As an art, it emphasizes on high imagination and artistic abilities; as science, it is logical and well planned strategies used to achieve effectively the aims and objectives of education and as an action art, it is a process of developing and reflecting creative abilities. The concept of teaching has been defined by many educationists in different ways. Simply put, it is the sum total of all the activities performed by a teacher to mould the behaviour of his students as per his desires which come from the aims and objectives of education.

A summary of the important characteristics of teaching is given below:

(i) Teaching is an effective interaction between a teacher and students.

(ii) The most important factor for effective teaching is teachers' communication skill and command over the subject.

(iii) Teaching is a tri-polar interdependent process as shown in Figure 2.2. Good teaching must have a very healthy two-way interaction between the teacher and students to attain the objectives of education. Teacher is the pivot of the education process of the child.

(iv) Effective teaching requires prior planning on the part of teacher. A teacher should plan lessons, decide teaching objectives, teaching methods and process of evaluation.

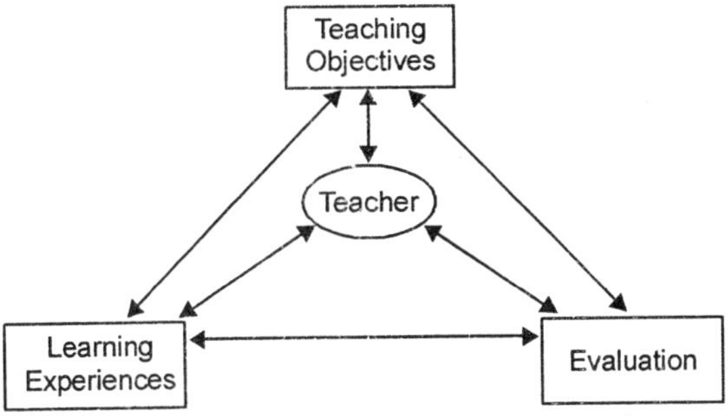

Fig. 2.2: Teaching as a Tripolar Interdependent Process.

(v) Good teaching is always based on democratic values and a good teacher is always compassionate and encourages learners to participate in the teaching-learning process.

(vi) Teaching provides encouragement, guidance and direction to the students.

(vii) Teaching develops power of thinking of students and shows them the path of self-learning.

(viii) Teaching is a remedial process and a teacher should solve the problems or learning difficulties of students.

(ix) Teaching is such a professional hobby that helps the children to fruitful their growth and development.

Teaching as a System

Consider the respiratory system which consists of many organs like nostril, nasal passage, trachea, lungs, etc. all are interconnected and interdependent and perform a unitary task of respiration. The system is a group of components which are interrelated and interdependent and work cooperatively to accomplish the unitary task. In any system there must be more than one components interconnected with each other, input, processing and output. In teaching, teachers provide input in the form of knowledge, content etc., the students process them through discussion, patient listening, perception, cognitive process of assimilation, accommodation and activity etc. and outcome is learning on the part of students. This establishes that teaching is a system (Fig. 2.3), for whose smooth functioning, all its components should work properly in orderly coordination.

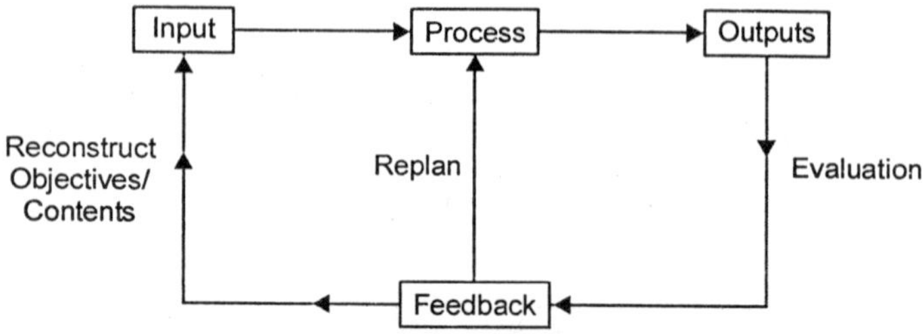

Fig. 2.3: Teaching as a System.

Learning is the development of memories and behaviour patterns acquired from the acquisition of knowledge, understanding, skills, values, and wisdom. It is the prime goal of education, and the product of experiences. Learning ranges from simple forms such as habituation to more complex forms such as play (activity) or dramatization, seen only in large vertebrates.

From the time of conception of an embryo to the birth of a child, behavioural changes occur in the embryo and the child. The changes or learning during embryonic stages are due to the hormonal influence and the interaction between the embryo and its environment in the embryo sac. After birth, the infant is surrounded by a biotic and social environment. The whole process of getting experiences, acquisition of knowledge and adaptation to the environment through formal, informal or non-formal means is called learning.

Different psychologists and educationists have defined learning in different ways. A few definitions are given here. According to B.F. Skinner, "Learning is a process of progressive behaviour adaptation", while Woodworth understands it as, "a process of acquiring new knowledge and new responses." Crow and Crow defined it as, "a process of acquisition of habit, knowledge and attitudes." For Gates *et al.*, "learning is the modification of behaviour through experience and training." Cronbach defines learning in this way, "learning is shown by a change in behaviour as a result of experiences."

Learning results in the development of cognitive, affective and psychomotor domains of an individual's personality. Behavioural changes are enduring in nature depending on the total experiences of the individual.

Approaches to Teaching and Learning

Different psychologists and educationists have different views regarding the process of learning. After studying these view, three approaches of learning, given by different psychologists have been shortlisted. Major theories of learning come under one or the other of these three approaches.

Constructivism: It works on the philosophy that there is no knowledge independent of the meaning attributed to experience (constructed) by the learner, or community of learners (Hein, 1991). Knowledge construction means that students construct their own knowledge through the active participation in the process of learning by seeking to find their own meaning in their experiences. Literally, learners construct/find/develop meaning in their subjective experiences that becomes their knowledge. Each person's subjective experience is just as valid as anyone else's, and no one has privileged viewpoint. It reflects that there are no objective criteria for what constitutes knowledge (Poerksen, 2004a). Knowledge acquired by one person may not be knowledge for another as no two persons have the same mental processes of constructions. Having the same constructions would carry with it a host of ontological presuppositions about the world and reality, one of which constructivists accept (Poerksen, 2004a, 2004b).

Constructivism replaced the position of a teacher from the centre of knowledge (objective), with the learner (subjective). Independent of the teacher each student's subjective experience has a special and unique meaning. It is both the pupils learning experience and their perceptions of those experiences that have educational significance.

Constructivist learning has emerged as a forceful approach to teaching and learning in this millennium. Based on the work of John Dewey, Montessori, Jean Piaget, Jerome Brunner, and Lev Vygotsky, it represents a paradigm shift from teaching-learning based on behaviourism to education based on cognitive theory. Behaviourists' epistemology focuses on intelligence, domains of objectives, levels of knowledge, and reinforcement. Constructivist epistemology assumes that learners construct their own knowledge on the basis of interaction with their environment. Four epistemological assumptions constitute the heart and soul of the constructivist approach of learning. These are:

1. Knowledge is physically constructed by learners who are involved in active learning.
2. Knowledge is symbolically constructed by those learners who make their own representation of actions.
3. Knowledge is socially constructed by learners who convey their meaning making to others.

4. Knowledge is theoretically constructed by learners who try to explain things they don't completely understand.

Constructivist Epistemology

Knowledge and its development in constructivism hinges upon the following assertions:

1. Knowledge is a way of making sense of experiences. The same process or product may be experienced by many. Knowledge about that process or product may vary for all individuals as they all may sense and perceive them differently. It is not something concrete outside the individual.
2. Knowledge is an interpretation that depends on individuals' ability, intelligence, previous experiences, past and prevailing situation, creativity, vertical and horizontal thinking etc. Therefore, knowledge is always open to uncertainty, that varies with time and is never permanent as it is always open to question.
3. Learning and knowledge is a personal and private activity.
4. Knowledge is a construction of reality. According to Taylor (1993), "Human knowledge is a process of personal cognitive construction, or invention undertaken by the individual who is trying to make sense of his social or natural environment".
5. Knowledge acquisition or learning is not the transfer of "nuggets of truth" (as referred by Kelly in 1995) to the individual but a personal construction.
6. Learning is determined by the interplay among learners existing knowledge, social context, teaching-learning environment and the problem that is to be solved.

Behaviourism: Behaviour of any organism or individual at any given time is nothing more than the product of his genetic endowment, personal experiences and the prevailing situation. Behaviourists believe that knowledge does not depend upon introspection. Behaviourism rejects the philosophy of internal mental states and focuses on the external observation of lawful relations between and among outwardly observable stimuli and their responses. In the eyes of behaviourists, the valid knowledge is that which is publicly observable and as such, behaviourists believe that the concept of mental states can be discarded (Freiberg, 1999).

Behaviourism was strongly influenced by positivism, a philosophical movement (Amsel, 1992), which only recognizes natural phenomena or properties of knowable things, along with their lawful relations of co-existence and succession. Positivists believe that relationships are discovered only by observation and experiment. Behaviourism and its base positivism, both are grounded in objectivism. Objectivism is based on the philosophy that there is a single reality external to the individual. Based on this objectivist worldview, behaviourists argue that learners "acquire" knowledge from outside world (Bichelmeyer & Hus, 1999, p. 3).

Pedagogical Analysis

Previously pedagogy was defined as a study of the methods of teaching a subject or methods of instructions given to the students to change their behaviour. It is perceived not merely as a science of instruction but as a culture or set of cultures that reflect different context and different teaching behaviours—inside as well as outside the classroom.

Using culture-sensitive pedagogy would mean incorporating different aspects of students' cultural background into the teaching-learning process. In the Curriculum Framework of NCTE (1998), it was pointed out: "Pedagogical analysis of school teaching subjects has been thought of as an essential component of practice teaching. By way of pedagogical analysis, a pupil teacher becomes conversant with the objectives of teaching a unit, the entry behaviour of students, classroom management and evaluation strategies. With this background of having looked into the pedagogical aspects of school teaching subjects, the pupil teacher is likely become more effective and confident in the classroom".

The conceptual frame of the concept 'pedagogical analysis' lies in the work of British researcher Edger Stones (1979, 1992) which can be broadly labelled as a 'psycho-pedagogical approach'. This model is founded on established principles from psychology that relate to human learning. Its view of effective teaching is framed in terms of ways and extent to which it facilitates learning.

The model has been systematically constructed and elaborated and hence it can be employed in a wide range or contexts. Its basic structure that gives it this flexibility and coherence and is also an important attribute of the model. It addresses all the three stages of the teaching-learning process:

i. Pre-active stage,

ii. Interactive stage, and
iii. Post-active stage; and treats them as related aspects of a teaching task.

A basic element of the model is the pedagogical analysis, also sometimes called as the task analysis, which is a major part of the pre-active (planning) stage. This emphasizes the need to undertake separate but linked investigations of the learners' and teachers' tasks and it proposes helpful procedures for affecting both of these. The analysis of the teaching task hinges on the teacher's ability to identify the 'type of learning' involved in the learning task. This requires sound knowledge and understanding of the learning theories, but with the employment of procedures stipulated in the model, the acquisition of this knowledge is through a reasoned inquiry into the relevance and usefulness of such theory. The interactive (implementation) stage is subsequently directly assisted by this analysis because it has 'classroom reality'. While doing pedagogical analysis of a unit or topic, we have to follow various steps; the most important among them is the method of teaching to be used to teach that topic. In the following paragraphs, a brief description is given on methods of teaching.

Important Methods of Teaching

Lecture Method: The most widely used method of teaching at higher education is the least effective method of teaching at school level. In this method, teachers play central role and they are the most active participant in the teaching-learning process. Students are the passive learners whose interest and participation are not taken into consideration. A Teacher simply delivers the lesson with the help of chalk and talk, so it is called chalk and talk method. It is the oldest conventional method of teaching. Higher order thinking, high level of understanding and creativity is least developed through this method.

Lecture-Demonstration Method: When a lecture is supported with demonstration, it becomes Lecture-Demonstration Method. Demonstration is a technique through which teacher shows various phenomena and processes to students so that they can have concrete experience and understand them properly. Demonstration is done with the help of 2-D/3-D models (static or functional), visual charts, flash cards, bulletin boards, Power Point presentation, multimedia presentation, film/CD/VCD shows etc. Demonstration helps in gaining student attention, motivating pupil and results in effective teaching and learning. Teachers and students both are active participants. Students assist teachers in setting up the stage appropriate for demonstration while the latter help students to draw inferences.

It helps in developing curiosity, interest and scientific attitude. Based on psychological principles of teaching and learning it develops higher order thinking, observation skill, listening skill, reasoning ability etc., and creates ground for healthy discussion in the class which results in life-long learning.

Problem Solving Method or Scientific Method: The most important objective of teaching and learning is to develop problem solving abilities among students. We face problems of various natures like scientific, social, economic, family etc. in our daily life. If we train students in scientific method, they will be in a position to solve them in the most rational way. It develops creativity, rationality, objectivity, reason based thinking, open mindedness and all other values which constitute scientific attitude or temper—the most needed attribute of a personality to bring peace and harmony in the world.

James Ross defined the method as, ".... an educational device whereby the teacher and the pupil attempt in a conscious, planned, purposeful manner to arrive at an explanation or solution to some educationally significant difficulty". According to Gerald A. Yokam and R.H. Simpson, "Problem-solving is a method in which a person uses his ability to solve the problems which confront him, enables a man to exercise control over his activities and his environment. Without it he is at the mercy of nature and cannot make intelligent social progress".

Problem-solving method of teaching is a process of raising a problem in the minds of pupil so as to stimulate purposeful, reflective thinking to arrive at a rational solution. It sharpens and trains the minds of the learners so that they can sense and perceive the problems around them and find their amicable solutions in a rational way.

To teach any topic or content through problem-solving method, a teacher should go through the following steps. It should be organized in such a way that students work on their own. Teacher acts as a guide, stage setter, motivator and a best friend to all students. He does not give ready-made solution to the problems but helps in finding the solution.

Step 1: Creating a Problem Situation/Condition/Environment

Teacher should create the situation having the problem to be studied or problem related concept which is to be developed. It can be done with the help of demonstration, discussion, question-answer etc. in the classroom or by taking students outside the class. Students will observe the situation carefully while the teacher help students in observing the situation in the right approach.

Step 2: Identifying the Problem

Students should identify the problem on their own through keen observation and queries with the teacher and peer group. Problem recognition or identification depends on the observation skill of an individual. Vice-a-versa, this method of teaching develops the skill of observation among the students.

Step 3: Defining the Problem

Students state the problem in a concise, definite and clear language and the Teacher may help students in doing this. There must be some key-words in the statement of the problem which should be defined operationally. Once the problem is well identified, the student attempts to learn as much as possible about it as an investigator goes to the web or library. This is called searching the relevant literature related to the problem. The investigator may find that others have already solved all or part of the problem. In this way, the investigator accumulates much background information. With these new ideas and facts, the researcher builds a firm foundation for attacking the problem.

Step 4: Analyzing the Problem

Students collect relevant information and data regarding the problem through various sources. They analyze the collected data and information. Irrelevant data is eliminated and relevant data gives direction in solving the problem.

Step 5: Formulating Hypothesis

On the basis of the analysis of the relevant data, a logical cause of the problem and its solution is worked out. It is an intelligent guess about the reason behind the problem and its tentative solution. This is called a hypothesis. Many hypotheses can be framed for a single problem starting from the strongest to the weakest hypothesis. Teachers assist in formulating the hypothesis.

Step 6: Testing the Hypothesis or Experimentation

Student selects the most likely hypothesis and performs experiment or conduct survey to test its significance. One by one all hypotheses are tested until a satisfactory reliable and valid is found. If all the hypotheses found non-significant, the student can go back to the previous stage, analyse the problem carefully and frame fresh hypotheses and test them. This process goes on until a hypothesis is found that can be validated.

Step 7: Collecting Data

While performing experiments or conducting survey, the student will collect the relevant data. At this stage high level of objectivity is needed to get the best i.e. reliable and valid result. If there is no experiment or if there is some field survey or library work in addition to experiment, student collect data from all relevant sources.

Step 8: Analyzing the Data

The data collected through performing experiments or from other sources are analyzed by the student with the help of the teacher. Statistical techniques and method and other parametric and non-parametric tests may also be used qualitatively or quantitatively.

Step 9: Drawing Conclusion and Making Generalization

On the basis of analysis and interpretation of data student draw conclusion. Some new demonstration may be arranged to arrive at the conclusion. A set of experiments may be arranged and if all or most of the experiments give the same result which was already reached out earlier, then the findings are generalized.

Step 10: Application of Generalization in New Situation

Students should be able to apply the generalization in their daily life and in learning more difficult contents. This helps in bridging the gap between the class-room and real life situation. It also helps in verifying the established principles by the student on their own. Students can also predict and explain different phenomena on the basis of the established principles and theories.

Benefits of Using Problem Solving Method

1. Helps in developing critical, logical thinking and reflective thinking, curiosity, imagination etc. (i.e. high order intellectual or cognitive skills or abilities).
2. Develops confidence and self-reliance in the students.
3. Helps in developing scientific attitude and train students so that they solve problems scientifically in their daily lives.
4. Develops cooperative and harmonious relationship between teacher and students.
5. Gives an opportunity to use the overall potential of the student and shapes their personality.

Project Method: This method is based on John Dewey's pragmatic philosophy which considers experience as ultimate reality. It was started by Kilpatrick and perfected by J.A. Stevenson.

This method gives children an opportunity to involve in the process of learning. 'Learning by doing', 'learning by living', and 'learning through association, cooperation and coordination' are the three guiding principles and foundation stone of this method. The essence of this method lies in carrying out a useful task cooperatively in a group which results in some physical outcome i.e. 'product'. The product may be in the form of a written report or display of the produced or developed object. Project must be challenging, interesting and affordable in terms of time, energy and resources. It should give real life experience to the students.

According to Kilpatrick, "A project is a whole-hearted purposeful activity proceeding in a social environment". Ballard defines a project in these words, "a project is a bit of real life that has been imparted into school". Stevenson defines project in this way, "a project is a problematic act carried to completion in its natural setting".

Benefits of Using Project Method of Teaching

1. This method is based on psychological principles of learning. It follows:
   a. Law of readiness.

   b. Law of exercise.
   c. Law of effect.
2. It is based on sound psychological approaches of teaching-learning like:
   a. Learning by doing.
   b. Learning by living.
   c. Learning by association, cooperation and coordination.
3. It promotes personal and social values like habit of thinking for common cause, tolerance, self-dependence, resourcefulness etc.
4. It is a democratic approach to teaching and develops democratic values in students.
5. It develops clear and permanent knowledge among students.
6. It nurtures positive attitude and dignity of labour among students.
7. It inculcates scientific attitude and train students in scientific method.
8. It gives an opportunity of correlated study. Depending upon the nature of project students learn various subject working on one project.
9. It reduces workload of one individual, distribute workload among many students and solves the problem of indiscipline.
10. It develops overall personality of the child-knowledge base (cognitive), values and ethics base (affective) and skill base (psychomotor).

Discovery Method: This method was advocated by H.E. Armstrong, Prof. of Chemistry in the Central Technical College, City of Guilds of London Institute. According to him, "Discovery method is a method of teaching which involves our placing the students as far as possible in the attitude of a discoverer". In this method instead of imparting facts, the teacher provides activities and situation where the students work independently to discover new facts and concepts. This method trains pupil in scientific method and inculcate scientific attitude.

Any method that excites children to work on their own, to think for themselves and to discover or try to discover something may be called as 'Heuristic' or 'Discovery' method. It makes pupils more exact, more truthful, observant, thoughtful, dexterous and laid the solid foundation for future self-education and encourages the spirit of enquiry and research.

Comparison of Problem Solving and Discovery Method

It is almost parallel to the problem solving method. The difference lies in the first step. In problem solving method teacher creates a problematic situation from which students are supposed to sense and identify the problem on their own. In 'Heuristic' or 'Discovery' method a problem is assigned to the class and each student is put in the place of a discoverer to find out something for themselves. The other steps like defining the problem, analyzing the problem, formulating the hypothesis, testing hypothesis or experimentation, data collection, analysis and interpretation of data and drawing conclusion are same as we have discussed in problem solving method.

Pupils can freely discuss the problem with the classmates, seniors and parents. Each student is given instructions regarding the problem in hand and of guidance from the teacher, but not so much so that the very purpose of discovery gets killed.

Discussion Method: Discussion is a process through which we exchange ideas, think critically and logically, have an opportunity to gain an understanding of some issues, solve problems with collective and reflective thinking. A discussion is based on the assumption that the views presented by different people are to be judged logically based on facts and empirical evidences. In discussion method the problems are solved through reflective thinking based on group agreement. It is best suited to those topics that cannot be easily explained by demonstration or other such methods.

Discussion is used for a variety of instructional purposes. It is a standard tool for reviewing information and ideas that have already been studied. Research shows that a review discussion after a lesson increased retention. Discussion is a way of helping students pull together their thoughts about material they have read. The method is also used to stimulate interest, build background, help students synthesize and evaluate experiences. Teachers use discussion mainly to find out what students know and think. Depending on the type of discussion, learners may gain the following advantages:

- Improved social skills necessary to carry out group work and to lead a good social life.
- Develop a sense of personal involvement.
- Increased ability to think critically and logically.
- Discussion stimulates analysis and encourages reasonable interpretations.
- Improvement in decision making ability in various situations.
- It develops democratic values through patient hearing of others,

evaluate their arguments, develop independent views and to continue focus on the problem.
- Development of organizing, synthesizing, summarizing and evaluating skills.
- Increased realization that most problems do not have simple, obvious solutions but require careful scrutiny.
- Increased ability to see more than one side of a problem.
- Develop confidence to ask questions, to assimilate and analyze information, draw inferences and face others.
- It develops an individual's personality into a dynamic type that is desired in today's society and by multinational organizations that will employ the students.
- Discussion leads to development of communication skills that is one of the most important keys of success.
- Discussion among students tends to increase mutual respect, self-esteem and cooperation.
- Discussion helps students become independent thinkers and good citizens in a democratic society.

Discussion may be carried out in many forms such as debate, class interaction or class meeting, evaluation, debriefing sessions, question and answer periods, panel presentation and interpretation, problem-solving small sessions, brainstorming, and so on.

Integrated Method of Teaching: Innovation, is an act of introducing something new, changes that create new dimensions of performance; a process of making improvements by introducing something new. Traditional formats like lectures, discussions, laboratories, etc. have become monotonous. For effective teaching and learning following points should be taken care of:

- Actively involve students in their own learning, a constructive approach.
- Help students to develop a conceptual framework and problem solving skills.
- Promote student discussions and group activities.
- Assess understanding at frequent intervals throughout learning process.
- Develop and conduct scientific investigation.
- Methods for making your class session more effective.
- Ways to encourage students' participation in the class.
- Promote activity based learning.

The integrated method involves complete integration of the content with nature and society where the teacher teaches how to study and participate in the classroom discussion, objectives to be achieved, subjects and methods to be evaluated, etc. For this the teacher needs to have relevant skills to create a conducive environment for teaching and learning. The teacher distributes responsibilities to students taking into consideration their strength, weakness and special needs.

A brief explanation of the lesson is given and then the grouping is done. The group must be heterogeneous headed by a group leader. Each group develops one activity and group leaders collect and arrange them. Each group performs the activities designed by them. All activities could be evaluated by whole class in addition to the experts or the subject teacher. Activities are evaluated in terms of the relevance, convenience, difficulty value, presentation, conceptual clarity, etc.

Conclusion

Education is a process of transforming the personality of learners through various approaches and methods of teaching and learning. Constructivist pedagogy relies on the philosophy that knowledge is created by learners themselves. A teacher is responsible for setting a stage for learning and act as facilitators. Contrary to this, behaviourists approach believes in transfer of knowledge from teacher to learners and hence the role of the teachers becomes active and that of learners, passive. Active participation in the process of learning makes learners understand concepts deeply and develop the ability of application and higher order thinking skills which are essentials of healthy and successful life in the present day competitive and innovative society. Problem solving, discovery, discussion, integrated, and project methods are such methods that should be used by teachers at all levels of education to make the learning interesting, joyful and result oriented.

References

Ahmad, J. (2009 and 2011). *Teaching of Biological Sciences*, PHI Learning Pvt. Ltd., New Delhi.

Amsel, A. (1992). "BF Skinner and the cognitive revolution", *Journal of Behaviour Therapy and Experimental Psychiatry*, *23*(2): 67-70.

Bichelmeyer, B. and Hsu, Y. (1999). Individually-Guided Education and Problem-Based Learning: A comparison of pedagogical approaches from different epistemological views, in: *Proceedings of Selected Research and Development Papers Presented at the National Convention of the Association for Educational Communications and Technology (AECT)*(21st, Houston, TX, February 10–14, 1999). IR 019 753.

Bruner, Jerome (1960). *The Process of Education*, Harvard University Press, Cambridge.

De Cecco, J.P. (1977). *The Psychology of Learning and Instruction*, Prentice Hall of India, New Delhi.

Freiberg, H.J. (1999). Consistency management and cooperative discipline. *Beyond behaviourism: Changing the classroom management paradigm*, pp. 75-97.

Hein, George E. (1991). The Museum and the Needs of People, CECA (International Committee of Museum Educators) Conference, Jerusalem Israel, 15-22 October 1991, Lesley College. Massachusetts, USA. (http://www.exploratorium.edu/IFI/resources/constructivistlearning.html)

Kelly, G.A. (1995). *The Psychology of Personal Construct*, Norton, New York.

Kilpatrick, W.H. (1918). *The Project Method.* Teachers College Record. Columbia.

Poerksen, B. (2013). *The Creation of Reality: A Constructivist Epistemology of Journalism and Journalism Education*. Andrews UK Limited.

Stones, E. (1979). *Psychopedagogy: Psychological Theory and the Practice of Teaching*, Methuen, the University of Michigan, USA.

Taylor, P. (1993). Collaborating to reconstruct teaching: The influence of researcher beliefs. *The practice of constructivism in science education*, 267-297.

Yager, R.E. (1991). "The Constructivist Learning Model: Toward Real Reform in Science Education", *The Science Teacher*, 58(6): 52-57.

3

Teaching and Learning and Effective Class room Interaction

K. Srinivas

Introduction

Most of the significant developments that one can observe today can be attributed to the impact of science and technology. The ICT increases the flexibility of delivery of education so that learners can access knowledge any time and from anywhere. Learning Management Systems (LMS) such as Blackboard, Moodle, SAKAI, and ANGEL, are now nearly ubiquitous in all spears of Education, and they represent a suite of technologies, tools, and processes that, when implemented and utilized skilfully, can have a positive effect on teaching and learning. The successes of the Learning Management systems are largely dependant on the teachers and students how effectively manage the resources consistently on regular basis. With ever-increasing information overload, web information retrieval systems are facing new challenges for helping people not only locating relevant information precisely but also accessing and aggregating a variety of information from different resources automatically.

Information and Communication Technology is a major driving force in contemporary education system. UGC has been utilizing the resources of its IUCs, specially CEC and INFLIBNET in providing ICT educational support for education and research, both in colleges and university sector. Researchers are likely to find material relevant to their subject in a variety of web-based resources: their own library catalogue, catalogues outside their own library, a national or union catalogue or a catalogue in another institution that specializes in similar subjects. The current process of information access for the sake of seeking information is cumbersome and requires some knowledge of the various resources, their access mechanism, the query interface they provide and the type of results they return. It also requires a manual comparison between the results returned from several resources and does not enable the user to move from one resource to another for further discovery and navigation.

Research and academic community are dealing with information and seek quick, authentic and latest information to pursue their studies and research works. E-resources in tertiary education are a means to provide scholarly and latest information to the research and academic community in India. Users are accessing around 8000 scholarly e-journals through this programme. Electronic mode of learning is gaining lot of momentum as a way of reaching the unreached both in quantum and quality. e-Resources can be in the form of e-books, e-journals as e-resources data centres contains substantial amount of data from diverse fields. For maximum benefit in conducting research and development, avoidance of duplication and the identification of promising opportunities, this data must be identified, retrieved, processed and integrated. Much effort is being applied to information identification and retrieval for which sophisticated processed tools exist. This is especially serious for the fields of higher education since intense specialization in every discipline needs in accessible referral material as new knowledge source as the academic communities interested in covering myraid topic areas that spread across the traditional disciplines. Far less effort is formalized to the information processing and integration problems, especially the cutting-edge areas of referral material to infer new discoveries and innovation.

Technology in Teaching and Learning

ICT allows new ways of teaching: explain, show, demonstrate, monitor and especially supervise learners in various adapted manners. At the same time, it allows learning by appropriating the knowledge in an individualized, interactive, cooperative, collective way by treating information in time and space. It question concepts of time and space by reducing the distance and by changing the present according to new interesting modalities for education.

Students can decide about their studies, learning time, place and resources in a better way. They can work in more supportive environments, seek help from teachers and fellows, and share their learning experiences and ideas in a productive fashion. Technology has invaded workplaces, homes and schools. It is not about understanding how to use a computer, it is about understanding how to access the information and use digital tools and create new forms of learning.

The technology can be used as a tool in the class room in the following ways:

Informative tool: provides vast amount of data in various formats such as audio, video and documents.

Situating tool: creates situations, which the student experiences in real life. Thus simulation and virtual reality is possible.

Constructive tool: manipulate data and generate analysis.

Communicative tool: to remove communication barriers.

There are many systems and tools available in today's market that can help teachers and administrators with many of their tasks. These technologies enable educators to improve communications, enhance student learning, controls costs and manage internet access in the classroom. Some technology tools directly impact teachers, students, and/or parents. Administrators and teachers alike however, will recognize the potential of these technologies to help them be more efficient and more effective in their day to day operations. For example:

Lecture Capture: Teachers can record their lectures that can be made available to students to replay and review complex concepts, or for students who couldn't attend class.

SaaS (Software-as-a-Service): is a web-based on-demand application with a provision that uses periodic, recurring subscription fees, and typically, a pay as you go model. In the SaaS model, costs are directly aligned with usage. As a result, depending upon specific contract terms, the cost is lower when an organization is smaller and will grow as the company grows and usage of the application increases.

Skype: Skype is one of the most popular Web 2.0 free application tool makes it easy to connect (using webcams, or just audio) over the Internet. Free video conferencing capability can really extend the reach of administrators, teachers, and students being requested and used in the school.

Open Educational Resources (OER)

Open Content/Open educational resources (OER)/Open Courseware are educational materials discoverable online and openly licensed that can be: used, improved, shared and redistributed. It includes texts, different forms of media, ideas, as well as documented teaching strategies/

techniques or practices. Advocates suggest that the value in OER lies in its potential to support learning in many ways and in many contexts. They are part of a larger movement that harnesses the affordability provided by the internet and aims to increase access to information, open availability of data, science for global collaboration and open source softwares.

Open Educational Resources enhances learning experience and enables learners to use different ICT tools, ensures repository of content accessibility anywhere, anytime. It provides the space for collaborative learning, motivate students to participate in pedagogical process.

OER is not synonymous with online learning or e-learning, although many people make the mistake of using the terms interchangeably. Openly licensed content can be produced in any medium: paper-based text, video, audio or computer-based multimedia. A lot of e-learning courses may harness OER, but this does not mean that OER are necessarily e-learning.

The most important reason for harnessing OER is that openly licensed educational materials have tremendous potential to contribute to improving the quality and effectiveness of education. The challenges of growing access, combined with the ongoing rollout of ICT infrastructure into educational institutions, indicates that it is becoming increasingly important for them to support, in a planned and deliberate manner, the development and improvement of curricula, ongoing programme and course design, planning of contact sessions with students, development of quality teaching and learning materials, and design of effective assessment – activities all aimed at improving the teaching and learning environment while managing the cost of this through increased use of resource based learning.

Some of the Indian OER initiatives are:

- A-VIEW (Amrita Virtual Interactive E-learning World)
- OER4S (Homi Bhabha Centre for Sc Ed.)
- OSCAR (IIT, Mumbai under Ekalavya Project).
- Shakshat
- NIOS-OER
- NROER
- NPTEL

E-learning Environments and Learning Management Systems

E-Learning environments may contribute to the teaching and learning process if the integration is done within the framework of proper pedagogy.

Building customized e-learning programmes places high demands on design, programming skills and time. An alternative to this can be deployment of courses within learning management systems.

Moodle — A Free Open Source Software for Web based Teaching and Learning

One such system that has been gradually gaining worldwide popularity is Moodle (Modular Object-Oriented Dynamic Learning Environment), a course management system for online learning. Moodle is "open source", allowing developers to tailor the system to individual needs. It communicates extremely well with many web-based resources (Facebook, YouTube, Wikipedia etc.), allowing developers creativity and versatility.

The design of Moodle is based on socio-constructivist pedagogy. This means its goal is to provide a set of tools that support an inquiry- and discovery-based approach to online learning. Furthermore it purports to create an environment that allows for collaborative interaction among students as a standalone, or in addition to, conventional classroom instruction.

Learning Management Systems: Features and Functions

Academics have taken the use of computer based applications in teaching and learning much more readily than they adopted audio-visual media. This is because of the strength of computer based applications and their power to manipulate words and symbols—which is at the heart of the academic endeavour. Today web has reached masses mainly due to its affordable cost and the convergence of PCs/Mobile/Multimedia and Communication technology. With advances in internet technologies, our dependence on ICT has increased allowing us to connect a variety of resources; also we have the opportunity to create new type of services. The focus of the Learning Management Systems is always on giving the educators the best tools to manage and promote learning. Many institutions are using the LMS platform like Moodle, to conduct fully online courses, while some are using it simply to augment face-to-face courses (known as blended learning.

Learning Management Systems has revolutionized the learning process by offering advanced and user-friendly solutions for encouraging the collaborative work of students and teachers. They come with a toolbox full of online teaching techniques that facilitate and enhance the proven teaching principles and traditional classroom activities. The philosophy behind LMS states that through an accent on collaborative learning, students get better motivated to engage themselves in the training process. Many of the LMS users love to use activity modules (such as forums, databases and wikis) to build richly collaborative communities of learning around their subject matter (in the social constructionist tradition), while others prefer to use LMS as a way to deliver content to students (such as standard SCORM packages) and assess learning using assignments or quizzes.

Moodle was designed by an educator and computer scientist, with "social constructionist" principles in mind. Moodle allows the integration of a wide range of resources, from chats and forums to online booklets, a variety of questions, collections of problems and exercises, lecture notes; including any kind of text-based or Html formatted documents, multimedia resources such as graphics, video or audio (e.g., MP3 files), PowerPoint, or Flash-based applications and Java applets "constructivist asserts that learning is particularly effective when constructing something for others to experience. This can be anything from a spoken sentence or an internet posting, to more complex artefacts like a painting, a house or a software package. The concept of *social constructivism* extends the above ideas into a social group constructing things for one another, collaboratively creating a small culture of shared artefacts with shared meanings. When one is immersed within a culture like this, one is learning all the time about how to be a part of that culture, on many levels."

A constructivist perspective views learners as actively engaged in making meaning, and teaching with that approach looks for what students can analyze, investigate, collaborate, share, build and generate based on what they already know, rather than what facts, skills, and processes they can reiterate.

Some of the tenets of constructivism in pedagogical terms include:

- Students come to class with an established world-view, formed by years of prior experience and learning.
- Even as it evolves, a student's world-view filters all experiences and affects their interpretations of observations.
- For students to change their world-view requires work.
- Students learn from each other as well as the teacher.
- Students learn better by doing.
- Allowing and creating opportunities for all to have a voice promotes the construction of new ideas.

- Allows students more control of their own learning.
- Allows lecturers to guide more, teach less.
- Allows student to build up knowledge, and become part of the teaching process.
- Can provide some really engaging learning experiences.
- Collaborating can be very well supported.

Conclusions

E-resources are increasingly important to all aspects of education—from teaching and learning to the student life cycle information. The Information and Communication Technologies (ICT) communities need to be made aware of the potential of information technologies for improving the Webgoggy through S&T and the research deliverance. LMS system is seen as a software platform which automates many of the processes associated with learning. It is a management software application enabling the delivery of learning content, resources and activities and also handles the associated administration tasks. With the extraordinary increase in information, increased student variety, new learning theories and ready access to the internet, teachers in today's classrooms are being presented with an opportunity to transform the learning in their classrooms from a traditional transmission model to a student-centred model, where students are more responsible for their own learning.

The key to understanding the difference between LMS and other computer education terms is to understand the systemic nature of LMS. LMS is the framework that handles all aspects of the learning process. LMS is the infrastructure that delivers and manages instructional content, identifies and assesses individual and organizational learning or training goals, tracks the progress towards meeting those goals, and collects and presents data for supervising the learning process of organization as a whole. LMS delivers content but also handles registering for courses, course administration, skills gap analysis, tracking, and reporting.

Introducing technology into the classroom can also bring a set of challenges. First is finding the time needed to incorporate new technology into courses. The technology itself can fail, leaving an instructor to resort to back up. Technology also changes rapidly and it takes time to keep up with technical changes that influence how equipment and software perform in the classroom. Need for institutional Support for the use of technology is also critical. Bringing technology into the classroom uses resources ranging from computers to classrooms to graduate assistants, and institution wide coordination is essential for ensuring an effective learning environment for students. Keeping the technology in working order is crucial but so are other issues such as ensuring a classroom's physical design supports the best possible use of the technology.

References

Alexander, S. (2005). E-learning: Blended directions. Paper presented at the E-Agenda Conference, Singapore.

Apedoe, X. (2005). The interplay of teaching conceptions and course management system design: Research implications and creative innovations for future designs. In A. Jafari and P. McGee (Eds.) *Course Management Systems for Learning: Beyond accidental pedagogy* (pp. 57-68). Hershey PA: Information Science.

Bailey, G.D. (1993). Wanted: A Road Map for Understanding Integrated Learning Systems. In G.D. Bailey (Ed.), *Computer-based Integrated Learning Systems* (pp. 3-9). Englewwod Cliffs, NJ: Educational Technology Publications.

Bain, J.D., and McNaught, C. (2006). "How academics use technology in teaching and learning: Understanding the relationship between beliefs and practice." *Journal of Computer Assisted Learning.*

Becker, H.J. (1993). A Model for Improving the Performance of Integrated Learning Systems. In G.D. Bailey (Ed.), *Computer-based Integrated Learning Systems* (pp. 11-31). Englewood Cliffs, NJ: Educational Technology Publications.

Blackboard Academic Suite brochure. (2006). Retrieved from http://library.blackboard.com/docs/as/bb_academic_suite_brochure_single.pdf Blackboard Company. (2006). from http://www.blackboard.com/company/

Brush, T.A., Armstrong, J., Barbrow, D., and Ulintz, L. (1999). "Design and Delivery of Integrated Learning Systems: Their Impact on Students Achievement and Attitudes." *Educational Computing Research*, 21(4): 475 486.

Carliner, S. (2005). Course Management Systems versus Learning Management Systems. Learning Circuits. http://www.learningcircuits.org/2005/nov2005/carliner.htm.

Connolly, P.J. (2001). A standard for success. InfoWorld, 23(42), 57-58. EDUCAUSE Evolving Technologies Committee (2003). Course Managment Systems (CMS). http://www.educause.edu/ir/library/pdf/DEC0302.pdf

Ellis, R., Calvo, R.A. (2007). "Minimum indicators to quality assure blended learning supported by learning management systems", *Journal of Educational Technology and Society.*

Survey of Learning Management Systems. (2006). Learning Circuits. Retrieved from http://www.learningcircuits.org/2006/August/2006LMSresults.htm.

4
Communication Skills for Effective Teaching

Shikha Kapur

Introduction

"To live is to communicate"—says the adage.

Simply defined communication is the act of transmitting knowledge, information, ideas, news, views, attitudes, influencing, convincing, entertaining, inspiring, frightening, spreading gossip, telling tales, stories, incidents, anecdotes, sharing feelings, passing skills from one person to another or between the source and the target group.

No organised life is possible without communication. Starting with grunts, signs, symbols and gestures that the primitive man used for communicating with others, today we have highly developed and sophisticated means of communication. Everett Rogers (1967) stated, "Communication is essential for social change." It is a prerequisite for progress, development and unity. It is an essential link between the individual and the innovation. Sapir (1931) opined, "... every cultural pattern and every single act of social behaviour involves communication in either an explicit or implicit sense."

Communication is derived from the Latin word "*communis*" (noun) meaning 'commonness' while '*communicare*' (verb) which means 'to make common' or 'to share' a piece of information, message, idea. The notion of 'commonality' and 'community' are both stressed in communication. According to Denis McQuail (1969) "Communication is the process which increases commonality and also requires elements of commonality to occur." In fact, the Sanskrit concept of communication is similar to that of McQuail (1986). "Communication is a relationship and mutual understanding and feeling that can be achieved amongst the '*Sahridyas*' or the people of one heart".

Communication is one of the most important processes for any species. Even the species that do not socialize have their prewired ways and means of establishing their territories, boundaries and the urge to mate.

Communication Among Humans

Communication among humans is the "production and reception of spoken, written, signed, or gestured information among human beings; it involves the use of symbols known as language received through the auditory, tactile, proprioceptive, and visual systems and generated through voice and speech, writing, manual signs, and gestures".

The foremost element in human communication is the sender or the person who initiates the process with an idea or an innovation and encodes the message and sends it through a channel. **Message** is the idea or innovation or information to be shared which can be presented in an oral form, written or non-verbal form as in a letter, an e-mail, etc. depending on the subject matter, purpose of communication, audience, the audience and their socio-cultural background. **Channel** is a vehicle or the media of transmission through which a message is carried *viz.* sound waves that

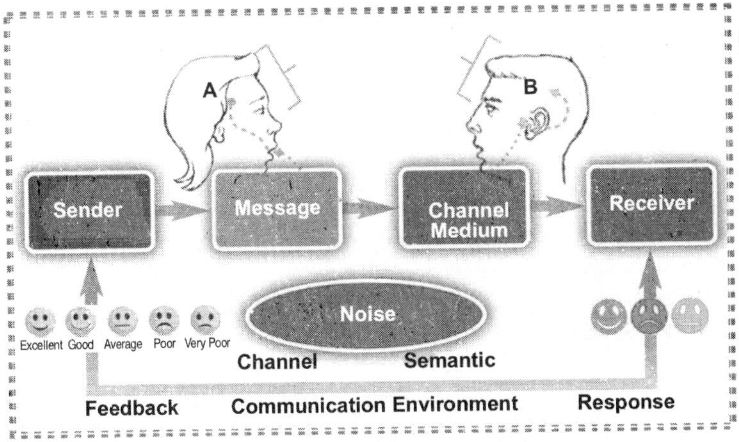

Fig. 4.1: Elements in Process of Communication.

Source: Talukder (2015). Five Elements of the Process of Communication.

carry the sound to the receiver either face to face or through mobile phone network, radio; or it may be a visual or a picture as in a hoarding, poster or magazine advertisement; or even a message flashed through an electronic audio-visual medium as television or a video call or a video conference etc. Selection of the channel is contingent upon the message, audience, situation and urgency of transmission of message. Wrong choice of channel can interrupt the process of communication.

The **Receiver** is the one who receives the encoded message, and then decodes it, interprets and understands it. The receiver sends a **Response** to the sender which is called **Feedback**. Feedback in communication is the indicator of 'effective communication' having taken place. Communication always takes place in a well-defined set-up called the **Communication Environment** e.g. an office or classroom or a social gathering. **Noise** is any unplanned interference in the communication environment which may be **Channel Noise** in the medium-loss of signal, crackling due to static or **Semantic Noise e.g.** illegible writing, or use of foreign language in communication.

Teaching and Communication

According to the Concise Oxford Dictionary, Communication means the 'act of imparting or the science and practice of transmitting information'. This clearly shows a close link between teaching and communication. Teaching plays a pivotal role in training of human resource specialists with necessary capabilities and also facilitates community development. Effective communication between teachers and students is the key to enhance the effectiveness of teaching and learning process.

Functions of Communication

Communication facilitates survival of individuals, evolution and sustenance of societies and organizations. Humans communicate for a variety of reasons. It is through communication that a teacher is able to establish relationships with the student/s relate to the surrounding/s and to each another. Some of the important functions served by communication include:

- Effective knowledge transaction
- Information sharing/receiving
- Educating

- Training
- Interacting
- Motivating
- Influencing and stimulating
- Persuading and coaxing
- Problem solving
- Providing Feedback
- Assist in Decision making
- Give Work/Job Instructions
- Establishing and sustaining relationships
- Group Building
- Sharing Emotions
- Integrating
- Relating
- Entertaining others

Types of Communication

The process of communication is complex (Hubley, 1993) as it uses different types of communication in the same situation. Communication may be one-way or a two-way. Teachers while using Lecture method use **one-way communication**. This is a less effective, but necessary means when a large body of technical knowledge has to be transacted between the teachers and students within a relatively short span of time. Many barriers to communication may crop-up in one-way communication that can be minimised through use of language easily understood by students, and Teachers speak slowly and as clearly as possible. As far as possible, the Lectures should be held in quiet, peaceful surroundings with classrooms that have good acoustics and are also well lit and ventilated.

Having **two-way communication** is the best strategy to overcome the barriers to communication between the teachers and student. Two-way communication entails getting regular feedback from the receivers in this case—the students. Students' feedback at regular intervals ensures that they are really able to understand what the Teacher is trying to put across to them (Fig. 4.2).

All teaching does not only take place through only **verbal communication** means that is through the use of words only with the students that maybe oral (spoken) or written. **Non-verbal communication** comprising of facial expressions, gestures, body language and even silence is equally important. Those teachers who are attentive to students' facial

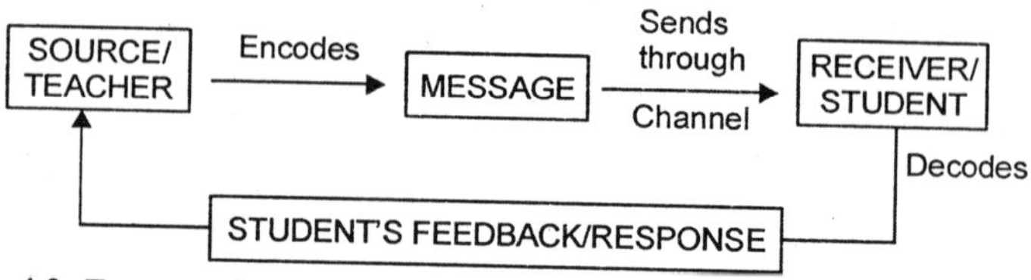

Fig. 4.2: Two-way Communication.

expressions and body language are clearly able to gauze and judge whether their students are alert, involved, confused, bored or disconnected. They can then change their strategies and styles of teaching-learning transaction with the students.

Verbal Communication		*Non-Verbal Communication*
• ORAL • WRITTEN	➢ Speaking ➢ Listening ➢ Writing ➢ Reading	➢ Facial Expression—frowning ➢ Sounds and Gestures—Giggling, waving ➢ Body Language—Eye, head, hand movements, slouching ➢ Proximity—sitting close to someone ➢ Touch ➢ Personal Appearance—Untidy ➢ Silence

Fig 3: Verbal versus Non-Verbal Communication.

Effective Communication Skills for Teachers

1. **Effective communication skill is neither region nor language specific.** It is not that people belonging to a certain part of the globe or particular linguistic groups have effective communication skills whereas the speakers of some other language are lacking henceforth.

2. **Effective communication skill is closely tied to the culture of the individual or group.** Teachers with similar cultural background as their students have a higher degree of acceptability by their students. However in case of students travelling abroad for education or teachers coming from foreign countries have to sensitize themselves and tune themselves to the elements of the new culture that they enter. Open-mindedness and flexibility on part of such students and teachers helps them accept cultural, regional, religious, gender and various other socio-economic differences.

3. **Display confidence in front of students.** Teachers need to establish eye-contact, not stammer and control classroom transaction.

4. **Know the students well.** The first step in effective communication is the teachers knowing the group of students they interact with in the classrooms. All the messages that a person receives is processed by a mental-filter also called the mind-set. This mental-filter is shaped by the process of socialization through family, friends, neighbours, school and society. This mental-filter or mind-set makes us understand each other better or can even be the cause of misunderstanding. Unless, we understand the attitude, the mind-set and the background of people with whom we are interacting, our communication skill would be imperfect and ineffective.

5. **Know the knowledge-level of the students.** Any learning process construed has to be based on the knowledge-level of the learners. They may vary in their age, experience, levels of knowledge, communication styles, that makes them distinct from the other and this diversity has to be respected and made an important resource in the learning situations (Kapur, 2015).

6. **Use different Presentation and Teaching Styles.** Each Teacher has a distinct teaching style. Some Teachers simply like to deliver Lecture and expect students to pen down what is being lectured. Some just like to dictate notes. These one-way authoritarian communication styles permit 'no questioning'. Learning through these styles is shallow, superficial, leading to rapid forgetting.

On the other hand, there are many other Teachers who encourage a lot of discussion and questioning as they transact concepts in their classroom. Student participation is at the core of their teaching style and this helps in acquiring in-depth knowledge by the students. The new ideas and concepts transacted through two-way participatory communication processes are better understood by students and they are also better equipped to apply them when they enter work situation. Certain key points in the Teachers presentation style include—

- Speak a language that the students are familiar with.
- Use terms and concepts that students will understand.
- Speak clearly and be loud enough; not too fast; facing the class and avoid all idiosyncrasies.
- Use appropriate non-verbal communication with appropriate gestures, expressions, eye contact and as far as possible move around the whole class.

- Keep tab of your speed of presentation so that the students are able to absorb the material that is presented.
- Have two-way communication—regularly taking feedback and checking whether students have understood.
- Teachers should listen well to their students.
- Develops good relationship with his students and respect each other.
- If Teachers communicate well with students they naturally do a better job of teaching.

7. **Take help of Teaching Aids.** According to a famous Chinese proverb—"What I hear, I forget; what I see, I remember; what I do, I know". According to researcher Dr Lawrence D. Rosenblum (2010), here's how much information each of our senses processes at the same time as compared to our other senses.

83.0%	Sight
11.0%	Hearing
03.5%	Smell
01.5%	Touch
01.0%	Taste

Teachers usually bank a lot on verbalism (both spoken and written) in their classrooms. But according to Rosenblum's research only 11 per cent students are ear minded therefore a large percentage of students are likely to develop ear fatigue, get bored and then disconnect from the teaching-learning situation.

The most common teaching aid available to each Teacher is the chalkboard or the blackboard. No teaching is possible without a chalkboard/blackboard. Several other teaching aids used by the Teachers include power point presentations, overhead projectors, pictures, charts, posters and interactive activity aids as practical demonstrations, tours, excursions, field trips and dramatics. All these teaching aids allow the Teacher to face the students while they use them.

The teaching aids used by the Teachers should be:

- Relevant to the subject—deal with the subject matter of the lesson, and clarify it.
- Are well prepared—contain only the highlights/main points; neat; different colours used for different points.

- Easy to read and comprehend—letters and pictures are large enough to be seen at a distance; not too much crammed up.
- Teachers uses them skilfully—with poise and confidence.
- Teaching aids if used properly can improve Teacher's communication with the students and lead to effective teaching.

7. **Have mastery of the subject.** Be equipped with scientifically accurate and up-to-date information that is in line with current thinking. For the students it's not the Teachers' experience but their mastery of subject, quality of teaching, and their teaching style is what the students find most important. The teacher should clear and emphasise important knowledge and leave out unnecessary details. The information should always be presented in a logical sequence. What is communicated in the class has to be comprehended and understood well by the students.

8. **Empathise with the students.** Empathy is the power to understand perspectives other than your own. It involves getting in the other person's shoes and know where the 'shoe bites'. Teachers must develop this skill as it leads to development of mutual trust. Empathy acts as a bridge between people and opens channels for two-way communication. It improves students' attitudes towards their Teacher and education, giving way to higher-order instructional strategies, and creating more effective academic experience.

9. **Develop a strong teacher-student relationship of mutual trust and understanding.** It is the underlying factor in effective communication (Obeidi, 2010; Espeland, 2001). This helps to increase students' confidence and their motivation to learn.

10. **Regular feedback.** Feedback should be continuous and on-going (Duncan, 2007; Hattie and Timperley, 2007). This helps in establishing a two-way communication between the Teachers and the students and helping to know the effectiveness of teaching.

11. **Listen with attention.** A good Teacher or communicator keeps encoding messages and sending them across to the students or receivers. To be a good communicator/Teacher one should be knowledgeable and be an active listener. Then only can one respond appropriately and establish a two-way communication. Only after listening well can a Teacher clear all doubts, answer questions and queries and provide appropriate solutions. Attentive and good listening skills are needed to develop empathy and understanding with the students and to assess whether they understand what they are being taught. Listening skills also help in negotiating with students and defusing any potential classroom conflicts.

12. **Keep an open mind.** India is a land of diversities. Our Colleges and Universities epitomize diversities—diversity of culture, region, religion, race, caste, gender. To be an effective Teacher, we have to keep an open mind free of all malice, bias and prejudice towards our students, peers and colleagues. This is the lesson which we not only follow as Teachers but also preach our students.

Conclusion

Teachers constantly impart new knowledge; transmit new information to their students hence bringing changes in their cognitive domain. They also usher in necessary attitudinal changes or changes in their affective domain along with helping students acquire skills necessary for the development of psychomotor domain pertaining to their discipline. In this process of transmission, the Teachers not only have to sharpen their existing knowledge but to also look for new strategies and ways to transact the new body of knowledge and skills to the students in an effective and efficient manner. Use of appropriate Communication skills is the key to effectiveness in the teaching and learning process between the teachers and the students. For effective teaching Teachers have to develop appropriate communication skills. They have to be both expressive as well as receptive. They have to be skilled in explaining concepts simply and clearly and also be skilled at listening. The complex, abstract concepts have to be broken down into small units and then transmitted to the students. They have to be versatile and be able to adapt their methods of communication to all students regardless of their ability or learning style. Effective communication includes transforming the boring into the interesting and having good presentation skills. If possible every Teacher should adopt the following **9 C's** as Communication Skills for effective teaching:

1. Confidence
2. Clarity
3. Correctness
4. Conciseness
5. Completeness
6. Considerate
7. Concreteness
8. Courteous
9. Concerned

References

Communis in Charlton T. Lewis and Charles Short (1879). Latin Dictionary. Oxford: Clarendon Press.

Duncan, N. (2007). 'Feed-forward': improving students' use of tutor comments, Assessment and Evaluation in Higher Education. 32(3): 271-283.

Espeland K. (2001). "Empowering versus enabling in academia." *J Nurs Educ* 40(8): 342.

Hattie, J. and Timperley, H. (2007). "The Power of feedback". *Review of Educational Research*, 77: 81-112.

Hubley, J. (1993). *Communicating Health*. London: Macmillan.

Kapur, Shikha (2015). "Understanding the Characteristics of an Adult Learner". *Jamia Journal of Education: An International, Biannual Publication*, 2(1): 111-121. ISSN: 2348 3490.

McQuail, Denis (1969). *Towards a Sociology of Mass Communication: Themes and Issues in Modern Sociology*, London: Collier-Macmillan.

McQuail, Denis (1986). *Mass Communication Theory: An Introduction*, London: Sage.

Obeidi N. (2010). "Factors on the communication between students and faculty members in the viewpoint of paramedical students." *Educational Strategies Journal*, 3(3): 133-136.

Rosenblum, Lawrence D. (2010). *See What I'm Saying: The Extraordinary Powers of Our Five Senses*. New York: W.W. Norton & Company Inc.

Sapir, E. (1931). *Communication in the Encyclopedia of Social Science*, 4:78-81, New York: Macmillan.

Talukder, Muhammad Jakirul Haque (2015, June 11). Five elements of the process of communication. [Blog post]. Retrieved from http://bdstudypoint.blogspot.in/2015/06/discuss-five-elements-factors-of.html

5
Inclusive Education as an Equitable Option for Disabled Children

Shabina Nishat Omar

Introduction

United Nations Convention on the Rights of Persons with Disabilities, Article 1 describes persons with disabilities as, "...those who have long-term, physical, mental, intellectual or sensory impairments which in interaction with various barriers may hinder their full and effective participation in society on an equal basis with others." This definition acknowledges the importance of the context and environment in enabling or disabling individuals from participating effectively within society. Any kind of substantial or extreme deviations from the accepted parameters of normalcy of the physical and mental ability of human beings resulting in obstruction or difficulties in social adjustment or professional performance is perceived as disability.

There are 150 million children across the world suffering from disabilities. Nearly one third of them are out of school. Most of these children live in Sub-Saharan Africa (43%) and South and West Asia (27%). In India, children with disabilities are five times more likely to be out of school than the national average, leading to an illiteracy rate among disabled people of up to 75 per cent.

Disabled children are often denied education as they are excluded, ostracised, marginalised and neglected. Even if they attend school, they are more likely to drop out early. The level of schooling they receive is usually inferior to that of their peers. The children with disabilities often do not go to school because of inadequate infrastructure and facilities suitable to their special needs. Also, there is insufficient comprehension about their learning needs, and attitudes triggered by prejudices around disability. Girls with disabilities are often doubly marginalised. They are often considered a burden on the family because they are seen as a non-productive member of society. Providing these girls with an education that meets their needs can address the root causes of their discrimination and remedy their situation.

Disability and Millennium Development Goals

Today, universal primary education has been established as the second of the Millennium Development Goals (MDGs). This is subscribed to by every country since 2000. It asserts the need for all children, including disabled children to successfully complete primary school in order to obtain quality education at par with that of their peers. This was outlined in the UN Convention on the Rights of Persons with Disabilities (CRPD). Although disability was not originally included in the MDGs, this was rectified in September 2010 when disability was officially acknowledged with regard to the MDGs. The second of the MDGs, universal primary education (UPE), was reiterated by a recent international human rights treaty, the United Nations Convention on the Rights of Persons with Disabilities (CRPD), when it came into effect in 2008. Article 24 states: States Parties recognise the right of persons with disabilities to education. With a view to realising this right without discrimination and on the basis of equal opportunity, States Parties shall ensure an inclusive education system at all level.

Inclusion is a way of thinking and acting that demonstrates universal acceptance and promotes a sense of belonging for all learners. It is not just about disabled children who are learners with special needs, but is an approach that embraces diversity and learner differences and promotes equal opportunities for all learners. Such an education system is built on a value-based approach to accepting responsibility for all children and students. Owing to lack of knowledge, educational access and technology, disabled children were initially treated as unwanted and segregated from other children. Later their education was carried out in special schools. In recent times there has been a shift towards having children with disabilities attend the same schools as non-disabled children. The educationists now feel that each child should be allowed to learn in his own way and at his own pace.

The concept of inclusive education has been clearly outlined in the Salamanca Statement and Framework for Action on Special Needs Education 1994. It states that all governments should "adopt as a matter of law or policy, the principle of inclusive education, enrolling all children in regular schools unless there are compelling reasons for doing otherwise". The democratic and human rights-based idea of Inclusive Education is defined in the Salamanca Statement and represented in the "recognition of the need to work towards 'schools for all'—institutions which include everybody, celebrate differences, support learning, and respond to individual needs." Inclusive Education is not only about issues of input such as access, and those related to processes such as teacher training, but it involves a shift in underlying values and beliefs, along with very specific approaches, positions, and solutions. Inclusive education is central to the achievement of high quality education for all learners and the development of more inclusive societies where difference is treated at par with sameness.

The basic premise of Inclusive Education is that the school should meet the educational needs of all children irrespective of their disabilities or limitations. Inclusive education can only occur when children with and without disabilities participate and learn together in the same classes. Research has proved that when a child with disabilities attends classes alongside peers who do not have disabilities, positive learning outcomes develop and major life goals are accomplished. However, simply placing children with and without disabilities together does not produce positive outcomes. Inclusive education occurs when there is commitment, advocacy, planning, support and joint hands on partnerships.

Inclusion in education is an approach to educating students with disabilities in a holistic and comprehensive way. Under the inclusion model, students with disabilities spend most or all of their time with non-disabled students. When children with disabilities learn in the same school as their non-disabled peers with the support necessary for them to be successful there, then the society is said to be "inclusive". All students in a school, regardless of their strengths and weaknesses in any area become part of the school community. A "team approach" is very crucial for inclusion. Some of the people instrumental in the success of the inclusive model of education could be regular teachers, parents, community, resource teachers, non-disabled children, Children With Special Needs (CWSN) and so on. Inclusive Education helps children with disabilities to prepare for full participation in community life.

The guiding principles of quality inclusive education are as follows:

- The mind of a child is shaped by diverse experiences and thus may have multiple intelligences. So each child can learn differently and be differently abled and selectively adept in various aspects of learning.
- Each child is a member of the larger society and thus by virtue of being a social citizen deserves equal opportunity and experiences of education so that in future equal opportunities of employment may be available to them. Inclusive Education must realise, value and support diversity and learner differences.
- Inclusive education is a child's right, not a privilege. The Individuals with Disabilities Education Act clearly states that all children with disabilities should be educated with non-disabled children of their own age and have access to the general education curriculum.
- Inclusive Education must set a high and positive expectation from its learners. Creating a culture of high expectations begins with an accessible curriculum and meaningful and relevant learning experiences. Educators and families must believe in and effectively implement the notion that with the right instructional supports, every learner can be successful.
- Education must seek to reduce barriers within learning environments. All education partners should collaborate in order to identify and reduce barriers within the curriculum, the learning environment and/or instruction that are interfering with students' ability to be successful learners and to participate in the learner community. All education partners, including school and jurisdictional staff, families, community service providers, post-secondary institutions, teacher preparation programmes and government should be committed to collaboration and to the success of all learners.
- Inclusive Education must include capacity building. School leaders, teachers, education professionals, families and community partners should be involved in as well as generate opportunities, relationships and resources that develop, strengthen and renew their understanding, skills and abilities to create flexible and responsive learning environments. Capacity building should ideally take place at the personal, school and system levels.

Inclusive Education has multiple benefits:

- It fulfils the aims of social adjustment and acceptance as children with disabilities are accepted by their peers, make friends and can be incorporated into mainstream society. Inclusive education can make this vision of families with disabled children a reality.
- *It enables the disabled children to develop a positive understanding of themselves and others.* When children participate in educational activities that mirror the real world, they learn to appreciate diversity and develop attitudes of tolerance and adjustment. Respect and understanding grow when children of differing abilities and cultures engage together.
- *Inclusive education makes children learn social skills* since they form friendships and bonds with other children. Children with and without disabilities learn with and from each other and co-operative task based learning is achieved.
- Inclusive education makes *children learn important academic and co-curricular skills.* Since children with and without disabilities are expected to learn to read, write and do math. With higher expectations and good instruction children with disabilities learn academic skills and this proves beneficial in future job opportunities.
- Since the philosophy of inclusive education is aimed at enabling all children to learn, children learn at their individual pace and style within a nurturing learning environment.

Every learner has unique needs. Some learners have profound and continuously changing needs while others have short-term or situation-based needs. Inclusive education thus requires flexible and responsive learning environments that can adapt to the changing needs of learners. For some learners, the most responsive and flexible learning environment may include:

- Instruction and support in a standardized classroom with peers of the same age where each person is attaining grade-level education.
- Individualized instruction supplemented by appropriate activity based in tasks in smaller group settings.
- A specialized classroom or setting fulfilling special needs of differently abled leaners.

- One-on-one instruction or a small student-teacher ratio.
- A combination of all the above or a selection from all the above as is suitable.

When teachers use evidence-based instructional practices and strategies to support student engagement, it can lead to greater achievement and success for all children and students. Flexible and responsive supports may include one or more of the following:

- Universal supports incorporated into the environment for all learners, such as flexible learning resources and technologies, differentiated instruction and positive behaviour supports.
- Targeted strategies or interventions especially for learners who need more specialized learning opportunities or access to more specialized expertise.
- Specialized/Individualized supports that directly relate to individual learning needs such as the use of sign language interpreters, alternate and augmentative communication systems (ACC), or mental health support.

Inclusive education and special school concepts are not competitive but complementary to each other. Inclusive schools must recognise and respond to the diverse needs of their students, accommodating both different styles and rates of learning and ensuing quality education to all through appropriate curricula, organisational arrangements, teaching strategies, resource use and partnerships with their communities. Inclusive education promotes child-to-child learning and participation of parents and community in planning and implementation of services for children in general and disabled children in particular.

In most countries, especially India, the educational opportunities for disabled children are either inappropriate or unaffordable or non-existent. Therefore, one of the best ways to impart quality education to all such children would be inclusive education, where all girls and boys, can study under the same roof and imbibe the same quality of education which will thereafter enable them to equal opportunity in later life such as a better job, more social and economic security, and more opportunities for full participation in society. This is an idealized vision in the world today as children with disabilities are still disproportionately excluded from school.

It is now widely acknowledged that to achieve the goal of universal education in India and in order to fulfil provisions laid out in the Right of

Children to Free and Compulsory Education (RTE) Act, 2009 (Ministry of Human Resource Development, 2009), the education of children with disabilities must be adopted in both ideology and practice to ensure equality and equity in education in India. Understanding Inclusive Education in the Indian context and developing a clear understanding of inclusion both as a concept and an ideology has been predictably difficult. Since Inclusive Education is a concept from the West it has been dismissed and often misunderstood. Singal (2005a) stated that inclusive education is "...a concept that has been adopted from the international discourse, but has not been engaged with in the Indian scenario" (p. 9). In another context, she says that the use of the term inclusive education appeared more fancy and politically correct and hence was adopted by practitioners and policy planners without necessarily developing a clear understanding of the notion behind it (Singal, 2006). Sharma (2010) too refers to it as a convenient term adopted by policy planners as it appears to be more child-centric. It was only as recently as in the nineties that some scholars wrote emphatically in favour of the ideals of inclusive education in India. Jangira (1995) and Kaur and Karanth (1993) warned against the disregard of the Western paradigm. They emphasized that this rejection of it was likely to hinder the total achievement of the governmental objective of Education for All. The obstruction to the development of a comprehensive understanding of inclusive education has also resulted from the obfuscation of the term has being often used interchangeably with integration. The use of terms like mainstreaming and integration with reference to education of the disabled is well-documented in policy and legal taxonomy. However, inclusive education has been a recent addition to the list. As Armstrong and Spandagou (2010) have elucidated, inclusive education originated as a challenge to the restrictions imposed by the existing models of mainstreaming and integration.

It has however often been misunderstood as being an alternative term for referring to integration. In a study of the understanding in the teachers of the concept of inclusion and inclusive education in Indian schools, Hodkinson and Chandrika (2009) used the term 'terminological ambiguity' to refer to a lack of clarity and elusiveness in its understanding. It is extremely essential that the two concepts be understood as clearly different not only in meaning and ideological affiliation but also in their multiple practical implications. Integration refers to a locational or geographical and social integration of children with special needs in regular classrooms, where readiness of the child with the disability is considered as a precondition for its success.

Inclusion subscribes to a "whole school" approach. Its genesis lies in the social model of disability and thereby inclusion advocates the schools' role in adapting and making accommodations within their system to assimilate children with varying learning needs (Lindsay, 2007). The importance of the school in empowering and playing a mitigating factor in the lives of children with special needs has been emphasized by several researchers such as Madan and Sharma, Vyas and Alur. According to Alur (2002), "inclusion is about minimizing exclusion and fostering participation for all students in the culture within a wider framework of support for all children in ordinary schools. Mittler (2006) explained that inclusion was based on a value system that celebrated diversity. Ainscow (1999) regarded it as a never-ending process that depended on continuous pedagogical and organizational development within the mainstream. Inclusion encompasses curriculum flexibility, pedagogy, infrastructural changes, sensitization of parents and peers as integral components of the accommodations that schools must make. Hence, initiative and commitment on part of a school must be viewed as imperative to the successful implementation of an inclusive education programme. Unless a school commits to the ideology of inclusion in principle and in practice, there are no guarantees for its success.

Apart from admitting children with mild disabilities who can be educated in regular classrooms, inclusion also addresses the needs of hundreds of children already present in regular classrooms who are affected by mild to moderate learning difficulties which go largely undetected and untreated. These children carry the risk of becoming dropouts due to poor school performance and may suffer from irreparable psychological and emotional trauma throughout their growing up years besides never being able to achieve academic success. Poor sensitivity of stakeholders (administrators, teachers, parents and peers) and lack of readiness of the system become additional factors contributing to their deprivation. Practice of inclusive education, therefore, also prevents exclusion of children with disabilities from the mainstream.

With the growing prevalence of children with various disorders, Inclusive Education can definitely benefit those children who have learning disability, mild or borderline intellectual functioning and other children with disabilities. Schools have to adopt a separate way of assessing these children instead of the normal writing assessments. Oral assessments, projects, experimental method, co-curricular assessments will prove beneficial. Resource rooms with a trained resource teacher and adequate learning aids should be made compulsory in all schools.

Today, with the availability of abundant opportunities across different fields, be it, music, sports, martial arts, art and craft, children, especially children with disabilities can excel across multiple myriad fields with basic academics and adequate life skills. And this is where we and the current education system of our country need to focus on to empower children with disabilities.

The Directive Principle of Indian Constitution, the National Policy of Education, The RCI Act, the Persons with Disabilities Act, The Sarva Shiksha Abhiyan (SSA) 2010 or Education for All ensures admission and education of all children in the age group of 6 to 14 years, including the disabled children. No normal school can deny admission to a disabled child. The Scheme of Inclusive Education for Disabled at Secondary Stage (IEDSS) has been launched from the year 2009-10. This Scheme replaces the earlier scheme of Integrated Education for Disabled Children (IEDC) and provides assistance for the inclusive education of the disabled children in classes IX-XII. This scheme is now subsumed under the Rashtriya Madhyamik Shiksha Abhiyan (RMSA) from 2013. The States/UTs are also in the process of subsuming under RMSA as RMSA subsumed Scheme. It aims at enabling all students with disabilities, to pursue further four years of secondary schooling after completing eight years of elementary schooling in an inclusive and enabling environment.

The scheme covers all children studying at the secondary stage in Government, local body and Government-aided schools, with one or more disabilities as defined under the Persons with Disabilities Act (1995) and the National Trust Act (1999) in the class IX to XII, namely blindness, low vision, leprosy cured, hearing impairment, locomotory disabilities, mental retardation, mental illness, autism, and cerebral palsy and may eventually cover speech impairment, learning disabilities, etc. Girls with the disabilities receive special focus to help them gain access to secondary schools, as also to information and guidance for developing their potential. Setting up of Model inclusive schools in every State is envisaged under the scheme.

The components of this scheme are:

- Student-oriented components, such as medical and educational assessment, books and stationery, uniforms, transport allowance, reader allowance, stipend for girls, support services, assistive devices, boarding the lodging facility, therapeutic services, teaching learning materials, etc.

- Other components include appointment of special education teachers, allowances for general teachers for teaching such children, teacher training, orientation of school administrators, establishment of resource room, providing barrier free environment, etc. The School Education Department of the State Governments/Union Territory (UT) Administrations are the implementing agencies. They may involve NGOs having experience in the field of education of the disabled in the implementation of the scheme. Central assistance for all items covered in the scheme is on a hundred per cent basis. The State governments are only required to make provisions for scholarship of a fixed amount per disabled child per annum.

In several parts of India, some pioneering experiments have taken place. One such instance is that of the Project Integrated Education for the Disabled (PIED) which has been functioning since 1987. A Composite Area Approach (CAA) is followed where regular classroom teachers, specialist teachers, parents and community members jointly work in the programme. The regular teachers are given training in handling disabled children.

Conclusion

For successful mainstreaming of the inclusive education in India it is imperative to improve the quality of teachers in relation to competencies required and in-service training. The emphasis should be placed on innovation and devising teaching and learning methodologies/strategies that fill the lacuna present in the system. There must also be a clear identification of training needs aimed at teachers in the context of their competencies to improve the quality of in-service training programmes. There must also be a clear highlighting of the shortcomings of present day in-service programmes. There is a major need in India for identification of the competencies of inclusive school teachers. There must also be a study of the competencies of existing teachers for imparting inclusive education. Only after a comprehensive understanding of the complete picture can any model of inclusive education be successfully implemented.

References

Ainscow, M. (1999). *Understanding the Development of Inclusive Schools.* London: Falmer Press.

Ainscow, M. and Cesar, M. (2006). "Inclusive education ten years after Salamance: Setting the agenda". *European Journal of Psychology of Education*, XXI, 3, pp. 231-238.

Alur, M. (2002). Special needs policy in India. In S. Hegarty and M. Alur (Eds.), *Education and children with special needs,* pp. 51-66, New Delhi: Sage Publications.

Armstrong, A.C., Armstrong, D. and Spandagou, I. (2010). *Inclusive Education: International Policy and Practice*. London: Sage Publications.

Forlin, C., Loreman, T., Sharma, U. and Earle, C. (2009). "Demographic differences in changing pre-service teachers' attitudes, sentiments and concerns about inclusive education". *International Journal of Inclusive Education*, 13(2): 195–209.

Hodkinson, A. and Devarakonda, C. (2009). "Conceptions of inclusion and inclusive education: A critical examination of the perspectives and practices of teachers in India". *Research in Education*, 82: 85-99. J

Jangira, N.K. (1995). *Responsive teaching*. New Delhi: NCERT.

Joshi, P. (2010). Developing a vision for inclusive education: A case-study. In N. Sharma (Ed.), *The social ecology of disability* (Technical series 3, Lady Irwin College, pp. 77-85). New Delhi, India: Academic Excellence.

Kaur, B. and Karanth, P. (1993). Education for young children with special needs. In T.S. Saraswathi and B. Kaur (Eds.), *Human development and family studies in India,* pp. 301-314). New Delhi: Sage Publications.

Lindsay, K.G (2007). Inclusive education in India: Interpretation, implementation and issues. Consortium for research on educational access, transitions and equity. Create pathways to access, Research Monograph, no. 15.

Madan and Sharma: *Inclusive Education for Children with Disabilities: Preparing Schools*, published by CORE Scholar, 2013.

Madan, A. (2013). "Inclusive Education for children with Disabilities: Preparing Schools to Meet the Challenge." *Electronic Journal of Inclusive Education.* 3(1).

Mittler, P. (2006). *Working Towards Inclusive Education: Social Contexts*. New York: David Fulton Publishers.

Mukhopadhyay, S. (2002). Whole-school approach and curriculum modifications. In S. Hegarty and M. Alur (Eds.), *Education and children with special needs,* pp. 141-146. New Delhi: Sage Publications.

Reid, G. (2005). Learning styles and inclusion. London: Sage Publications. Ministry of Human Resource Development, Government of India (2009).

Right of children to free and compulsory education (RTE) Act, 2009. Retrieved from http://mhrd.gov.in/rte Ministry of Social Justice and Empowerment (2011).

Sanjeev, K. and Kumar, K. (2007). "Inclusive education in India". *Electronic Journal for Inclusive Education*, 2(2).

Sharma, N. (2010). Education for children with disability: Reflections on 'best practices' to assimilate children in the mainstream. In N. Sharma (Ed.) *The social ecology of disability* (pp. 125-149). Technical Series 3, Lady Irwin College. Delhi: Academic Excellence.

Sharma, N. and Sen, Sharma, R. (2012). Children with disabilities and supportive school ecologies. In M. Ungar (Ed.), *The social ecology of resilience: A handbook of theory and practice*. doi: 10.1007/978-1-4614-0586-3_22. New York: Springer

Sharma, U., Moore, D. and Sonawane, S. (2009). "Attitudes and concerns of pre-service teachers regarding inclusion of students with disabilities into regular schools in Pune, India." *Asia Pacific Journal of Teacher Education*, 37(3): 319-331.

Singal, N. (2005a). Responding to difference: Policies to support 'inclusive education' in India, paper presented at the Inclusive and Supportive Education Congress 2005, University of Strathclyde, Glasgow.

Singal, N. (2006). "An ecosystemic approach for understanding inclusive education: An Indian case-study." *European Journal of Psychology of Education*, Vol. XXI, 3, pp. 239-252.

The draft Rights of Persons with Disability Bill 2012, Retrieved from http://socialjustice.nic.in/pwd2011.php.

6

E-Content Development

A New Paradigm Shift in Higher Education in India

S.K. Tiwari

Introduction

The MHRD, under its National Mission on Education through ICT (NMEICT) launched in 2009, allocated funds to the UGC on 29th September, 2011 for development of e-content in 77 subjects at postgraduate level. It proposed to create high quality, curriculum-based, interactive content in different subject across all disciplines of social sciences, arts, fine arts and humanities, natural and mathematical sciences and linguistics and languages. E-content, so developed would be available in open access through a dedicated Learning Management System (LMS) as well as through *Sakshat* Portal.

The best form of learning is where the student is kept engaged through the process of imparting education. In the traditional classroom situation, there are a number of ways to assess whether or not students are actually assimilating instruction, e.g. the teacher may pose questions or conduct formal assessments to gauge the level of understanding of each student. Likewise, for an online learning session to be effective, the courseware must include interactive features that facilitate "immersive learning". This might be in form of "interactive elements" that students can engage with as they progress through the conceptual learning materials, or it may be a full-fledged simulation that tests both understanding and skills within the context.

Development of e-content is a specialized job requiring skills of a web designer and instructional designer. However, a faculty or a scientist involved in teaching and research is perfectly capable of preparing basic materials that can be transformed into e-content with intervention of web designer and professionals with ICT skills. A guideline is designed to guide author/content writer to write an e-content module for a given paper along with description of multimedia contents, as instructing to graphical designer/animator.

The project sanctioned by the MHRD under NME-ICT provides for development of e-content for all modules and sub-modules in 77 subject areas at PG level. On average, each subject would have 16 (max) or less core papers in 2 years PG course. For this initiative, each paper, in turn, would consist of 40 modules, roughly equivalent to 40 hours of lectures delivered for a paper in a semester. The UGC has constituted a Standing Committee, *e-PG Pathshala*, on e-content creation to monitor and coordinate the activity of content creation in a most effective and efficient manner and in order to have uniformity of the e-Content. The Standing Committee is the apex level decision making body.

NME-ICT is a Centrally Sponsored Scheme to leverage the potential of ICT, in teaching and learning process for the benefit of all the learners in Higher Education Institutions at any time any where mode. Its motto being "to provide connectivity up to the last mile", the NME-ICT aims to extend computer infrastructure and connectivity to over 38,000 colleges existing at present and each of the departments of over existing 550 universities/deemed universities and institutions of national importance in the country.

NME-ICT seeks to bridge the digital divide, i.e., the gap in the skills to use computing devices for the purpose of teaching and learning among urban and rural teachers/learners in higher education domain and empower those, who have hitherto remained untouched by the digital revolution and have not been able to join the mainstream of the knowledge economy. This will enable them to make best use of ICT framework for teaching and learning.

NME-ICT is focused primarily on development of high quality e-content in all disciplines and subjects at various levels. The projects under NME-ICT can broadly be classified as:

(a) e-Content Development, (b) Infrastructure Development, and (c) Social Impact

Objectives of E-content Development

1. Web enabled, High quality content for web based learning (for all subjects) (not to replace traditional teaching).
2. Any time/Anywhere/Anyone can access/receive same content on the web.
3. For formal/non-formal modes, to supplement/complement teaching/learning.
4. Develop partnership between Universities and IT industry for development of new content and method (contemporary technology).

Benefits of E-Content Development

1. Can be Customized for different learning needs/Groups
2. Cuts travel expenses
3. Takes less time to train people
4. Eliminate/Reduce need for classroom infrastructure
5. Instant up dating, accurate and useful for long period
6. Enables to make communities to share knowledge
7. Motivates for organizational learning
8. E-learning solutions are highly scalable
9. Programme can be for 10/100/1,00,000 with little effort or incremental cost

EMMRCs: There are 22 *Educational Multi Media Research Centres* (EMMRCs) which are responsible for (I) subject specific academic content development and (II) Programme development of e-Content, Video based productions and production of LoR's in 17 subjects (Phase-I) as well as EMMRCs also supervise production of e-content (specific to other 60 subjects) with the help of academicians and production agencies other than the Media Centre (EMMRCs) itself (Phase II).

Table 6.1: 17 UG Subjects Undertaken (Phase-I, 11th Plan)

S.No.	*Subjects*	*Programme to be produced by EMMRC*
1.	Maths	Calicut
2.	Physics	Poona
3.	Chemistry	Roorkee

4.	Botany	Srinagar
5.	Zoology	Ahmedabad
6.	Political Science	Manipur
7.	History	Kolkata
8.	Economics	Osmania
9.	Commerce	Jodhpur
10.	Language (Eng.) TEFLU,	Hyderabad
11.	Geography	Mysore
12.	Psychology	Sagar
13.	Environmental Sc.	Chennai
14.	Computer Sc.	Indore
15.	Communication and Journalism	JMI, New Delhi
16.	Sociology	Madurai
17.	Agriculture	Patiala

Fig. 6.1: 22 EMMRCs in India.

35 PG Subjects for which Proposals are invited in the 2nd Phase

• Anthropology	Biochemistry	Biotechnology
• Botany	Chemistry	Commerce
• Computer Sc.	Computational Sc.	Zoology

• Computational Social Sc.	Law	Economics
• Education	English	Environmental Sc.
• Food technology	Forensic Sc.	Geography
• Psychology	History	Earth Science
• Sociology	Management	Statistics
• Mass comm. and Journalism	Mathematics	Hindi
• Microbiology	Philosophy	Physics
• Political Sc.	Public Adm.	Social Work
• Lib and information Sc. Linguistics		

Detailed Subject-wise Breakup for 2nd Phase

- Actuarial Science (Risk/Disaster Management)
- Education; Adult Education/Continuing Education; Non Formal Education
- Analytical Sciences/Instrumentation Architecture
- Bioinformatics
- Buddhist Studies; Comparative Study of Religions
- Business Economics
- Computer Science
- Computational Social Science
- Defence and Strategic Studies
- Electronic Science; Information Technology
- French, Japanese, Russian, Urdu, German, Spanish, Chinese, Comparative Literature
- Population Studies
- Genetics
- Home Science; Food and Nutrition
- Human Resource Management
- Human Rights and Duties
- Museology and Conservation
- Nano-Science and Nanotechnology
- Pharmaceutical Science
- Physical Education, Sports and Health; Social Medicine and Community Health
- Visual Arts (including Drawing and Painting/Sculpture); Graphics/ Applied Art/History of Art); Performing Arts (Dance/Drama/Theatre); Music and Fine Arts; Indian Culture
- Gender Studies

Table 6.2: Tablet Aakash-IV (Launched on March 2014)

	Aakash I	*Aakash II*	*Aakash IV*
Memory (GB)	2	4	4GB (internal) + 32GB card DDR3 SD RAM memory
OS (Android Application)	Android 2.2	4.03	Android 4G tablet PC 7" touch screen
Sensor	—	G - Sensor	
Battery (Mh)	2100	3000	4 hr
Processor (M hz)	366	512 (Fast)	Dual core 1.2 GHz
Camera	—	Front VGA Camera	0.3 mega pixel or more
Internet	Wi – fi connection	Wi – fi connection Multi Touch Panel U-Tube-Video Download	Rs. 3999/- Wi – fi connection USB Port: support for 2G, 3G, 4G phase and data connecting

Aakash-1: Low Cast computing cum access Tablet device (launched on Oct., 5, 2011, Vigyan Bhawan, N. Delhi); @ Rs. 2276/- (Rs. 1138/-); 11th Plan-Rs. 700 crores to provide 50 per cent subsidy.

Aakash-2: 20,000 by Nov., 2012; 50 lac tablets in 1st phase (1.1 crore by Dec., 2013); @ Rs. 1500/- (expected).

Aakash-4: @ Rs. 3999/-; 17,000 tablets delivered; 10 vendors – HP, Lenovo, Dell.

- Support reading and editing in many languages: Hindi, Sanskrit, Devnagri, Urdu, Kanadda, Telugu, Malyalam, Tamil, Punjabi, Gujrati, Bengali, Oriya, Assamese, Bishnupriya, Manipuri.

Method of hour estimation: Estimated on the basis of number of hours required to transact the content in class room *e.g.* A course in class room requires 1 credit (1 credit = 15 hours).

So, content of the course will be 15 hours.

Stable knowledge (linguistics) will be valid for 10 Years while Dynamic knowledge (social science, Science, technology) will be valid for 3 Years.

PROPOSAL SUBMISSION FOR E-CONTENT DEVELOPMENT

Eligibility/Target Group for E-Content Development

- Teachers/Professionals of College, University
- College/University Department
- College/University
- Consortium of Universities
- Commercial establishments/production houses having experience in production of e-Content, LoR's and Video; and ties with university/college

"e-content development" is an entirely new project initiated by MHRD/UGC. It is quite possible that PIs/Co-PIs may not have prior experience in the field similar to that of audio-visual programmes. Proposals for e-Content development under e-PG Pathshala by a PI & CoPI may be submitted, through the Host Institute under which the PI(s) are working. The proposals may be submitted to Chairman, UGC, New Delhi by any:

(a) PG teacher, engaged in teaching in an Institution recognised by UGC, for at least ten years, in the particular discipline.
(b) Educational institution in India imparting higher education, who agrees with the aims and objectives of NME-ICT/UGC, shall be eligible to submit proposals.
(c) Agency/Institution/Individual through invitation of NME-ICT/UGC.

The Host Institute, where the PI(s) is/are working may forward an application of PI(s) for e-Content development under e-PG Pathshala by a PI or PI & Co-PI(s) in accordance with the 'Guidelines for e-content development' and 'Proforma for submitting a Project proposal' for seeking financial assistance from UGC, under e-PG Pathshala, NME-ICT programme for development of e-content of a subject/course.

The Standing Committee, e-PG Pathshala, UGC having reviewed the application in prescribed format and forwarded by the Host Institute, shall call the PI and/or Co-PI(s) to present their proposal before it. The Standing Committee, e-PG Pathshala, may offer its comments for modifications of the proposal, if any and approve the proposal.

The funds on this are transferred by the UGC to the Host Institute. In order to ensure that a number of projects sanctioned to PIs working at different Host Institutes are developed uniformly and in according with the Guidelines and Norms set by the Standing Committee, e-PG Pathshala, it is important that common set of understanding is arrived between UGC, all the PI(s) and the Host Institute. Accordingly, a uniform Memorandum of Understanding is to be signed between the UGC, all the PI(s) and Host Institutes.

Evaluation of Proposals: The procedure for evaluation of the proposals would be more or less the same as adopted by funding agencies like UGC, DST except the benchmarks for judging the project would be suitably modified in view of above mentioned issues. Proposals can be submitted online on e-PG Pathshala website. Each Standing Committee, e-PG Pathshala, UGC member gets an opportunity to go through the Project and review the proposal. All the projects sanctioned under e-PG Pathshala, shall have an expert group for monitoring projects called *Project Review and Supervisory Group* (PRSG). The PI is required to submit names of 10 Subject Experts to the UGC and the Standing Committee, e-PG Pathshala, constituted by the UGC shall chose few or add some more experts to form a PRSG for each Subject. These expert groups indentified for sanctioned projects shall monitor the progress periodically and submit the report to the SC, UGC.

While submitting fresh proposals, the Project Investigator (PI) on behalf of the implementing Institution has to submit an undertaking to the SC, UGC, that the proposal being submitted by them has not been submitted elsewhere, nor is it a repetition of any other project for which they have received funding from any other agency. However, if they want to submit the same or similar proposal to any other funding agency, they should inform SC, UGC.

Principal Investigator and Co-Investigator(s) and Implementing Institution(s)

Principal Investigator (PI) has the primary responsibility for implementation of the project. The project team consists of the PI, Co-Investigators (up to 2) and the project personnel appointed as per the sanction order, if any. It is necessary to ensure that the project is carried out by the project team in a cohesive manner. Periodic meetings of the PRSG are essential for this purpose.

1. In case of PIs who would be superannuating during the duration

of the project, a "in service" Co-Investigator may be ensured by the Institute authorities. In such cases, the Institute should inform to the SC, UGC, well in advance, about their "no objection" for providing the infrastructural facilities to the PI for implementation of the project after his superannuation.

2. Having accepted the responsibility for implementation of project, PI should be committed to implement the project over its duration and should not go on long leave.
3. PI may engage teachers with 10 years of PG teaching experience who are in service or retired, as content writers.
4. In case, PI is shifting to another institution on new appointment/ transfer/long term deputation, the project could be transferred to that institution with the mutual consent of both the institutions and of the SC, UGC. Such requests for transfer of the project should be sent well in advance and should be accompanied with 'No Objection' certificates (NOC) from both the institutions and the Endorsement Certificate from the new Institution.
5. In case the PI leaves the project due to unforeseen circumstances, the Co-Investigator could be considered as the PI, subject to the approval of Head of the Institute and the SC, UGC. Such a request should be sent at least 4-6 months in advance along with a detailed bio-data of Co-Investigator.
6. The PI as well as the implementing institution has the responsibility of informing the SC, UGC about any change in the status of the PI/Co-Investigator including relieving them on short term deputation for a continuous period of 3 months or more.
7. The project stands terminated in the absence of PI/Co-Investigator for a continuous period of 3 months without intimation to the SC, UGC.
8. The implementing institution has an important role to play and in consultation with the SC, UGC take steps to ensure successful completion of the project, before relieving the PI.
9. The implementing Institute should provide full infrastructural facilities such as accommodation, water, electricity, and communication facilities etc. for smooth implementation of the project.
10. Payment towards Project overhead charges to implementing institute is not admissible.

Project Staff and Honourarium

1. All personnel including Research personnel appointed full/part time under the project are to be treated as temporary employees and will be governed by the Administrative rules/service conditions of the implementing Institute. No reference on these issues be made to this UGC. The UGC will have no liability, whatsoever, for the project staff after completion of the project.
2. Scale and emoluments for the posts not covered under this order are governed by norms prevalent in the implementing Institution or as may be decided by this Department. Total emoluments spent on—engaging personal, work outsourced, honourarium to regular staff and procurement of Hardware and/or Software required for development of e-content should not exceed the budget allocated for the project.
3. Honourarium, to PI(s) if any, shall be payable only after completion of the project and acceptance of deliverables by the Govt. of India, Department of Higher Education, MHRD. The Honourarium shall be regulated strictly as per rules and regulations in force from time to time.
4. Further the Honourarium to PI(s) in no case stall exceed 10 per cent of the cost of project and no one individual would get more than 20 per cent of his/her annual Salary as honourarium for the whole year including honourarium received from any other source whatsoever.

Pilot Project/Detailed Project

(a) Every PI/Co-PI is required to give a presentation before the Standing Committee, e-PG Pathshala. In view of fairly wide range of available domain expertise among SC members as well as in the areas of teaching methodology, content development and other aspects of education. However, if the Standing Committee, e-PG Pathshala, UGC feels that expertise in certain areas is not available, the committee may associate some external experts.

(b) Based on presentation and critical examination of the proposal, the Standing Committee, e-PG Pathshala, UGC shall either recommend sanction of the project or may make suggestions for further improvement. The maximum duration of completing a Pilot project would be one year or as approved by SC, UGC.

(c) It is decided to adopt 2-step approach of considering a pilot process and then request a comprehensive evaluation of the full proposal within a few months to sanction the full project by the time the pilot project can be reviewed and assessed as successful by PRSG (domain experts).

(d) On completion of pilot project, the SC would invite some external experts or follow the PRSG recommendation on review of the project. Based on the feedback of the experts, the SC would invite PI for presentation for the detailed project.

Funding and Duration of Projects: Rule for funding of the Pilot project (under content development) is restricted to Rs. 7 lakhs or 10 per cent of the total cost of detailed project, whichever is more. The funding guidelines to be followed by SC are advisory in nature. However, in special cases, the SC may use its discretion to deviate from these guidelines so that mission objectives can be achieved. These guidelines may be reviewed from time to time by the UGC.

Content Development: It consists of (i) Academic content writing and (ii) e-Content production. The Academic content may be written by the Subject Experts. However, the services of INFLIBNET and CEC including its EMMRCs spread across the country or Production Houses, having experience in production of e-Content and Video programmes, especially for education may be sought by the Implementing Institution. Proposals for e-Content development may be submitted keeping in mind that the product is developed and delivered to SC, UGC in an integrated form, following Guidelines with regard to Template and Technical parameters:

However, if it is found that the quality of e-Content is not as per Technical and Production Guidelines, the Implementing Institution/ individual assigned to produce the e-Content shall have to get it corrected within budget sanctioned.

E-Content Module and Content Duration: Content duration is estimated on the basis of the number of hours that are required to transact the content in the classroom. For example, a course in the classroom requires one credit and a credit is equivalent to 15 hours classroom teaching. The content of a course will be taken as 15 hours. On an average, UG students have to take 6 - 8 papers in an academic year. Therefore, during the study period of 3 years a student may take 18 - 24 papers. A paper shall comprise of 40 modules, each module of one hour duration.

E-CONTENT MODULE AND CONTENT DURATION

A course in classroom requires	1-credit = 15 hrs
UG student, 6 - 8 papers	1 year
PG student 16 papers	2 years
18 - 24 papers	3 Years
1- paper (20 - 25 lessons)	1 - lesson : 3-hrs. of teaching
1- paper (40 modules of 1 hour)	40, 60 - 75 hrs of teaching (in 1 semester)
2.5 hrs of classroom lecture	Normally covered by an e-content Module of 30 minutes.

Project Management and Monitoring: An Academic Content Advisory Committee is constituted by the Implementing Agency, i.e., UGC, comprising of a panel of Subject/Technical Experts and Media professionals, Managers to monitor and review the progress of implementation of the e-Content Scheme assigned to the Institute Agency.

The committee shall be responsible for selecting and engaging (i) a Course Coordinator for each e-Course assigned and (ii) Production House/ Agency for production of e-content Development. The Academic Content Advisory Committee meets once in three months, or more often if needed, to review the quality of Academic Content delivered by the Subject Experts and quality of Production delivered by the Production Agency/ Implementing Agency of each e-Content course and recommend the corrections, changes etc., that are required in accordance with the Guidelines issued.

Nature of Product: The Programme Production Agency shall take the Academic content from Subject Coordinator/Subject Expert, engaged by the Implementing Agency and shall produce e-content Module as per Academic and Technical criteria and provide Graphics, Animation and MM inputs, wherever needed. The Production Agency shall also incorporate necessary modifications as indicated by Subject Coordinator or Academic Content Advisory Committee.

The text may be divided into sections, subsections and, where necessary, sub-subsections.

Text is formatted using "Times New Roman" or "Arial" font (size 11). Fonts should be provided in separate folder in case of font in regional language. Uniform font size and style is maintained throughout the text with single line spacing. Pages are assigned sequential numbers. The first section is normally an introduction, which should state clearly the objective of the work, its scope and the main advances reported, with brief references to relevant work.

The preferred format for numbering the sections: 1. 2. 3., etc. with Times New Roman Bold. The subsection should be numbered as 2.1., 2.2., 2.3., etc. with Time New Roman Italics and the sub-subsection should be numbered as 2.3.1., 2.3.2., etc. with Time New Roman Italics.

Content delivery through Video is an essential component of each module of the e-Content that needs to be incorporated to explain the topic. It may include Multimedia (MM), Animation, Documentary, Simulation, Virtual Lab. The duration of Video should be 30 Minutes (or more). However, it is presumed that a content writer/domain expert is not fully acquainted with art of creating MM and above mentioned types of video. As such, content writer is required to describe his/her MM requirement using a story board. The process is described in detail at point 6 and get the video part generated.

Script for the MM Content: If the Content Writer is unable to provide the multimedia files, they have to submit script for preparing the MM using storyboard. The Content Writer has to visualize the concept to be presented in MM.

- *i.* ***Image** (2D&3D):* The Content Writer may provide a hand drawn image or a reference to an image available publicly on the web that need to be modified. Otherwise he/she may also give a brief description of the image to be developed through out-source services.
- *ii.* ***Video**:* A brief description of the video content to be included. *Example*: Water pollution, Video on industrial wastage flowing in the river.
- *iii.* ***Animation** (2D&3D):* The nature and purpose of animation needs to be explained in the module with specific movements (fade in, fade out; zoom in, zoom out, etc.) of different elements or flow charts describing the process. *Example*: Generation of Hydroelectricity.
- *iv.* ***Simulation**:* It is the imitation of the operation of a real-world process or system over time.

Multimedia Content Format

***I. Audio**:* Audio is of 3 types—*Narration or Voice Over* (VO), *Music/*

Speech (M) and *Sound Effects* (SFX). Specify the types of audio to be used. Specify the kinds of music and sound effects required. If voice over is to be used, prepare the script of the voice and write it on the module. It may be noted that the chunk text would be delivered as audio.

II. Visual: Visual can be of 2 types—static and motion, the former is called *graphics* and the later *video*. It is very important to give a description of the graphics or video used. Then a description of what it will show, its purpose, etc. are required. The Content Writer may provide graphics including pictures, maps, hand-drawn images, etc. as is done in case of print publication. However, Content Writer may not have the skill to make animation, simulation or audio-visual content. The INFLIBNET Centre or other out-source service provider has developed expertise that would help Content Writer to enrich their content with multimedia. However, the Content Writer is expected to describe the MM enrichment that he/she requires for the content.

(a) *Format* for Images (Graphics)

- In order to obtain high quality output, image resolution should be 600 dpi at the actual finished size. Ensure to embed images or supply linked image files.
- Number the illustrations/Figure/Graphic/Map/Table according to their sequence in the text.
- Submit each figure as a separate file.
- For easy identification of source files in terms of figure numbers and format used, ensure that the name of file should contain figure number as well as format type.
- Provide captions to illustrations separately. A caption should comprise of a brief title (not on the figure itself) and a description of the illustration. Keep text in the illustrations to a minimum but explain all symbols and abbreviations used. Figure captions should be understandable without reference to the main text.
- Convert figure or save as the image file in following formats: EPS: Vector drawings. Embed the font or save the text as 'graphics'. TIFF: Colour or grayscale photographs (halftones): always use a minimum of 300 dpi. TIFF: Bitmapped line drawings: use a minimum of 1000 dpi. TIFF: Combinations bitmapped line/half-tone (colour or grayscale): a minimum of 500 dpi is required.

***(b) Video*:** Content Writer has to submit in flash format (flv) with following specifications: (i) To use good quality Video Camera, 1/3" 3X-CMOS/CCD Camera or better. Preferred format should be HD video (ii) Resolution: 1080p recommended.

(c) Animation: Animation is the rapid display of a sequence of images of 2-D or 3-D artwork or model positions to create an illusion of movement.

(d) Simulation: It is the imitation of the operation of a real-world process or system over time. The act of simulating first requires that a model be developed that represents the key characteristics or behaviours of the selected physical or abstract system or process. The model represents the system itself, whereas the simulation represents the operation of the system over time. Good simulations provide the maximum level of interactivity as they allow the user to explore a Guideline for e-Content Writer concept, process, relationship, etc. by changing input parameters and watching the outcome in a graphical representation. A computer simulation is an attempt to model a real-life or hypothetical situation on a computer so that it can be studied to see how the system works. By changing variables in the simulation, predictions may be made about the behaviour of the system. It is a tool to virtually investigate the behaviour of the system under study.

Navigation: The navigation is the mechanism through which a multimedia programme moves from one shot to another. Some of the important navigation buttons are start/begin; end, next, previous/back, home, etc. Specify the type of navigation button and its action.

Citation Style and Bibliography: References to publications in a thesis should be rendered in a standardized form using style manuals such as: APA (American Psychological Association), Chicago, Harvard Style Manual, etc. References should be carefully checked for completeness, accuracy and consistency. This is very important in electronic environment because it enables researchers to exploit the 'Reference Linking' facility and link back to the works that are cited through Cross Ref. Ensure all bibliographic details of citations are reproduced exactly as they are given in the original document. In case of author/editor, surname should precede 1st name and 2nd name (if available) and separated by a comma. For example Jagdish Chandra Bose should be rendered as Bose, Jagdish Chandra. Bose, Jagdish Chandra (surname) (1st name) (2nd name).

Meta-Data and Information Bank: The e-content Development Project under NME-ICT envisages development of a large number of e-modules, video programmes, etc., related to a number of subjects of UG and PG and e-PG Pathshala. It is important that key words appearing in each module are recorded on a Production Detail Report (PDR format to be provided) by the Subject Expert/Production Agency. This information is then tagged with the e-Content and stays with it forever. A Computerized Library Management Software (CLMS) created to handle such information proves to be boon in churning out data out of an infinite number of programmes stored. Such Meta-data (data about the programmes) can be surfed by anybody on the net by pressing a keyword and the person can seek any of the information related to the programme, its synopsis, etc.

Quality Control: The content authenticity shall be the responsibility of the PI, however: (i) Technical quality, (ii) Subject/Academic Content, (iii) Editorial quality (iv) Pedagogical values etc. shall be the responsibility of the Production agency and should follow instructions on this laid down above. Further, issues concerning copyright aspects/intellectual property rights are to be taken care of by the e-Content production agency and PI. The final products in the form of e-Content modules shall finally be reviewed and approved by the Academic Content Advisory Committee before making it available to public.

Intellectual Property Rights (IPR) and Copyrights: The IPR and Production Copy Rights of the e-Content and other products developed shall rest with the NME-ICT, however the Subject Expert delivering the lecture(s), text, diagrams, Chart(s) etc. shall submit an undertaking in writing to the SC, UGC that he/she has not violated the Copyright issues.

Release of Grants in Yearly Instalment and Financial Management

The grants for the project shall be released on the basis of yearly requirements taking note of the progress and expenditure incurred. The first sanction order indicates the budgetary allocation for the duration of the project under various heads like *Equipment, Manpower, Travel, Consumable, Contingency etc.* In specific cases, the item, apart from these heads, for which an allocation is made, will be indicated separately.

i. The first instalment of grant shall be released along with the first sanction order.
ii. Diversion of funds from non-recurring head i.e., Equipment to Recurring head like Manpower, Consumable etc. is normally not allowed. However, reallocation/re-appropriation of grants under different heads require prior approval of SC, UGC.

iii. All the assets acquired from the grant will be the property of Govt. of India and should not be disposed of or encumbered or utilised for purpose other than those for which the grant had been sanctioned, without the prior sanction of NME-ICT.
iv. After completion/termination of the project, NME-ICT will be free to sell or otherwise dispose of the assets, which are the property of the Govt. The Institute shall render to the Govt. necessary facilities for arranging the sale of these assets. The NME-ICT also has the discretion to gift the assets to the Institute or transfer them to any other Institute if it is considered appropriate and justified.
v. The SC, UGC reserves the right to terminate the project at any stage if it is convinced that the grant has not been properly utilised or appropriate progress is not being made.

Objectives of the guideline are as follows:

- To develop e-teaching materials in a creative way without IT expertise.
- Enable exploration of more usable presentation in context of e-learning content creation through models, practical examples and checklist.
- To develop e-content using contemporary ICT technology.
- To maintain uniformity and follow appropriate standards for inter-operatibility.

Criteria for Monitoring the Scheme: The proposals will be evaluated by the Academic Content Advisory Committee, keeping in mind the following criteria:

(a) *Technologically Friendly*: so as to download and use on any computer either independently or in a LAN situation;
(b) *Learner Friendly*: for easy navigation;
(c) *Learner Centric*: to be useful in self-instructional mode;
(d) *Teacher Friendly*: so as to use in various teaching-learning methods *viz.* classroom lectures, tutoring to a group, lab session, etc.
(e) *Employing Learner Centric Pedagogy*: specifically, designer of e-Content should pay attention to the teaching model—such as simple information communication, exploratory approach,

discovery approach, mastery learning etc. Many types of interactive methods should be included to make the learning process effective and efficient.

(f) *Self-evaluation*: Have plenty of evaluation material to give feedback to the learner as to his/her achievements on a given topic of the course and including formative as well as summative evaluation.

(g) *Object Based Learning/Teaching*: to specifically state the objectives of learning/teaching and employ different strategies for skill, competency and functionality developments.

Incentives for Creation of E-Content Programme: The teachers/ subject experts who put their rich experience in the development of e-content will be given due recognition by considering their work on development of *ten e-content modules as equivalent to a publication of a paper in an International peer reviewed journal/Referred Journals*, subject to the condition that an appropriate notification in this regard is to be decided and issued by the MHRD/UGC.

Pre-requisites, Roles and Responsibilities of Content Writer: Content Writers (selected by the PI) is required to provide the following details about him/her prior to offering his/her services as content writer:

(i) Personal Details: Name(s), Designation, Organization, Brief Biography, Contacts, Mobile, LL, e-mail ID, etc.

(ii) Transfer the copyright to the UGC/NME-ICT/MHRD and sign Creative Commons License Agreement. All e-content created will be available in open access under the Creative Commons License.

(iii) Ensure that content are original and are not plagiarized, and submit. Content Writer/Subject Expert delivering the lecture(s), text, diagram(s), Chart(s) etc. shall submit an undertaking in writing to the SC, UGC that he/she has not violated the Copyright issues on this.

Conclusion: E-Content Development is an ambitious and extremely important area that requires the attention of the government, teachers and the external stakeholders. As the wold moves towards digitization, education needs to not just incorporate but also embed the proccesses in the system. It is not just the students, but teachers and policy makers who need to learn adaptation of new technologies.

The aim of E-content development is to create an information rich society where everyone is empowered to create, receive, share and utilize information for their development. Well designed, developed and validated e-content depending upon the nature of the content and the learners, will provide access to high quality meaningful digital content and serve as an effective virtual teacher. Various instructional design models are available according to our requirements to design the content for the programmes. Most of the models involve the process of analyzing the learner needs and goals of the instructional material development, development of a delivery system and content, pilot study of the material developed, implementation, evaluating, refining the materials etc.

As access to information becomes easy due to the World Wide Web (www), it makes the task of the teacher easier and challenging at the same time. As the quality of teaching and students' learning are determined by the teachers it becomes imperative to upgrade the knowledge base of the teachers. Well trained teachers with required knowledge, skills and commitment can develop scientific and critical thinking, promote tolerance, and develop cultural and social values in them. Innovative technologies, while allowing teachers to acquire new knowledge and skills, place additional demands on them be as innovative and creative in their teaching and learning processes. ICT provides new opportunities for capturing, storing, disseminating and communicating a wide variety of information. The availability of variety and rapid expansion of databases has made inclusion and integration of ICT in teaching and learning inevitable.

7

Some Issues and Challenges in Higher Education

Fauzia Khan

Introduction: Over the years higher education is not only facing the challenges of catering to a rising population, it is also posing a problem in a fast changing socio-economic-political world order. Some of the issues that this chapter addresses are those of improving the institutions providing education through investments in research, leadership, faculty and internationalization.

Since Independence, higher education in India has expanded manifold. There were only 20 universities in 1947, the number increased to 711 in 2014-15 and the number of colleges increased to 40,760 (2014-15) from 500. The number of teaching staff also grew from 15,000 to 12.61 lakhs during the same period, as did the number of students enrolled in higher education that went up from 1 lakh in 1950 to 265.85 lakhs provisional students enrolled in various courses at all levels in 2014-15. The enrolment ratio increased from less than 1 per cent in 1950 to 23.6 per cent for age group 18-23 years in 2014-15. In 2014-15, Gross Enrolment Ratio registered an increase of 11.87 per cent compared to 2013-14, demonstrating the significant increase in the institutional capacity of higher education. The aim of the present Five-Year Plan is to increase the Gross Involvement Ratio by 15 per cent to 30 per cent.

During the past two decades both private and government institutions are drawing their interest from higher education. A large number of colleges, university level institutions and deemed universities have been established by state legislatures, but still there is a need for further expansion of higher education to meet the growing demands and increasing aspirations of the new generation.

National Policy on Education 1986 asserted that higher education should provide people with an opportunity to reflect on the critical, social, economic, cultural, moral and spiritual issues facing humanity. The 12th plan instilled a rejuvenating spirit in the scenario of higher education in India. The main focus being promotion of inclusive and sustainable economic growth ascribed by the philosophy of social justice and equity. Various stakeholders felt that higher education needed to be integrated with global knowledge economy for the dissemination of research based knowledge. Research based knowledge has potential of generating productive human resources.

Higher education in India covers all the post senior-secondary education after class 12th in different subject areas. There are different professional courses like engineering and technology, medicine, agriculture, teaching and so on. There are four levels of courses, *viz.*, Undergraduate programmes, Masters/Postgraduate programmes, Pre-doctoral (MPhil) programmes and Doctoral programmes (PhD). The most recent initiatives in higher education include the integrated graduation programmes and lateral entry of three-year bachelor's degree holders in science in the third year of the four-year engineering degree programmes. The significance of such academic restructuring is a very important step in higher education reforms.

The UGC was assigned the overall responsibility for the whole of the higher education system, but it is observed that there exists very little coordination among the statutory bodies with respect to approval mechanisms, nomenclatures, degree durations, accreditation process etc.. The Knowledge Commission proposed to establish the Independent Regulatory Authority for Higher Education (IRAHE) to overcome this limitation. A good regulatory system can facilitate and promote innovation and quality or a bad one can discourage initiative and destroy the quality. Mehta (2003) reaffirms the need to have a clear distinction between control and regulation for higher education institutions by bringing transparency.

The UGC Annual Report 2014-15 provides a level-wise and subject-wise enrolment data for the year 2014-15. It shows that majority student enrolment is at the undergraduate level. There are 86.26 per cent (2,29,33,295) of total students enrolled in undergraduate programmes, only 11.09 per cent (29,46,670) in the post-graduate programmes and a mere 0.67 per cent (1,78,781) in doctoral programmes. The remaining

1.57 per cent (4,16,979) students were enrolled in various types of diploma and certificate programmes in the formal system of higher education.

In the academic year 2014-2015, the total number of teachers in Universities and colleges was 12.61 lakhs as compared to 10.49 lakhs teachers in the previous year. Out of the 12.61 lakh teachers, 84.66 per cent teachers were in colleges and the remaining 15.34 per cent in University Departments/University Colleges. Most of these colleges have a small number of enrolled students and less than a dozen teachers. Fixed courses are available to students and the students do not have much choice. The teaching-learning process followed in Indian higher education remains essentially teacher-centric.

Today teachers undertake this challenging work without any training and accountability. Further, there is limited exposure for the faculty of institutes of higher education to any quality professional development programmes. Existing programmes are dull and ineffective; in-house mentoring is usually non-existent and intra-institutional politics, are a hindrance for creating an academic ambience that is suitable for bringing out implicit talent of the faculty. The exposure of faculty to international seminars and conferences is also limited as a result of which they remain oblivious of any new development in their respective fields. Recently, the government has taken measures to improve the academic contribution of the teachers by means of their upgradation and adaptation through various courses.

Academic Leadership and Leadership in Higher Education

> "A leader is the one who knows the way, goes the way and shows the way".
>
> —*J.C. Maxwell*

All organizations require a leader and the same is true of the educational institutions.

Academic leadership transfers knowledge and skills to human capital. The term has not been discussed so far. Most faculties are reluctant to involve in academic administration perceiving the job as changing career (Moore, 1983). Some researchers believe that academic administration is a job of intellectuals and faculty and administration are same role and mix of academic career (Martin, 1988). Today, the enriched role of academic faculty is almost confirming the Martin's (1988) thought. Burns (1978) commented that, "leadership is one of the most observed and least understood phenomena on earth." So, there is a need to study leadership in academic setting and train teacher educators and teachers in this area.

Industry and Education

The driving forces of innovation and globalization are pushing business organizations and companies to revamp their managerial personnel skills and hire people with creative thinking and education in new skills. Educational institution too want people who are comfortable with complexity and uncertainties.

After independence education tended to concentrate more on socialistic pattern of development. Since the 1990s, the education system has been striving for quality in education. Resource constraints have slowed development of education. Different measures suggested by plans, programmes and policies have not achieved targets in stipulated time. Presently, greater amount of challenges are demanding academic leadership from many fronts. Academic leadership is influencing the behaviour of teaching staff to achieve academic goals which includes both scholastic and co-scholastic areas. The current situation of higher education and researches reveal a need for the educational system to create an added emphasis on leadership skills.

Leadership in higher education institutions is increasingly becoming a complex and a challenging task in the present scenario. Management and leadership institutions primarily concern themselves with management of personnel, finance and infrastructure. It is necessary to train people, especially those in leadership positions, in methods and techniques of management of quality. Delegation of leadership is based on the tenure of in-service rather than the quality of leadership. There is a need for effective leadership. In general, academic leadership draws a lot from literature of various disciplines but it does distinguish epistemology and pedagogy. The educational institutions demand improvement and reformation of the institution with an aim of achieving higher levels of student successes along with accountability at the level of the institution.

The impact of an effective leader has far reaching consequences. A leader has to have high expectations regarding progress, development and success of students, teachers and other staff as well. He/she has to focus relentlessly on the improvement and the facilitation of the teaching-learning process, cultivate partnerships with parents and the community, supervise the daily operations of the institution, manage and oversee the hiring and appraisal of the staff. He/she has to continuously monitor disciplinary problems and resolve issues, play an important part in the long-term planning and setting budgets for the institution, ensure efficient resource utilization of physical resources and human resources.

The responsibility of teacher educators is two fold: (1) to train their students and fulfil the responsibility as teachers and, (2) prepare and train teachers.

So why do we need to groom teachers as leaders? Answer to this question is first we are preparing them for a future education system and secondly giving them skills to adapt to ever changing scenario in the world. This need is an urgent and critical in educational institutions for teacher educators and teachers, where an accelerating growth in size and complexity of the educational enterprise has given rise to problems never before encountered.

Growth of higher education since 1950-51 in terms of degree awarding Universities/Institutions registered 24.7 fold increase, number of colleges had 58 fold increase, student enrolment had 67 fold increase and teacher's strength had 52 fold increase as observed during 2014-15. There is increasing competition in the field of higher education. Commercialization of higher education has increased. A person's success is based on his/her occupation or career. Thus, there is an urgent need of the people to increase the levels of their vocation.

Success of an institute of higher education is being measured on the basis of the number of student placements. The international ranking of higher education institutions is a controversial and a widely debated aspect.

According to Singh and Ahmad, a general complaint from employers is that a large number of graduates are not employable and they have to be trained extensively after recruitment. In today's global village national boundaries have no relevance as far as the job market is concerned. With thousands of our graduates looking for job opportunities abroad, the Indian universities have to be more conscious about the quality of their product.

Excellence

In the present scenario, the earnings and status of people in their respective work-places determine the standard of education they have received. There are many stakeholders in higher education i.e., students, parents, teachers, non-teaching staff, government funding agencies, regulatory bodies and educational agencies as well as future employers. All have their own views about the quality of education.

The deterioration of quality is visible in the output of universities. Few universities, colleges and deemed universities have managed to maintain their standard of quality since their inception. With the advent of globalization, there was concern regarding the quality of Indian Universities and Colleges. Consequently, National Assessment and Accreditation Council (NAAC) was established in 1994 to address the issue of quality in Higher Education. It assessed 179 universities and 4096 colleges till March 2010 and found that 37.65 per cent universities were A grade, 58.65 per cent were B grade and 3.70 per cent were low grade. International level Assessment was worse. Only 20 Indian Universities are ranked among the BRICS top 200, in the new edition of the QS University Ranking: BRICS. The six highest-ranked are all members of the prestigious Indian Institute of Technology (IIT) group: IIT Delhi (13th), IIT Mumbai (15th), IIT Kanpur (16th), IIT Madras (17th), IIT Kharagpur (20th) and IIT Roorkee (37th) with the close places of the first five in particular reflecting a strong consistency in quality Universities and Calcutta also made it to the BRICS top 50 and seven Universities within the top 100.

While a quarter of top 20 spots is certainly respectable, the ranking is likely to fuel concerns about the country's failure to keep pace in International University rankings, especially in comparison with China. The latter has a total of 71 institutions in the BRICS top 200, including six within the top 10.

National Policy of Education

The National Policy of Education (NPE, 1986) had observed that the available machinery was unable to maintain the standard of higher education in the country. Various options were examined and the NPE and the conclusion reached was that an external agency was required to assess the practices of higher education systems.

At present there are many agencies responsible for assessing the quality of education in the country, e.g., NAAC (National Academic Accreditation Committee) set up by UGC in 1994 to accredit institutions of higher education, NBA (National Board of Accreditation) established by the AICTE in 1994 to accredit programme of engineering and related areas, AB (Accreditation Board) established by agriculture department and ICAR in 1996 to accredit agriculture institutions. The function of these agencies is to assess the higher education institutions on predetermined criteria and they try to maintain quality assurance. Accreditation in India was voluntary, but many state governments have made it mandatory for the institutes of higher education. The impact of accreditation on quality of education is quite visible on the output of institutions that opted for voluntary accreditation process, but many reputed universities and colleges have so far not volunteered themselves for accreditation. The recent efforts of the MHRD/UGC to create multiple assessment bodies in the country are a welcome sign and highly desirable action.

Research and Innovations

Despite a poor performance in basic research (as measured by publications and education counts) and applied research (measured by Patent Control), there is a general optimism about India's political co-operative research (Agarwal, 2009).

Indian Higher Education institutes fail in the area of research, largely due to lack or inadequacy of funding by the government. There are hardly any instances of path-breaking research by Indian faculty. Recently several measures have been taken by the UGC to improve the quality of research. One such step is of granting stipend for research scholars. Also, several regulations have been developed by the UGC to define systematic creation, collection and compilation of categorized information.

The need to improve teaching and research has also been emphasized by the National Knowledge Commission (NKC) (2006). NKC also considered faculty members as important elements for improving the quality of universities through knowledge creation and enhanced teaching performance. Synergies that exist between research and teaching mutually enrich each other. Universities are the natural home for teaching and research, as well. NKC therefore emphasizes that the research output of these institutions will be vital contributors to India's socio-economic development and progress in science and technology.

The quality of research depends on the easy and ready access to scholarly communication. Most of the scholarly journals are Scholarly communications through the internet provides an innovative solution to the problem of affordability and almost no cost in distribution.

Sometimes in certain institutes, research collections are kept closely guarded so candidates who want to pursue research are not able to consult them and are selecting the research problems without knowing what type of work already exists in the area of their interest resulting in duplication of work.

Multiple linkages interconnecting institutions or groups that are regional, national, international or subject specific, are rare. This usually leads to a 'reinvention of the wheel' resulting in wastage of money, time and energy.

There is now an international trend to preserve thesis and dissertations electronically and make them accessible. This helps to not only prevent duplication of work but also improve the quality of doctoral research. Establishing DELNET and INFLIBNET in our country is an effort in this direction.

The National Policy on Education 2016

The National Policy on Education 2016 draft recommends that India must strive to find a respectable place in the field of research and innovations, for which faculty induction and promotion procedures must be transparent, rigorous and designed to accept only the intellectually inclined. The API must be replaced by more scientific procedures of assessing the quality of contributions which need not necessarily be only publications and attendance in seminars. A task force of seasoned experts and scholars should be appointed to study recruitment, promotion and retention procedures like those followed by internationally renowned universities and institutions.

Internationalization of Higher Education

Internationalization of Higher Education means the migration of students from one nation to another nation to get a desired qualification at the level of higher education as advancements in the field of technology and education also make international education possible. There are many reasons contributing to the growing number of enrollments in foreign universities. One is the unavailability of seats in courses desired by sudents. Another is the expectation of parents and students regarding carrer options and job opportunities.

UNESCO (2009) presented a report on the 'World Conference on Higher Education'. According to the report:

- There were more than 2.5 million students in the world studying outside their own country.
- It was also predicted that the number of international students might rise approximately to 7 million.
- The main preferred destinations of international students are The United States, The United Kingdom, Germany, France and Australia.
- In recent years, some Asian countries have started attracting more international students.

Despite informal internationalization, exchange of scholars and students and a number of collaborative programmes in place, we have not been able to develop a national policy on this vital issue. A national policy needs to be developed in this regard.

The Draft National Policy on Education of 2016 recommends 'globalization' of higher education without compromising on basic needs of access, equity and quality for the student. At the same time the policy also emphasizes encouragement be given to 'high quality' foreign universities and educational institutions to collaborate. While the nature of cooperation and collaboration may vary, the foreign university should be in a position to offer its degree to the students in India that would be valid in the country of origin. It is recommended that the top 200 universities be facilitated to have collaboration arrangements with Indian universities.

Efforts of the Government in the Field of Higher Education

The outlay of government policies for higher education has seen a many-fold increase in the recent past.

- During 12th Five Year Plan RUSA was launched to provide strategic funding to eligible state higher educational institutions.
- The 11th Five Year Plan had focused on the establishment of new universities and colleges.
- The Technical and Medical Education Bill was passed in 2010 aiming to discourage malpractices prevalent in technical and medical education. Engineering, medical and management institutions recieved direct funds from the MHRD. Common admission tests on a national scale were sanctioned IIT-JEE, CPMT, CAT etc. to select candidates for professional courses.

Privatization of Higher Education

There are several types of private institutions for higher education. While most of these are colleges, some are deemed universities. These institutions include:

1. Institutions established by State Legislatures.
2. Institutions established by religious and linguistic minorities.
3. Old private institutions substantially funded by the government.

- The General Agreement on Trade and Services (GATS) of World Trade Organization (WTO) education has been identified as a service. This gives particular importance to the higher education and its Internationalization.
- Different modes of delivery by foreign providers have been identified. These modes include — Branch Campuses; Double/joint Degree; Twinning; Franchised Programmes; Validated Programmes and distance and open learning, e-learning, etc.
- The Foreign Educational Institutions Bill (2010) has finally got the green signal by the government. The MHRD has termed a milestone in education, which will help benchmark quality education in a new way altogether, by enhancing the choices for students and increasing competition. If this Bill becomes a law, then it will gain following advantages:
    a. Different universities of the world are eager to open their campuses in India. These foreign universities will be granted the status of deemed universities under the UGC Act.
    b. It will increase healthy competition, improve the standard of education and open up more seats in higher education.

On the Flip Side

1. These institutions can poach faculty from Universities with better pay scales and perks.
2. There will be no reservation policy for SC, ST and OBC students and teachers.
3. The main aim of these foreign institutes will be to increase their profits as a result of which they will launch the courses the market needs, and charge a high fee.
4. There are no criteria prescribed for the assessment and accreditation of the foreign universities in India. They are assessed on the basis of their reputation. Higher education system needs a comprehensive internationalization strategy at both national and institutional levels. A systematic approach is required to internationalize higher education, best practices should be introduced for better functioning, and close monitoring is required to check over commercialization.

Conclusion

Education democratizes by demolishing the barriers and is capable of obliterating inequalities that are imposed by birth and other circumstances. This is true not only for the local environment but also for the larger global environment. Higher education has pervasive and substantial impact on development, since it arms an individual with necessary knowledge, attitudes, skills and competence for realizing important personal and social. One of the most important needs of higher education is to reformulate the curriculum in accordance with the demands of the present. The political, social, scientific and technological landscape of the world is changing very fast and the curriculum has to be sensitive to this change for it to stay relevant.

There is a need for teachers also to constantly update their knowledge, attitudes and skills through professional development programmes. These programmes should not only be limited to acquaint the teachers with new developments in their respective fields but they must also cater to the problems faced by the teachers in their day-to-day academic life. There is a need to shift the professional development programmes from the usual lecture mode to workshop mode. The teachers and the administrative staff should be exposed to the good and innovative practices in higher education within and outside India.

The research scenario in India too has been an area of concern. The M. Phil. and Ph.D. programmes must be combined so that a research scholar has a firm foundation in research before he/she could select a topic and its related methodology. The selection of the topic should be based on a thorough analysis of the national and international researches available in that area. It is, therefore, imperative that both the national and international bodies must make the researches freely available to all so that duplication and waste of funds and time may be avoided. The politicisation of higher education is another area of concern. The effect of internal and external politics of higher education is counterproductive to the quality of higher education. Appointments of Vice-Chancellors, teachers and students are often influenced by the politics. As pointed by UNESCO every candidate's qualifications, aptitude and passion for the subject, course and job must be given due consideration before appointments are made.

Teachers need to update their knowledge and advance their pedagogic competencies. Excellent teaching needs to put student's effective learning at the centre of the teaching process (Floud, 2010).

There is an immediate need to craft progressive policies for higher education. The government should have a clear vision of policies. It should have the wisdom to understand and appreciate new realities and courage to take bold decisions regarding the educational system. "The single most important thing needed now is to get out of the rigidity of the system. In the rapidly changing world of today, one thing is certain; yesterday's education system will not meet today's need and even less so the need of tomorrow" (Kirpal, 1994).

It was commonly believed that leadership skills are a gift of nature so competent leaders are born and not made. While this may be true in a few cases, but in majority of cases proper education and training in educational leadership and administration can equip existing or prospective leaders with the tools and skills to navigate myriad issues that arise with leadership roles. J.F. Kennedy once pointed out that learning is indispensable for leadership, hence a successful leader needs to learn and to change and adapt oneself with the changes in time, after all, diamonds were once rocks and butterflies were once caterpillars.

References

Aggarwal, P. (2009). *Indian Higher Education—Envisioning Future*, New Delhi: Sage Publication Pvt Ltd.

Floud, S.R. (2010). The Professionalization of Academics as Teachers in Higher Education. Retrieved on www.esf.org/fileadmin/public.../professionalisation_academics.pdf on 06 Jan. 2015.

Mehta, V.R. (2003). "The Killing of Higher Education" in Golden Jubilee Lecture Series of University Grants Commission.

Ministry of Human Resource Development (1986). National Policy on Education-1986, New Delhi: Government of India.

Singh, K.P. and Ahmad, S. (2011). *Higher Education in India: Major Concerns.* Association of Indian Universities, Vol. 29, pp. 1-5.

University Grants Commission (2009-10). UGC Annual Report 2008-09.

University Grants Commission (2009-10). UGC Annual Report 2009-10.

University Grants Commission (2009-10). UGC Annual Report 2010-11.

8

Higher Education in India

Policy Contestations

Aarti Srivastava and *Soumini Ghosh*

Introduction

Higher Education in India has come a long way from the establishment of three universities at Calcutta, Bombay and Madras in 1857 to today. It has witnessed significant changes, both at macro and micro level. Education sector is guided by policies and commissions that lay foundations and chart the way for onward journey. According to A. Mathew (2016), India after independence adopted a strategy of appointing Committees and Commissions to reform education. Post-independence India has witnessed only two Education Policies at the national level. The first one being in 1968 and a second one in 1986 followed by a Programme of Action in 1992. The process for a new Education Policy has been initiated (through recommendations made by the TSR Subramaniam Committee, in 2016). This chapter undertakes a study of two of the indices—Perception on Expansion and Research, and Quality and Teaching through the policy lens in the context of higher education in India. There are two sections in this chapter. The first section will re-visit the two Education Policies i.e. 1968 and 1986 and their perceptions on Expansion and Research, as well as on Quality and Teaching; the second section will include a brief study of recommendations of the Committee on New National Education Policy, 2016, headed by TSR Subramaniam, again with respect to the two indices being selected for study, i.e. Perception on Expansion and Research and extent of focus on Quality and Teaching.

The first Commission appointed in independent India was the Radhakrishnan Commission (1948-49), which focused only on higher education. Later, several Commissions/Committees were appointed to make recommendations on higher education to enrich its functioning. The reports of these Commissions/Committees formed the basis for initiating many reforms which circumvented its development.

According to Mathew (2016), discourses on Higher Education after independence can be distinguished by four major trends. The first being the reluctance to expand and restrict admission without improving current facilities available in Higher Education Institutions (HEIs) and diverse views on continuity and change in the ways in which research is organized in higher education. The second concerned academic improvement related to curriculum, content, assessment, and evaluation. The third concerned with discourses on reorganization of governance of HEIs for purposes of greater accountability. The fourth related to the privatization and private participation in higher education. Mathew further pointed to how even a cursory glance of the various committees and commissions on higher education highlighted two divergent views about higher education in India. One that it has been and continues to be viewed as the major instrument of national transformation and the other that the system of higher education is in deep crisis, progressively deteriorating over the last six decades.

Policy Dynamics: NPE 1968 and NEP, 1986

According to K. Sudha Rao (2002), Education was the key instrument of national development and individual welfare. A critical input for economic development, particularly human resource development. The fact that the first Education Commission, i.e. the University Education Commission or the Radhakrishnan Commission (1948) focussed only on Higher Education points to its critical role in consolidating the beginnings made during British rule in post-independent India. However, the initial enthusiasm did not lead to an education policy with equal speed. In fact, when the Constituent Assembly was actively piecing together India's Constitution between 1948-1950, education took a backseat and there was no parallel Steering Committee on education.

It was only in the 1950s that the Radhakrishnan Commission was followed by the Mudaliar Commission on Secondary Education (1952-53). The turning point came with the Kothari Commission (1964) which led to the first National Policy on Education (NPE) in 1968.

Expansion and Research

The NPE, 1968 was a result of the recommendations of the Kothari Commission of 1964-66, appointed to advise the Government on "the national pattern of education and on the general principles and policies for the development of education at all stages and in all aspects to enable an educational reconstruction. As Mathew (2016) points out, the NPE, 1968, follows the Kothari Commission's suggestion for planned expansion of higher education on the basis of trends of manpower needs and employment opportunities. Replacing open door access to admission in arts and commerce courses, by a policy of selective admission according to the number of teachers and facilities available while selecting the best among eligible students. Both the National Education Policy (NPE), 1968 and New Education Policy (NEP) 1986 suggest "Selective Expansion" and "Focussed Research."

Science and research got high priority for accelerating growth of the national economy. "Special Emphasis" was placed on the development of education for agriculture and industry with at least one agricultural (single campus) university in every State; practical training in industry for technical education; a continuous review of the agricultural, industrial and other technical manpower needs of the country and maintaining a balance between the output of the educational institutions and employment opportunities. (NPE, 1968)

Even on University Education, the NPE, 1968 states that, the number of full-time students to be admitted to a college or university department should be determined with reference to the laboratory, library and other facilities and to the strength of the staff; new universities should be established only after an adequate provision of funds has been made for the purpose and due care has been taken to ensure proper standards; special attention is given to the organisation of postgraduate courses and to the improvement of standards of training and research at this level; centres of advanced study are strengthened and a small number of 'clusters of centres' aiming at the highest possible standards in research and training are established. Increased support is given to research in universities generally, and institutions for research should, as far as possible, function within the fold of universities or in intimate association with them.

Though both the policies of 1968 and 1986 make a case for limited expansion, the NPE of 1968 preferred planned expansion. It appears to be more realistic as on the one hand it emphasizes on the consolidation and expansion of facilities in the existing institutions while arguing for urgent steps for protecting the system from degradation, on the other hand suggesting a "Reorganization of Education at Different Stages". The NEP 1986 points to the context of the unprecedented explosion of knowledge and how higher education has to become dynamic by constantly "entering unchartered areas." The "universal character" of universities and other institutions of higher education was underscored, even if on a selective basis. (NEP, 1986). The open learning system was initiated in order to augment opportunities for higher education and as an instrument of democratising education and to make it a lifelong process. (NEP, 1986/1992)

Enhanced support to ensure high quality research were suggested by the NEP, 1986, apart from efforts to encourage the setting up of national research facilities within the university system with proper forms of autonomous management. Research in Indology, humanities and social sciences was promised support. Synthesis of knowledge, and inter-disciplinary research was encouraged. (NEP, 1986/1992). The NEP, 1986 also suggested a national body covering higher education in general, agricultural medical, technical, legal and other professional fields, in the interest of greater co-ordination and consistency in policy, sharing of facilities and developing interdisciplinary research (NEP, 1986/1992). The NEP of 1986 in its section on "Innovation, Research and Development" states that research as a means of renovation and renewal of educational processes will be undertaken by all higher technical institutions primarily aimed at producing quality manpower capable of taking up R&D functions. Research for development focussing on improving present technologies, developing new indigenous ones and enhancing production and productivity, along with suitable systems for watching and forecasting technology were suggested. (NEP, 1986) Network arrangements between different institutions in the country to pool their resources and participate in projects of national importance was also suggested (NEP, 1986). The Education Policy of 1986 was more receptive to changes that might accrue in higher education.

Quality and Teaching

A. Mathew looks at Quality and Teaching from the point of view of three sub-categories of analysis: Content, Curriculum and Standards of Teaching; Assessment and Evaluation; and Teachers, Recruitment, Working Conditions and Accountability.

According to the NPE, 1968, teachers must be accorded an honoured place in society as they are important in determining the quality of education and its contribution to national development. The academic freedom of teachers to pursue and publish independent researches and to speak or write about national and international issues should be protected. Education of teachers, particularly in-service education, should receive due emphasis. NEP of 1986 states that in order to promote teacher orientation, teachers will be prepared at the beginning of the service as well as continuing education thereafter. Teacher's performance must be systematically assessed.

Recruitment must be reorganised to ensure merit, objectivity and conformity with spatial and functional requirements. A system of teachers' evaluation—open, participative and data-based would be created and reasonable opportunities of promotion provided. Teachers should have the freedom to devise appropriate methods of communication and activities relevant to the need and capabilities of and the concerns of the community, and continue to play a crucial role in the formulation and implementation of educational programmes. Networking arrangements between institutions of teacher education and university departments of education are encouraged.

The NPE of 1968 does not directly delve much on higher education. The focus remains on science and technology, with special focus on agriculture and industry. Production of Books is recommended. The NEP of 1986 also suggests courses and programmes to be redesigned to better meet the demands of specialisation. Special emphasis was laid on linguistic competence and increasing flexibility in the combination of courses. Efforts for transformation of teaching methods with use of audio-visual aids and electronic equipment were suggested as were Linkages between the University system and institutions of higher learning in arts, archaeological studies, oriental studies, etc. was also suggested (NEP, 1986)

NEP of 1968 and 1986 suggest continuous evaluation. The NPE of 1968 states that, a major goal of examination reforms should be to improve the reliability and validity of examinations and to make evaluation a continuous process aimed at helping the student to improve level of achievement rather than merely 'certifying' the quality of his performance at a given moment of time. For NEP of 1986 as part of sound educational strategy, the objective was to re-cast the examination system, ensure a method of assessment that is a valid and reliable measure of student development and a powerful improvement for improving teaching and learning; elimination of excessive element of chance and subjectivity;

de-emphasize memorisation; continuous and comprehensive evaluation that incorporates both scholastic and non-scholastic aspects of education, spread over the total span of instructional time; effective use of the evaluation process by teachers, students and parents; introduction of concomitant changes in instructional materials and methodology; instruction of the semester system from the secondary stage in a phased manner; and the use of grades in place of marks.

The education policies of 1968 and 1986 offered perspectives to offer on critical issues of expansion, research, quality and teaching. The NPE 1968 suggested a uniform education structure, a common school system, free and compulsory education for children up to 14 years of age, equalizing educational opportunity, development of languages, spread of literacy, community approach at school level, education of minorities, and gradual investment of 6 per cent GNP on education. NEP of 1986 lay greater emphasis on school education. The National System of Education (NSE) is the highlight of the policy that implied all students, irrespective of caste, creed, sex or location would have access to education of quality. Based on a National Curricular Framework, institutions like the UGC, AICTE, ICAR, Indian Medical Council would be strengthened to play an important role in giving shape to the National system of education. An integrated planning among all these bodies would establish functional linkages and reinforce programmes of research and postgraduate education. The NEP of 1986 called for improving quality of existing institutions, equality of opportunity, and access, quality, quantity, utility and financial outlay be tackled.

What followed the Education Policy of 1986, and the Programme of Action of 1992 was a period of no-policy or as JBG Tilak (2012) puts it, "having no policy on higher education has itself been the policy".

The period post-1992 saw the opening up of the higher education system to private and foreign players. These changes called for major policy reforms but there were none. Commissions on Higher Education, notably the National Knowledge Commission or NKC (2006) and the Yashpal Commission Report (YPC) on Renovation and Rejuvenation of Higher Education (2008) attempted to discuss reforms. The NKC suggested a kind of an overhaul of higher education based on five concepts of: Access, Concepts, Creation, Application and Services to develop a knowledge society. The YPC made a case for world class universities. Both the NKC and YPC suggested reforms of regulatory institutions, however none concretely suggested the need for policy, nor did they garner enough attention from the government to think through policy reforms.

In 2016, after an interregnum of three decades, a Committee headed by TSR Subramaniam was constituted to provide inputs for a New Education Policy. The next section examines at some ideas of this Committee.

TSR Subramaniam (Committee for Evolution of the New Education Policy)

The TSR Subramaniam Committee for Evolution of the New Education Policy picks up strands from where the last policy left, by pointing to the changing educational scenario: loaded with new concepts such as rights-based approach to elementary education, student entitlement, shift in emphasis from literacy and basic education to secondary, higher, technical and professional education, the endeavour to extend universalization to secondary education, reshaping the higher education scenario. Unlike the previous Education Policies (of 1968 and 1986) the new Committee's recommendations suggest Quality as the over-arching guiding principle.

So, it is Quality of Expansion, Quality of Research, Quality of Teaching and Assessment that is being suggested and not Quality as different from these Expansion, Research, Teaching and assessment. The "way forward" would be to improve the quality of education and restore its credibility, ensuring transparency in the management of education. The difference between the earlier policies and the draft new policy recommendations can be attributed to circumstances. During 1968 and 1986, higher education was still nascent, but the TSR Committee, 2016 looks at a time when higher education has evolved over three decades, enough time to have attained some level of quality. The TSR Committee, 2016 explains Expansion through some facts from the UGC and All India Survey on Higher Education (AISHE) reports, whereby Universities has grown from 27 in 1950-51 to 621 in 2010-11 and further to 712 in 2013-14. The number of Institutes has grown from 11,095 in 2010-11 to 11,443 in 2012-13. The number of colleges has shown phenomenal growth, from 578 in 1950-51 to 32,974 in 2010-11; 34,852 in 2011-12; 35,829 in 2012-13. In 2014-15, there were 711 universities, 40,760 colleges (UGC Annual Report 2014-15) and 11,922 standalone institutions in higher education sector in India (AISHE 2014-15). As against 2 lakh students in 1950-51, the total enrolment in higher education in 2014-15 was 3.33 crore, comprising 1.79 crore boys and 1.54 crore girls. The number of teachers stood at 14 lakh, with 39 per cent female teachers. The Gross Enrolment Ratio (GER) in higher education was 23.6 per cent (24.5% for boys,

22.7% for girls; 18.5% for SCs and 13.3% for STs) (AISHE, 2014-15). The largest number of students (around 80%) is enrolled in Under-Graduate courses, followed by Post-Graduate (11.4%) and Diploma (7.2%) courses. During the academic year 2014-15, out of the estimated total enrolment of about 3.33 crore, 37.41 per cent students were enrolled in Arts, 17.59 per cent enrolled in Science, 16.39 per cent enrolled in Commerce and Management, and the remaining 28.61 per cent were pursuing professional courses, including Engineering/Technology (16.27%), followed by Medical courses (4.02%).

The private sector has played a major role in the growth of educational institutions in India. In 2011-12, 63.9 per cent of the total number of colleges and institutes were in the private sector and 58.9 per cent of the total number of students was enrolled in private colleges and institutes. State institutes accounted for 35.6 per cent and Central institutes for 0.5 per cent of the total number of colleges and institutes. Enrolment in these institutions was 38.6 per cent and 2.6 per cent respectively. Though regional disparities have increased in terms of Inter-state disparities in the Gross Enrolment Ratio (GER). In 2002-03, the GER spread varied between 5 per cent (Jammu and Kashmir) and 29 per cent (Chandigarh). In 2011-12, the variation in GER was much larger, between 8.4 per cent (Jharkhand) and 53 per cent (Chandigarh). Also now the number of Affiliated Colleges should not exceed 100.

The Committee states that while issues of accessibility and enrolment have dramatically improved in the past decades, and much advance has been made in relation to equity in opportunities, issues relating to quality of education, both at the school and higher levels have not been addressed adequately either in policy or in practice. Even on Research, the Committee observes that quality has been a casualty, resource squeeze often demoralizing those who are sincerely inclined towards serious research and innovations.

It talks about how the Academic Performance Index (API) has led to low quality publications and organization of national seminars with the sole intention of giving the participants a chance to enhance their API score. The committee further goes on to show how despite increase in India's overall share of research publications in the world (between 2006-2016) from 2.8 to 3.4 per cent, Indian higher education continues to have limited research capacity and the research output is generally of low quality. Despite some 800 universities and 40,000 colleges employing 8 lakh faculty and teaching almost 3 crore students, not many significant scientific or technological innovations have emerged from an Indian institution since independence barring some spectacular achievements in the field of Space and Atomic Energy. Significant research is concentrated in the IISCs and IITs, which are also short of doctorates, as well as around 41 per cent and 22 per cent faculty shortages respectively. Central universities have around 38 per cent vacancies of faculty positions. Faculty induction and promotion procedures must be transparent, rigorous and designed to accept only the intellectually inclined. The API must be replaced by a task force of seasoned experts and scholars, in order to redefine recruitment and promotion procedures for professionals in higher education. The Committee also points to how the utility of higher education in assuring employment is questionable. Seen from a clear gap between the focus and quality of education in academia and the actual skills required by industry. As far teaching is concerned, the Committee maintains that with the rapid increase in the number of higher education institutions, the recruitment process should be so structured as to ensure the entry of quality of teachers into the system.

Though there has been improvement in the quality of candidates as a result of NET examination, special centres need to be established, to promote research in various aspects of teaching-learning processes in the higher education sector—on pedagogical practices, the development of teaching skills, the use of modern technology, evolving methods to assess quality of teaching and learning, creating feedback mechanisms to assess teaching effectiveness, etc. The Committee suggests improvement in the system of assessment and accreditation which in practice, face qualitative and procedural gaps in the implementation process.

Internal quality assurance (IQA) mechanisms remain more as a unit to collect data on various aspects of teaching-learning and prepare reports than functioning as an effective mechanism to monitor and improve quality.

Assessment, according to the Committee must focus on developing an easily implementable and operationally feasible Quality Assurance Framework for Higher Education, in-line with local requirements but also alive to international developments and best practices; encouraging self-evaluation, accountability, autonomy and innovation in higher education with an emphasis on high quality research; involve all competent stakeholders in the higher education sector to join in creating a system to undertake quality evaluation and help institutions realize their academic objectives and place each higher education institution in a category-wise hierarchy of institutions according to the evaluated level of achievement. While there is enough to look forward to in the recommendations of the Committee, some suggestions leave much to be desired.

The Committee has been critical of the rise of too many sub-standard institutions of higher education. Even though the committee states that such institutes of excellence may include upgrading existing institutions to levels of excellence, a big goal of 100 such mixed centres is unrealistic. Bringing the issue back to square one, i.e. is quantity really the answer to quality? Also, the idea of Centres of Excellence is blurred.

Secondly, even though the Committee points to a "mushrooming growth" of private colleges and universities, or "teaching shops", mostly of indifferent quality, it suggests significant privatization of higher education. Be it the 100 Excellence Centres in public and "private" sectors. Or vouching for full freedom for a private entrepreneur/philanthropist interested in doing so, based on a commitment.

It recommends that the top 200 universities should be facilitated to collaborate with Indian universities. Indian higher education must globalize without compromising the basic needs of access, equity and quality for the Indian student. Too much openness is being suggested. And the aim of balancing expansion as well as ensuring equity appears idealistic. Repeated emphasis is on improving global rankings over laying down some indigenous standards.

Conclusion

From the discussion what we see is that there has been a policy paralysis with respect to Higher Education. Whether the three-decade in-action was a deliberate 'policy' of the Indian State, or the influence of stakeholders which could not find middle-ground still remains unanswered. Expansion and Research as well as Quality and Teaching find a mention in both the education policies of 1968 and1986, as well as the *Report of the 'Committee for Evolution of the New Education Policy, 2016'*. However, the two education policies were very idealistic in nature but left much to be desired in reality. The 2016 Committee also suggests for "mindless expansion." While "Quality" appears to be the buzzword, the Committee in no way suggests measure to improve the quality of the existing institutions. And the committee's recommendations have still not lead to a policy. Despite some of its ambiguous recommendations, the 2016 Committee should be considered as a starting point, and a New Education Policy needs to chart out a realistic roadmap for Higher Education.

References

GOI: Government of India (1968). *The National Policy on Education:1968.* New Delhi. GOI.

GOI: Government of India (1998). *National Policy on Education, 1986: Programme of Action.* New Delhi: GOI.

GOI: Government of India (1962). *The Report of the University Education Commission: December 1948-August 1949.* Volume I. New Delhi. GOI

GOI: Government of India (1952). *Report of the Secondary Education Commission: October 1952-June 1953.* New Delhi. GOI.

GOI: Government of India (1964). *Report of the Education Commission: 1964-66.* New Delhi. GOI.

Mathew, R. (2016). *Reforms in Higher Education in India: A Review of Recommendations of Commissions and Committees on Education*; Research Paper 2, Centre for Policy Research in Higher Education.

MHRD: Ministry of Human Resource Development (2008). *Report of the 'Committee to Advise on Renovation and Rejuvenation of Higher Education.'* New Delhi. MHRD.

MHRD: Ministry of Human Resource Development (2014). *Report of the 'All India Survey of Higher Education.'* New Delhi. MHRD.

MHRD: Ministry of Human Resource Development (2016). *Report of the 'Committee for Evolution of the New Education Policy.'* New Delhi. MHRD.

NKC: National Knowledge Commission (2006). *Report to the Nation.* New Delhi: NKC.

Rao, Sudha. K. (2002). Eds. *Educational Policies in India: Analysis and Review of Promise and Performance*; NIEPA (now NUEPA: National University for Educational Planning and Administration).

Tilak, J. B. G. (2012). "Higher education policy in India in transition". *Economic and Political Weekly, 11*(13), 31 March, 36–40.

UGC: University Grants Commission (2014). *Annual Report.* New Delhi. UGC.

SECTION-II
Democracy, Globalization and Development

9

Evolution of Parliamentary Democracy in India Today

S. Prabhakar

Introduction

After Independence, in the Constituent Assembly deliberations, we had opted for a parliamentary form of Government in which Parliament is the supreme legislative body. Under parliamentary system, Executive is accountable to Parliament. The Parliament exercises control over the formulation and implementation of public policy, that includes both domestic and foreign policies. This is evident in Clause (3) of Article 75 of the Constitution which proclaims that "the Council of Ministers shall be collectively responsible to the House of the People." Article 246 (1) of the Indian Constitution gives Parliament exclusive power to make laws with respect to any of the matters enumerated in List I in the Seventh Schedule to the Constitution. The actions of government are questioned and scrutinized by Parliament in its functioning.

Not only during the debates in the Constituent Assembly immediately after Independence in 1947 but also in the 1st and 2nd Lok Sabha, debate took place on why we had chosen parliamentary democracy instead of presidential system. For example, on March 28, 1957, Prime Minister said, "we chose this system of parliamentary democracy deliberately; we chose it not only because to some extent, we had always thought on those lines previously, but because we thought it was in keeping with our own old traditions, not the old traditions as they were, but adjusted to the new conditions and new surroundings. We chose it — let us give credit where credit is due — because we approved of its functioning in other countries, more especially in the United Kingdom."[1] There is no doubt that parliamentary democracy has served us so well so far. We could see smooth transition of governments, elections after elections, since 1957 when the 1st Lok Sabha term ended.

Today, India has earned the glory of being the largest working parliamentary democracy in the world. Parliament of India is the highest legislative body representing the people in implementing the provisions of Constitution and its goals. Apart from legislating laws, Parliament performs the functions of scrutinizing and passing the Budget, conducting oversight of the activities of the government and representing citizens are some of the essential functions.

Hopes, aspirations, interests, welfare and well-being of the people are taken care of by the Members of Parliament through their participation which ensures accountability of Executive to Legislature.

Efforts have been made from time to time to promote transparency, accountability and good governance. Role of Legislature has increased tremendously over the years. Population of India as per 1951 Census was 36 crore, now in 2017, our population is 133 crore. There is a need to increase the number of seats of Members of Parliament in Lok Sabha. In the first Lok Sabha, we had 489 seats; in the 16th Lok Sabha, we have 545 seats, including 2 Nominated Members from Anglo-Indian community. Hence, there is a need to increase the number of seats of Lok Sabha commensurate with the rise in population to the tune of 133 crore from 36 crore in the 1st Lok Sabha. Recently, the President of India too brought out this fact by saying, "it was time to take a look at the legal provisions on delimitation of parliamentary constituencies with a view to increase their number."[2] The current number of seats in Lok Sabha is based on 1971 Census. Since then, we could find huge increase in our population.

Parliament should generate public awareness about its role, powers and functioning. Views expressed in Parliament should always reflect the public opinion and lead to public good. Securing greater degree of accountability of the Executive to the Legislature and the people is one of the main responsibilities of Parliament. Parliament is a vehicle of social change. With its deliberations, Parliament brings about changes in the governmental activities. Parliament's role in framing of the legislation is of paramount importance. Though draft legislation emerges from the Executive, Parliament after due debate and discussion accord the seat of approval to the legislative proposal.[3] If necessary, it amends the draft.

When a Bill is passed in both Houses of Parliament, Lok Sabha and Rajya Sabha, and assented by President, it takes the shape of a law, which is binding on everyone.

Parliament had the opportunity to introspect on its functioning on many occasions in the past. Commemorative functions in Parliament were held on the 25th and 40th anniversaries of Independence. During the 13th Lok Sabha, Lok Sabha celebrated the 50th anniversary of the adoption of the Constitution of India and of the Indian Republic on the on 26th November, 1999 in the Central Hall of Parliament House. Sincere tributes were paid to the Founding Fathers of the Fundamental Law of the Land by the Secretary General. The Lok Sabha Speaker, G.M.C. Balayogi, in his Foreword said, "Over the last half-a-century, the treasured heritage bequeathed to us by the Founding Fathers has been a beacon to the nation in the challenging enterprise of building a modern and vibrant India, responsive as well as responsible to the millions who make up this country." On such solemn occasions, efforts have been made to introspect on the functioning of parliamentary democracy in the country and to strengthen it. It is indeed a matter of pride for all of us that we could move ahead on the growth path, pending issues and concerns that challenges us as a nation, which we strive harder to address in order to overcome them and to fulfil the hopes and aspirations of the people.

A general feature over the last three decades is that precious time of Parliament is being wasted on disruptions and pandemonium. Kuldip Nayar, an eminent member of the Fourth Estate had stated while addressing the Bureau of Parliamentary Studies and Training (BPST) under Lecture Series for Members of Parliament, on 30th November, 2007, "....roughly 25 per cent or 27 per cent of our time in Parliament is wasted because of pandemonium or somebody trying to bring something which is not relevant there." There is an urgent need to address this issue on priority. It has rightly been said by the former Secretary-General, Lok Sabha, "democracy is not a finished product but it is a continuing and dynamic process. On the road to democracy, there is no end in the journey. A perfect democracy has never existed anywhere in the world."[4] Evolution of parliamentary democracy has started in 1952 and is continuing with changes taking place at regular intervals, which we are going to see in this chapter.

When Lokpal is in place, we would usher in a new era of accountability. Ultimately, what people aspire for is good governance. The fundamental duty of any government is to provide basic amenities to the people. As one author stated, "Parliament and Parliamentarians have to justify themselves. The people need good, corruption-free and citizen-friendly governance."[5] To ensure such an exalted goal, various initiatives have been undertaken right from 1952 to strengthen parliamentary democracy. It would be of vital interest to know as to what Parliamentarians in Lok Sabha has been doing specifically in the last two Lok Sabhas (14th and 15th) since 2004, and the current 16th Lok Sabha.

Parliamentary Initiatives in the 14th Lok Sabha (2004-2009)

Many important legislations were enacted in the 14th Lok Sabha. Right to Information (RTI) Act, which vested in the citizens the right to call governance to account, was enacted. The Mahatma Gandhi National Rural Employment Guarantee Act (MGNREGA), which gave the right to work to every rural household for 100 days of guaranteed employment, was enacted too. Likewise, 24-hour Lok Sabha Television channel came into being during the 14th Lok Sabha.

Other developments too took place in the 14th Lok Sabha like 11 MPs were expelled on the ground of improper conduct of accepting money for asking questions in 2005; suspension of a few MPs involved in alleged improper conduct of MPLADS Fund in 2006. This clearly shows that the Speaker with the powers bestowed in him can take stern action to stop corrupt and unethical practices by the elected representatives. This strengthens the parliamentary democracy. MPs indulging in cross voting during the discussion on Confidence Motion on 22nd July, 2008 too took place during 14th Lok Sabha.

During the 14th Lok Sabha, a function was held in the Central Hall of Parliament to commemorate the 150th Anniversary of First War of Independence on 10 May, 2007. Somnath Chatterjee, the 14th Lok Sabha Speaker initiated Parliamentary Forums to help Members to know better about the topical subjects from the experts in the field to perform and contribute better during debates in Parliament.

Parliamentary Initiatives in the 15th Lok Sabha (2009- 2014)

During the 15th Lok Sabha, Rules of Procedure and Conduct of Business are made gender neutral. Till now, only masculine gender words were used in legislations. From now onwards, such words will be used in the rules of Lok Sabha which are same for both masculine and feminine genders. There are many other initiatives taken in the 15th Lok Sabha.

Legislation of laws is one of the preliminary functions of Parliament. Bills form an important device. In the 15th Lok Sabha, as many as 181

Bills were passed. Out of which some are very significant Bills like Prohibition of Employment as Manual Scavengers and Their Rehabilitation Bill, 2013; Sexual Harassment of Women at Workplace (Prevention, Prohibition and Redressal) Bill, 2012; The Andhra Pradesh Reorganization Bill (Telangana) Bill, 2014; the National Food Security Bill, 2013; the Right of Children to Free and Compulsory Education (Amendment) (RTE) Bill, 2009; The Protection of Children from Sexual Offences Bill, 2012; The Lokpal and Lokayuktas Bill, 2011; The Right to Fair Compensation and Transparency in Land Acquisition, Rehabilitation and Resettlement Bill, 2013; and The National Green Tribunal Bill, 2013. Apart from Bills, 372 Private Members' Bills were introduced, out of which, 10 on important subjects were also moved.

Many procedural reforms were undertaken like moving of Cut Motions in respect of outstanding Demands for Grants were allowed which were not discussed by the House. Local MPs were invited during the study tours of Parliamentary Committees keeping in view the importance of their contribution. Earlier, MPs were not invited. During the 15th Lok Sabha, three Parliamentary Fora on Disaster Management, Artisans and Crafts people and Millennium Development Goals were set up which provides opportunity to MPs to discuss contemporary issues and their wider ramifications on the debates in Lok Sabha and in Committee proceedings.

During 15th Lok Sabha, Lok Sabha commemorated the 60th anniversary of the first sitting of our Parliament by calling a sitting on May 13, 2012.

It is relevant to state that in 2010 in the 15th Lok Sabha (UPA-II Government) a complete Winter Session of Lok Sabha was washed out. The Opposition wanted the Government to set up a Joint Parliamentary Committee on 2G Scam. Speaker, Lok Sabha had expressed deep sense of anguish on the frequent disruptions leading to adjournments with an entire session being washed out. She expressed pain by the failure in the 15th Lok Sabha which has not been as productive as the previous Lok Sabhas. But at regular intervals efforts were made to strengthen parliamentary democracy.

First Round Table Discussion on 'Strengthening Parliamentary Democracy'

In order to strengthen parliamentary democracy and the relevance of parliamentary democracy, Lok Sabha had organized two Round Table Discussions are organized so far. During his inaugural speech of the First

Round Table Discussion on 'Strengthening Parliamentary Democracy' on 4th September, 2008, Somnath Chatterjee, the Speaker of the 14th Lok Sabha had lamented about the frequent disruptions of the Question Hour, forced adjournments, etc. Many eminent personalities like Fali S. Nariman, Kuldip Nayar, M.S. Swaminathan, Inder Malhotra, Shanti Bhushan, Jaswant Singh, Bimal Jalan, Anil Divan, Era Sezhiyan, H.K. Dua, B.G. Verghese, etc. Fali S. Nariman had reminded of the oath taken by MPs at the Millennium meeting that they would never disrupt Question Hour but repeatedly Question Hour was disrupted. In the end, Hon. Speaker appealed to the participants of the Conference to strengthen this great institution of parliamentary democracy by working together.

Second Round Table Discussion on 'Strengthening Parliamentary Democracy'

Somnath Chatterjee, Speaker of the 14th Lok Sabha had convened the Second Round Table discussion on 'Strengthening Parliamentary Democracy' on 1st November, 2008. In his keynote address, he remarked that "it is the institution of Parliament, which occupies the pivotal position and the rest of the polity revolves around the Parliament." This has set the tone for the Second Round Table discussion. Many eminent personalities like Justice A.M. Ahmadi, Shashi Tharoor, N.R. Narayana Murthy, Vasant Sathe, Shyam Benegal, etc. participated in this discussion. Very valuable suggestions were made.

These two Round Table Discussions on 'Strengthening Parliamentary Democracy' would go a long way in understanding the parliamentary democracy in the right perspective. Speaker has shown great statesmanship and wisdom by inviting even non-MPs to participate in the discussions. It is a step in the right direction because valuable suggestions from media veterans, corporate magnates, eminent jurists, academicians would add to the overall contribution in not only strengthening the parliamentary democracy but also bringing forth altogether new ideas and solutions for varied issues being dealt by Parliament.

Parliamentary Initiatives in 16th Lok Sabha

Till 12th April, 2017, the end of the Budget Session, 52,028 questions, both Starred (Oral) and Unstarred (written) Questions were asked and answered. As can be seen in the 16th Lok Sabha, disruptions have come down drastically due to the single party majority Government in place since 1984. This augurs well for the parliamentary democracy as can be seen from the output during the just concluded Winter Session of Lok Sabha in 2014 where you could find very little disruption took place.

In the Winter Session of 2016 of the 16th Lok Sabha, due to opposition's demand of PM's response to demonetization and the response of the Government is at variance, business could not be transacted and is considered as the least productive Session of the 16th Lok Sabha. But in the Budget Session of 2017, in 29 days of sittings, business has been transacted for 176.39 hours; 24 Government Bills were introduced and 23 Bills were passed. Some of the important Bills which were passed are — The Maternity Benefit Bill, 2016, the Mental Healthcare Bill, 2016, the Motor Vehicles Bill, 2016, the Goods and Services Tax (GST) Bill; 560 Starred questions were slated and 136 were responded on the floor of Lok Sabha; 541 Matters of Urgent Public Importance were raised, discussion on Short Duration Discussion under Rule 193 on Sustainable Development Goals (SDGs) remain inconclusive; 158 Private Members Bill were introduced; Members raised 494 matters under Rule 377; Ministers made 51 Statements. Productivity of Lok Sabha is over 100 per cent (to be precise 108%); and that of Rajya Sabha is 86 per cent.

One of the major parliamentary initiatives is the Committee, which is also called Mini Parliament, have been performing extraordinarily and its contribution has increased manifold in the recent past as we venture to see below.

Department-Related Parliamentary Standing Committees

Committee system plays a vital role in furthering the parliamentary democracy. Departmentally Related Standing Committees (DRSCs) came into existence in August, 1993 primarily to ensure effective parliamentary scrutiny over the administration, especially on matters relating to the Budget and vital policy formulations. This was the reason for conceptualizing these DRSCs. Initially only 3 subject Committees — Agriculture, Science and Technology and Environment and Forests — were set up in the 8th Lok Sabha, in 1989. Later, on 31st March, 1993 17 DRSCs covering almost all the Ministries and Departments of the Union Government were set up. In 14th Lok Sabha, in July, 2004, 7 more DRSCs were added. Altogether, we have 24 DRSCs at present. We find in the Committee meetings elaborate deliberations on legislative and financial business, which in the Lok Sabha Chamber is difficult due to time constraints and other compulsions.

Functions of the Committee are—(a) to consider the Demands for Grants of the concerned Ministries/Departments and make Reports on the same to the Houses; (b) to examine such Bills pertaining to the concerned Ministries/Departments as are referred to the Committee by the Speaker, Lok Sabha or the Chairman, Rajya Sabha as the case may be, and make Reports thereon; (c) to consider Annual Reports of the concerned Ministries/Departments and make Reports thereon; and (d) to consider national basic long-term policy documents presented to the Houses, if referred to the Committee by the Speaker, Lok Sabha or the Chairman, Rajya Sabha as the case may be, and make Reports thereon.[6]

Evolution of committee system and parliamentary function over the decades lead to Minister concerned laying a statement regarding the status of implementation of the recommendations contained in the Report of the Standing Committee on Demands for Grants pertaining to the concerned Ministry. Department-related Parliamentary Standing Committees has been contributing immensely in making the Government accountable to Parliament. Though the recommendations made in reports of the Committee are not mandatory for the Government to accept *in toto,* and are advisory in nature, of late, recommendations have been accepted up to 60-70 per cent.

Deliberations in the Committee amply bring out the concerns of Parliament in an elaborate manner and also put forth the measures to be taken by the Executive to act on the comments, recommendations, observations and suggestions of the Legislature with due diligence.

In the US, Germany and UK, the committee system is strengthened by having its own independent staff to provide expertise to the elected representatives sitting as the committee members.... In the US, committee staff is not only very strong but it is further supported by such independent institution like the Congressional Research Service, General Accounting Office and the Office of Science and Technology.[7] It is high time, we adopt some such method to enhance the contribution to the committees in a better way.

Reports of the Committees

To showcase the success of parliamentary democracy, one can also sight the role played by the Committees. In the 13th Lok Sabha, 934 Reports (both Action Taken Reports and the Standing Committee Reports put together) were presented; in the 14th Lok Sabha, it had presented 1092

Reports (626 Reports of Standing Committees); and in the 15th Lok Sabha, it had presented 1167 Reports, out of which 652 were Reports of Standing Committees). In the 16th Lok Sabha, till 23rd December, 2015, it has presented 90 Reports. This clearly shows that the output emanating from Lok Sabha has increased over the 15 years in spite of coalition Governments in place, which means that Committee system in Parliament has been doing extraordinarily all this while.

Limitations

It is a stark fact that only a miniscule portion of the policy aspect is scrutinized by Parliament and committees with the result majority of the important aspects of different ministries and departments are left out and never come in the domain of discussion and debate in the committees.

First Lok Sabha sat for 135 days; second Lok Sabha about 125 days; even the Eighth Lok Sabha sat for 97 days but over the past 2 decades or so, the number of days of Session has come down drastically. In the 14th Lok Sabha, it sat for just 66 days and 15th Lok Sabha, only 71 days. In the 16th Lok Sabha it has come down drastically to 60 to 70 per year. Of late, it has met even lesser number of days, particularly in 2008, and in 2006 and 2011, when States elections were held — serious and discernible discussion fail to find a place in the agenda of the business of Parliament. Parliament is bestowed by our Constitution with powers to oversee the functioning of the executive. This very purpose would be defeated if the sittings of Parliament are few and far between. In the above mentioned Conference, Vice-President of India, Hamid Ansari, while quoting statistics about the decline in sittings of Lok Sabha and Rajya Sabha, called for the restoration of the deliberative role of Parliament by increasing the number of sittings to about 130 days a year.[8]

It is pertinent to point out here how disruptions during the Session days lead to passage of importance Bills with no discussion or debate. Disruptions over the past two decades or so, particularly since 1991, in the 9th Lok Sabha, resulted in passing of 18 Bills in less than two hours. Likewise, in 13th Lok Sabha, in 2003, 33 Bills were passed in 32 hours. In the 14th Lok Sabha, 8 Bills were passed in 17 minutes. In the Winter Session of 14th Lok Sabha, on 23 December 2008, nine Bills were passed in 15 minutes. This trend has to change. Bills should be passed only after due deliberations and the studied response from the Government. Efforts should be made by the Government and the Opposition to send all the

Bills to the Committee, as is the case in USA and UK, so that more detailed discussion could take place. Pre-legislative scrutiny process should be given emphasis as in the UK where every draft Bill and its Explanatory Notes are made publicly available for pre-legislative scrutiny.[9]

Conclusion

Parliament is bestowed with many constitutional provisions to bring up issues of national importance concerning the policies, schemes, programmes and plans of the government. Parliamentary debates, interventions should be made more effective to protect the interests of India. There is a need to strengthen public faith in the democratic institutions. With a single party Government at the Centre, public faith in parliamentary democracy is restored but to strengthen it, much more needs to be done.

The functioning of Lok Sabha has improved over the years. In the 16th Lok Sabha, we could see discernible changes. Though parliamentary interventions by way of debates and discussions on various burning issues are not considerable, there is no denying of the fact that Parliament's efforts, as enumerated in some detail, is not negligible too.

As explained earlier, Parliament is bestowed by our Constitution with powers to oversee the functioning of the executive. Whether this prime function of Parliament is being carried out is debatable. Till the last few Lok Sabhas, coalition governments faced pulls and pressures, also resulting in too much of disruptions, which had immensely affected the smooth and orderly conduct of the proceedings of Lok Sabha. In the 16th Lok Sabha, with a clear mandate to a single party, we can expect Lok Sabha would function smoothly for the rest of the two years, and would not only contribute towards fulfilling hopes and aspiration of the people but would also serve the national interests.

End Notes

1. Palmer, Norman D., *The Indian Political System*, Boston: Houghton Mifflin Company, 1961, pp. 93-94.
2. https://en.wikipedia.org/wiki/1951_Census_of_India, Retrieved on 22nd April, 2017.
3. https://en.wikipedia.org/wiki/Demographics_of_India, Retrieved on 22nd April, 2017.

4. http://www.hindustantimes.com/india-news/need-to-look-into-increasing-lok-sabha-seats-says-president-mukherjee/story-S1Mph6NTy14glusu YlBadN. html, retrieved on 22.4.2017.
5. Publication of Lok Sabha Secretariat, "Parliament as a Vehicle of Social Change", New Delhi, January, 2003.
6. 50th Anniversary of the Republic of India (Lok Sabha Secretariat, New Delhi: January, 2000)
7. Chapter 2 — *The Working of Indian Parliamentary Democracy: Experiences and Prospects*, p. 12 by Subhash C. Kashyap in "Parliamentary Democracy in India — Experiences and Prospects" (Eds. Batskhem Myrboh (Akhansha Publishing House: New Delhi: 2014)
8. *Ibid.*, pp. 27.
9. Rajya Sabha Debates, 15th Lok Sabha, http://164.100.47.134/committee/commitee_main.aspx
10. Kamath, P.M. "Foreign Policymaking in India: Need for Committee System to Strengthen the Role of Parliament", *Strategic Analysis,* Vol. 11, No. 10, May 1987, p. 231.
11. http://www.hinduonnet.com/thehindu/thscrip/print.pl Retrived on 3.4.2008
12. Pre-legislative scrutiny, Commons Library Standard Note, http://www.parliament.uk/briefing-papers/SNO2822/prelegislative-scrutiny.

References

Anil Kumar Jha, Satya Narayan Prasad, Shatrughna Prasad, Rabindra Choudhary, Eds. *Democracy in India — Challenges and Prospects* (Axis Books: New Delhi: 2012).

Batskhem Myrboh, Airpeace Well Rani, Eds. *Parliamentary Democracy in India—Experiences and Prospects* (Akhansha Publishing House: New Delhi: 2012).

Choudhary, N.P., Ojha, A.K., Eds. Chapter 25 — Challenges before Parliamentary Democracy — Upendra Mishra in *Indian Democracy: Contemporary Challenges* — (Shipra Publications: New Delhi: 2013).

Democracy and Politics in Modern India — Dr. N.S. Gehlot (Deep & Deep Publications: New Delhi: 2012).

Future of Parliamentary Democracy in India, Ed. G. Gopa Kumar, Icon Publications, New Delhi, 2007.

Godbole, Madhav, *India's Parliamentary Democracy on Trail* (Rupa Publications: New Delhi: 2011).

History of the Parliament of India (Vol. 1), Subhash C. Kashyap, (Shipra Publications: New Delhi: 1994).

Jain, C.K. Ed. *Triumph of Democracy — An Overview of World Parliaments.* CBS Publishers: New Delhi: 1993).

N.P. Choudhary, A.K. Ojha, Eds. *Indian Democracy—Contemporary Challenges* (Shipra Publications: 2013).

Publication of Lok Sabha Secretariat, *Parliament as a Vehicle of Social Change*, January, 2003.

Rajya Sabha Debates, 15th Lok Sabha, http://164.100.47.134/committee/commitee_main.aspx.

Singhvi, L.M. *Parliamentary Democracy* (Ministry of Information and Broadcasting, Government of India Publication Division: New Delhi: 1973).

10
Debating Gandhi

Anil Dutta Mishra

Introduction

Mahatma Gandhi popularly known as Bapu or Father of the Nation is remembered all over the world for his love of peace, non-violence, truth, honesty, pristine purity, compassion and his success in using these instruments to bring together the entire population and helping the country to attain independence from the colonial power and show the new way to the world. Gandhi was a creative man and responding to the challenges of his time and setting example for present and future generations. Albert Einstein, the great scientist rightly said that "Generations to come will scare believe that such a one as this ever in flesh and blood walked upon this earth".

Louis Fischer points out, the year in which Gandhi was born 1869, was also the year in which the "Suez canal was opened, Thomas A. Edison patented his first invention, France celebrated the hundred anniversary of the birth of Napoleon Bonaparte, and Charles W. Eliot became president of Harvard University. Karl Marx had just published Das Capital, Bismark was about to launch the Franco-Prussia war", and Victoria ruled over England and India.

Gandhi changed the course of history and created history. He was a man of principles, great convictions and always practiced what he preached. There was no dichotomy between theory and practice and between public and private life. He left an everlasting impact on the world at large because he always spoke and understood the language of the masses, socially deprived and downtrodden. Even after sixty- eight years of his death Gandhi continues to attract the attention of scholars, social activists, media, policy makers and dreamers not only in India but throughout globe. He motivated millions of people during his lifetime, continues to inspiring people around the globe.

Relevance of Gandhi

Today the world is passing through a critical phase of human history and is in search of an alternative. Liberalisation, privatisation and globalisation are not only reshaping the economy of the people and nation but fundamentally reshaping culture, ideology, attitude and lifestyle of the people across the world. Everywhere one can see the fundamental change. Small is being replaced by mega. Invisible became visible. There is a mad race for materialistic development resulting in alienation of people from society and nature and resorting to violence of different type. Everywhere structural violence has increased. Service and need is replaced by greed. Ethics and honesty is no longer pivotal in public life. Marxism provided an alternative to Capitalism. Due to inherent contradiction Marxian experiments failed. Liberalism and neo-liberalism are also not able to solve the human miseries.

Gandhian principles are capable of mitigating the challenge of human suffering. His philosophy becomes pertinent in the present world due to the complexity of human behaviour. His philosophy, laying stress on the goodness of human nature, unity of mankind, service of man, application of moral principles considered valid for individuals to group life and inter-state relations, the non-violent process of change, social and economic equality, economic and political decentralization, tries to resolve the various kinds of tensions that disturb domestic and international harmony. It is capable of strengthening the forces of love, creativeness and joy of life and beauty. It takes an integrated view of man and emphasizes his spiritual nature. Gandhi provides an answer and an alternative, which is above all, a ray of hope, a vision for future and a blueprint for individual, state and society. The interpretations of Gandhian thought and perspective needs to be reiterated again and again till the masses learn to adopt and practice it in their thought and deed.

Gandhi provides solution to the contemporary dilemmas and conflicts arising out due to failure of developmental paradigms and failure of leadership. Even the welfare state is not responding as it was expected. The tragedy of modern India is that the important aspects of the Gandhian philosophy are not given serious attention. The ruling elite never realized that Gandhi was much ahead of time. The quest of humanity for social justice and sustainability will remain a dream until and unless humanity realizes what Gandhi meant when he said, that economics is untrue which ignores and disregards moral values. Gandhi in his various speeches and in his articles written throughout the freedom struggle spoke highly of democratic decentralization and rural development.

In the issue of *Harijan*, dated 22nd July, 1946 Gandhi stated that 'Independence must begin at the bottom'. He said, "the swaraj of my dreams is the poor man's swaraj. The necessaries of life should be enjoyed by you in common with those enjoyed by the princes and the moneyed men. But that does not mean that you should have palaces like theirs. They are not necessary for happiness. You or I would be lost in them. But you ought to get all the ordinary amenities of life that a rich man enjoys. I have not the slightest doubt that swaraj is not Poorn Swaraj until these amenities are guaranteed to you under it".

Gandhi was an author, thinker, philosopher, though not in modern sense but beyond that. His writings, running into volumes, known as *Collected Works of Mahatma Gandhi*, contain a wide range of views on different issues concerning humanity, spirituality and cosmology.

He led a simple life and committed to moral and political values. His life is symbol of pristine purity and based on highest order of transparency. His relentless experiment after experiment with truths and changing contexts may not have lent his writings a propositional form. However, it contains deep philosophical proposition containing all aspects including man, nature and spirituality. Works on Mahatma Gandhi are both voluminous and diverse. More than 450 biographies are written by well known authors including Nobel laureates and in almost all the languages of the world. There are works on him which present him from different perspectives such as Marxism, Liberalism, Feminism, Subaltern, *Dalit* or Human Rights.

There is a need to provide a platform and forum where different interpretations of Gandhi can be brought together in debate, thereby elevating the understanding of Gandhi. One must come out from the cocoon of caste, class, gender, regions, ideology and religion. There is no need of garlanding of Gandhi rather need of the hour is to follow the basic tenets of Gandhi that is love, compassion, honesty, self-esteem and integrity. One must go beyond the comparative, expository, and even dialogical axes, to bring to centre stage the idea of debate.

Differences are the pre requisite to a debate, and a living debate involves intellectual activity. Truth is not seen as given but has to be arrived at through arguments and counter-arguments.

A.L. Basham, "Traditional Influences on The Thought of Mahatma Gandhi", in Ravindra Kumar [Ed], *Essays on Gandhian Politics: The Rowlatt Satyagraha of 1919*, Oxford: 1971 suggests that many concepts in Gandhi's thought are derived from 'Indian tradition' and were absorbed by him during his childhood and youth. The contact with the West only brought to fruition these already existing traditional aspects.

He recognizes no resonances of the past, as in his view 'Gandhi is a relentless explorer of immediacy'; the terrifying thing about him is the 'dimensionless now which he inhabits'. In situating the influences on Gandhi outside the fold of colonial knowledge systems and influences, it thwarts those attempts. In fact Gandhi took the pearls of wisdom from every source which enlightened his thought and action. Gandhi was by product of global culture. He beautifully assimilated ancient wisdom in modern context.

We must carefully read the following postures in Gandhi: though he was a 'nationalist', he 'fought the nation-state'; though an 'anti- colonialist' he wished to redeem the British; a Hindu who happily by- passes the shastras; a congress leader who wanted to preside over the dismantling of the Indian National Congress. Gandhi did not deny the Nehru in him; he only wanted Nehru and his modernists to recognize the voice of Gandhi's India. Akeel Bilgrami argues that Gandhi repudiates this entire tradition, though without necessarily relapsing into social solipsism.

Gandhi was a thinker and as a phenomenon need to be understood and analyzed. He was travelling from one truth to another truth and experimenting on it. He believes that there is no finality in truth. Mahatma Gandhi was a creative man, concurrently writing history for himself and rest of the world to follow. Being a constructive activist throughout his life, he was continuously experimenting with his ideas and actions in the face of ever evolving contemporary challenges. He experimented with truth in plurality rather than in singularity. His concept of truth was not a static phenomenon. It varied in perspectives, person to person, and hence became a relative concept. He was most simple in thought process but adduced the complexities of thinking in a unique way by combining theory with practice, words with deed and non-violence with action. He was greatly admired both in India and abroad but this did not leave him from being misunderstood by his own people and colleagues. Gandhi became global necessity but perhaps increasingly less followed in India including in the Gandhian Institutions and the Institutions established by Gandhi himself or in his name.

Through his creativity Gandhi became a great man in diverse sense and in many ways. It is difficult to understand a great person. Bhavbhuti, a great scholar of Sanskrit, rightly said 'who indeed can claim to know and understand the mind of the great?' This is true in case of Gandhi.

Gandhi inspired masses and masses inspired him. Being a leader, he used to write and reply the letters every day. These letters are treasure of information and functions like a light house in the journey of thought in the ocean of knowledge. There is a lot of misconception about Gandhi. Neither his political mentor [Guru] Gopal Krishna Gokhle, nor his political heir, Pandit Jawaharlal Nehru could fully understand him. Gandhi's adherence to truth and pristine purity demonstrated by his own conduct is perhaps the most transparent way, may seem Brahamanical to many. But apparently in this way, the supposedly Brahamanical way led Gandhi to record every event of his life truthfully and honestly, that forms the single major source of knowledge about him. Hence, it is hardly surprising when Gandhi interacts with his followers, opponents, critics, fence sitters and detractors with equal ease.

Gandhi's relationship with whosoever came in contact with him was simple, honest and free from psychological and sociological encumbrances. He was at as much ease with the Viceroy as with other grassroots level party worker. He was as considerate to Brij Kishore Shukla, who invited him to Champaran in Bihar, as was he towards Albert Einstein or Romain Rolland, his great personal friends. There was something unique in him that enabled him to interact as confidently with Lord Irwin, as with Madeline Slade [Mira Behn] or Sarojini Naidu. However, in the pre- independence era, his interaction with women was still a matter of great curiosity and enigma if not an outright stigma.

Gandhi was doing something fundamentally original and unique for aspiring women. Gandhi's relationship with women is well-known, but highly controversial and misunderstood due to various reasons. Lack of proper understanding of Gandhi and lack of knowledge of Indian culture and traditions were the main reasons for such misconception. Gandhi's understanding of women was based on Indian tradition of spirituality and concomitant four *purusharthas*—*Dharma*, *Artha*, *Kama* and *Moksha*. Such an understanding indeed formed the worldview of Gandhi. If one misses this vantage point of Gandhi, one might end up trivializing his strong sense of gender equality and holding him responsible for his undue attraction towards women. In fact everything was open and transparent in Gandhi's life, and anybody could have ever put it to public scrutiny. In this sense, Gandhi epitomises finer values of truth, dignity and integrity in public and private life. Gandhi's extraordinary experiment of celibacy and non-coercion towards women was misconstrued as his degeneration by both his mistaken friends and foes. However, it might be inconvenient to those women Gandhi shared his bed with. But hardly there is any evidence of such women ever raising any doubts on his intention. In fact, the answer is simple and straight-Gandhi's relationship with women can be explained as one based on spiritual or platonic love where physical attraction and sex are not even a remote reference. Therefore, Gandhi's relationship with women can be easily understood by keeping the Indian tradition in mind.

In fact, *Hind Swaraj* is the Gandhian Bible. Through *Hind Swaraj* Gandhi wanted to establish **self esteem of individual** and **moral regeneration of India**. In other words Gandhi through *Hind Swaraj* wanted to transform (a) **India as a nation and polity and** (b) **Indians.** *Hind Swaraj* is a **source book for evaluation of India and Indians.** It is a manual of action for people. *Hind Swaraj* is a critique of excessiveness of materialistic western society. It is a pointer to downside of modern civilization i.e. colonialism, neo-colonialism, violence, alienation etc. It is also a pointer to Political democracy because political democracy without social democracy is not a democracy at all. Criticism on Railways, Lawyer and doctors must be seen as downside of colonialism and neo-colonialism. *Hind Swaraj* provides an alternative how a oppressed class can fight. It provides a way to fight against oppression, injustice, extremism, violence etc. It also provide alternative to individual, society and state. One can honestly say that Indians love to talk about *Hind Swaraj* but not understood it properly nor transformed its idea or philosophy on ground. It is a source book for evaluation of India and Indians in the post independent India.

Among the tributes received in New Delhi within hours of Mahatma Gandh's assassination on 30 January, 1948 was one from Sarojini Naidu who said: "May the soul of my master, my leader, my father, rest not in peace. Not in peace my father do not rest. Keep us to our pledge. Give us strength to fulfill our promises to our heirs, your descendants, guardians of your dreams, fulfillers of India's destiny."

The force of her words reminds us that we should not rest till we are able to internalize in ourselves the twin principles of Truth and Non-violence in our thought and action. We should be optimistic and hope that we would be able to overcome the present crises facing the world.

According to Gandhi, real democracy should have meaning not for a few but for all including the poorest and even for the maimed, the blind, and the deaf. He did not believe in mere lip sympathy for the ideal which comes so easily to most present day politicians and leaders. The entire social order should be such that this ideal should be achieved in practice. A genuine democracy calls for a higher degree of seriousness of purpose and a sense of urgency. Gandhi realized that once people are awakened, they would become a revolutionary force. Their minimum expectations would have to be satisfied, otherwise they would explode. This explosion could take many unpleasant and ugly forms.

Of course, in order to come out of the present malaise and dilemma, the only remedy lies is in adopting Gandhian path to resolve conflicts. Arnold Toynbee observed: "At this supremely dangerous moment in human history, the only way of salvation for mankind is the Indian way Emperor Ashok' s and Mahatma Gandhi's principles of non-violence and Sri Ramakrishna's testimony to the harmony of religions. Here we have an attitude and spirit that can make it possible for the human race to grow together into a single family and in the Atomic Age this is the only alternative to destroying ourselves."

Indians by and large tolerate injustice and unfairness with feudalistic servility and fatalistic resignation. On 15 August, 1947, India achieved Independence. But Gandhi was not present in New Delhi. At that time, he was working among the poor people of Bengal. The reason for his absence was simple. He had two dreams in his life. The first dream was liberation of India from the British rule, while the second was liberation of Indians from oppression and injustice, from inequity and inequality, from discord and disharmony. To quote his own words: "I shall work for an India in which the poorest shall feel that it is their country in whose making they have an effective voice, an India in which there should be no rich class and no poor class of people, and an India in which all communities shall live in perfect harmony. This is the India of my dream."

His first dream was fulfilled but the second was not. According to the Mahatma, the true time for celebration would be when the second dream is fulfilled. Gandhi was a leader of his people, unsupported by any authority; a politician whose success rested, not upon craft or guile, but simply upon the moral grandeur of his soul; a fighter who pushed back the mightiest empire on earth without the use of force; a spirit of profound wisdom and captivating humility, armed with only an iron will and inflexible resolve; and a frail man who confronted the brutality of military strength with the dignity of a simple human being. To the Mahatma, Truth was God and non-violence was religion. At his memorable trial for sedition in 1922, he said: "Non-violence is the first article of my faith. It is also, the last article of my creed. In non-violence bravery consists of dying, not in killing". His compassion and humanity were as boundless as the universe. "Gather together", he said, "under one banner all men from all religions and races of India and infuse into them the spirit of solidarity and oneness to the utter exclusion of all communal and parochial sentiments." And again: "My Hinduism is not secularism. It includes all that I know to the best of Islam, Christianity, Buddhism, and Zoroastrianism. Truth is my religion and *Ahimsa* (the principle of non-violence) is the only way of its realization." Gandhi held the view that the life of a good citizen was the life of *Karma* action in the service of the country. "My writings should be cremated with my body", he said. "What I have done will endure, not what I have said or written."

The hatred and fanaticism which consumed the body of the Mahatma did not touch his soul. Indian systems and ideologies may be relevant at one time and irrelevant at others. But teaching of this great and benign lamp of wisdom and humanity are for endless time. He gave us the priceless gift of self-respect and the sense of dignity as a nation. The last interview which the Mahatma gave was in the early afternoon of 30 January, 1948 to Margaret Bourke an American from the *Life Magazine*. She asked him whether he would persist in his theory of non-violence in the event of a nuclear attack on a city. The Mahatma's reply was that if the defenseless citizens died in a spirit of non-violence, their sacrifice would not go in vain. They might well pray for the soul of the pilot who thoughtlessly sprayed death on the city. This was his last message of compassion to mankind. He completely identified himself with the Indian masses. He observed: "We must first come in living touch with them by working with them and in their midst, we must share their sorrows, understand their difficulties and anticipate their wants. With the pariahs we must be pariahs and see how we feel to clean the closets of the upper classes and have the remains of theirs to be thrown at us. We must see how we like being in the boxes, miscalled houses, of the labourers of Bombay. We must identify with the villagers who toil under the hot sun beating on their bent back and see how we would like to drink water from the pool in which the villagers bathe, wash their clothes and pots, and in which their cattle drink and roll. Then and not till then shall we truly represent the masses and they will, as surely as I am writing this, respond to every call."

The Indian masses responded to the Mahatma's call in a spirit of total surrender. He said to them that **"real Swaraj will come not by the acquisition of authority by a few but by the acquisition of the capacity**

by all to resist authority when it is abused." He repeatedly used to mention that through realization of freedom for India, we would try to carry on and fulfil the mission of the universal brotherhood. He was really involved in achieving the broadest good of humanity at large.

Gandhi shows the way to harmonize the values of *artha* and *moksha*, secularism and spirituality, power and justice. *Purusharthas*, as interpreted by Gandhi, provide a set of values and ideals within which public discourse in India can (and should) be conducted. He presents a balanced view of life. Wealth, power, pleasure, aesthetic beauty, ethical integrity and freedom of the spirit, the *purusharthas*, are goals that all Indians seek. Gandhi explains how and why that seeking should be the basis of modern India's public philosophy.

The concept of *purushartha* has three related meanings. First, it means any human striving, secondly, it refers to human striving directed towards overcoming fate and *karma*. And thirdly, it refers to anyone of the four canonically recognized aims of life, *viz.*, *dharma* (ethics and religion), *artha* (wealth and power), *karma* (pleasure) and *moksha* (liberation from *samsara*, the cycle of birth, death and rebirth.

The moral authority of most of the politicians has almost disappeared, since they are seen as opportunists, in league with criminals and crooked businessmen. It is, therefore, not possible for politicians to impose discipline in a society which sees them as examples of indiscipline. The common man is alarmed at the moral sickness that is enveloping the world and lowering our ethical standards. Money power seems to have an all pervasive effect. One hopes that we do not reach a level where indifference by contagion or where lassitude slowly engulfs the nation and after a certain point of conditioning violence becomes acceptable, scandal becomes routine, and militant resistance turns into a film script. Education must be shaped as a potent weapon to reverse the process from seeking pleasure, acquisition, and violence to self-control, sharing, and compassion.

India's success will be measured not by homogenizing a heterogeneous situation, but by the success with which diverse societies can be harmonized and co-exist and become mutually reinforcing and supportive; where traditions and modernity are appropriately blended, and where man-made capital does not become destructive of the natural capital. Both models have their specific constituencies in India.

Gandhi was a simple person and whatever he has written can be understood by the illiterates and literates alike. Yet his was a complex personality. Behind the veneer of simplicity, there was a complex Gandhi, a Gandhi who can be understood only if we tune our life to that of Gandhi. His mind, methods and mission were old, nay ancient indeed, but they went against the main currents of his times. They made history, and set the agenda for generations to come. He could interact with kings and prime ministers with the same ease as he could with peasants and artisans. He was not an academic in the ordinary sense of the word but he has become one of the major subjects of academic discourse. He was a practical philosopher, an applied social scientist, a grassroots social worker, a revered national leader, a scientist and a saint, all at the same time. His was a simple but complex personality. No matter how deep we penetrate his writings and life, we fail to understand him for we can neither relive his times nor can we disentangle ourselves from the myths, experiences, and prejudices of the past. To understand him, we have to read and re-read Gandhi, meditate over what he said and did and why and above all experiment with truth and non-violence to resolve the problems we face with similar, if not the same, resolve, dedication, and mission. Gandhi changed the world he lived in and gave new direction to what is now known as development. This series is being published to enable the reader to know Gandhi first hand, in his own words.

To understand Gandhi we have to be objective and analytical but at the same time synergic, interdisciplinary, and holistic. Unfortunately, we are trained to be specialists; we see the parts but not the whole. But if everything is related to everything else, and nothing stands apart, knowing the part alone would lead to knowing the whole. Universe is a system of which the solar system is a sub-system; in the solar system, the earth is sub-system; in the earth as a system, lithosphere, hydrosphere, ionosphere, atmosphere and biosphere are sub-systems; in the biosphere, human species form a sub-system; in the human species each family and individual forms a sub-system. This being the case, to understand even an individual in full, we have to treat his as a part of the whole universe. True he is more closely related to the systems nearer him but he is influenced and he influences by his thoughts and deeds not only his fellow human beings, but also all that surrounds him, nature included. All that we do has its implication far wider than we realize. This is how the problem of global warming and climate change has emerged. Real Gandhi is a systems man and unless we see him that way, we cannot understand him.

Further, Gandhi is so much an inseparable part of our modern history that we tend to be emotional about him and refuse to hear anything critical of him although those who see nothing great in him are not few. On the one hand, he is treated as the father of Indian Nationhood, on the other there are many who think that he wanted to take India to primitive days; who consider him an impractical man, and a man who mixed up religion, politics, and economics. We can understand Gandhi only if we distance ourselves, both physically and intellectually from dogmatism, fanaticism, and barren logic; if we see life in its all manifestation, and as a part and parcel of other life forms in general and human beings in particular.

Gandhi worked all through his life to liberate India from British colonialism; but this mission of his was only a part of a larger and more encompassing mission of liberating humanity from the mythos that grip its soul, mind, and body. He lived so simply not only because he wanted to identify himself with the poorest of the poor, but also because he followed the dictum of simple living and high thinking. Gandhi saw unity in diversity; unity of souls and diversity of bodies with oscillating minds in between. Gandhi had no enemies: he had no hatred for anyone. He accepted differences of opinions, perceptions, thoughts, and approaches natural for each individual saw the truth differently. These and other differences can be transcended and ironed out when the contenders are overflowing with love for each other and talk to each other as brothers and sisters.

He was at once saint and revolutionary, politician and social reformer, economist and man of religion, educationist and *satygrahi*; devotee alike of faith and reason, Hindu and inter-religious, nationalist and internationalist, man of action and dreamer of dreams. He was a great reconciler of opposites and he was that without strain or artificiality.

Rabindranath Tagore called him Mahatma, Subash Chandra Bose 'Father of the Nation'; Lord Mountbatten, 'One Man Boundary Force'; Hindu fundamentalists — 'Pro Muslim', Jinnah 'Pro-Hindu', and Western Churchill called him 'naked fakir'. Whenever he went wrong, he stopped, looked around, retraced his steps and then moved again. What Gandhi did was to all around him. Each of us has the potential to become something like him by experimenting with Truth as we move forward on the road to higher levels of consciousness.

When people asked him to put his experiments in writing, he replied: "I am not built for academic writings. Action is my domain." (*Harijan*, 3-3-1946, p. 28). Yet he wrote copiously. As we scan through the 100 volumes of his *Collected Works*, we are struck by the depth and breadth of his reach. We wonder how this man of action wrote so much in so short a time. Even a four line letter he wrote contains pearls of wisdom. Yet, he was so humble as to say "There is no such thing as 'Gandhism' and I do not want to leave any sect after me, I do not claim to have originated any new principle or doctrine. I have simply tried in my own way to apply the eternal truths to our daily life and problems... Well, all my philosophy, if it may be called by that pretentious name, is contained in what I have said. You will not call it 'Gandhism': there is no 'ism' about it" (*Harijan*, 28-3-1936, p. 49). He climbed step by step to transcend all isms and proclaimed Truth is God.

Gandhi tried to solve problems as they arose, following the law of Truth (morality), keeping in view the cultural background of the people, and good of the society at large. He was often accused of being inconsistent, which he indeed was because "At the time of writing I never think of what I have said before. My aim is not to be consistent with my previous statements on a given question, but to be consistent with truth as it may present itself to me at a given moment. The result has been that I have grown from truth to truth; I have saved my memory an undue strain; and what is more, whenever I have been obliged to compare my writing even of fifty years ago with the latest, I have discovered no inconsistency between the two. But friends who observe inconsistency will do well to take the meaning that my latest writing may yield unless, of course, they prefer the old. But before making the choice they should try to see if there is not an underlying and abiding consistency between the two seeming inconsistencies" (30-9-1939, p. 228).

Not many have been able fathom his depth. Gandhi believed in the unity of human life, which is a synthetic whole. It cannot be divided into separate, watertight compartments — religious, moral, political, economic, social, individual and collective. Gandhi said "Drops in separation could only fade away, drops in cooperation made the ocean which carried on its broad bosom ocean greyhounds." [CWMG: 89: 97] "A drop torn from the ocean perished without doing any good. If it remained a part of the ocean, it shared the glory of carrying on its bosom a fleet of mighty steps." [CWMG: 87: 23]

Gandhi changed his approaches to conflict resolution depending on the nature of problem, people involved, and the circumstances surround it; certain timeless laws he followed and adhered to ever remained his guiding stars. *One*, he firmly believed that the process of evolution Darwin unraveled did not stop with the chimpanzees turning into Homo sapiens. Once the physical evolution was over, the evolution of the inner self began and it would continue until the humans evolve into super-conscious beings. Anything that took man backward to his animal past was regressive, and that which took him to the next milestone of consciousness was progressive. *Two*, Truth and non-violence were the driving forces of this evolutionary journey to higher consciousness. *Three*, everything was related to everything else, and hence nothing stands independent and isolated. All that we feel, think, and act upon, has wider implications. Those nearer us are affected more than those at distant places. *Four*, since the journey of life adds new experiences, truth is not absolute; it is relative. As such all of us can be victims of truth or untruth depending on our perception of the reality. One should therefore change one's views as new truths come to light. One should not be dogmatic. *Five*, all life is a united whole; humans have to love not only their fellow human beings but also the nature—the plants, insects, and animals, and all that is created by the cosmic force otherwise known as God. And *Six*, there is enough on this earth to satisfy everyone's need but not everyone's greed" and hence follow the dictum of simple living and high thinking.

Gandhi lived in a world of wars, colonialism, survival of the fittest, and eye for eye, Gandhi's truth and non-violence appeared to many, as weapons of the weak. They gathered around him as co-workers and followers only when it appeared to work as a potent force against violence appearing in different garbs: injustice, exploitation, colonialism, and wars, to mention a few. Gandhi's weapons proved more powerful but least destructive *vis-a-vis* the conventional weapons of war. His *satyagraha* evoked worldwide attention and crossed the borders of India to reach many other countries, the USA, Russia, China, EU, and South Africa included. It proved beyond doubt that his means of fighting injustice ennobled both sides and left them in win-win situation. Globalization of Gandhian praxis did not go far enough to usher in a civilization of peace and harmony. It remained a movement which petered off when war mongering returned with a big bang in the form of modernization and globalization. Modernization means westernization and globalization means deprivation of the rights of the people to fully participate in production and consumption of the goods and services they need and use. It converts people from being producers to consumers.

Rejection of the Gandhian ways began soon after India became independent. It proved too difficult for the leaders of the time, even though they followed Gandhi during the freedom struggle, to carry forward his legacy of truth and non-violence. Gandhi was soon enshrined in museums spread over different parts of the country, and Gandhi Bhawans of select universities. He became a research topic and a name to be prefixed with institutions, organizations and individuals to acquire prestige. Many development schemes sponsored by the Central and State governments are being named after Gandhi. But in all these cases it is name, not the spirit of Gandhi that pervades.

A number of approaches to study of Gandhi's thought are in practice today — the Nationalist, the Marxist, the Oriental, the Post-colonial and the Subaltern, etc. To understand Gandhiji amidst his conflicting statements, one has perhaps to go into the meaning of meaning. To know their deeper significance, going by the literal meaning of the words would be futile and burdensome (CWMG: 93: 153). Even Vinoba Bhave, the spiritual heir of Gandhi failed to comprehend his *guru*. "Gandhiji...laid bare his mind in its fullness before the world. For his part, he had permitted no secrecy. Even so, I must confess, the last chapter of his life, which I have called the 'Swargarohan Parva', or the chapter of the 'Ascent to Heaven', remains a mystery to me. Indeed, in my eyes, it stands equal to the last phase of Lord Krishna's Leela. To unravel its mystery, it may become necessary for Gandhiji himself to be born again". [CWMG: 86: IX-X].

Conclusion

The need of the hour is that leaders and people of the country be inspired by the ideals and teachings of Mahatma Gandhi. We need a man of values at the head of a government. If the policies of tomorrow are to be freed from the corrosiveness of purely personal ambition and raised to the level of serving great causes — such as liberating men from poverty, disease and hunger, both of body and mind—then Nehru is of relevance. If kindness, magnanimity, gentleness, and concern for others are the virtues which should inform public life, then Gandhi is of relevance. With the passage of time, Gandhi will be of greater relevance, and not merely to my country, but to the world at large. I have no doubt that so far as my own countrymen are concerned, more especially the younger generation to whom Gandhi is a mere name, they will, in the fullness of time and in the measure they address themselves to the real problems of India's historic transformation.

The relevance of Gandhi remains undiminished today. In fact, his ideas and approach to political, economic and social issues are more relevant now than even in his life-time. The policy makers, politicians, intellectuals and scientists must remember in thought and action the Talisman of Mahatma Gandhi: "Recall the face of the poorest and the weakest man whom you may have seen, and ask yourself, if the step you contemplate is going to be of any use to him? Will he gain anything by it?

Will it restore him to a control over his own life and destiny? In other words, will it lead to swaraj for the hungry and spiritually starving millions? Then you will find your doubts and yourself melting away."

Gandhi's spoken words, writings, and work done by him will resonate for centuries to come. At the same time we must remember the **seven social sins** which Gandhi wrote in **Young India of 22.10.1925.**

Politics without principles
Wealth without work
Pleasure without consciences
Knowledge without character
Commerce without morality
Science without humanity
Worship without sacrifice.

What breath is to life, Gandhi is to humanity and civilization. As long as there is strife, hostilities, ethnic cleansing, religious unrest, internal conflicts and threats of military occupation, people will turn to Gandhi. His usefulness will not end unless conflict ceases, radical discrimination ends, women are empowered and poor live with dignity.

11
The Quest for Real Independence

D.K. Giri

I was invited to a meeting on social justice by *Dalits*, largely, the scavengers, who sounded very exasperated with the state of their affairs. They were lamenting that there was no real freedom for them even after seven decades of Indian independence. They were so aggrieved that they began invoking some subdued idea of *Achhutstan* (land of untouchable) before the Poona Pact of 1932 between M.K. Gandhi and Ambedkar. It was an unsettling experience. That is why it is in order that, as we brace up to celebrate 70th anniversary of India's independence, we should talk of and work for real independence. It is true that Indians got political independence from United Kingdom, but without certain fundamental values political independence becomes vacuous. In order to enjoy real freedom, the citizens across the social or cultural spectrum must be guaranteed the following 5-set of integrated values. These values can be ensured by political systems, policies, and personal, social and moral education (PSME), and movements.

Equality

This is the most desirable value for citizens in any democracy. This is also the most difficult concept to understand and implement, because human beings are born different from each other. So equality does not mean levelling out or uniformity. That is not possible. One is talking about recognising equally the essential worth of human beings, irrespective of such differences as may be observed in abilities, aptitudes and other variables that are innate or acquired through birth, family or profession.

Some argue that freedom and equality conflict with each other. As people enjoy their unbridled freedom, it may lead to unhealthy competition and inequality. Conversely, the first step towards greater inequality is also the first step towards less freedom. Hence, freedom and equality are not to be made opposites, but mutually re-informing.

Conceptually there are two aspects of equality—that is, equality of rewards, and equality of opportunities. The first aspect of equality is not acceptable to most people. How can people get the same salary irrespective of the differences in what they do? How can a CEO of a company and the peon in the same company draw the same salary? What one is suggesting here is that people should get same wages if they are doing same kind of work irrespective of their caste, class, or gender. The other aspect, the equality of opportunity, should be given to all irrespective of their backgrounds—gender, caste, class, religion or language. But, even this aspect of equality cannot be applied mechanically. For instance, in an unequal society like India, people cannot access equal opportunities because of their inherent disabilities. We must create equality of condition—a level playing field. That is why the Indian constitution gives reservations to Scheduled Castes and Scheduled Tribes. Yet, people from these communities could not enjoy equality because of other associated problems discussed below.

Identity

Karl Marx had prescribed that after the overthrow of capitalism, a "new man" will emerge with one identity; that is a worker. The liberal democracy confers another identity; that is "a free man". Both these formulations are limited. People acquire different identities on the bases of social and cultural affinities. We are not just talking of individual identities, but group identities. Identity and equality are closely linked. In those countries where everyone belongs to the same religion, same linguistic group, etc. it is not much of a problem, but in a country like India which is heterogeneous, culturally and racially, group identity becomes very salient. In India, where groups are unequal, identity poses a problem i.e. identity itself is not a problem but identity coupled with inequality is.

The only overarching identity for all Indians is citizenship. Indian citizens are distributed into religious, linguistic, racial, caste, and other identities. In many countries, citizens are required to abjure their identities in order to get the benefits as a citizen. But this is not true in India. Not only do we recognize identity, we celebrate it. Therefore, we can say

Indian citizenship is in a way multicultural citizenship. People of various backgrounds are having citizenship entitlements. Take the example of religion. India does not have an official religion. We have several important religious communities — Hindus, Muslims, Christians, Sikhs, Zoroastrians, Baha'is — all enjoy freedom of religion. Except for one group — Hindus, Buddhists, Jains and Sikhs, who have a common civil code, all other religious communities have their separate civil codes. They can maintain their own worship places, they can establish and run their own educational and health institutions. These are all indications of the constitutional recognition of identity groups. So citizenship and identity are not juxtaposed, not seen in contradictory terms but as a continuum as it were. We have 22 recognized languages; many countries have just one. Every child in the country is entitled through the constitution to be educated till the age of 14 in his/her mother tongue. In India, we have taken identity as a serious issue because we are endlessly diverse and that is why we have to reconcile the citizenship entitlements along with identity entitlements. When we fail to do so, we have social tensions and sectarian strife. All identities are recognised constitutionally, but in practice, there are discrimination and alienation. The reason for such distortion is lack of pluralism, the next principle.

Pluralism

Secularism has become controversial in India. Congress and other parties have been accused of minority-ism or pseudo-secularism, whereas BJP is said to be promoting *Hindutva*, or majoritarianism. It is perhaps because secularism in India is different from what the Western countries understand it to be. That is where it seems to have got muddled and become nebulous. In the West, secularism, in French *laicite,* meant separation of state from the religion. Secular meant non-religious. But, in India, although we do not have a state religion, state gets involved in religious matters. In Indian constitution, secularism means, (i) equal respect for all religions, (ii) and equal distance from all religions. Whether it was possible, even in principle, for the state to maintain those (equi-distance and respect) is a matter of debate, which we do not engage in here. Secularism as it has been explained, understood, and practiced, seems to be a failed concept. We need to substitute it with a more viable concept—pluralism.

Many countries in the world are diverse by nature, but they do not practice pluralism. They do not recognise multiple identities, suppress the weaker ones. Pluralism essentially means co-existence of multiple identities. Plurality or diversity is a fact, but pluralism is a value orientation, an attitude, and a principle. In order to build a pluralist society, there has to be recognition and celebration of identities, and an order of equality. In a plural society, identity groups are different but equal, not inferior or superior. For instance, religious majority does not treat a minority as inferior, or a bigger linguistic group does not suppress a smaller linguistic one. In India, the people from North call those from North-east as *Chingi,* or from South India as *Madrasi*, These are pejoratives, undermining the identity of people. Muslims seem to be more stigmatised than others. They are treated as outsiders, as descendants of Babur, and are often discriminated. To be sure, discrimination is the enemy of pluralism, whereas practice of egalitarianism leads to pluralism.

Dignity

The problem of dignity exists in all societies. This is, in fact, is the next level of pluralism. We may not discriminate or stigmatise a group, but we do not always bestow on them their human worth: we can treat somebody as equal, recognize their identity but that does not mean we really give them dignity. The groups or communities which are denied dignity are many in our country. How do the urban people look upon the rural people, how do they treat women, how white collar workers deal with manual workers, how the physically and mentally differently-abled people or aged are denied dignity in addition to the traditionally disadvantaged groups such as *dalits*, *adivasis*, fisher folks, OBCs and similar groups. So every human being wants to be treated with dignity irrespective of his/her class. One might not be earning much money but that does not mean that their dignity can be compromised. The manner in which we deal with our domestic servants for example our drivers. There is no equality in terms of their wages but yet we have to treat them as human beings i.e. treat them with dignity. So we have to think in terms of extending the idea of dignity to all contexts, which is a lot more than equality.

Dignity essentially means mutual respect. One cannot think in terms of legislating on that. One cannot have a law that states that you must give respect to somebody. For example, the constitution talks about fraternity. But, one cannot say that if you are not fraternal you will be punished. The difference between other political values and dignity is that it goes beyond discrimination and stigmatization. Suppose one does not discriminate or one does not stigmatise, that does not mean one is showing dignity or the other is getting dignity. So accepting pluralism is the prerequisite for bestowing dignity just as recognizing identity is a prerequisite for pluralism. So, they are all interlinked, one cannot have one without the other. The only technical difference is that dignity cannot be bestowed through a process of legislation, it is a matter of mutual understanding. People feel degraded when denied dignity. Lack of dignity is a social and cultural evil. Many from lower social strata feel frustrated when they denied dignity despite their professional and material success. So we need a dignitarian society for people to feel free and self-confident.

Solidarity

Solidarity is the glue that binds all the principles mentioned above. Solidarity again has two aspects — one, to acquire a sense of overarching community; a feeling that all citizens inhabiting a country is like a large community. Our Constitution also starts with, "We the people of India give ourselves a Constitution…." The word "we" implies community-ness. And a community is based on the principle and practice of "caring and sharing", which is really the expression of solidarity. The second is the fight for justice. This refers to solidarity within the community not necessarily across the communities. This is when solidarity becomes a weapon for the weak in their fight for social justice. Karl Marx had famously said, "Man exploits man." This really brilliantly characterizes the history of mankind, when strong has dominated and exploited the weak. It is true that most constitutions in democratic politics do not put the dominant, and the dominated, the strong and the weak, the rich and poor in antagonistic terms. They seek to maintain equality and order through regulation and distributive justice. But human nature being what it is, acts of solidarity are critical in maintaining a plural society. The American theologist and intellectual Karl Paul Reinhold Niebuhr said, "Man's capacity for justice makes democracy possible, but man's inclination to injustice makes democracy necessary"; without solidarity, justice is impossible to secure or deliver. Let us remember John Ruskin's legendary essays titled "Unto This Last". The title was taken from the Bible, "The Parable of the workers in vineyard" in Mathew 20:14-15, "I will give unto this last even as unto thee… So, the first shall be last, and the last first." Gandhiji translated it into "sarvodaya" (well-being of all), and later Vinoba Bhave called *sarvodaya* is *antyodaya* (well-being of the last or the poorest). Both these concepts entail solidarity. Rich and the privileged must care for the poor. Solidarity also implies tolerance, love and compassion. Many countries including India lack compassion.

The idea of embracing solidarity is to bring compassion to the forefront of public life.

To conclude, freedom enables people to live their lives as they want, without fear or insecurity. In an unequal society, security comes through equitable development. Nobel laureate Professor Amartya Sen says, "Development is Freedom". So in order to be free, we need to have development with all its social and economic dimensions. Development cannot be secured for all if the five values discussed here are not ensured. Based on experience of social and political processes in many countries including India, ensuring the set of five integrated values is integral to "real freedom" for a vast majority of people in India.

12
Rearticulating the Notion of Communalism in Post-2014 India

Mujibur Rehman

Introduction

The issue of communalism has been largely debated in the context of Hindu-Muslim relation for past several decades since colonial days. Additionally, a very animating debate in India has unfolded in past few months on subjects like intolerance to the recent arrest of the JNU student leader, Kanhaiya Kumar, under a Sedition Act framed during colonial rule. A few these issues have received global attention. There are other incidents pertaining to Love Jihad, Ghar wapsi, Award wapsi reflecting rather a new set of phenomenon on the issue of communalism and challenges it is posing to Indian society. In particular, it has demonstrated a heightened sense of politics of polarization in Indian polity.

But the manner in which the intolerance debate has unfolded, it appears as if the notion of "intolerance" has a greater explanatory power than communalism. I would disagree with this formulation. The "notion of intolerancec", I would argue, is only one of the many tendencies of communalism.

The Hindu Right has responded by saying that such things have been occurring for a long time, there is history to it, and there is some truth to this claim of the Hindu Right. More than 30 books were banned long before the BJP came to power. At the same time, it is hard to believe these are all aberrations as the Hindu Right wants us to believe; instead there is a pattern to it. In a recent lecture Amartya Sen said that Indians have become "tolerant of intolerance" more than what they used to be in the past. This pattern is a reflection of the ideological shift India is experiencing in contemporary time—with a goal to set up a *Hindu Rashtra*/Hindu state that has been a political ambition of the Hindu Right since 1930s.

My volume, ***Communalism in Post Colonial India: Changing Contours (Routledge 2016)*** arose out of my concerns on the dominant argument advanced by historians of varied ideological persuasions. The argument/their narrative always about the role of the colonial state and the communal question—largely was located in the Hindu-Muslim question. Since we continue to have communal violence in post-Independent India, and modern Indian state is not colonial state, we cannot apply the same explanation. It is true modern Indian state has "colonial impulses— which is why we have such a large scale human rights violence in various parts of India.

Therefore, my communalism volume makes two-fold claims: firstly, it recognises that forms of communalism in modern India has changed from the 1940s and the 1950s due to the changing roles that political parties, state, media and civil societies in recent years. Secondly, new conceptual tools arising from interdisciplinary traditions are needed to advance our understanding of this question.

The notion of communalism is employed in monolithic sense in dominant formulations in scholarly as well as in popular narratives. In simple terms, whatever *communalism* meant in 1930s and 1940s in India—remains unaltered in subsequent periods such as in 1980s and 1990s. It continues to have the identical meanings in contemporary times. Conceptually, it is seen as time and context independent. This formulation is challenged by our research. It urges scholarly community not just to be adaptive but respond imaginatively to the new era of communalism with its changing forms by virtue of new concepts and methodologies.

In the arena of theoretical analysis, the more effective interrogation of the notion of communalism is conducted in conjunction with other ideas such as secularism, nationalism, minority rights, democracy etc. Often how these relationships are defined and interpreted has determined the nature, quality and impact of scholarship. For instance, Amartya Sen seeks to explain the idea of communalism by unravelling various criticisms of the idea of secularism. Luois Dumont has sought to achieve the same by analysing the idea of nationalism. Martha Nussbaum has explained it also with help of other dimensions such as democracy and tolerance. The methodological insight indicates that incisive analysis on democracy demands serious understanding of political parties. However, often scholars have made profound statements on democracy without alluding to role of political parties at all. An important example of this genre of analysis is the writings of Amartya Sen on democracy.

Fortunately, on the subject of communalism and secularism also, scholars of various disciplines have recognised the role and position of political parties as crucial to study of Indian democracy. Again, the understanding of the relationship between secularism and minority rights is indispensable for explaining the puzzles of democracy. In Indian case, this could be most effectively explored by asking a question such as: What has the democratic practice done to this relationship between communalism, secularism and minority rights in last more than six decades? There is a general realization that the imperfections in the practice of secularism has made it less desirable making minorities particularly more and more vulnerable. And, political parties have played decisive role contributing to this development. Also interestingly, noted historian Perry Anderson has following observations, "Indian secularism is Hindu confessionalism by another name."(Anderson: 2012, 142)

The rise of the BJP and Ayodhya movement has inspired western scholarship on the subject of communalism, minority rights and secularism in recent years. The writings of Amrita Basu, Christopher Jaffrelot, Thomas H. Hansen, Steve Wilkinson, Paul Brass, and several others represent this trend.

The Hindu right, however, has remained rather steadfast in its attack on secularism mainly because it presents the ideological threat to the idea of *Hindu rashtra* or the *Hindutva*. It was thus necessary to delegitimise and question it under all circumstances to make it a completely an irrelevant idea. To this end, it seems the Hindu Right devised a systematic strategy and executed it with great efficacy over the years. As the idea of secularism gained wide currency—the Hindu right chose not to attack the idea itself instead focussed on its practice. Out of this strategy came out the notions such as "positive secularism" and "negative secularism." These distinctions were widely used during 1980s and 1990s India's public discourse by the Hindu Right, signalling that it alone knows what is a good secularism; though no evidence of it was found in the decisions of its governments either at the Centre or at the State. To present itself as a legitimate secularist; the Hindu Right ridiculed other supposedly secular parties and organizations as "psuedo secular." 2014 parliamentary election saw a new strategy of the Hindu Right to deal with secularism. For the first time in India's modern history, a Prime ministerial candidate unleashed an unprecedented attack on the idea of secularism speeches after speeches, a practice he continues even as the Prime Minister.

As the BJP's Prime Ministerial candidate, Narendra Modi did go to address a rally near Muzaffarnagar (in a place called, Bulandsahar only 100 kilometers away), it was attended by scores of Muslims according to media reports. In his speech, Narendra Modi used data from the *Sachar Report* (2006) to argue that Muslims of Gujarat are better off than Uttar Pradesh. He mocked those who use secularism to attack him. He said the Congress brand of secularism has destroyed Muslims:

> Aaj Kal Fashion Ho Gaya hai, when Modi says Vikas, They say secularism ko Kya Hoga?
>
> When Modi says aparadh, Secularism ko kya Hoga.
>
> Secularism, Secularism, Secularism.
>
> I ask you: Do you want corruption, crime free development oriented government?

This attack on secularism continued even after he became India's Prime Minister and even after he took oath to protect and preserve India's Constitution. Secularism is part of India's Constitution. Here is an interesting recollection from Prime Minister Modi's speech at a reception in Berlin on April 14, 2015 for the Indian Community hosted by India's ambassador. He said the following: "Decades ago, German radio had a news bulletin in Sanskrit when there was none in India. Our country did not because of secularism. India's secularism is not so weak that it will be shaken just because of a language. One should have the self-confidence. That should not be shaken." Another interesting story emerges from the speech given by Rajnath Singh, India's Home Minister, on November 26, 2015, initiating a two day debate on "growing intolerance" in India's parliament. Rajnath Singh said "secular" is the most misused word in India. In his words, "Secularism is the most misused in the country. This must stop. Because of the rampant misuse of the word, there has been instances of tensions in society." He further argued that B.R. Ambedkar did not consider it necessary to include the words "secular" and "socialist"—that were added later to the Preamble in the Congress regime of Indira Gandhi. According to Mr. Rajnath Singh, "these values are core to the Indian ethos." On this debate, the Hindu Right enjoys considerable advantage. Scholars have sought to explain this. One recent work is the Presidential Speech by Prof. Sabyasachi Bhattacharya who apparently believes it was the larger commitment to justice and equality was the reason for the omission. My argument is it is the fear by Nehru to face stiff resistance from Patel and Rajendra Prasad who were closer to the Hindu Right thinking forced Nehru keep it for a suitable political time. Political time is an important aspect of Nehru's political strategy on all issues.

What is "communalism" according to the Hindu Right? The Hindu Right has no notion of communalism at all; because communalism is nationalism. For it, Muslims are eternally disloyal people and outsiders. Over last seven decades and more, Indian Muslims have voted for secular parties, national or regional, with the exception of Kerala's Muslim League. For many decades, Muslims remained loyal to the Congress party and later since mid-1970s began to shift their loyalty to other secular regional parties. There was some evidence of some of them voting for the BJP in 2014 election—particularly in Uttar Pradesh, Karnataka and Gujarat. Though issues such as cow slaughter/beef etc. in recent months have hardened their resistance toward BJP, part of which were reflected in the voting pattern in Bihar.

Another front for attack on secularism was launched by branding Indian state policy toward minorities as appeasement. It is mainly aimed towards Muslims. Apparently, this criticism has been in existence in India for a very long time. One of its early evidence could be noted in a letter by Prime Minister Nehru written to Chief Minister on 15 October, 1947. This accusation continues floats around in Indian public debate. Its presence, and continuation as a part of the active language of discourse on secularism and minority rights does weaken the foundations of Indian secularism, and contributes to the creation of hostile attitude towards Muslims and other minorities. Interestingly, Gopal Singh Panel report (1983) contains enormous evidence of extremely abysmal socio-economic conditions of Indian Muslims. The failure of India's supposedly secular political elites, intellectuals and activists, to use these resources to counter the onslaught on Indian secularism lent legitimacy to the appeasement accusation by the BJP and its sister organizations during the late 1980s and early 1990s when this accusation gathered momentum. Sachar Report (2006) has given further resources to substantiate to Gopal Singh Panel findings.

Mr. Modi, as Gujarat Chief Minister, resisted the implementation of the Sachar Report, however, appeared quite enthusiastic to use its data to his advantage during the 2014 campaign. In a Hunkar Rally in Purnia, Bihar on March 12, 2014; he cited following data to make his point that how Gujarat model has not only helped Muslims; and how Gujarat Muslims have been doing much better in life compared to Bihar Muslims. He said, "In Bihar 45 per cent Muslim are poor compared to 24 per cent in Gujarat in urban areas; and in rural areas 38 per cent in Bihar are poor compared only 7 per cent in Gujarat." During the Bihar election campaign, Mr. Modi used all the opportunity to spread the rumour that Nitish/Lalu were planning to steal the *dalit* reservation and give them to Muslims. In one of the parliament debates, he did say he does understand that it is important for all parts of the body to remain healthy, so Muslims from the outset, BJP and its predecessor Jana Sangh, devised a political strategy based on its agenda in which Muslim voters were consciously excluded. Hindu Right viewed Muslims as disposable voters, and its electoral and political exclusion as inconsequential in its attempt to capture India's state power. In the post- 2014 election period, various activities, campaigns and programmes by various organizations of the Hindu Right has not only alienated Muslims but encouraged Muslims elites to work out new strategy to deal with the growing threat posed by the Hindu Right. Some of these programmes include: Love Jihad; Ghar Wapsi programmes; Beef ban and Lynching of Mohammed Aqlaq in Dadri, UP etc. During this period, BJP and its sister organizations at a rather dramatic speed unleashed various programmes that contributed to self-unmasking its own Hindu agenda that its critics often hailed as its true face.

There are incidents of communal violence in recent years, say for example, Muzaffarnagar 2013; Kokrajhar 2012; Kandhamal 2008; and Gujarat 2002. The Gujarat 2002, among all of these cases, is widely discussed and researched, also seen as example of Indian style of ethnic cleansing or fascism. Since the political ideology of secularism play a crucial role in Indian electoral politics, Indian political elites are sensitive to their secular image. Some political elites are conscious to endorse interreligious conflict as a communal violence. They feel more comfortable to describe it as ethnic conflict as if the latter is a conflict of lesser kind. Hoping that this attempt lend a new label to communal violence would not tarnish their secular image, these political elites view it of less consequential electorally. There was prominent use of this conceptual manoeuvring by political elites during Kandhamal violence in 2008. The leaders of Biju Janata Dal (BJD) including its Chief Minister, Naveen Pattnaik, explained it as an ethnic conflict often. The political leaders of Samajwadi Party (SP) in Uttar Pradesh was made to explain Muzzafarnagar violence in 2013.

For Indian polity, the big question is how the relationship between communalism and violence is perceived? And how the future discourse on secularism is going to unravel around this relationship. In 1992, at the time of Babrij Masjid demolition, the BJP that led Ayodhya movement was running a few state governments that remained riot free under BJP rule. When the Narasimha Rao government (1991-1996) decided to dismiss these governments owing to the BJP's connivance in the demolition of the Babri Masjid, a debate erupted around the question: What is a good evidence secularism? Does it mean that a political party claiming to be secular but fails to contain riots or violence against minorities/Muslims during its reign over a political party that does not claim to be secular but its regime is riot or violence free? These arguments questioning the meaning of secularism in Uttar Pradesh were raised with regard to Samajwadi Party (SP). This is going to be a dominant question in the Indian public debate in coming years. What is good for minorities/ Muslims? A secular regime with frequent eruption of violence/riot or a regime that claims non-secular but its rule is not marred by violence or riot?

In my view, Communalism could exist without violence, and riot is its violent manifestation There could be non-violent communalism showing signs of normalcy at the surface, but could practice discrimination and prejudices covertly or overtly. Absence of violence or riot does not offer concrete evidence of absence of communalism from a society. Such prejudicial attitudes has a tendency to accumulate, it could explode at a critical time leading to some of the worst forms of ethnic violence or riot as evident in Gujarat 2002 or Muzzafarnagar 2013.

Implications for Muslims

There is enough evidence to suggest that the Hindu Right has a systematic design to restructure the relationship of Indian Muslims both at the state as well as at the level of society. This would, in turn, not only perpetuate Muslims suffering of a new kind; it would also lead to compromise, accommodation and backlash from the Muslim community.

At the state level, the Hindu Right seems to be keen to pursue a strategy of disempowerment of Muslims from the political power structure by preventing them to compete for political offices and keeping them away from any decision making processes. The decision not to let any Muslim to run for Assembly in Gujarat or allowing only a few Parliament seats in 2014—mostly when in constituencies where it had little chance to win. The decision by the Modi government not to offer any significant portfolio in its Cabinet to a few Muslim faces it is another evidence of this trend. Not to celebrate *iftar* party etc. only deepens the suspicion that restructuring of Muslim relationship is very central to its agenda. More-ever, Gujarat 2002 or Muzzafarnagar 2013 were not conventional riots instead these were riots engineered more to defang the Muslim community. In a way, it is meant to send a message that era of victimhood or that of equal right is over. Or else, how would one explain the conduct of the Prime Minister who has all the time of the world to travel to virtually all the capitals of the world, but no statement or visit or policy response for the victims of Muzzafarnagar riots, located less than 100 kms from New Delhi?

At the societal level, the Hindu Right seems to be keen to send a message that Indian Muslims must have the obligation either to explain and pay for historical atrocities committed during the Muslim rule. Furthermore, the community should be prepared to bear the consequences of the atrocities inflicted on the Hindus across the border particularly in Pakistan and Bangladesh, partly owing to being the member of a community that had the audacity to create two nations out of Akhanda Bharat. Indian Muslims should also learn to adapt their lifestyles, food habits and religious rituals consistent with the majoritarian sensibilities. Haryana CM's statement, a former RSS member like Mr. Modi's is reflective of this mindset.

Evidently, all of this will lead to substantial polarization and violence contributing to the processes of democratization of Indian polity. Consequently, Muslim question in the era of the *Hindutva* would pose greater challenge to the issues of multi-culturalism and democracy given that the designs of the *Hindutva* would cause more violence and polarization raising fresh issues of human rights and minority rights for outside world, but in the domestic arena institutions and political elites would look at these more as a new normal in changing world. Some of its evidences are seen in Gujarat society for past decade or so.

References

Anderson, Perry (2012). *Indian Ideology*, New Delhi: Three Essays Collective.

Basu, Amrita (2015). *Violence Conjectures in a Democratic India*, New Delhi: Cambridge University Press.

Grover, Vrinda and Saumya Uma (2017). *Kandhamal: Introspection of Initiative for Justice 2007-2015*, New Delhi: United Christian Forum and Media House.

Mander, Harsh and others (2016). *Living Apart: Communal Violence and Forced Displacement in Muzaffarnagar and Shamli*, New Delhi: Yoda Press.

Rehman, Mujibur (2016). *Communalism in post-colonial India: Changing Contours*, New Delhi: Routledge.

Rehman, Mujibur (2017 forthcoming). *Rise of Saffron Power: Reflections of Indian Politics*, New Delhi: Routledge.

13
Globalisation: An Analysis

Amna Mirza

Globalization is a complex and controversial term, when discussion goes on its definite meaning and content, it further gets contentious. Although the globalization can be seen as the buzz word for our time, yet there is debate on what it is actually about. Globalization can be defined as the complex web of interconnectedness that affects all aspects of modern lives.

Globalization is not new, it is the 'scale and nature' of interconnectedness under discussion that makes it essential to analyze in current times. This article intends to depict the process and idea that globalization involved and different aspects of this multifaceted phenomena. The paper will also try to analyze the process of globalization, its significance and implications in economic, political, cultural, ecological terms. Lastly, a discussion on the impact of globalization on third world countries is also done by using the views and counterviews of various economists and then look uopn what is the way forward.

Most of us believes that globalization is a recent phenomena and refers current time as "the era of globalization". But the real fact is that globalization is not a new phenomena, the world was moving towards globalization from a very long time. For instance if we talks about silk road during middle ages, an interconnected network of trade routes across central Asia or trade system of European nations in other countries in the time of imperialism, it can be stated that the process of globalization was in existence since earlier time. Thus it is not totally a new phenomena. It's only in 21st century that globalization gained momentum due to the advancements in technology and communication.

In late 1980s, through innovations and advancements in science and technology, travel and transportation, communications and IT world became interconnected. The disintegration of USSR, end of bi-polar world and the rise of uncontested capitalism brought several socio-political changes in the world system. The world had to reshape itself to the new conditions. There was the introduction of neo-liberal policy, Bretton woods conference which resulted with Structural Adjustment Programme (SAP) and liberalization programme. This time the eruption of new forms of technology, mainly the Internet, increased the intensity of global contracts and migration of people to different parts of the world looking for better prospects. As the industrial revolution giving rise to a kind of global integration beyond the boundaries of nation states, these events created a new global situation seeking a fundamental redesigning of economic and political arrangements. Friedman has mentioned that "Globalization is the integration of markets, finance and technologies in a way what is shrinking the world from a size medium to size small and enabling each of us to reach around the world farther, faster and cheaper than ever before.

With forces of integration at work, being in isolation is no longer a luxury for nations today. As things move, one cannot ignore the fact that new constellations emerge. New contours are being chalked out, an example here can be that nobody thought in the past that Data and algorithm will be emerging as new currency of power. Further, there are contestation too, which explains the multifaceted nature of globalization process.[1]

Globalization and Its Dimensions

Economic and Political

Globalization is often understood primarily in economic terms. There is a tendency to confine the discussion over globalization to economic realm and define the process as the integration of all economies of the world, it's political, social, cultural implications are usually ignored. The real fact is that globalization is a complex multi- dimensional phenomena. As we know that globalization is the process of integration, interdependence and interaction of world's economies, population, culture, companies worldwide, it has many aspects to discuss. Because of cross border trade in goods and services, technology, people and information, globalization has multiple implications in economic, political, cultural, technological and ecological terms. Thus the interconnectedness that globalization has generated is multi-dimensional, we can capture different aspects of multifaceted phenomenon in following ways:

National economies, more or less, have been absorbed into a single unified global economy. The process of global integration has impacted almost every aspect of contemporay life- markets began to work on more efficient lines, diminishing warfare and face to face military conflicts, increasing competition between buyers and sellers.

Certain developments like Foreign Direct Investment, technological advancements, rise of economies of sale facilitated in better technology transfer and enhancing industrial restructuring. Though the interdependence between nations also affected by market instability. The lack of accountability of foreign actors, fluctuations in economic cycle posed a threat to national sovereignty. The rise of nationalistic or protectionist tendencies posits new dangers of de-globalization.

MNCs and transnational corporations do not operate in vacuum, they don't drive globalization on their own. They operate on the guidelines setforth by World Bank and IMF. International groups like OECD and the World Economic Forum serves as a platform to determine the rules for capitalist global governance.

It is argued that Globalization did not suceed in removing poverty nor did it usher in stability. It did not lead to adequate growth in erstwhile Soviet economies as they dismantled socialist communist models on hopes of growth. Western banks made unscrupulous gains by relaxation capital market controls. Further the outcome that one can see is that the process of globalisation did not yield adequate returns, regardless of how well intentioned the act was of.[2]

One major aspect of globalization is declining the sovereign status of nation states. It refers to de-territorialization of politics, rule and governance. In political terms, globalisation implies- loosening of national boundaries, limiting the power of nation state with widespread flow of capital, goods, people and technology across borders, rise of super power and global governance and increase in the role of International Non-Governmental Organizations (NGOs). The interconnectedness of the world has intensified to the extent that a decision taken in one part of the world leaves its impacts in others. For example, recession in IT sector in US affected the career of software professionals in Asia. Supranational institutions like WTO, IMF affected the domestic policies. The policies which were usually called internal are being regulated by some invisible hands of an external power. Daniel Bell stated that Globalization is linked with 'crisis of territorial nation-states.'

Globalization is seen to be significant for ushering kantian order of eternal peace and respect for human rights, democracy as it's the people element that is the focus of any interaction. Since these are also linked to the essence of humanity, it is argued that thereby globalisation becomes an important interesting project. However, looking at its impact, it requires right coordination and control too.[3]

Cultural: As a result of popular media, global travel, tourism there is increased cultural interconnectedness across the world. Global economic and political institutions has also given rise to similar life patterns in different parts of the world. Local culture is exposed to other ways of living and alternatives. Globalization opens up the local culture to new methods of production, new products for consumption and new leisure style and ideas like human rights, democracy. MNCs and impact of markets gave rise to new forms of consumer culture. The transfer of ideas and values have affected the social relations too.

Transmission of ideas have also led to standardization of cultural expressions which further led to hegemony of a particular form over the other. Globalization implies the dominant western culture that has been prominent all over the globe. Some call it "Americanization of the world". George Ritzer used the term Mcdonaldization for the increasing popularity of fast food restaurants all over the world.

Globalization is related to culture and culture is an important dimension of globalisation. Within this argument are the inseparable twin concepts of connectivity and proximity, which have made forces of interchange and exchange to something that can be described as 'unicity'. The idea that culture signifies meanings that human Attatch to their idea of social and political order, then definitely gets impacted by myriad forces at work leading to blurring of spacial and time differences.[4]

Technological: Technology is the main driving force behind the process of globalization. In the era of globalization, technology is described as the socialized knowledge of producing goods and services. Market is the main force behind technological advancements. The latest technical innovations like nano technology, plastic money and optic fibres has given rise to new horizons on trade and exchange. The immediate access to goods and services enhanced by technology have led to 'distributed intelligence'. However globalization is seen as moral necessity, but since we have unequal accessibility and affordability of technology then what kind of vision we seek for the global system.

Transnational lives are most visible faces that not only depict various realms of globalization but also point towards one of the drivers of globalization. It was the second industrial revolution that witnessed new development and innovation in the realm of technology and globalization is debated to be emerging as an offshoot of it.

As technological advances become rampant, today network of experts are working at various realms and avenues and this has a bearing on reconfiguration of world economy too.[5]

Ecological: As globalization accelerates industrialization, it produces multiple serious threat to ecology such as resource scarcity, global warming, climate change, melting of glaciers, rise of sea level, loss of biodiversity, pollution on land, air, water and so on. As environment do not respect national boundaries, these are hardly taken seriously by anyone. For instance, instead of taking joint responsibility to curb the danger of acid rain, nation states blame each other. This is the globalization of environmental threats. It is extremely important for all countries to make a balance between economy and ecology and to set the goal of sustainable development is only alternative left with us. Various steps have been taken at global level for the consolidation of sustainable development such as 1972 Stockholm Conference, 1992 Rio De Janerio Summit, Rio+20 in 2012. Sustainable development brought with it the notion that economy and environment are not necessarily anti-thetical.

Though it cannot be denied that globalization has led to crisis of environment but on the other hand it has contributed in creating awareness about environmental issues at global level. It has began the age of transnational environmental groups and helped in spreading "ecological sensibility". The transnational environmental organization "Green Peace" working on problems like toxic substances, energy, nuclear issues, ocean is a case in point. Globalization can be blamed for environmental degradation but environmental groups have become successful because of globalization only.

Looming crisis of climate change, biodiversity, desertification, have become focus of international attention. At the same time, one must take into account that many environmental problems are not quickly recognized if they are seen as manageable and discrete. This points towards limits of human understandings and complex nature of ecological issues that have a global impact.[6]

Globalization: Contested Terrain

There are various viewpoints over the question- Is globalization actually happening? There has been intense debate on the impact and significance of globalization. David Hell *et al.* (1999) has made an influential attempt to outline the various positions on this debate over globalization. There are three school of thought which percieved globalization in different ways- Hyperglobalists, also called global optimists, believes that globalization is a positive action because it brings economic advancement, huge prosperity and the spread of democratic values. They sees globalization as a new point in human history which gives rise to denationalising economies through the establishment of transnational networks of trade, production and finance. They believed in the notion of 'borderless world' which means national borders have become irrelevant and world is dominated by transnational forces. Therefore, national economies are unworkable in a global context.

Sceptics, by contrast, are sceptical about the idea that globalization or global economic integration is anything new. They believes that if we look back to the 19th century, there are higher evidences of developed flows of trade and investments. Sceptics argues against the exaggerating the benefits of economic integration, states still holds importance, globalization is only a process of intense internationalization. They views globalization as a fantasy and dismissed the idea of global integrated economy.

Transformationalists, falls between hyperglobalists and sceptics, offers a middle road view of globalization. It admits that profound changes have come in the patterns and processes of global politics without its traditional features having been withered away.

Globalization has provided immense opportunities and choices, promoted economic growth and yield profits. It has increased employment opportunities, free trade has opened the doors for developed nations to invest money in developing countries, market competition has decreased the prices of goods and services. Reduction in cultural barriers is also a great benefit of globalization. Thus globalization has given rise to integrating economy, culture and governance.

Globalization has brought huge disadvantages also. It has increased gap between rich and poor, developed and underdeveloped and issues of inequality, injustice, insecurity, poverty and malnutrition increased at massive scale. Rampant cases of non-traditional security issues such as narcotics, terrorism, pandemics etc has emerged. Labour are forced to work under unfair conditions, many MNCs have been accused of social injustice in less developed countries. Indigenous industries face extinction as these small scale industries couldn't compete with large scale industries or MNCs. As international mobility is a direct consequence of globalization, the danger of chronic disease or commuicable disease like AIDS persists.

Divergent Viewpoints

David Held posits globalization as a process of widening, deepening and speeding up of global interconnectedness at all levels of contemporary life. The driving forces behind the process are international trade and finance, de-territorialization (time and space compression), communication and technology. It involve a process of spatial organization of social relations which can be seen in the form of transnational and transcontinental networks. The increasing number of supranational forces challenges the authority of nation-states.

For Anthony Giddens, globalization is a product of modernity. Both local and global have been couched to each other to produce a new configuration but it doesn't mean than that local has lost its significance. Both affect each other. He presents 4 intersecting dimensions of globalization- capitalism, the inter-state system, militarism and industrialism. The contradictions of capitalist economic system influences the pattern of economic globalization and "Universalism" of nation state, on the other hand is responsible for a single world economy. Globalizing of military power is,similarly, behind the idea of militarism and the changing global division of labour is behind the idea of industrial development.

Martin Wolf feels that globalization isn't as an ideology, but as a journey towards undefined destination. The factors like reduced costs, quicker communication and economic liberalization are responsible for greater integration. The reason what makes globalization work is quest for better life by individual, anti-globalism is anti-liberty. The remedy to deal with the issues of globalization calls for greater globalization itself. Martin Wolf has pointed out that as history teaches us we have choices so if mankind has to choose better world then state must focus on its long-term interest in co-operative global economic order.

Susan Strange holds that power has become an important factor that determines the relationship between state and market. Corporations that have acquired global character and new finance structure impacts power beyond national boundaries. She opines that the globalization of production, knowledge and finance has left the nation-states only as regulative powers.

James Rosenau titled the process of connecting global and local as 'fragmegration'- a combination of two processes: fragmentation & integration. Fragmentation signifies weakened states by shifting their power upward to supranational bodies or downward to local ones. The driving forces behind fragmegration are skill revolution, mass migration, new technology and transnational institutions. This period is theorized as a period of turbulence as disturbances occured by weakening of long standing authority.

Jagdish Bhagwati,who is a supporter of free trade, in his work In Defense of Globalization (2004) posits that free trade has promoted economic efficiency. Though it also has some negative affects on workers but that doesn't mean we should shut our doors to free trade. Rather we must work to tackle these problems. He recommended Adjustment Assistance Programmme for relief, it is better than protection. He feels that cost involved in compensating the workers is much less than the profits incurred in free trade. Bhagwati defines globalization as an opportunity to develop, all the hurdles involved within it will occur even without it.

Joseph Stiglitz, an eminent economist, in his work Globalization and its Discontents (2002) argues that the process of globalization can prove beneficial if country adopts it according to its local conditions. For instance, East Asian countries such as Korea and Taiwan took advantange of globalization of knowledge and invented their own technology, it ultimately made them self-sufficient.These countries rejected the Washington's advice of liberalization and privatization and didn't follow the process of free trade blindly. Thus countries must accept the process of globalization by closely analysing the situation and judging what is best for them.

Walden Bello in his work, Deglobalization: Ideas for a New world Economy (2002) holds that global economic institutions like WTO and others imposes certain rules over developing countries that further the interest of corporations of developed nations. These institutions poses threat to development, social justice, equality and environment. He calls for a 'anti-corporate globalisation' and suggested the deconstruction process by abandoning these giant multilateral institutions.

Walden Bello endorses the concept of 'deglobalisation' aims to bring about decentralized, local economies and communities across the world.

He recommended that our focus must be on production for the local market rather than production for exports. So 'deglobalization' signifies re-empowerment of the local and national.

Conclusion

Though globalization has several positive implications like increased economic growth, economic efficiency, high living standards but it is not same for developing countries. There is a lack of consensus on norms of global governance, as seen in case of climate change regime or agricultural subsidies. In addition, there have been isolationist reactions of certain nations that impact and obstructs the positive side of globalization. There are concerns of lack of infrastructure of globalization and inadequate sound institutional foundation. Thus, in current volatile environment, globalization and deglobalization often co-exist.

As the international system is going through a phase of transition, profound changes are taking place in the form of protectionism, populism. The need of the hour is to promote equitable development while ensuring inclusive growth and achieving various socio-economic goals mainly for less developed and developing nations in the world.

Notes

1. Michael O'Sullivan, The Levelling: What's Next After Globalization, Public Affairs, New York 2019.
2. Joseph Stiglitz, Globalization and Its Discontents, Penguin, 2012.
3. Jan-Erik Lane, Globalization and Politics: Promises and Dangers, Ashgate, 2006.
4. John Tomlinson, Globalization and Culture, Polity Press, Cambridge UK, 2013.
5. David Pretel, Lino Camprubí, Ed. Technology and Globalisation: Networks of Experts in World History, Palgrave Macmillan, Switzerland, 2018.
6. Peter Christoff, Robyn Eckersley, Globalization and the Environment, Rowman and Littlefield, UK, 2013.

References

Anthony Giddens, Runaway World, Profile Books, London, 2002.

Anthony Giddens, The consequences of Modernity. Polity Press, Cambridge, 1991, pp. 71-75.

David Held & Anthony McGrew, Globalization/Anti-Globlaization: Beyond the Great Divide, Cambridge, 2007, pp. 10-15.

David Held and Anthony McGrew, with David Goldblatt and Jonathan Perraton, Global transformation: Politics, Economics and Culture, Stanford University Press, California, 1999, pp. 5-8.

James N. Rosenau, Dynamics Beyond Globalization, Princeton University Press, 2003, pp. 10-20.

Susan Strange, States and Markets, Bloomsbury, UK, 2013.

Susan Strange, The Retreat Of the State: The Diffusion of power in the World Economy, Cambridge University Press, 1996.

'The Future of Globalization', World Economic Form, Davos, 2013.

Thomas L.Friedman, The world Is Flat 3.0: A Brief History of 21st century, Picador, 2007.

14
India's Neighbourhood Policy

Tabasum Firdous

Introduction

India shares a border with Pakistan to the west, Bhutan, China and Nepal to the north-east, and Bangladesh and Myanmar to the east. Besides it, the Indian Ocean on the south, the Arabian Sea on the south-west and the Bay of Bengal on the south-east and Sri Lanka and Maldives in the Indian Ocean. The Andaman and Nicobar islands of India share a maritime border with Thailand and Indonesia. In terms of her population, size, economic development, technological advancement and military capabilities, India has a predominant position in South Asia, and accounts for 76 per cent of the population of South Asia living in 73.25 per cent of the total land area of the region.

Since the last decade of the twentieth century, the broadening concept of security from traditional to non-traditional threats including religious extremism, international terrorism, drug trafficking, arms smuggling and aggressive nationalism has led the nation-states to alter their foreign policies. India also reoriented her foreign policy for the non-traditional security threats present in her immediate and extended neighbourhood. The country is cooperating with the regional and global initiatives to face the unconventional threats. For the last two decades India has attempted new endeavours in her foreign policy in the quest for attaining the status of a global power. The Post-Cold war era witnessed India reformulating her foreign policy while following the major determinants as economic growth, energy security, nuclear capability, democratic tradition and soft-power capability. Today, the driving forces of her foreign policy are the need for sustained economic growth, energy, maritime security, access to technology and innovation, as well as internal and external security.

India is facing the conventional challenges are active in the form of 'Big Brother' syndrome, Indo-Pak rivalry, lack of regional economic integration, persistent instability and conflicts among the regional countries etc. New challenges are securing grounds in the form of China's involvement in the region, widening developmental gap between India and other South Asian nations, and lack of effective integration of South Asian countries with the global economy. The current developments and shifts at global order suggest that the country has to work for creating the external environment conducive to her transformation and development.

Challenges and Responses

India has to address the three sets of challenges, i.e. ensuring a peaceful neighbourhood, establishing and balancing the relations with the major powers, and addressing the issues of food security, water, energy and environment. It is in this context that India's foreign policy since early 21st century added an intermediating level between the regions and global outlook. The country is pursuing policies to restore her ties and reintegrate with adjacent regions. Acknowledging the significance of the regional economic cooperation, the country has engaged the regional countries in the framework of 'neighbourhood' and 'extended neighbourhood' policy. India sought the cooperation of her immediate neighbours while supporting the cause of South Asian Association for Regional Cooperation (SAARC) that includes Afghanistan, Bangladesh, Bhutan, India, Maldives, Nepal, Pakistan and Sri Lanka. Her framework of extended neighbourhood stretches from the Suez Canal to the South China Sea including West Asia, Central Asia Republics, Southeast Asia, East Asia, Asia-Pacific and Indian Ocean Rim. This 'extended neighbourhood' policy first engaged the Southeast Asian nations under the "Look-East Policy" framework and now the Central Asian Republics under the policy framework of "Connect Central Asia Policy" (CCAP). Thus, the 'Look East Policy' since 1990s and now the 'Connect Central Asia Policy' since the beginning of the 21st century reflects India's 'Extended Neighbourhood' orientations.

With the involvement of external powers in South Asia, particularly the US and China, the strategic interests of India has increased manifold. In order to sustain economic growth, the country has to ensure adequate supplies of energy resources and raw materials. For this, the country has acknowledged the need to promote regional economic integration. However, her primary aspiration of socio-economic development, security and peace is dependent on a peaceful and prosperous neighbourhood. All this necessitates the policy designs to provide a space for the political, economic and cultural links with all her neighbours.

India also has to deal both her core and peripheral neighbourhood in different manner while taking into account the regional diversities due to geo-strategic and geo-political nature. Taking into consideration these necessities and requirements for regional integration, Afghanistan provides a suitable route for India to achieve her objectives. Besides the geo-strategic significance, Afghanistan is also essential to contain the non-traditional security threats within the region. Thus, India's 'Afghan Policy' since 9/11 forms an essential part of her neighbourhood and extended neighbourhood orientations.

Today India's foreign policy has shifted from NAM to NAM 2.0, a policy approach seeking "Strategic Autonomy" to replace "Strategic Neutrality" of decision making which was supposed to be essence of previous non-alignment that today sounds redundant. What is more relevant to describe India's foreign policy in post-Cold War era is the term "Multi-alignment" as used by Shashi Tharoor to describe the maturity of India in balancing the relations with world powers. Successive governments of India in 21st century globalized world have focused multi-alignment, realizing that in contemporary interdependent and interconnected world, foreign policy cannot be based on the orthodox principle of 'either-or', but a matrix of 'and' too is needed.

Basic Determinants of India's Foreign Policy

India's foreign policy rests on some basic determinants that include: Geography, History and Tradition, National Philosophy, Political Organization, Economic Condition, Military Strength, Domestic Milieu, Indian Diaspora, Changing International Trends and Nature of Leadership. A foreign policy is prone to change in accordance to the changing nature of these determinants. India's foreign policy also witnessed continuity and change since the country's inception as an independent nation-state in world politics. The foreign policy of the country has changed in due course of time with the changing nature of leadership, domestic requirements, international trends and situations. Almost all the leaders have influenced the country's external relations according to their varied outlooks and party ideologies. This argument can be validated by the following discussion regarding the impact of personality of leaders and regimes based on different party ideologies.

Jawaharlal Nehru

Pandit Jawaharlal Nehru, the first Prime Minister and Foreign Minister of independent India, was the real architect of the country's foreign policy. An internationalist in outlook, Panchsheel was a typical representation of his way of approaching problems with other countries. Nehru has the credit of adoption of Non-Alignment policy as integral to Indian foreign policy. He shaped India's foreign policy, which he believed was firmly rooted in India's civilizational tradition, freedom struggle and quest for peace and development. His preferences were to build a stronger neighbourhood i.e., countries bordering India by land and sea rather than concentrating on the developments in Europe. During his tenure, India also reached out to the struggling countries in Africa and emerged as a leading voice against racialism and colonialism. Nehru also attempted to force a negotiation with Pakistan through the UNO. However, Chinese invasion in 1962 had far-reaching effects on India's foreign policy. It made India to rethink for enhancing military strength of the country to deal with such situations.

Lal Bahadur Shastri

Lal Bahadur Shastri succeeded Jawaharlal Nehru in 1965 and immediately met a war with Pakistan. The response to the Pakistan's aggression while directing the Indian Army march towards West Pakistan and the subsequent defeat of Pakistan gained Shastri reputation of capable leader after Nehru, bearing the fresh memories of India's defeat in 1962 against China. India under Lal Bahadur Shastri and Pakistan under Field Marshall Ayub Khan (then President of Pakistan) signed the Tashkent Agreement in 1966. However, Shastri's demise soon after the agreement gave independent India her first woman Prime Minister in January 1966.

Indira Gandhi and Morarji Desai

Indira Gandhi has recognition for being more pragmatic and realistic in her foreign policy. Her proactive stand in terms of pragmatism and her sensitivity to the imperatives of vital national interest left an imprint on reorienting the foreign policy along the lines of realism. Liberation of

Bangladesh, non-accession to Nuclear Non-Proliferation Treaty (NPT) and strengthening ties with the former Union of Soviet Socialist Republics (USSR) under her leadership substantiates the stand of being more pragmatic and realistic in promoting national interests. The major highlights of foreign policy during Indira Gandhi's era are as reflected in the Treaty of Friendship with the Soviet Union, India's role in liberation of Bangladesh and Nuclear explosions at Pokhran.

Though Indira Gandhi reaffirmed the faith in non-alignment, she did not hesitate to criticize the United States for its excesses in Vietnam even when India was dependent chiefly on US for food supplies and Indian economy was shrinking due to droughts and floods. One of Indira Gandhi's greatest efforts was to increase India's self-sufficiency in food grains through the Green Revolution to reduce the country's dependence on imports and thus stabilize India's economic condition. Even after the US support to Islamabad, the India-Pakistan War of 1971 helped in the liberation of East Pakistan as a new nation of Bangladesh. China too was turning towards the US to end its isolation. China used USA against India and USA was using China against Soviet Union. This consequently paved the way for Indo-Soviet Treaty of Peace Friendship and Cooperation in August 1971. The treaty brought in criticism that India was abandoning the path of non-alignment. When Z.A. Bhutto became the Prime Minister of Pakistan, a summit between Indira Gandhi and Bhutto in Simla brought an accord signed on 1st of July, 1972, known as the Simla Agreement. This agreement stipulated that Kashmir issue should be resolved peacefully through bilateral negotiations. However, India and the US witnessed troubled relations due to the Pakistan factor and by India's nuclear explosion at Pokhran on 18th of May, 1974.

With Morarji Desai, India retained special relationship with the Soviet Union, but what was striking was the change in the US attitude exemplified in Jimmy Carter's visit to India. Desai government also worked for improving relations with archrival Pakistan and China. The visit of then Foreign Minister A.B. Vajpayee to China heralded a new beginning of relations between the two countries.

However, Indian foreign policy under Desai was shortlived with the return of Indira Gandhi who now focused to continuing rapprochement to the United States. Her meeting with the then US President Ronald Reagan at Cancun in October 1981, succeeded in convincing US that India was not a client follower of Moscow. She affirmed India's neutral stand towards the two superpowers. Indira Gandhi also tried to mend relations with China to make her neighbourhood stable and peaceful.

The emphasis on developing relations with ASEAN heralded the process of 'Look East Policy', which was later on carried by subsequent Prime Ministers.

Rajiv Gandhi

Rajiv Gandhi era has an impact on foreign policy with respect to the Indian Peace Keeping Force (IPKF) in Sri Lanka, further improvements in Indo-Soviet relations and the transfer of computer technology from the US to India. Indian Peace Keeping Force was the Indian military contingent performing a peacekeeping operation in Sri Lanka between 1987 and 1990. It was formed under the mandate of the Indo-Sri Lankan Accord in 1987 that aimed to end the Sri Lankan civil war between militant Sri Lankan Tamil nationalists such as the Liberation Tigers of Tamil Eelam (LTTE). Rajiv Gandhi also preferred to carry forward the traditions of his grandfather (Jawaharlal Nehru) and mother (Indira Gandhi) in consolidating the policy of non-alignment, but tried to give it a contemporary dimension. Despite some initial disturbances, Indo-US relations interchanged in almost all aspects of political, economic, cultural and social. He also prioritized India's policy towards his neighbours particularly Sri Lanka and Pakistan.

Vishwanath Pratap Singh and Chandrashekhar

V.P. Singh's government focused the neighbourhood policy to re-engage the surrounding countries for cooperation in building confidence. First, due to the pressure of Sri Lankan government under Ranasinghe Premadasa and the loss of Indian Peace Keeping Force (IPKF) in Sri Lanka, V.P. Singh immediately withdrew the force. India also welcomed the success of mass movement for multi-party democracy in Nepal. The country also praised the restoration of democratic rights to the people of Bangladesh and extended her support as well. India's next Prime Minister Chandrashekhar also continued this approach and visited Nepal in 1991. However, the Prime Minister denounced Iraq's occupation in Kuwait during Gulf war. The government also allowed the US aircrafts to land on Indian soil for re-fuelling.

Pamulaparti Venkata Narasimha Rao

P.V. Narasimha Rao sustained relations with the Russian federation on one side, and consciously developed relations with the emerging powers including the US, Western Europe and Japan. He also signed the landmark accord for maintaining peace and tranquility on the Sino-Indian border Line of Actual Control (LAC) in September 1993 during his visit to Beijing. He also tried to stabilize relations with Pakistan and met then Prime Minister of Pakistan, Nawaz Sharif for several times in between 1991 and 1994. This resulted in a number of agreements on Confidence Building Measures (CBMs). The government also initiated an extensive and dynamic programme of economic liberalization and reforms commonly known as LPG-Model. A part of this programme was to give highest priority to economic objectives in India's foreign policy. The main objective of economic reforms was to mobilize flows of investment and technology from abroad to India. It also aimed at implementing policies that would expand the Indian market and improve the country's access to foreign markets.

Inder Kumar Gujral

P.V. Narsimha Rao was followed by the short-term Prime Ministerships of H.D. Devegowda, I.K. Gujral and A.B. Vajpayee. During this period, however, India's foreign policy was dominated by the 'Gujral Doctrine' considered to have made a substantial change in the manner in which India's bilateral relations were conducted with its immediate neighbours, especially the smaller ones. Gujral Doctrine is a set of five principles to guide the conduct of foreign relations with India's immediate neighbours as spelt out by I.K. Gujral, first as India's Foreign Minister and later as the Prime Minister. These five principles are:

> *With neighbours like Bangladesh, Bhutan, Maldives, Nepal and Sri Lanka, India does not ask for reciprocity, but gives and accommodates what it can in good faith and trust.*
>
> *No South Asian country should allow its territory to be used against the interest of another country of the region.*
>
> *No country should interfere in the internal affairs of another.*
>
> *All South Asian countries must respect each other's territorial integrity and sovereignty.*
>
> *They should settle all their disputes through peaceful bilateral negotiations.*

I.K. Gujral largely relied on the Nehruvian tactics and vision. However, he carved out a foreign policy of his own in accordance with the changed circumstances. India under Gujral preferred constructive responses to have a beneficial impact on bilateral relations with neighbours. The country tried to strengthen India-Bangladesh ties, which were deteriorated by the 1992 demolition of the Babri Masjid. Gujral also took major initiatives to strengthen ties with Sri Lanka and intended to carry forward the India-Pakistan dialogue. The most striking development came in the relations between India-China. During Chinese President and General Secretary of the Communist Party Jiang Zewin's visit to India in November 1996, an agreement was signed to maintain peace and tranquility at the border and provided a mechanism for maintaining it. There was also pressure from the US for signing the Comprehensive Test Ban Treaty (CTBT). Gujral government, however, explained India's security concerns, economic perspectives and requirements and succeeded in establishing cordial relations between India and USA.

Atal Bihari Vajpayee

A.B. Vajpayee's tenure began with India conducting successive underground tests at Pokhran, which made clear that India had become a nuclear weapons state. Subsequently, the government declared that India had no need for more tests and undertook a voluntary moratorium on further testing. The government also declared that India would not be the first to use the atomic weapons and the recourse to them would only be in the self-defense. India's diplomatic attempts at nuclear disarmament brought India under international sanctions. The World Bank and the International Monetary Fund under US pressure withheld new assistance and the ban was extended to a number of other financial institutions. However, India withstood international pressures, and the Vajpayee regime later on improved ties with the US and sustained the international economic pressures. The government also focused to engage Pakistan on different tracks. Vajpayee inaugurated the bus service between Delhi and Lahore in February 1999. In certain aspects, the Vajpayee government tried to move beyond the Gujral Doctrine through the Bus Diplomacy with Pakistan. The bus service preceded a MoU reaffirming their unilateral moratorium on further nuclear testing and a host of Confidence Building Measures (CBMs). However, Kargil war and the Kandahar hijacking of 1999 jolted the relations again. After Musharraf consolidated his control in Pakistan and gave indications of his desire to revive talks with India, the two countries held Agra Summit in July 2001. Nevertheless, the event of 9/11 and 13th December attack on the Indian Parliament further deteriorated India-Pakistan relations.

Dr. Manmohan Singh

Manmohan era is known for strengthening India's world affairs with much focus on multilateral world order and regional engagements. The era witnessed improvement of relations with China, Indo-US Civil Nuclear Cooperation and new phase of Cooperation with Russia. Economics lies at the centre of the Manmohan Doctrine. India also pushed for the reforms in the UNO and WTO. Indo-US Civil Nuclear Cooperation (also known as 123 Agreement), has its framework in a joint statement issued by India's then Prime Minister Manmohan Singh and then US President George W. Bush on 18th of July 2005. With this, India agreed to separate its civil and military nuclear facilities and to place all its civil nuclear facilities under International Atomic Energy Agency (IAEA) safeguards. In exchange, the United States agreed to work towards full civil nuclear cooperation with India.

Indian Foreign Policy showed marked continuity under Manmohan Singh in its relations with important neighbours like China, Pakistan and big powers like USA. Manmohan Singh government made efforts to intensify peace process. During the Manmohan-Musharraf meeting on the sidelines of the UN General Assembly on 24th of September 2004, peaceful solutions to all the problems including Kashmir was focused. Manmohan Singh government repeatedly emphasized the need to work towards a situation in which borders would become irrelevant. Many CBMs were undertaken to normalize border issues with Pakistan. Besides the Kashmir issue, the two countries discussed Sir Creek, Wullar Barrage and the Tulbul navigation project. The demilitarization of Siachen and the Baglihar dam issue was also the part of agenda. The most remarkable change was the shift in public opinion in both the nations. At least, the change was evident that mostly opinion was growing against war in both countries. However, the peace dialogue was seriously disrupted by a series of terrorist acts including Mumbai Attack in 2008.

Narendra Damodardas Modi

The analysts have described Modi's style of engaging the world nations as a proactive foreign policy. Analyst S.D. Muni is of the opinion that

Modi has brought in dynamism and activism in foreign policy while reaching to the countries that were ignored and meeting local people of different nations. The government has attempted to resolve some disputes with other nations as is evident with the signing of historic Land Boundary Agreement with Bangladesh. He is also re-energizing India-US Relationship. The government also remained active in rescue and post-disaster operations in Yemen and Nepal.

Bigger shifts are visible with the method of how India is conducting itself on the world stage and the tools of statecraft it is using in this process. S. Jaishankar, Foreign Secretary of India, while terming India's foreign policy as a new proactive foreign policy, provided a detailed list of five "innovations" in the way India was using the tools of statecraft i.e. developing narratives, creating lexicon and imagery, using soft power, utilizing Indian diaspora and seeking a link between foreign policy and national development. The government is developing a narrative as part of a transition to make India a leading power by bringing the world attention towards India's sacrifices in World War I, or its record in peacekeeping operations. The creation of a new lexicon and imagery has been utilized by Modi government as a significant tool to promote national interests. For instance, the government has shifted focus from "Look East" to "Act East" policy. Similarly, the image of a "first responder" in humanitarian assistance and disaster relief has been critical in signaling and driving foreign policy change. The government has also emphasized the use of soft power in the foreign policy of country. This is evident with the emphasis and success of Narendra Modi at the UN General Assembly meeting in 2014 for observing 21st of June as the International Day of Yoga and its links with the country's culture and heritage.

S.D. Muni also opines that Modi is using religion as a foreign policy tool while visiting the Temples and Mosques in foreign nations. The emphasis is also on utilizing the Indian diaspora to promote India's national interests abroad. Efforts are on to bring resources, technology and best practices from international arena to further the country's own development. The 'Make in India' initiative justifies the process of linking foreign policy with the national development.

Narendra Modi invited all SAARC leaders to attend his swearing in ceremony as an unprecedented gesture of friendship and cooperation. Since then, the government has attempted to discourage all the conflicting issues with the neighbours and boost the economic, social and cultural ties. Mr. Modi has visited almost all the neighbouring countries to encourage a robust relation with all of them. However, mistrust with

Pakistan continues as per the cross-border infiltration and cease-fire violations are concerned. There are also some diplomatic games going on within the region providing enough space for the bilateral relations to deteriorate further. China-Pakistan nexus for regional designs and in particular to shape the future of post-ISAF Afghanistan is viewed as a strong challenge for India. Nevertheless, the government has signaled a positive gesture to improve relations with Pakistan as well. In March 2015, the new Foreign Secretary of India, S. Jaishankar commenced on a SAARC Yaatra and visited Pakistan as a part of the Yaatra. Thus, the Foreign Secretary talks were held on the 3rd of March 2015 after about 7 months from their previous cancellation. However, while both sides insisted on peace and cooperation, Pakistan made it clear that it would once prioritize Kashmir over other issues in the Indo-Pak dialogue. Pakistan also reemphasized its will and effort to abolish terror with the ongoing 'Zarb-e-Azb' campaign on the western frontier. India also assured Pakistan of the fact that 'talks and terror' cannot go hand in hand. Sushma Swaraj, India's External Affairs Minister paid a visit to Pakistan to attend Heart of Asia Summit. Much delayed National Security Advisers meeting was held at Bangkok in which they discussed, in the words of India's External Affairs Minister, "peace and security, terrorism, Jammu and Kashmir, and other issues including tranquility along the LOC". Apart from the routine diplomatic statements, no substantial progress was made in the recently held meetings. Prime Minister Narendra Modi's surprise visit to Pakistan was a goodwill gesture to improve the relations. However, the year 2016 was inaugurated with the Pathankot attack that once again created hurdles in carrying forward the talks.

Like any emerging power, India too has an ambitious but complicated relationship with its neighbouring countries as well as world powers. The country, however, has rightly understood that to play a major role in global politics, first it needs to be able to have a consensus among its neighbours. With the status of the largest country in South Asia and an influential player in the wider Asia-Pacific region, the smaller countries of the region view India as a mentor in foreign affairs. Though India tried to address this issue bilaterally as well as multi-laterally, there is no doubt that enough was left behind for the country to catch up especially when China has started to expand its range and horizon particularly since 1980s. Post-Cold War world has witnessed the most profound technological, economic and geopolitical change in the most compressed period of history.

Given its strength and strategic location, India can shape Asia's balance of power. Nevertheless, at the same time, the country is wary of

China. The gap in power and stature between China and India has widened significantly. There is a perspective in India that Mr. Modi faces major regional challenges due to failing states near abroad. The entire belt to Indian west from Pakistan to Syria suffers from instability and extremism. Thus, the challenge before Indian leadership and foreign policy makers is to promote India as a more competitive, confident and secure country aimed at gaining its rightful place in the world. The leadership has to evolve more dynamic and innovative approaches to diplomacy and national defense, demanding an active involvement of India in the region. India cannot rely on SAARC, as the organization is likely to remain a stunted one.

Changing circumstances and leadership has put several challenges for India in her foreign policy formulations. The analysts are focusing the international affairs of the country with utmost concerns and queries. How India will maintain the traditional foreign policy instruments such as Non-alignment policy and Panchsheel? How the country will sustain to maintain an independent foreign policy as a leader of developing countries? How India's unique geographical position and large Diaspora can be capitalized? How the country will balance the US factor without antagonizing Russia? How India will achieve the growing demand for energy, technology and find global market for her skilled workforce and products when neo-liberal economic interests of great powers overpower the international politics? How the country will deal the issues like human rights, violence, terrorism and environmental concerns?

Modi has succeeded to show a new orientation for pragmatic international engagement at global level with his frequent foreign visits. Indo-US strengthening relations are evident with Mr. Modi and President Obama's mutual visits to the respective nations. Nevertheless, there are some challenges for India to balance her interests with the US as well. It is true that both the countries are capable to sort out differences over nuclear deal to its full implementation. However, Modi's 'Make in India' initiative to boost the country's national interest at global level can contradict with when the US view India as a 'market' and 'counterweight to China' in Asia. In addition to that, the growing proximity among China, Pakistan and Russia pose challenge to India's strategic interests. This is so because of India's heavy dependency on Russia's military know-how in its military complex, China's growing influence in South Asia and Pakistan's sustained efforts to export terrorism to India. A stronger relation with the US could have far-reaching implications on energy, sharing of technology, poverty reduction and counter-terrorism efforts. The United

States and Japan both want to build strategic, long-term relations with India as a part of new Asian architecture that would balance China. At present, India is in a better position to be able to enjoy the benefits of managing all the relationships without a formal commitment with China, Japan or the United States which are competing for India's friendship. However, the situation is not same with Russia. It will be a real test for India's foreign policy to make in-roads into age-old India-Russia relationship. Russia has recently approached Pakistan with concluding a deal to sell Mi-35 helicopters to Islamabad. Again, Russia is aware of the fact that it has very limited friends especially in post-Crimean annexation and direct involvement in Syrian crisis. Thus, Moscow is getting closer to and dependent on Beijing, which is again raising concerns for India. India's permanent membership in SCO is a positive development. However, it is not easy to change an age-old foe like China into a trusted partner.

India's involvement in Afghanistan is of utmost concern for the regional as well as global politics. India's role in rebuilding Afghanistan has gained the country reputation all over the world, but has dissatisfied some key national actors including Pakistan. India has some considerable interests in this war-torn nation. The country wants to assure a stable and peaceful Afghanistan, which will enhance inter-regional trade ties and economic links. Not only this, a peaceful and democratic Afghanistan for India means the country will not be used against India's interests in the region by any state or non-state actor. However, the Taliban resurgence and ISAF drawdown has further complicated the situation and put the economic and security interests of India at risk. Now, it is again a test for India's foreign policy to stand with the changing circumstances in Afghanistan to secure her interests.

There are various grounds that India can exploit for her benefits while assuring Sino-Russian cooperation as the three Eurasian giants' share wide ranging interest on many major international issues. There is a recognition in India for the strategic needs of Russia in getting friendlier with Pakistan in post-ISAF situation to assure that the terrorist outfits should not make a safe haven in Afghanistan, which in turn would affect Russia's regional security and instability into the Central Asian Republics. With the strengthening of BRICS nation's solidarity, United States is emphasizing more on building a trilateral mechanism with India and Japan to curtail the growing influence of China in the region. Here India can utilize the situation to get more benefits from both China and the US.

Conclusion

Regarding India's present foreign policy dynamics, S.D. Muni expressed that "India, today, has stable relations with the US, China and Russia. The country is also maintaining good relations with ASEAN nations with widening framework that include Japan, South Korea and Australia as well". John Cherian has expressed the opinion in relation to India's policy response to Middle East crisis with these words that "The country (India) is maintaining a delicate balance in its relations with the three crucial countries of Middle East including Iran, Israel and Saudi Arabia". Thus, India has to use the strategy of what Shashi Tharoor termed as 'Multi-alignment' that advocates an alignment with all nations for serving the national interests in this globalized world. This strategy has the potential to balance the power equations with respect to India's regional and global concerns. It will help to boost economic growth and create jobs by attracting foreign investment from Western Europe, Russia, Japan and China. It will also help in maintaining India's advantages of defense ties with Russia and will provide access to the US military technology as well. There is also the scope to engage Iran and other Middle East countries for gaining access to the resources therein. Sino-Russia cooperation will also help the country to share maximum advantages of hydrocarbons in Central Asia. Engaging Pakistan will compel Islamabad to act on Mumbai Terror Attack case and adopt measures to prevent Pak soil from nurturing terrorism. The strategy will also help in assuring a peaceful drawdown of ISAF from Afghanistan and restoration of peace thereafter. The multi-alignment strategy also has the potential to strengthen India's position for a permanent seat in the UNSC. Thus, the foreign policy makers can explore new ways to engage with the regional and global powers to promote the national interests while balancing the power equations in the country's favour.

References

Bajpai, K.P. and Mattoo, A. (2007) (Eds.). *Engaged Democracies: India-US Relations in the 21st Century*. New Delhi: Har Anand Publications, p. 221.

Bajpai, K.P. and Pant, H.V. (Eds.) (2013). *India's National Security: A Reader*. London: Oxford, p. 98.

Chawla, A. (2015). "Review of Indo-Pak Relations in 2014 and Beyond", *FPRC Journal*, Foreign Policy Research Centre, New Delhi, (1), p. 169.

Dulat, A.S. (2015). *Kashmir: The Vajpayee Years*. New York: HarperCollins, p. 49.

Jaishankar, S. (2015). "Indian Foreign Policy—Seminal Shift or Continuity", available at: http://gurughantal.net/2015/09/27/indian-foreign-policy-seminal-shift-or-continuity/, (Accessed on 10th of November 2015, at 22:10).

Karnad, B. (2005). *Nuclear Weapons and Indian Security: The Realist Foundations of Strategy*. India: Macmillan Publishers, p. 76.

Mistry, D. (2014). *The US-India Nuclear Agreement: Diplomacy and Domestic Politics*. Cambridge: Cambridge University Press, p. 56.

Pant, H.V. (2011). *The US-India Nuclear Pact: Policy, Process and Great Power Politics*. India: OUP, p. 132.

Paul, S. and Iyer, N. (2015). "Renewed Hope of India's Foreign Policy under Modi Government: A Critical Appraisal of Challenges and Opportunities." *FPRC Journal*, Foreign Policy Research Centre, New Delhi, 2015 (1), p. 100.

Ramesh, J. (2015). *To the Brink and Back: India's 1991 Story*. New Delhi: Rupa Publications, p. 215.

Sethi, M. (2009). *Nuclear Strategy: India's March towards Credible Deterrence*. New Delhi: Knowledge World International, p. 110.

Sridharan, E. (2007). *The India-Pakistan Nuclear Relationship: Theories of Deterrence and International Relations*. India: Routledge, p. 238.

Wolpert, S. (2010). *India and Pakistan: Continued Conflict or Cooperation*. California: University of California Press, p. 86.

SECTION-III
Human Rights, Media and Gender

15
Understanding the Concept of Human Rights

Abdulrahim P. Vijapur

Introduction

Human rights have emerged as the most powerful concept of our age. It has become, in the opinion of former Secretary-General of the United Nations, Boutros Boutros-Ghali, a common language of mankind and the ultimate norm of all politics. Adopting this language allows all peoples to understand others and to be the authors of their own history. Two other great men—a scholar and a statesman—have more eloquently on the importance of human rights. A statement of Sir Hersch Lauterpatch, a noted protagonist of human rights and one of the most eminent international lawyers of the 20th century rightly captures the spirit of modern laws and functions of the States. He had observed in 1947: "The protection of human personality and of its fundamental rights is the ultimate purpose of all law, national and international". Similarly, Adlai Stevenson of the USA once had remarked, "human rights are at the core of everything we do and try to do." These two statements — made by a jurist and a statesman — candidly reveal that the concept of human rights has acquired a significant place in human life/civilization, as it is true that a large part of our time is devoted, in the ultimate analysis, to the promotion and protection of human rights. Moreover, it needs to be recalled that both the classical as well as contemporary political theories have affirmed and reaffirmed the significant principle that it is the "individual" for whom the State (or for that matter, any social or legal order) exists, and not *vice versa*.

Since 1948, the United Nations has adopted more than 100 human rights documents covering the entire gamut of human relationships. These, among others, deal with the rights of women, children, refugees, migrant workers, stateless persons, minorities, indigenous peoples and prohibition of racial or religious discrimination, genocide, slavery, torture, stateless persons, minorities, and indigenous peoples. Among all of these documents three are most important and basic. They are the Universal Declaration of Human Rights (UDHR) adopted on 10 December, 1948, the International Covenant on Economic, Social and Cultural Rights (ICESCR) and the International Covenant on Civil and Political Rights (ICCPR) adopted in 1966.

These three documents together constitute what is popularly known as the "International Bill of Human Rights", i.e., the first international bill in human history. December 10 is celebrated as Human Rights Day throughout the world as UDHR was adopted on this historic day. On the importance of human rights one should recall the often neglected Preambular paragraph of the UDHR, which stated that "whereas it is essential, if man is not to be compelled to have recourse, as a last resort, to rebellion against tyranny and oppression, that human rights should be protected by the rule of law..." With the introduction of the international protection of human rights there appeared an institutional mechanism of international human rights laws capable of becoming the basis and the framework for the full development of man's personality, represent for his standing as a human being and the equality of citizens before the law within the various States.

The importance of human rights is such that it can truly be asserted that, with their emergence and the first steps taken to promote and protect them, human society has taken a qualitative leap forward. In any event, human rights represent a new element in the development of mankind, and in the life of human society, because they signify the end of a period and the beginning of a new era in national and international governance.

Meaning of Human Rights

The concept of rights though is central to Social Sciences it is poorly understood. There is no agreement on its meaning, nature, and content. It is a concept very much contested not only between the East (Representing former socialist States) and the West (representing liberal - democratic States) but also between developed and developing countries. Each group of nations has a different perception of human rights.

The so-called first world countries of the West believed in the supremacy of the individual, while the communist countries of East focused on the community and the unconditional priorities of class interest. Hence, the individual benefited from these group rights, as his/her rights were better provided for, within the community. The communists gave priority to economic, social and cultural rights and insisted that they could not be separated from the class character of society in which they existed, while the liberal-democratic States of the West asserted the primacy of civil and political rights. This debate of priority of one set of rights over another continued to occupy the agendas of national and international governance during major part of the 20th century.

The newly emerging States of the Third World, while adopting the Eastern or Western model of human rights paradigms in their constitutions, or a combination of both, focused on solidarity or group rights such as right to self-determination of peoples, including sovereignty over their natural resources, the right to development, the right to a healthy and ecologically balanced environment, the right to peace and the right to ownership of the common heritage of mankind. They also insist on interdependence and indivisibility of civil and political rights to economic and social rights.

Thus, the modern concept of human rights is comprehensive in its nature and content. It includes three types of rights: civil and political, economic, social and cultural and the emerging collective or group rights. In fact, the catalogue of rights is expanding everyday. Moreover, it must be noted that no catalogue elaborating specific human rights will ever be exhaustive or final. Its content goes hand in hand with the state of moral consciousness, or development of civilization at any given time in history.

It is gratifying to note that in general the East is now shifting more towards the West in their perception of human rights, and civil and political rights are given greater attention than ever before. The collapse of communism and the end of the "Cold War" in 1990s suggests that arguments over divergent concepts of human rights are no longer a subject of mutual accusation and a spirit of cooperation between East and West is evolving gradually.

Let us discuss some important questions: What is the importance of rights? Why do we need them? How can we define rights? Which is the most appropriate term for rights? Whether terms such as natural rights, civil rights, political rights and fundamental rights are same or have different meanings? Here we explore answer to these questions.

There exist definitional problems of the concept of rights. Many definitions of the concept of rights are found in the literature. Each of the following definitions helps us in understanding different facets of rights. Let us look at them.

1. According to Ernest Barker, "Rights are the external conditions necessary for the greatest possible development of the capacities of the personality."
2. Harold J. Laski defines rights as "those conditions of social life without which no man can seek, in general, to be his best". On their importance he remarked, "the state is known by the rights it maintains".
3. In the words of Bernard Bosanquet, "we have a right to the means that are necessary to the development of our lives in the direction of the highest good of the community of which we are a part".
4. Wilde considers that "Rights are reasonable claims to freedom in the exercise of certain activities". He further says: rights depend upon duties. "It is only in a world of duties that rights have significance". They are like the two sides of a coin.
5. Prof. Hohfeld calls the *four things* which the term 'a right' covers: "claims", "privileges or liberties", "powers" and "immunities". Examples of "claim rights" are the right of an old-age pensioner to a pension and an unemployed to get his social security benefits. Examples of "Liberty rights" are the right of a man to spend his leisure as he pleases, and to grow a beard if he wants to. A "Power right" entitles the right-holder to require other people to do certain things at his discretion. Examples are the right of a landlord to alter the rent paid by his tenants, and the right of a policeman to question eyewitnesses at the scene of a crime. An "immunity right" entitles the right-holder to be exempt from something—an MP (Member of Parliament) to be exempt from the law of libel for what he says in Parliament, a conscientious objector to be exempt from military service.

In short, rights are nothing but claims against the State or government or individual persons. In other words, human rights are those conditions of life that allow us to develop and use our human qualities of intelligence and conscience and to satisfy our spiritual needs. We cannot develop our personality in their absence. They are fundamental to our nature; without them we cannot live as human beings. James Nickel rightly states that human rights aim to secure for individuals the necessary conditions for leading a minimally a good life. According to Scot David, the concept of human rights is closely connected with the protection of individuals from the exercise of State, government or authority in certain areas of their lives; it is also directed towards the creation of social conditions by the State in which individuals are to develop their fullest potential. Plano and Olton have stated that human rights, which are considered to be absolutely essential for the survival, existence and personality development of a human being. To deny human beings their rights is to set the stage for political and social unrest, wars, hostility between nations and between groups within a nation—and that denial leads to urgent demands for a better life in larger freedom. Human rights, far from being an abstract subject for philosophers, political scientists and lawyers, affect the daily lives of everyone—man, woman, and the child.

Rights are also used in a variety of ways indicating differences in ideological and philosophical perceptions. For some, rights are "normative attributes" that belong to a self-conscious person who perceives himself as an agent of purposive creative action. For others, rights are entitlements to choose from. McCloskey describes rights positively, as entitlements, to do, to have, enjoy or have done. For MacCormick rights "always and necessarily concern human goods", that is, concern with what it is good, at least, in normal circumstances, for a person to have. Feinberg and White asserted that rights can be "possessed, enjoyed, exercised and claimed, demanded and asserted".

The term "human rights" is all comprehensive—it includes civil-political (negative rights) and economic, social and cultural (positive rights) and collective or group rights. On the other hand, the term natural rights implies that nature has endowed human beings certain inalienable or natural rights like right to life, liberty and property. The terms civil rights or political right have narrow connotation. The term "fundamental rights", which we find in the Indian constitution, refers to certain basic/ core civil and political rights. Socio-economic rights are not made fundamental in the constitution. Since the constitution is the fundamental or basic law of the land, rights included in it are known as fundamental rights.

There are two other terms—legal rights and moral rights. The former refers to rights laid down in law and the latter refers to rights based on general principles of fairness and justice. Moral rights may or may not be enforced and supported by the law of the land. For example, a teacher may claim that he/she has a moral right to discipline their pupil, offer them advice about their academic and mo1.l development or about their choice of career. Sometimes people claim certain rights because of what they earn through their work (by writing a book an author may gain both a moral and legal right to a percentage of the proceeds from sales).

It should be acknowledged that rights and duties are two sides of the same coin. One's rights impose duties on others. Allegiance to the State, where a citizen resides, obeying the State laws, payment of taxes, exercising right to vote, rendering compulsory military service, parental duty towards their children when they are young and the duty of adult persons to take care of the needs of their old parents, etc. are some of the duties which have been recognized in different countries.

Kinds and Categories of Rights

Rights can be of many kinds, such as legal rights, moral rights, civil rights, political rights, social rights, economic rights, cultural rights and so on. Those rights which are provided in law and protected by it are called legal rights **Enforcement of rights is important. But it is quite possible to have a right to something without the right being enforced. For example, if my car is stolen and the thief is not caught or arrested, I still have a right to car.**

Three kinds of human rights have emerged at the international level. They are: civil and political rights, economic, social and cultural rights and group/solidarity rights. The UDHR and ICCPR recognizes many civil and political rights, such as right to life, liberty and security of persons, prohibition of slavery, torture, arbitrary arrest, detention or exile, right to fair trial, freedom of movement, religion, freedom of expression, right to privacy, right to seek asylum, right to nationality etc. These rights are sometimes known as first generation rights, as they found their first formulation in the Western socio-political thought and governance in 17th and 18th centuries.

The UDHR and ICESCR have given recognition to many socio-economic rights such as the right to work, favourable conditions of work and equal pay for equal work; right to form and join trade unions; right to social security; right to an adequate standard of living including adequate food, clothing and housing; right to protection of the family; the right to highest attainable standard of physical and mental health; right to education and participation in cultural rights. These rights are called second generation rights because they emerged at national and international level only in the 20th century due to socialist revolution in Soviet Russia.

In the 1970s, another set of rights have evolved at the international level. They are known by different names — third generation rights, group rights and collective rights. Such rights include —the right to development; the right to peace; the right to clean natural environment; the right to one's own natural resources; and the right to one's own cultural heritage.

It should be noted that the term "generation" of rights is a misnomer. It suggests a succession of phenomena, whereby a new generation takes the place of the previous one. That is, however, not the case with the three generations of human rights. On the contrary, the idea is rather that the three "generations" exist and be respected simultaneously. Moreover, there is the curious phenomenon that one particular right — that of self-determination — belongs both to the first and the second generations. It needs to be noted that, according to the Vienna Declaration and Programme of Action, 1993, all rights are indivisible, interdependent and essential. **In fact, the term generation of rights is not coined by the United Nations. It is suggested that the word "generation" should be replaced by "categories".**

Nature of Human Rights

Following salient features mark the concept of human rights:

1. Human rights are universal moral rights; they belong to everybody because they are human. **By definition, rights are not earned, bought or inherited. They are inherent in human dignity. They are inalienable.**
2. One of the guiding principles is that rights are available to all persons in the State irrespective of race, colour, sex, language, religion, political or other opinion, national or social origin, property or other status (Article 2 of the UDHR). They are universally applicable to all persons. In other words, non-discrimination is an important principle of contemporary human rights.
3. They are universal in the sense that they transcend the national boundaries or ideologies. They are designed to be culturally and ideologically neutral; they are not specifically liberal or socialist, Eastern or Western, Northern, developed or developing, Christen, Buddhist, Islamic or Hindu.
4. The concept of human rights is comprehensive in its nature and content. It includes all categories of rights, such as civil and

political, economic, social and cultural and even the newly emerging group or collective rights like, rights of minorities, indigenous peoples, right to development, right to peace and right to clean environment etc. In fact, the catalogue of rights is very detailed and comprehensive. The list of rights is expanding everyday. Moreover, no catalogue elaborating specific human rights will ever be exhaustive or final. The content of human rights goes hand in hand with the state of moral consciousness, or civilizational development at any given time in history.

5. Also, all rights and freedoms are indivisible and interdependent. The United Nations does not rank them in any hierarchy or any order of priority. Though we may classify rights in different categories, they are all complementary to each other. They are also interrelated. No set of rights has priority over the other.
6. Rights are not absolute or unlimited. Some of them can be suspended during war or public emergency. Justifiable and reasonable limitations can be imposed on their exercise, which are necessary to protect national security, public order, public health or morals or the rights and freedoms of others.

Evolution of Rights—Developments at Domestic level

The idea of "rights" and "duties" of citizens is as old as the concept of the State. The concept of rights in those systems was not fully developed and understood in the sense we know it today. It suited those socio-political milieus. To have a better understanding of the concept of rights, it is essential to look at their history.

The idea of rights is as old as human species. As man is a social being and cannot live outside society (as he/she is not self-sufficient for one's needs), the problem of rights arose involving man's relations with other individuals in a society, and his relations with State/government. Through these relationships men evolved certain norms of social behaviour, which got crystallized, over centuries' struggles, into what we call today as human rights.

Many important events and revolutions contributed towards the development of human rights. First, the earliest charters of human rights are to be found among the three British constitutional documents, namely, **the Magna Carta (1215), the Petition of Rights (1628) and the Bill of Rights (1689) adopted after the Glorious Revolution of 1688**. These three documents were the forerunners of the modern bills of rights. They imposed restrictions on the powers of the King and his arbitrary rules. It may be recalled that in the 17th century England there were conflicts and tensions between the Parliament and the King over the latter's arbitrary rule. These struggles led to the "Glorious Revolution" of 1688. This revolution is also known as Bloodless Revolution. James II, i.e., the King was forced to abdicate the throne. Fearing for his life the King fled the country with his neck in fact paving the way for the accession to the throne of William (of Orange) III and Mary II (the King's daughter who sided with the Parliament in this struggle). Following the revolution the Parliament passed the Bill of Rights in 1689. This Bill declared illegal the claimed suspending and dispensing powers of the Crown. It prohibited the levying of taxes or the maintenance of standing army in peacetime by the Crown without Parliamentary consent. The Bill also provided that "excessive bail ought not to be required, nor excessive fines imposed, nor cruel and unusual punishment inflicted". It further provided that "jurors ought to be duly impaneled and returned" and that "all grants and promises of fines and forfeitures of particular persons before convictions are illegal and void". **Moreover, it may be noted that the Glorious Revolution provided a precedent that rulers could be removed by popular will if they failed to observe the requirements of constitutional legitimacy**.

It was in the late 17th and the 18th centuries that the necessity for a set of written guarantees of human freedoms was felt as a new philosophy of governance. The dignity and rights of man was the dominant theme of political philosophy of the 18th century. This theme flowered into practical significance with such historic documents as **the Virginia Declaration of Rights, 1776, the America Declaration of Independence, 1776, the French Declaration of the Rights of Man and Citizen, 1789** and of more lasting importance, the series of Amendments to the U.S. Constitution, adopted in 1791 as the American Bill of Rights. Let us elaborate the rights proclaimed in these documents. The American Declaration of Independence contains ideas of human rights, such as:

That all men are created equal, that they are endowed by their creator with certain unalienable rights that among these are life, liberty and pursuit of happiness... that to secure these rights, Governments are instituted among men, deriving their just powers from the consent of the governed. That whenever any form of government becomes destructive of these ends, it is the right of the people to alter or abolish it.

The Virginia Declaration of Rights included specific liberties that were to be protected from State interference. These included freedom of press, the free exercise of religion and the obligation that no person should be deprived of their liberty except by the law of land or the judgment of their peers. The Virginia Declaration had a great influence on the drafters of the U.S. constitution (1787), as these minimum rights were included in it subsequently.

The French Declaration of Rights of Man and Citizen, 1789, recognized many rights, such as, all men are born equal; the State shall preserve the natural rights of man, which are liberty, property, security and resistance to oppression; no one may be indicted, arrested or detained except in cases determined by law; all men should be presumed innocent until judged guilty; freedom of thought, opinion and press; freedom of religion; no taxes without consent of all citizens; no one shall be denied right to property except for an obvious requirement of public necessity, certified by law, and on condition of just compensation in advance. The Declaration proclaimed that liberty consists in the ability to do whatever does not harm others; hence the exercise of rights of each man has no limits except those which assure to other members of society for the enjoyment of the same rights. Law can only determine these limits. **Therefore, it is generally said that my right to swing my hand ends where someone's nose begins.**

The Bolshevik Revolution of 1917 of Soviet Russia was another milestone in the development of the modern concept of rights. It introduced socio-economic dimensions to the concept of rights, which were neglected in the events and documents of English, American and French revolutions. While the three revolutions emphasized the first generation civil and political rights (which are also called negative rights), the October revolution of Russia popularized socio-economic rights which are positive rights. These rights are called positive because their implementation requires resources and positive action by the State.

Thus it should be acknowledged that each of these declarations, events and revolutions discussed in this section have made important contributions in advancing and shaping the concept of human rights. However, being product of their times and specific circumstances, they lacked totality of the concept and were narrow in their scope and applications. For instance, Magna Carta yielded concessions (not rights) only to the feudal lords, though it set limitations on arbitrary rule and laid the foundation for the rule of law. The American Declaration and Bill of Rights were applicable only to those who constituted what was abbreviated as WASP (White, Anglo-Saxon and Protestant). Slaves did not have rights in USA until slavery was abolished in 1864, and the rights of women were not part of the conception of rights at the time of American

Revolution. Similarly, although French Revolution was more egalitarian than the American, the question of the rights of women was raised, only to be quickly suppressed, and slavery was abolished, only to be restored by Napoleon. Moreover, Western States like United Kingdom and France did not extend the notion of rights to the "subject" people in their colonies. In sum, human rights had not become universal during then.

Humanitarian Intervention (HI)

The doctrine of HI has been expounded by many international lawyers, including Hugo Grotius, the father of International Law, in the 17th century. This doctrine recognizes as lawful the use of force by one or more States to stop the maltreatment by a State of its own nationals when that conduct was so brutal and large scale as "to shock the conscience of the community of nations". It is true that the principle of HI was frequently misused in the past and often served as a pretext for occupation or invasion of weaker countries. But it was the first to give expression to the proposition that there were some limits to the freedom States enjoyed under international law in dealing with their own nationals. Many great Powers have invoked the principle during the 19th century to prevent the Ottoman Empire from persecuting minorities in the Middle East and the Balkans. In the recent past India invoked it in 1971 while it intervened in East Pakistan (which emerged as Bangladesh) to put an end to massive violations of human rights of East Pakistanis.

International Humanitarian Law (IHL)

Through many treaties concerning laws of war IHL was developed. Treaties of 1864, 1906, and 1929 regulated the rights of the wounded in armies in the field, the wounded at sea in times of armed conflict. The 1864 treaty also protected medical personnel and hospitals. And also the protection to civilian population was provided by 1907 Hague Convention and prisoners of war were dealt with by treaty in 1929. From time to time, the laws contained in these treaties have been revised and modernized. Much of that law is codified in four Geneva Conventions of 1949 and the two 1977 additional Protocols to these Conventions. It must be noted that the creation of the International Committee of the Red Cross (ICRC) in 1864 by Henry Dunant contributed greatly to the development of the laws of war.

The four Geneva Conventions aim to protect the sick and wounded members of the armed forces, prisoners of war (POW) and civilian population. For instance, the Geneva Convention on POW requires that prisoners be treated "humanely" and that they not be subjected to physical or mental torture to secure from them information of any kind. It prohibits "measures of reprisal against POW" and provides that all POW be treated alike by the detaining Power, without any adverse distinction based on race, nationality, religious belief or political opinion. The fourth Geneva Convention, which seeks to protect civilian populations, establishes a massive code of conduct for the Occupying Power. It prohibits "not only murder, torture, corporal punishment, mutilation...of a protected person, but also...any other measures of brutality whether applied by civilian or military agents." It outlaws the taking of hostages, collective punishment and reprisals as well as "individual or mass forcible transfers" of protected persons or their deportations to the territory of the Occupying Power.

Abolition of Slavery

The first international treaties concerning human rights were linked with the acceptance of freedom of religion (e.g., the Treaties of Westphalia of 1648) and the abolition of slavery. Slavery had already been condemned by the Congress of Vienna in 1815 and a number of international treaties on the abolition of slavery appeared in the second half of the 19th century (e.g. the Treaty of Washington of 1862, documents of the Conferences in Brussels in 1867 and 1890 and in Berlin in 1885). The practice of slavery was first condemned in the Paris Peace Treaty (1814) between Britain and France. Under the League of Nations the Convention to Suppress the Slave Trade and Slavery was adopted in 1926. This Convention still remains the basic document prohibiting the practice of slavery, although it was amended by a Protocol in 1953 and supplemented in 1956 to deal with problems of defining the acts which constitute slavery in the modern world.

International Labour Standards

International Labour Organization (ILO), which has been in existence since 1919 and became a Specialized Agency of the United Nations in 1946, seeks to achieve social justice through its activities in the social and labour fields. The basis of ILO action for human rights is the establishment of international labour standards and the supervision of the implementation of these standards by ILO member States. ILO has adopted more than 150 Conventions and Recommendations on labour standards. These Conventions, when ratified by States, they are binding upon them. The Conventions relate to the basic human rights concern of ILO, such as freedom of association, abolition of forced and child labour, freedom from discrimination in employment and occupations. They also lay down standards in such fields as conditions of work, occupational safety and health, the provision of paid holidays and social security, industrial relations, employment policy and vocational guidance, and provide for the protection of special groups, such as women, migrants and indigenous and tribal peoples.

Protection of Minorities under League of Nations

The League of Nations was given a mandate to supervise the enforcement of the minorities' treaties emerging from the 1919 peace agreements with Eastern European and Balkan States. These treaties included provisions relating to the protection of the minorities. The minorities' regime of the League consisted of five special treaties binding Poland, the Servo-Croat-Slovene State, Romania, Greece and Czechoslovakia; special minorities' clauses in the treaties of peace with Austria, Bulgaria, Hungary and Turkey; five general declarations made on admission to the League by Albania, Lithuania, Estonia and Iraq; a special declaration by Finland regarding the Aaland Islands and treaties relating to Danzing, Upper Silesia and Memel.

The League agreed to serve as the guarantor of the undertakings that the Parties assumed in these treaties. It exercised those functions by developing a system for dealing with petitions by minorities charging violations of their rights. It is pertinent to note that during 1930-32, the League received 305 petitions from the minorities out of which only 153 were admitted. These petitions, among others, pertained to matters such as suppression of private schools, use of biased historical texts, restrictions on minorities' languages, agrarian reforms to the detriment of minority landlords, discriminatory policies in a job placement, denial of pension rights, denial of citizenship and acts of violence, repression and terror on the part of the authorities. The League system for dealing with these petitions was relatively effective and quite advanced for its time. Although the League was quite effective in redressing the grievances of minorities on smaller issues and everyday friction, it failed to solve the wider problems of peaceful living and amicable cooperation. Nonetheless, its decision to ask the Permanent Court of International Justice (PCIJ) for

Advisory Opinions on contentious issues of minorities rights were a welcome development in international law/relations. The decision of PCIJ on the Minority Schools in Albania Case (1935) have been assayed. All major national and international developments concerning the evolution of rights have been examined.

Conclusion

During the last 350 years many international efforts were undertaken in conferences and international organizations which contributed towards the evolution of human rights norms and standards. Following are some of the major landmark developments at the international level, which have brought the protection of human rights on the agenda of international politics and law. With these revolutionary developments, the process of internationalization of the concept of human rights began.

The idea of rights is as old as human species. As man is a social being and cannot live outside society (as he/she is not self-sufficient for one's needs), the problem of rights arose involving man's relations with other individuals in a society, and his relations with State/government. Through these relationships men evolved certain norms of social behaviour, which got crystallized, over centuries' struggles, into what we call today as human rights.

References

Baehr, Peter R. (1999). *Human Rights—Universality in Practice*, London: Macmillan

Cranston, Maurice (1973). *What are Human Rights?* London: The Bodley Head.

Freeman, Miacheal (2002). *"Human Rights—An Interdisciplinary Approach"*, Cambridge: Polity.

Levin, Leah (2009). *Human Rights — Questions and Answers*, 5th edition, Paris: UNESCO.

Vijapur, Abdulrahim P. (2008). *Human Rights in International Relations*, New Delhi: Manak Publications, this book has subsidized by Government of India through NBT, India, for the benefit of students and priced at Rupees 88.00.

—— (ed.) (2008). *Implementing Human Rights in the Third World— Essays on Human Rights, Dalits and Minorities*, New Delhi: Manak Publications.

—— (co-edited) (1999). *Perspectives on Human Rights*, New Delhi: Manak Publications.

—— (co-authored) (1997). *Pluralism, Minorities, National Integration: Problems and Prospects*, New Delhi: South Asian Publishers.

—— (1996). *The United Nations at Fifty: Studies in Human Rights*, New Delhi: South Asian Publishers.

—— (2012). "Laying the Foundations of Rights: The Role of ILO in Evolving Rights of Working Class", In Jose George, Manoj Kumar and Dharmendra Ojha (eds.) *Working Class Movement in India in the Wake of Globalization*, New Delhi: Manohar Publishers and Distributors.

—— (2015). "The Question of Domestic Jurisdiction and the Evolution of United Nations Law of Human Rights", In Sam Daws and Natalie Samarasinghe (eds.), *The United Nations*, Vols. (Sage Library of International Relations), Vol. 6: *Rights, Justice and Protection*, London: Sage Publications.

—— (1993). "The Principle of Non-discrimination in International Human Rights Law: The Meaning and Scope of the Concept", *India Quarterly: A Journal of International Affairs*, 49(3). Available at: http://iqq.sagepub.com/content/49/3/69.full. pdf+html

—— (2006). "International Protection of Minority Rights", *International Studies* (New Delhi/London/Thousand Oaks), 43(4). Available at: http://isq.sagepub.com/content/43/4/367.full.pdf+html

—— co-authored (2006). "The International Covenants on Human Rights: An Overview", *India Quarterly: A Journal of International Affairs*, New Delhi, 62(2). Available at: http://iqq.sagepub.com/content/62/2/1.full.pdf+html

—— (1993). "The Islamic Concept of Human Rights and the International Bill of Rights: The Dilemma of Muslim States", *Turkish Yearbook of Human Rights*, Vol. 15. Available at: http://yayin.todai.gov.tr/dergi.php?cilt=15&Dergi=5

—— (ed.) (1991). *Essays on International Human Rights*, New Delhi: South Asian Publishers/Absecon Highlands, N.J.: International Book Company.

—— (co-authored), *Comparative analysis of conceptions of human rights, democracy and the rule of law in selected third countries* (Utrecht, the Netherlands: Utrecht University, 23 December 2015), available at: http://www.fp7-frame.edu

16

Status of Right to Information in India

Prabodh Saxena

Introduction

The Twentieth Century, particularly the second half of it, witnessed an unprecedented spate of decolonization. Nation after nation gained independence in quick succession. The majority chose democracy as the form of governance. After about three quarters of a century, the experiment with democracy has yielded mixed results. While it suffered an untimely death in some countries, many nations are still struggling to stabilize it. Notwithstanding this, there are a few exemplary success stories as well. Undoubtedly, the finest and at times the most amazing example is India.

As Indian Democracy evolves amidst trials, tribulations and successes, it both influences and gets influenced by various international developments. One such celebrated development, occurring all over the world, is the recognition of a basic human right i.e. **'The right to Information'**. It is now accepted that democracy does not simply mean that the Executive remains responsible to the Legislature and that people should sink into passivity after exercising their franchise during elections.

Accountability and Democracy

Democracy now has a more positive and dynamic nature. Meaningful and constant dialogue between the political executive and the governed class is increasingly considered a *sine qua non* of a vibrant system of governance. Participation in governance is the catchword and this can only be ensured if there is an effective right to information. Let us remember the golden words of Justice Louis Brandies of the US Supreme Court that "A little sunlight is the best disinfectant."

In legal terms, Sweden's experiment with access and openness, dating back to 1766 is undoubtedly the earliest.[1] Even Denmark had an Act, as far back as 1865, allowing the losing party in a court case to see the administrative file. In 1888, the Colombia Code of Political and Municipal Organization allowed individuals to request documents held in government agencies and archives, unless another law specifically forbade the release of these documents.

As a matter of fact; the history of right to information can be divided in two phases, namely pre- and post-Cold War era. Till 1989, only 14 countries had enacted access legislation over a period of a quarter century. The law was confined to rich countries, mainly stable democracies in the West. The prerequisites for operating such a law were a professional civil service, human rights traditions, an independent judiciary, an assertive media, and active non-governmental organizations. Support of technologically advanced and modern record keeping was also an essential requirement. It was considered to be luxury which could only be afforded by the rich and the advanced countries at a huge cost.

The end of the Cold war saw a spurt in access legislations. The Nineties themselves accounts for 28 of them. 2005 was another watershed year. An old democracy like United Kingdom enacted the law and we saw Uganda, a major African country legislating the access law along with the one billion plus strong country, India.

In pursuance of an international trend and domestic demand, the Government of India enacted the Freedom of Information Act, 2002.[2] Prior to that, the credit for the pioneer legislation on the matter goes to the states of Tamil Nadu and Goa.[3] Few other states[4] were also quick to follow suit. Before the Central Act could be notified to have come into force, there was a regime change. The United Progressive Alliance, on the recommendation of National Advisory Council, decided to kill the earlier Act on the ground that it did not fully conform to the international standards and thus the Right to Information Act, 2005 (hereinafter the RTI Act) was born.[5]

This short note makes an attempt to present the status of the RTI Act. Section II very briefly introduces the main features of the law. Sections III, IV and V give an account of the positive attributes, namely, the international standing of the RTI Act, its strengths and impact over the years, respectively. Sections VI and VII look at the weaknesses of the law and its implementation respectively. Section VIII concludes.

SECTION-II
Salient Features of the RTI Act

The RTI Act prescribes mandatory disclosure of certain information to citizens within a specified period of time and creates a legal-institutional framework for setting out the practical regime of right to information for every citizen to secure access to information under the control of Public Authority. The Act extents to the whole of India except the state of Jammu and Kashmir.[6]

It empowers every citizen to not just ask any question but also to take copies of or to inspect any government document and/or government works and take samples of materials of any government work.[7] Information has to be provided within 30 days.[8] Moreover there is also a provision for an "urgent request", where the information requested concerns the life and liberty of a person, it should be provided within 48 hours of receipt of the request.[9]

At times, the power of inspection and sample collection is more effective than the power to demand copy of documents.[10] If used intelligently, it can directly assault corruption, particularly in the engineering departments. Some years back, a group of IIT Delhi students used this provision of the RTI Act to inspect repair works of Delhi roads with effective results.[11]

Section 4 of the Act has been enacted with the intention that the Public Authorities self-publish sufficient information to limit the requirement for additional information sought out by RTI activists. It gives a very elaborate list of categories of information, which should be *suo motu* published and updated regularly.

The RTI Act also lays down specific obligations on the appropriate governments[12], competent authorities[13] and public authorities[14]. Under the RTI Act all constitutional bodies, statutory bodies, bodies created by government notifications and local self-government bodies are classified as public authorities. The ambit thus covers the high and mighty like the two Houses of Parliament, State Legislatures, office of President/ Governors, the secretariat of the Prime Minister/Chief Ministers/Supreme Court/High Courts/Subordinate Courts, Election Commission, Comptroller and Auditor General, Union Public Service Commission, Information Commissions etc. In addition, bodies owned, controlled or substantially financed directly or indirectly by the government are also classified as public authorities. Finally, non-Government organizations substantially financed by the government are also within the definition of public authorities. Only domestic and foreign private bodies working within the country have been excluded from the purview of the RTI Act.

Certain categories of information have been exempted from disclosure under Sections 8 and 9 of the RTI Act. The categories, by way of illustration, include information likely to affect the State's security, strategic, scientific or economic interests of the State, information forbidden by courts, detection and investigation of offences, source protection, conduct of international relations and Cabinet papers. Trade or commercial secrets, information the disclosure of which would cause breach of privilege of Parliament or State Legislature, information received in fiduciary relationship and personnel information, are also exempted from disclosure. However, the exemptions provided above are not absolute and withholding of information must be balanced against disclosure in the public interest and information has to be released even if harm is shown to the public authority if the public benefit in knowing the information outweighs the harm that may be caused by disclosure. The bottom-line of disclosure is that any information that cannot be denied to parliament or legislative assembly cannot be denied to the requester.[15]

Subject to these exemptions, the RTI Act also contains a provision for reveal of information, which is otherwise, exempted from disclosure under section 8, on completion of 20 years after the conclusion of the event except in exemptions mentioned in section 8(a), 8(c) and 8(i)[16]. The only absolute exemption is in favour of copy right of a person (State is excluded from the protection)[17]. Intelligence and security agencies specified in Schedule II to the RTI Act have been exempted but they have the obligation to provide information in matters relating to corruption and human rights violations.[18]

The RTI Act sets up an information delivery mechanism through appointment of Public Information Officers (PIOs) in the public authorities and mandates the appointments of Information Commissioners[19] to inquire into complaints[20], hear second appeals[21], and guide implementation of the RTI Act[22]. The Information Commissions are empowered to levy penalty[23] and can also award damages and compensation. The decisions of the Commission are binding.[24]

The RTI Act also incorporates the unique principle of severability[25] and takes care of third party interests[26]. The jurisdiction of subordinate courts has been barred expressly[27] and it is explicitly laid down that the provisions of the RTI Act, in case of conflict, override the Official Secrets Act, 1923, and any legal instrument.[28] By inclusion of the word 'instrument', there is an obligation to bring all the rules, guidelines, manuals etc. in conformity with the RTI Act.

SECTION-III
The Global Standing of the RTI Act

Those that have had the chance of analyzing the major access legislations of the world will have no issue in agreeing that the RTI Act of India is the most progressive access legislation anywhere. Some even prefer to call it the most ambitious as it can only be fully realized under ideal conditions.

Not surprisingly, the Indian law has been rated very high globally. Centre for Law and Democracy and Access Info Euro has developed a rated index for the last five years. As per the latest information released by them on the International Right to Know Day on September 28, 2016. Indian law is the fourth best law with 128 points (it was third in 2015) among the 112 countries which have access law as of 2016.[29] According to them the Mexico Law with 136 points is the best followed by Serbia with (135 points) and Slovenia (129 points). However in terms of country size and establishment of democratic institutions and reach, the comparison between India and the three countries above it is not very convincing. Be that as it may be, it reconfirms the superiority and strength of Indian law globally. It is also interesting to note that the top laws are from developing countries.

SECTION-IV
The Points of Strengths

In a country where laws are far too many to count, why is it that the RTI Act is celebrated? There are even award ceremonies to honour RTI activists. There is definitely a distinguishable aspect to the law. Following is an illustrative list of strengths of our law, some of which are unique:

(a) It covers every institution from the office of the President to the patwari of the village.[30] The reach is absolute—executive, legislature and judiciary. Even in countries like USA and Japan, the reach is not total.

(b) Besides the applicant's contact details, he/she not required to either give any reason for requesting the information or any other personal details.[31]

(c) The law is perhaps the only Indian law that has a provision for levying a penalty against defaulting officers. Even if it is Rs. 25, 000, it is an effective feature because the penalty has to go from one's pocket and it does pinch. The threat of disciplinary proceedings against an erring officer is also real. The information seekers can also receive compensation or damages, if so warranted. Now other laws are following.[32]

(d) There is a legal obligation on the PIO to assist the requester.[33]

(e) In general litigation, onus is on the applicant and the appellant to prove his case. The rule is relaxed only in extreme circumstances. The RTI Act, however, provides that the onus to prove that the information was rightly denied lies on the PIO.[34]

(f) It mandates information technology, digital record keeping, networking and e-governance, subject to availability of resources.[35]

It is interesting to note that even seasoned politicians who are well versed in law and parliamentary affairs are, at times, using the RTI Act rather than asking questions in the Parliament.[36] This is because requests can be made anytime and there is a time limit for their reply. The public authority can neither give an interim reply nor can it take the ground that the matter is sub-judice which is often invoked in legislature to stall a discussion or answer. On top of this, the information that cannot be denied to a legislature cannot be denied to a requester. The only limiting factor is that under the RTI Act there is no requirement to generate the information or answer to questions/clarifications etc. Aware persons have quickly realized the immense power of the RTI Act.

SECTION-V
The Power of Impact

The RTI Act has emerged as the showpiece legislation of India. It has completed eleven years amid success stories, enthusiasm, hope and on the other extreme, protest and ridicule. If we look at the jurisprudence generated by CIC, the reactions are mixed. Activists are demanding blood because they think that the CIC lacks the necessary 'killer instinct' of ruthless compliance. On the other hand, the information givers are overwhelmed with the reach of the law and its loose recourse in purely personal issues.

Newspaper and electronic media recounts on a daily basis the success stories of the law. Its impact is all pervasive. It has exposed scandals of misuse of PDS ration at many places and has resulted in correction of systems in the exposed places. Ordinary citizens have been able to secure long delayed pensions, house allotment letters and passports despite the fact that the RTI Act is not a redress law. Even political parties are using it vigorously to score points over their opponents.

In particular, the RTI Act has helped expose some of the most infamous scams in the history of India. Some of them are presented below:[37]

(a) RTI applications filed by activists Yogacharya Anandji and Simpreet Singh in 2008 exposed the Adarsh Housing Society scam, which eventually led to the resignation of the then Maharashtra Chief Minister. The response revealed that flats in the Adarsh Housing Society originally meant to provide residence for war widows and veterans, were used to house politicians, bureaucrats and their relatives.

(b) In the 2G scam, an RTI application by Subhash Chandra Agrawal revealed that Ex Telecom Minister had a "15-minute-long" meeting with then Solicitor General in December 2007 after which a "brief note was prepared and handed over to the minister", but the minutes of the meeting were not recorded.

(c) RTI application filed by non-profit Housing and Land Rights Network showed that the then Delhi Government had diverted Rs. 744 crore from social welfare projects for *Dalits* to the Commonwealth Games from 2005-06 to 2010-11.

The impact of the RTI Act augurs well towards the creation of a system which will be more accountable, transparent and citizen-friendly.

SECTION-VI
The Weak Spots

India is operating this flagship legislation with inadequate budgetary support, embryonic e-governance at selective places, primitive record keeping, limited rural penetration and low capacity building of both the information seekers and information providers. The modes of payment of fees are also somewhat limited.

The weak proactive disclosure has been identified as the biggest handicap. Public authorities in our country still have a long way to go in proactive disclosures. They must endeavour to voluntarily put out in the public domain information that is of use to citizens. This will be a major challenge for public authorities in the arena of Information Housekeeping in view of lack of availability of dedicated manpower to update the information regularly and also in absence of earmarked budget for the same. However, to be fair to the Public Authorities such information, how so ever widespread, may not answer the curiosity of information seekers who have a particular interest in mind.

In India, a citizen can ask for any and every information subject to the limitation prescribed by the RTI Act. It is a no holds barred right.[39] It has been noticed that that parties involved in private litigation wantonly use the provisions of the RTI Act to open confidential information of one another.

The capacity of the PIOs to discharge their job efficiently remains a challenge. There can be no second opinion that government servants need to be trained and sensitized regarding their duties towards the citizens under the RTI Act.

It is also important to discuss the unease of judiciary with the RTI Act as it is the only law that addresses the issue of accountability in judiciary as there is no immediate possibility of Judges (Inquiry) Bill becoming an Act. The High Courts have much restrictive Rules and steeper fees. Public reactions have forced some of them to take corrective measures, albeit reluctantly. Unfortunately, judiciary has fallen short in its actual implementation of the RTI Act. It is important for the full realization of the right that the judiciary is on board.

The appointment of ex-bureaucrats and some politically aligned people to Commissions all over the country has attracted sharp criticism. The activists are very unhappy with the working of the CIC, particularly their 'reluctance' to impose penalty and for disposal of appeals without hearing the appellant. The activists have also frequently raised the issue of alleged victimisation and discrimination, including physical action against requesters by authorities for using the RTI Act notwithstanding the whistle Blowers Protection Act, 2011[40].

While discussing gaps in the implementation of the right in India, it is not out of place to flag the issue of extending the ambit of the RTI Act to private entities. With the opening of the economy and consequent liberalization, the government is withdrawing from its conventional and even sovereign functions, and the private sector is increasingly assuming important public functions like electricity supply, communication and public transport. The 2008 Global Meltdown has demonstrated how highly paid and educated Chief Executives have mismanaged the funds of their depositors because of greed and propensity to indulge in 'kite flying operations' at the cost of someone else's money thus destroying both the funds and faith of the common people. After South Africa[41], the Bangladesh Act, 2009 has made an elaborate definition of public authorities[42] covering non-government bodies or bodies administered with public finance, or conducting public work on behalf of the government, or under contract with anybody from the government. The Nigerian law also includes private companies performing public functions, reflecting the emerging school of thought about what good access legislation should be.[43]

Recently, the Sri Lankan access law has incorporated a similar provision.[44] To keep itself in tune with the progressive norms of modern day access legislation, India should seriously and urgently consider a similar provision in the RTI Act.

SECTION-VII
The Problem of Plenty

A study conducted by the Commonwealth Human Rights Initiative (CHRI)[45] in 2014 revealed that over 1.75 crore RTI applications have been filed from 2005 to July 2014. The CHRI study also noted that there has also been a ten-fold increase in the number of RTI applications to the Prime Minister Office (PMO) between 2006-07 and 2014-15. The number of RTI applications per day increased from 3 in 2006-07 to 35 in 2014-15. The filing of RTI applications in the PMO makes for an interesting though sad commentary. Unfortunately, many of these applications were frivolous and some even ridiculous, amounting to a criminal waste of public resources and money. Few samples are:

(a) "What is the speed of internet of Wi-Fi in the PMO?"
(b) "Has the Principal Secretary to Prime Minister, Shri Nripendra Misra, ever taken his subordinates, in the PMO, on a picnic?"
(c) "Enclose all the proper records and documents which show that the present Prime Minister of India is The Prime Servant of India and not the Prime Minister."

Similarly, Research, Assessment and Analysis Group (RaaG) and Satark Nagrik Sangathan (SNS) in a report[46] have stated that around 1,87,974 cases are pending, which comprise collective backlog in the disposal of appeals and complaints, in the 16 State Information Commissions (SICs) as of December 31, 2015, The report also revealed that in 9 of the 16 SICs, for which data was available, the waiting time for a hearing was more than an year. It also recorded that the pendency in the Central Information Commission (CIC) saw a rise of 43 per cent during the period of the study.

According to the Annual report of CIC of 2014-15[47], during the year 2014-15 the total number of disposed cases was 20,181 whereas the pending cases for disposal as on 01 April 2015 were 37,323.

The situation may appear alarming and yet it does not capture the complete picture. Latest statistics of many SICs are not in public domain and if anyone succeeds in painting an updated and consolidated sketch of CIC and all SICs, I am afraid, the numbers will be frightening.

Further, this is the state of affairs at a time when the Act is being used by a miniscule portion of the population of the nation. If the use of the RTI Act becomes widespread, which it must, it is apprehended that Commissions will succumb to the problem of arrears just as the courts have in the past. All the stakeholders including information seekers must wake up to the reality and the impending crisis and without wasting any time create a roadmap to chart out recovery and reforms.

SECTION-VIII
Conclusion

Access legislations, all over the world, have brought discomfiture to the powers that be.[48] They have helped to uphold the spirit of openness, transparency and accountability in public life. The Indian experience is no different. It has given 1.25 billion people the right enjoyed so far by few thousand legislators and has empowered the weak and the vulnerable. Second Administrative Reforms Commission has rightly termed 'Right to Information' as a 'Master Key to Good Governance'.[49] The incorporation of RTI into Sustainable Development Goals Target 16.10 can be expected to provide even greater impetus to this trend.

Indiscriminate and unhealthy use of the legislation is a worldwide phenomenon prevalent in the initial years of enactment. Busy bodies, professional middlemen and lazy journalists have used access legislations for their own end. Though it is a concern, it should be taken in its own stride[50]. It cannot dilute the ultimate truth that access right, properly implemented, is a multidimensional human right that can make a huge difference to both the people and their government. A great journey has commenced. There are many formidable tasks yet to be accomplished but the whole world should know that the Access Age has arrived. It is a matter of satisfaction and pride that in the twenty-first century, India is leading this movement.

Notes

1. Access to Public Records Act, 1766.
2. Act No.5 of 2003.
3. The Tamil Nadu Right to Information Act, 1997, The Goa Right to Information Act, 1997.
4. The Rajasthan Right to Information Act, 2000, The Karnataka Right to Information Act, 2000, The Delhi Right to Information Act, 2001, Maharashtra Right to Information Act, 2000.
5. Act no 22 of 2005 enacted on 15 June 2005 came into force fully on 12 October 2005. Some provisions like section 4(1), section 5 (1) , section 5 (2) , sections 12, 13, 15,16, 24, 27 and 28 providing for setting up of delivery mechanism came into force with the enactment.
6. Jammu and Kashmir has its own Right to Information Act of 2004, which was replaced by the Jammu and Kashmir Act of 2009. The rules were notified in 2012. The framework is weak as compared to the national law but it can now be said that the whole country is under information regime.
7. Section 2(j)
8. Section 7
9. Proviso to Section 7 (1). Recently the Center Information Commission in a judgment has held that the information relating to sexual harassment should be provided within 48 hours. See Sushma Rani Tirkey v. PIO, Council of Scientific & Industrial Research. CIC/CSIRD/A/2016/306867
10. Section 2(f) defines record.
11. See http://git.net/ml/politics.antibriberycampaign/2007-05/msg00006.html
12. Defined in section 2(a)
13. Defined in section 2(e)
14. Defined in section 2(h)
15. Proviso to Section 8(1).
16. Section 8(3)
17. Section 9
18. Section 24
19. See Chapter III and IV of the RTI Act
20. Section 18
21. Section 19. The first appeal lies to an officer of the department who is senior in rank than the PIO within 30 days of the decision; the time limit for disposal of appeal being also 30 days extendable to 45 days.
22. Section 19(8)(a) and Section 25(5)
23. Under Section 20 if a PIO, without any reasonable cause, refuses to receive an application, does not furnish information within the prescribed time limit, denies the request with mala fide intent or knowingly gives incorrect, incomplete or misleading information or destroys information or obstructs the process, the officer becomes liable for a penalty of Rs. 250 per day, subject to a ceiling of Rs. 25,000. Moreover, the law provides that in such

cases the Information Commission can also recommend disciplinary action against the PIO under the applicable service rules.

24. Section 19(7)
25. Section 10
26. Section 11
27. Section 23
28. Section 22.
29. Accessible at www.rti-rating.org
30. Lowest government functionary
31. Section 6(2)
32. For instance, the Nepal Right to Information Act, 2007. The Sri Lankan law has gone even further, providing for imprisonment beside fine. (See Section 39 of the Right to Information Act, 2016 of Sri Lanka)
33. Section 5(3).Also see Section 6(1) which provides that all reasonable assistance be given to a requester for reducing his oral request inwriting.
34. Section 19(5)
35. Section 4(1)(a)
36. Reference is invited to RTI appeals of eminent Parliamentarians. For instance Mr. Varun Gandhi filed RTI application to know identity of MP's with Swiss Bank accounts. See http://indiatoday.intoday.in/story/mp-swiss-bank-accounts-varun-gandhi-black-money/1/158603.html
37. http://www.firstpost.com/india/right-to-information-what-11-years-of-the-rti-act-of-2005-have-done-for-india-3047286.html
38. Though it is very difficult to arrive at the precise cost of complying with the access request, yet one can get an idea from an old study titled "Freedom of Information in the U.K., U.S. and Canada". By Sarah Holsen published in "The Information Management Journal" in May/June 2007 (Page 50-55). It states that according to the U.S. Department of Justice Office of Information and Privacy, the total cpst of administering the U.S. FOIA in 2003 was just over $23 million. According to the government of Canada, its annual FOI cost is estimated to be around $30 million (Cdn.) or approximately $25 million in U.S. dollars.
39. Such a broad window is not available even in the developed countries, operating such laws for decades. Contrast this to US where the Government in 1996, *owing to limited resources* (emphasis mine), recognizing that as requests are very broad and complex, established procedure for the department to discuss with requesters ways of tailoring large requests and made corresponding amendment in their requests. The RTI act does provide in Section 7(9) that the information shall ordinarily be provided in the form in which it is sought unless it would disproportionately divert the resources of the public authority or would be detrimental to the safety or preservation of the record in question. However because of lack of understanding or due to fear of penalty this provision is not being used much in practice. For a detailed analysis of the problem, refer to the article of the author titled, "The Flip Side of the RTI Act," published in Vol L,

June 2007, Pg 21-38 issue of Administrator, a publication of Lal Bahadur Shastri National Academy of Administration, Shimla.

40. The Act received the assent of President on 9 May, 2014
41. Part 3 of Promotion of Access to Information Act ,2000 deals specifically with access to records of private bodies.
42. Section 2 of the Bangladesh Right to Information Act , 2009
43. See Section 3(7) of the Nigeria Freedom of Information Act, 2011
44. See Section 43 of the Sri Lanka Right to Information Act, 2016
45. http://www.humanrightsinitiative.org/publications/rti/ICs-RapidComp Study-finalreport-NDelhi-ATITeam-Jul14.pdf
46. Available at http://www.news18.com/news/india/1-9-lakh-cases-pending-in-state-information-commissions-study-1308355.html
47. latest available on their website http://www.cic.gov.in/reports/37
48. Ian Paisley Jnr. became the first government minister in the UK to resign as an access request revealed that Mr. Paisley Jnr. had also lobbied in support of a massive government land sale plan. US was compelled to disclose that 558 men from 41 countries are in detention at Guantanamo Bay.
49. Accessible at http://arc.gov.in/rtifinalreport.pdf
50. In a recent article former Chief Information Commissioner Mr ShaileshGhandhi has, on the basis of his experience, claimed that Right to information is misused, but those who do so make up less than 5% of total applicants. The full article can be reached at https://scroll.in/article/827689/right-to-information-is-misused-and-thats-all-the-more-reason-why-this-law-should-not-be-weakened.

17
Protection of Consumer Rights in India

Sheetal Kapoor

Introduction

Consumers play a vital role in the development of a nation. Gandhiji in the light of the above rightly said, "A customer is the most important visitor on our premises. He is not dependent on us. We are dependent on him. He is not an interruption in our work—he is the purpose of it. We are not doing him a favour by serving him. He is doing us a favour by giving us the opportunity to serve him." Modern technological developments have made a great impact on the quality, availability and safety of goods and services but unfortunately the consumers are still victims of unscrupulous and exploitative trade practices.

As consumers we face huge problems relating to defective goods, deficiency in service, adulteration, spurious goods, hoarding, use of deceptive and fractional weights, late deliveries, variations in the contents of the pack, poor after sales service, misleading advertisements, hidden price components, price discrimination, ATM and credit card frauds, financial frauds, real estate problems and problems related to public utilities. These problems arise because unscrupulous sellers take an unfair advantage of the ignorance and helplessness of the consumers. Since the business does not always act responsibly there is a need to educate and protect the consumers to enable them to look after their own interests and interests of the society at large.

A recent study by ASSOCHAM has revealed that 40 per cent of Indians are not aware about how and where to file a complaint if the manufacturer gives them a defective product or deficiency in service or an adulterated food item. The consumer movement in India is still in its nascent stage in the second decade of 21st Century. It requires a big fillip to become a mass movement. Consumers today want value for money, a product or service that would meet reasonable expectations is safe in use and there is full disclosure of the product specification. These expectations are termed as 'Consumer Rights'.

World Consumers' Rights Day—Genesis

15th March is observed as the World Consumers' Day in different parts of the World. This day has a historic importance as it was on this day in 1962, when the Bill for Consumer Rights was moved in the US Congress by John F. Kennedy. He equated the rights of the ordinary American consumer with national interest. During his speech President John F. Kennedy had remarked: **"If a consumer is offered inferior products, if prices are exorbitant, if drugs are unsafe or worthless, if the consumer is unable to choose on an informed basis, then his dollar is wasted, his health and safety may be threatened, and national interest suffers."** He gave the American consumers four basic rights such as right to safety, right to choose, right to information, right to be heard.

The Consumers International (CI), formerly known as International Organization of Consumer Unions (IOCU), the umbrella body, for 240 organizations in over 120 countries, began observing 15th March as an occasion to promote basic rights of consumers since 1983.

The Consumer Protection Act, 1986

The Consumer Protection Act, 1986 was enacted by the Parliament to protect the interests of consumers against substandard products, increased prices through market manipulation, failed warranties, poor after sales service and unfair trade practices on 24th December. Since then, 24th December is observed as National Consumer Day in India. Consumer Protection Act (CPA) is considered as a benevolent social legislature for protecting consumers from the malpractices of manufacturers. CPA provides simple, speedy and inexpensive redressal to the grievances of the consumers. This Act is not only preventive but also compensatory in nature. Unlike other laws, it is civil and focuses on undoing the wrong to a consumer by way of remedial action or payment of compensation or damages to the aggrieved consumer. The Act has set in motion a revolution in the field of consumer rights that perhaps cannot be paralleled anywhere else in the World. The Act applies to all goods and services unless specially exempted by the Central Government, in all sectors whether Private, Public or Co-operative.

The Act enshrines all the consumers rights which are internationally accepted. As per the Act, the consumer protection councils have been established at Central, State and District levels to promote and protect the consumer rights. They are:

- Right to Safety: To be protected against the sale of goods and services which are spurious/hazardous to life.
- Right to information: To know the quality, quantity, weight and the price of goods/services being paid for, so that one is not cheated by unfair trade practices.
- Right to Choose: To be assured, wherever possible, access to a variety of goods and services at competitive prices.
- Right to be heard: To be heard and to be assured that the interest would receive due consideration at appropriate fora.
- Right to Seek Redressal: To seek legal redressal against unfair or restrictive trade practices or exploitation.
- Right to Consumer Education: To have access to consumer education.

The Consumer Protection Act is a progressive, comprehensive and unique piece of legislation enacted by India. It enshrines all the consumer rights which are internationally accepted. As per the Act, the consumer protection councils have been established at Central, State and District levels to promote and protect the consumer rights. Section 2 (1) (d) defines the term 'consumer' under the Consumer Protection Act, 1986, as any person who buys, hires or avails of any goods or services for a consideration which has been paid, or promised or partly paid or promised or paid under a system of deferred payment. The term consumer, however, does not include a person who obtains goods and services for resale or for any commercial purpose. Thus, the term consumer includes buyer, user, hirer and beneficiary of goods and services. In the proposed fourth Amendment of the Consumer Protection Act, 1986, the term 'consumer' would include buying of goods, hiring/availing of services made through any mode, inclusive of but not limited to offline, online through electronic means, teleshopping, direct selling etc.

Thus, 'consumers' includes the following heads:

1. **Buyer of goods or Purchaser of goods:** Any person who purchases products for consideration that has been paid, or promised or partly paid and partly promised, or under any system of deferred payment for final consumption is a consumer. The position of the buyer depends upon the 'contract of sale'.
2. **User of the goods:** Any person who uses goods with the approval of the buyer, who has bought goods for consideration is a consumer. Thus all family members are beneficiaries of a contract and included as consumers.
3. **Hirer of services:** Any person who hires or avails of any service for a consideration which has been paid or promised or partly paid and partly promised, or under any system of deferred payment is included as a consumer. The service sector includes banking, telecom service, postal service, insurance, railways, air travel, doctors, caterers, contractors, transport operators, etc.
4. **Beneficiary of services:** In respect of services, the beneficiary of such service is also a consumer. According to *Indian Medical Association* vs. *V. P. Shanta* case it was decided that medical practitioners are not immune from a claim for damages on the ground of negligence. The patients who are rendered free service are the beneficiaries of the services hired by the patients who paid for the services. In *Spring Meadows Hospital* vs. *Harjit Ahuluwalia* (1998) (2), the Supreme Court held that a consumer would mean a person who hires or avails of any services and includes any beneficiary. Therefore, when a young child is taken to a hospital by his parents and treated by the doctor then the parents and the child would come under the definition of a consumer.

A trader or businessmen who buys the goods or services for resale is not a 'consumer'. The Consumer Protection Act Amendment in 2002 excludes persons who buy goods or services for a 'commercial purpose'. However, 'commercial purpose' does not include the following:

- Goods bought and used for the purposes of earning livelihood by means of self-employment. This means that if an individual or a family buys goods for professional or vocational use s/he will be a 'consumer'.
- Services availed for the purpose of earning livelihood by means of self-employment. This means that if a person or family buys

services for professional or vocational use s/he will be a 'consumer'. Thus, any person who buys goods either for resale or for making profit is not a 'consumer' under the Consumer Protection Act. In *Raj Kumar* vs. *S.C. Verma*, 2001 (1) CPR 437 it was held that persons buying goods either for resale or for use in large scale profit-making activity would not be 'consumers' entitled relief under the Act.

A complaint can be filed in the consumer Forum by a consumer to whom goods are sold or delivered or agreed to be sold or delivered or such services provided or agreed to be provided or by a Voluntary Consumer Organization (VCO) or by the Central Government or the State Government, Union Territory Administration or by one or more consumers where they are of same interest. In case of death of consumer, his legal heir or representatives have the right for filing a complaint. A complaint can be filed within two years from the date on which the cause of action has arisen. However, a complaint may be entertained after the period if the complainant had sufficient cause for not filing the complaint within such period by recording its reason for condoning such delay. A complaint should contain the following details:

1. The name, description and address of the complainant.
2. The name, description and address of the opposite party or parties.
3. The facts relating the complaint, when are where it arises.
4. Documents, if any, in support of allegations.
5. The relief sought.
6. The complaint should be signed by the complainant or his/her authorized agent.

   No lawyer is required for filing a case in consumer forum.

Adjudicatory Bodies Set Up under CPA

In order to provide speedy and simple redressal of consumer grievances, Chapter III of the Consumer Protection Act makes provision for the establishment of Remedial Agencies for settlement of consumers' disputes and for matters connected therewith. There is a three-tier system in the Act, which has been set up at district, state and national levels. They are:

1. A Consumer Disputes Redressal Forum also known as the

"District Forum"

2. A Consumer Disputes Redressal Commission also known as the "State Commission"
3. A National Consumer Disputes Redressal Commission also known as the "National Commission"

While the National Commission is set up by the Central Government, the State Commissions and District Forums are set up, in each, State and District, respectively by the State Government concerned. Provided that the state government may, if it deems fit, establish more than one District Forum in a state.

At present there are 35 State Commissions, one in each State/UT and 629 district forums besides the National Commission at the apex. The government is monitoring the disposal of cases by the consumer courts through National Commission.

The pecuniary jurisdiction of the District Forum is up to Rs. 20 lakhs, and that of the State Commissions is above Rs. 20 lakhs and below Rs. 1 Crore and claims involving more than Rs. 1 crore are to be filled directly before the National Commission.

The law provides for the complaint to be decided within a period of 3 months from the date of receipt of notice by the opposite party where no analysis or testing of commodities is required to be done by the laboratory. If it requires analysis or testing of commodities the period for giving final order is five months. Till 30-11-2016, the Consumer courts at National, State and District level have together registered **46,87,864** cases and **42,73,208** cases have been disposed. Thus there are still **4.1** lakh cases which are pending within various consumer foras and the disposal rate is 91.36 per cent.

Total number of Cases Disposed by Consumer Forums Since Inception

Table 17.1 depicts that **1,05,916** cases were registered since inception up to 30th November, 2016 with the National Commission out of which 89 per cent cases were disposed of, while 11 per cent were still pending with the National Commission. In case of State Commission 7,28,526 cases were registered since inception up to November 2016 and 86.1 per cent cases were disposed of. A staggering number of 38,53,422 cases were registered throughout the District Consumer Forums in the country and performance of District Consumer Forums was better as 92.17 per cent cases were disposed of. This indicates that consumer redressal system is now being utilized at the district levels, which is a positive sign of generating awareness to seek redressal.

Table 17.1: Total Number of Cases Disposed by Consumer Forums Since Inception (Update on 30-11-2016)

Sl. No.	*Name of Agency*	*Cases filed since inception*	*Cases disposed of since inception*	*Cases Pending*	*% of total Disposal*
1.	National Commission	105916	94270	11646	89.00%
2.	State Commissions	728526	627289	101237	86.10%
3.	District Forums	3853422	3551649	301773	92.17%
	Total	**4687864**	**4273208**	**414656**	**91.15%**

Statement of Cases Filed/Disposed of/Pending in the National Commission and State Commissions

A state-wise analysis indicated in Table 17.2 shows significant variations in the number of cases registered and per cent cases disposed by the State and District Consumer Forums. The total number of cases registered up to 30-11-2016 with various State Commissions was higher for Uttar Pradesh followed by, Maharastra, Rajasthan Gujarat and Delhi. Thus, it signifies consumer awareness is associated with consumer movement as in case with Rajasthan, Kerala, Himachal Pradesh and Delhi literacy rates are higher. Per cent cases disposed of both by the State and District Consumer Forums also depicts regional variations. States with poor disposal system were Telangana (11.2%), Uttar Pradesh (66.71% disposal), Odisha (72.85%), at the State Commission level.

Statement of Cases filed/disposed of/pending in District Fora

Table 17.3 shows the statement of cases filed/disposed in various District Forums since inception (update as on 31-11-2016). Performance of District Forums was better across the states except for Lakshadweep (with 80.46% of disposal of cases), Uttar Pradesh (with 88.58% disposal of cases). If we see the average percentage of disposal of cases in case of District Forums since their inception we find that 92.17 per cent of cases have been disposed, which is a positive sign.

Table 17.2: Statement of Cases Filed/Disposed of/Pending in the National Commission and State Commissions (Update on 30-11-2016)

Sl. No.	*Name of State*	*Cases filed since inception*	*Cases disposed of since inception*	*Cases Pending*	*% of Disposal*	*As On*
	National Commission	105916	94270	11646	89.00	30.11.2016
1.	Andhra Pradesh	32513	31648	865	97.34	30.11.2016
2.	A & N Islands	111	106	5	95.50	30.06.2015
3.	Arunachal Pradesh	96	85	11	88.54	31.10.2016
4.	Assam	2930	2509	421	85.63	30.11.2016
5.	Bihar	18764	15412	3352	82.14	31.10.2016
6.	Chandigarh	16982	16476	506	97.02	30.11.2016
7.	Chattisgarh	11674	11244	430	96.32	30.11.2016
8.	Daman & Diu and DNH	25	20	5	80.00	31.03.2011
9.	Delhi	44605	38598	6007	86.53	30.11.2016
10.	Goa	2869	2775	94	96.72	30.11.2016
11.	Gujarat	54302	49379	4923	90.93	30.11.2016
12.	Haryana	48110	46690	1420	97.05	30.11.2016
13.	Himachal Pradesh	9473	9332	141	98.51	30.11.2016
14.	Jammu & Kashmir	9038	7549	1489	83.53	31.05.2016
15.	Jharkhand	5884	5367	517	91.21	30.09.2016
16.	Karnataka	53800	46115	7685	85.72	30.11.2016
17.	Kerala	29313	27278	2035	93.06	31.10.2016
18.	Lakshadweep	18	16	2	88.89	31.10.2016
19.	Madhya Pradesh	51000	42666	8334	83.66	30.11.2016
20.	Maharashtra[1]	69113	58003	11110	83.92	31.01.2016
21.	Manipur	170	164	6	96.47	31.12.2015
22.	Meghalaya	300	285	15	95.00	31.03.2015
23.	Mizoram	223	216	7	96.86	31.08.2016
24.	Nagaland	165	136	29	82.42	30.09.2015
25.	Odisha	24257	17672	6585	72.85	31.01.2016
26.	Puducherry	1074	1019	55	94.88	30.11.2016
27.	Punjab	36043	34537	1506	95.82	31.10.2016
28.	Rajasthan[2]	62672	55723	6949	88.91	30.11.2016
29.	Sikkim	57	54	3	94.74	31.03.2015
30.	Tamil Nadu	27698	24497	3201	88.44	30.11.2016
31.	Telangana	2116	248	1868	11.72	30.11.2016
32.	Tripura	1728	1690	38	97.80	31.12.2016
33.	Uttar Pradesh[3]	79617	53109	26508	66.71	30.09.2016
34.	Uttarakhand	5925	4905	1020	82.78	30.11.2016
35.	West Bengal[4]	25861	21766	4095	84.17	31.12.2015
	Total	**728526**	**627289**	**101237**	**86.10**	

Note: [1] Maharashtra is having one additional Bench
[2] Rajasthan is having one additional Bench
[3] UP is having one additional Bench
[4] WB is having two additional Benches

Table 17.3: Statement of Cases Filed/Disposed of/Pending in District Fora (Update on 31.11.2016)

Sl. No.	Name of State	Cases filed since inception	Cases disposed of since inception	Cases Pending	% of Disposal	As On
1.	Andhra Pradesh	117244	115248	1996	98.30	30.11.2016
2.	A & N Islands	767	720	47	93.87	30.06.2015
3.	Arunachal Pradesh	515	486	29	94.37	31.10.2016
4.	Assam	16157	14736	1421	91.21	30.06.2016
5.	Bihar	100605	86188	14417	85.67	31.10.2016
6.	Chandigarh	55750	53986	1764	96.84	30.11.2016
7.	Chattisgarh	47318	41989	5329	88.74	30.11.2016
8.	Daman & Diu and DNH	162	144	18	88.89	31.03.2011
9.	Delhi	254168	236589	17579	93.08	31.03.2015
10.	Goa	7156	6770	386	94.61	30.11.2016
11.	Gujarat	209792	194038	15754	92.49	30.11.2016
12.	Haryana	250342	238873	11469	95.42	30.11.2016
13.	Himachal Pradesh	63941	61245	2696	95.78	30.11.2016
14.	Jammu & Kashmir	20792	18855	1937	90.68	31.12.2007
15.	Jharkhand	39096	34978	4118	89.47	30.09.2016
16.	Karnataka	188849	178511	10338	94.53	30.11.2016
17.	Kerala	205185	194457	10728	94.77	31.10.2016
18.	Lakshadweep	87	70	17	80.46	31.10.2016
19.	Madhya Pradesh	225500	208401	17099	92.42	30.11.2016
20.	Maharashtra	371772	334075	37697	89.86	30.09.2016
21.	Manipur	1297	1240	57	95.61	31.12.2015
22.	Meghalaya	1005	925	80	92.04	31.03.2015
23.	Mizoram	3771	3733	38	98.99	30.06.2015
24.	Nagaland	652	598	54	91.72	30.09.2015
25.	Odisha	104439	96325	8114	92.23	31.01.2016
26.	Puducherry	3177	2982	195	93.86	30.11.2016
27.	Punjab	188689	183249	5440	97.12	31.10.2016
28.	Rajasthan	361568	326902	34666	90.41	30.11.2016
29.	Sikkim	338	324	14	95.86	31.03.2015
30.	Tamil Nadu	114623	105926	8697	92.41	30.11.2016
31.	Telangana	90028	85557	4471	95.03	30.11.2016
32.	Tripura	3522	3394	128	96.37	31.10.2016
33.	Uttar Pradesh	660199	584825	75374	88.58	30.09.2016
34.	Uttarakhand	40328	37475	2853	92.93	30.11.2016
35.	West Bengal	104588[1]	97835	6753	93.54	31.12.2015
	Total	**3853422**	**3551649**	**301773**	**92.17**	

Notes: [1] Data of Bankura DF not included.

Information Regarding Functional/Non-Functional (State Commissions/District Forums)

Unlike the civil courts, the consumer courts are quasi judicial authorities that have to follow simple, summary procedure for quick disposal of complaints. The Presidents and Members of the District Forum constitute the backbone of the Forum. They play a major role in enhancing the faith of the consumers in the redressal mechanism. Table 17.4 shows the

Table 17.4: Information Regarding Functional/Non-Functional (State Commissions/District Forums) (Update On 30-11-2016)

Sl. No.	*States*	*Whether SC Functional or Non-Functional*	*No. of District Fora*	*Func-tional*	*Non-Func-tional*	*As On*
1.	Andhra Pradesh	Yes	17	17	0	30.09.2016
2.	A & N Islands	Yes	1	1	0	30.06.2015
3.	Arunachal Pradesh	Yes	18	18	0	30.06.2016
4.	Assam	Yes	23	21	2	30.09.2016
5.	Bihar	Yes	38	33	5	30.06.2014
6.	Chandigarh	Yes	2	2	0	30.09.2016
7.	Chattisgarh	Yes	27	18	9	30.09.2016
8.	Daman & Diu	Yes	2	2	0	31.03.2011
9.	Dadra & Nagar Haveli	Yes	1	1	0	31.03.2011
10.	Delhi	Yes	10	10	0	30.06.2015
11.	Goa	Yes	2	2	0	30.09.2016
12.	Gujrat	Yes	30	30	0	31.03.2015
13.	Haryana	Yes	21	21	0	30.11.2016
14.	Himachal Pradesh	Yes	12	8	4	30.09.2016
15.	Jammu & Kashmir	Yes	2	2	0	30.06.2014
16.	Jharkhand	Yes	24	24	0	30.09.2016
17.	Karnataka	Yes	31	31	0	30.09.2016
18.	Kerala	Yes	14	14	0	30.09.2015
19.	Lakshadweep	Yes	1	1	0	30.06.2016
20.	Madhya Pradesh	Yes	49	49	0	30.09.2016
21.	Maharashtra	Yes	40	40	0	31.12.2015
22.	Manipur	Yes	9	4	5	31.12.2015
23.	Meghalaya	Yes	11	7	4	31.03.2015
24.	Mizoram	Yes	8	8	0	30.06.2015
25.	Nagaland	Yes	11	11	0	30.09.2015
26.	Orissa	Yes	31	31	0	31.03.2015
27.	Puducherry	Yes	1	1	0	30.09.2016
28.	Punjab	Yes	20	20	0	30.09.2016
29.	Rajasthan	Yes	37	37	0	30.09.2016
30.	Sikkim	Yes	4	4	0	31.03.2015
31.	Tamil Nadu	Yes	30	25	5	30.09.2016
32.	Telangana	Yes	12	12	0	30.09.2016
33.	Tripura	Yes	4	4	0	31.12.2016
34.	Uttar Pradesh	Yes	79	79	0	30.09.2016
35.	Uttarakhand	Yes	13	13	0	30.11.2016
36.	West Bengal	Yes	23	23	0	31.12.2015
	Total		**658**	**624**	**34**	

information regarding whether State Commissions or District Forums are functional in every state or not. It is a big relief to note that in 2016 the State Commissions are functioning in all the States. Further analysis of the Table 17.4 shows that out of 654 district forums only 624 are functional. Delays in appointments affects the speedy adjudication of consumer complaints.

Information Regarding Vacancy Position in the State Commissions and District Forums

Table 17.5 shows that as on 30-11-2016 there were one vacancy of the President and 20 vacancies of members of the State Commission lying vacant. In case of District Forums there were 95 posts of Presidents and 301 members of the District Forum lying vacant. For law to be effective there should be no posts in the District Forums and State Commission lying vacant otherwise consumers would lose faith in the system.

In order to ensure expeditious disposal of complaints, Section 13(3A) of the Consumer Protection Act provides for disposal of cases within 90 days where no analysis or lab testing of the products is required. Where testing of products is required the disposal of case can be done in 150 days. In reality cases run for many years and this clause is often breached. Adjournments according to the CPA amendment in 2002 should be allowed in exceptional circumstances and if given the court should record the reasons for it in writing and justify it.

In order to meet the changing requirements of consumers in the emerging market environment, the Act has been amended three times with the last amendment in 2002, providing more teeth to the law and to cut down delays in disposal of cases by the Consumer Courts at various levels. The Bill for the Fourth Amendment in the Act is pending in the Parliament which would widen the horizon and deal with the problems related to online purchases, product recalls also.

Recent Schemes started by the Government

A separate Ministry of Consumer Affairs promotes and protects the welfare of consumers. To meet the objective the Department is undertaking various measures involving all concerned to strengthen the consumer movement in the country. Some of the steps recently taken by the Ministry of Consumer Affairs, Food and Public Distribution, are:

Table 17.5: Information Regarding Vacancy Position in the State Commissions and District Forums (Update on 30-11-2016)

Sl. No.	States	State Commission		District Forum	
		President	Member	President	Member
	National Commission	0	2		
1.	Andhra Pradesh	0	2	1	26
2.	A & N Islands	0	1	0	0
3.	Arunachal Pradesh	0	0	0	11
4.	Assam	0	1	3	8
5.	Bihar	0	0	9	24
6.	Chandigarh	0	0	0	0
7.	Chattisgarh	0	0	1	23
8.	Daman & Diu and DNH	0	0	0	2
9.	Delhi	0	0	2	4
10.	Goa	0	0	0	0
11.	Gujrat	0	0	8	4
12.	Haryana	0	0	0	7
13.	Himachal Pradesh	0	0	0	12
14.	Jammu & Kashmir	1	0	0	0
15.	Jharkhand	0	0	0	0
16.	Karnataka	0[1]	0	4	14
17.	Kerala	0	0	1	1
18.	Lakshadweep	0	1	0	1
19.	Madhya Pradesh	0	1	0	33
20.	Maharashtra	0	2	10	17
21.	Manipur	0	3	0	0
22.	Meghalaya	0	0	1	4
23.	Mizoram	0	1	0	0
24.	Nagaland	0	0	0	0
25.	Odisha	0	0	0	0
26.	Puducherry	0	0	0	0
27.	Punjab	0	1	8	15
28.	Rajasthan	0	0	10	17
29.	Sikkim	0	0	0	0
30.	Tamil Nadu	0	2	11	12
31.	Telangana	0	1	10	19
32.	Tripura	0	0	0	0
33.	Uttar Pradesh	0	0	11	33
34.	Uttarakhand	0	0	0	6
35.	West Bengal	0[2]	4	5	8
	Total	**1**	**20**	**95**	**301**

Notes: [1] President retired on 19.05.2009.
[2] President take charge on 07.05.2008.

- GAMA portal has been launched in 2015 to curb the menace of misleading advertisements. Consumers can lodge their complaint regarding misleading advertisements on www.gama.gov.in

- Grahak Suvidha Kendras have been started also in 2015 in six states to help the rural consumers regarding filing of complaints in local language.
- Under CONFONET scheme the consumers who have filed complaints in District Fora/State Commission/National Commission can see the cause list, case status and judgment through online sitting at their home or elsewhere.
- Under the multi media 'Jago Grahak Jago' campaign a radio serial has been designed by the Ministry of Consumer Affairs in 2016 in which advice was given to consumers in local and regional language on consumer related problems.

Conclusion

The welfare of consumers remains in their own hands. If the consumers are responsible, vigilant and are able to assert their rights and responsibilities, resist/reject substandard goods/services wherever required and do not hesitate to seek justice through consumer forums if needed, the manufacturers, traders and service providers cannot afford to take them for granted while selling a product or rendering service on payment or to adopt any unfair trade practice. An alert consumer aware of his rights and responsibilities not only can protect himself but can also make consumer sovereignty a reality.

References

Aggarwal, V.K. (2003). *Consumer Protection Law and Practice*, 5th Edition Delhi: Bharat Law House.

Consumer Protection Judgements (CPJ) relevant cases

George, S. Day and A. Aaker (1970). "A Guide to Consumerism", *Journal of Marketing*, 34: 12-19.

Girmaji Pushpa (2002). *Consumer Rights for Everyone*, Penguin Books.

Goodwin Cathy (1991). "Recognition of a Consumer Right", *Journal of Public Policy and Marketing*, 10(1): 149-166.

Gupta, Joyeeta (1986). "Consumerism: Emerging Challenges and Opportunities", *Vikalpa*, II(2): 149-158.

Kapoor, Sheetal *et al.*, (2007). *Consumer Affairs*, Delhi: Universities Press.

Rao, Rajyalakshmi (2012). *Consumer is King*, 3rd Edition, Delhi: Universal Law Publishing Co..

www.consumeraffairs.nic.in

www.ncdrc.nic.in

18

Role of Media in Society

Syeda Afshana

Introduction

We live in a society that is saturated with media. In our everyday life, we navigate through a mass media environment on a scale that is unprecedented in human history; so much so that media has become a dominant sociological institution alongside family, religion or educational systems, in 21st century. The level of involvement of media in our everyday lives has become so pervasive, that we take them for granted, like the air we breathe; ever present but rarely considered.

Our media and our society as we know are fused: media/society. One way to recognize the importance of media in our lives in to imagine life without media; imagine you wake up in a sort of parallel universe where everything is same except that media do not exist. No television, no movies, no radio, no recorded music, no cell-phones, no computers, no internet, no books, no magazines or newspapers. We would not watch sports on TV, catch videos or stream programmes online, or go to a movie for fun. We would not listen to recorded music for relaxation, we would not use our cell phones to call or text friends, we would not post news and information about ourselves or communicate with others on social networking sites, blogs, or other internet forums. Our understanding of politics and the world around us would be different because we would not have newspapers, television, magazines, and websites. Even our perceptions of ourselves would probably be different, because we would not have television characters and advertising images to compare ourselves against. Our social lives—how we interact with other people—would also change in the absence of media. Of course, changes would reach well beyond our private lives. The behaviour of politicians, business executives, and leaders in other fields would change without media. Government would operate differently. Without advertising, business would be fundamentally different. Education, religion, and every other institution would also be different without media, as would social movements and citizens' organizations (Croteau. *et al.*, 2011).

Given the level of involvement and role of media in our daily lives and society, questions have been raised by some scholars and historians regarding the positive as well as negative effects of our dependency on media. In order to dwell deeper in to the role and impact of media in society, we first need to understand the word media itself. The media itself is a plural of medium, further communication media differs from technological communication.

There are different types of media in any society at any given point of time and as such to speak of media as a uniform concept will be misleading. There are various standpoints which need to be considered when we try to understand the dynamics of media and society. Within that broad framework it takes up various themes. These include the importance of the context — political, social, cultural, economic — in which mass media have developed and been adopted; the interaction between technological and social change; the relationships between media institutions and the state; and the interrelationships of different media (Gorman & Mclean, 2002).

Our starting points are the three basic levels of any consideration of society:

(1) The *State* and related governmental institutions,
(2) The *Market* and related property and commercial phenomena, and
(3) The *Civil Society* made up of people and citizens apart from the two preceding spheres.

This articulation of society can be illustrated in Fig. 18.1.

The figure is borrowed from the Norwegian social scientist and peace research pioneer Johan Galtung (1999), who places the mass media floating between the three pillars (he calls the Market pillar "Capital"). In the history of European countries the media have found their place first close to both the State and the Capital, emerging from late-feudal patronage and boosted by mercantile capitalism. With the rise of modern democracy and party structure, the press became part and parcel of the

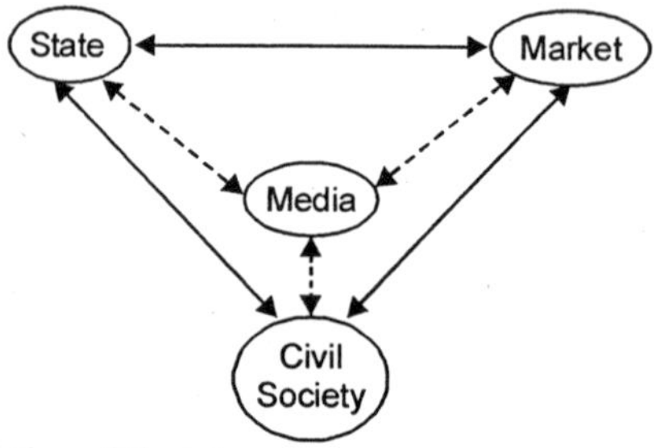

Fig. 18.1: Articulation of Society

Civil Society, while broadcasting remained closely tied to the State. The second half of the 20th century has brought the media — both print and electronic — increasingly towards Capital-driven markets (Hamelink & Nordenstreng, 2007)

The classic example to understand media as an intermediary between the state, civil society and the market can be understood by following example. The government decides that the prices of petrol and diesel will either be increased or decreased. That decision needs to be conveyed to the people. This is done by the media. The media not only inform the people about it but also explain the effect of that decision taken by the government on the people. But this is just one facet of media and because media is such an integral part of our lives, it generates a great deal of debate about the workings, role and impact of media itself. Like are the news biased? Do movies have too much obscenity or violence? Does media only sensationalize things?

To address these questions we need to look both media and society from a sociological perspective which allows us to consider the role of media in our individual lives but in context of broader social forces likes economy, politics and technological developments. Thereby allowing us to understand the dynamics of media and society from a multi-pronged approach.

The sociological approach to communication theory is based on assumption that there exists a definite relationship between mass communication and social change. Some of the relevant theories which are going to be discussed here are:

The cultivation theory: Developed by George Gerbner in 1967, it is based on the assumption that mass media have subtle effects on audiences who unknowingly absorb the dominant symbols, images, and messages of media. He calls it "cultivation of dominant image pattern". According to this theory a long persistent exposure to TV is capable of cultivating common beliefs about the world.

Social Learning Theory: It is one of the most widely used theories in mass communication. According to this theory, the media are active but subtle educators in teaching readers, viewers, listeners about the world. An important component of this theory is that it explains how people can learn from observations alone.

Agenda Setting Theory: The term was coined by Maxwell McCombs and Donald L. Shaw in 1972. This theory tries to describe and explain as how stories are selected: (a) Packaged and presented—a process known as Gatekeeping, (b) by resulting agenda, and (c) how this agenda affects what people think about the relative importance of the issues presented. This theory also "predicts" that of particular news item is presented prominently and frequently by the press, the public will come to believe that it is important.

Uses and Gratification Theory: This theory has emerged out of the studies which shifted their focus from what media do to the people to what people do with media (Katz, 1959). The uses approach assumes that audiences are active and willingly expose themselves to media and that the most potent of mass media cannot influence an individual who has "no use" for it in the environment in which he lives. The uses of the mass media are dependent on the perception, selectivity, and previously held values, beliefs and interests of the people.

We have ample examples and incidences in our contemporary times that corroborate the claims made by these sociological theories and also point to the role and impact of media on society. The Watergate scandal, which is till date one of the most controversial Presidential scandals and that also led to the downfall of Richard Nixon is the prime example of how media uncovered the truth and played the role of the watchdog. Author Rick Perlstein on the impact of Watergate on American society says, *"Watergate got us to think of leaders as mere mortals. America began to think of itself in a very different way — I would say a salutary." Similarly if it wouldn't have had been for images which media personnel captured in the Vietnam War, a popular civilian agitation wouldn't have taken place, which pressurized the American government to withdraw its troops. In more recent times, the use of media in Arab spring is widely documented.* According to experts, social media played a significant role during the Arab Spring because it facilitated communication and interaction among participants of political protests. Protesters used social media to organize demonstrations (both pro- and anti-governmental), disseminate information about their activities, and raise local and global awareness of ongoing events (Fadi, 2011) Research from the Project on

Information Technology and Political Islam found that online revolutionary conversations often preceded mass protests on the ground, and that social media also played a central role in shaping political debates in the Arab Spring (Phillip, *et al.*, 2011). In some cases, governments used social media to engage with citizens and encourage their participation in government processes; but in others, governments monitored Internet traffic or blocked access to websites or the entire Internet, according to a study conducted by the Dubai School of Government (Fadi, 2011).

In India the role of media has been aggressively seen. There have been many instances where media has interfered into various issues, and then reshaped the public opinion, forcing law enforcing agencies to take up the action. At various instances the media has forced judiciary to take up decision regarding any issue. The murder of Delhi model Jessica Lal by Manu Sharma is one of the most known cases of media interference resulting in justice. The incident took place on April 29, 1999 when Jessica Lal was shot dead in a party hosted by socialite Bina Ramani, in her restaurant. Lal was working as celebrity barmaid in Ramani's restaurant. The main accused was Siddharth Vashisht, known as Manu Sharma, the son of Venod Sharma, a prominent Congress leader in Haryana.

Media took up this case and initiated a media trail. The final verdict, which was passed on this case, was a shining example of media interference. NDTV channel received numerous text messages from masses, urging that immediate action be taken against Sharma and the others. Given the incident and the poor proceedings of the judicial system, people were losing faith in the judiciary and the media was able to shed some light on this very fact. The media, along with Sabrina Lal (Jessica's sister) organized a candle light vigil in New Delhi. Various support groups were formed to support the cause of "miscarriage of justice", as termed by the media.

On 9th September, 2006, news magazine *Tehelka* organized a sting operation on the witnesses of the case. The sting operation revealed that Venod Sharma had bribed them to make sure that they won't speak in the court. This video coverage of the sting operation was then aired by news channel STAR News. A poll was carried by *Hindustan Times* that revealed that on a scale from 1 to 10, the faith that Indians had on the judiciary was near about 2.7. With pressure building up from all the corners and media, Delhi High Court was compelled to take notice and the case was reopened after an appeal made by Delhi Police. The accused, Manu Sharma, was finally pronounced guilty of killing Jessica Lal, and the court pronounced life sentence in his favour on 20th December, 2006.

The efforts of the media helped the case to be reopened and justice was finally delivered. (Kathakali Nandi, 2011)

There are many other examples which showcase how media in India impacted both the state and the civil society. Priyadarshni Matto rape case, Bofors Scam or the Operation West End—all these point to the various roles and also the kind of impact media has. These examples show that media not only acted like a information disseminator, but adopted several roles like:

(1) "Monitoring" for reporting the use and power,
(2) "Facilitative" for serving civil society,
(3) "Radical" for questioning the political system, and
(4) "Collaborative" for serving the state and other power institutions.

However, the role and impact of media is not always positive; the accident of Princess Diana caused by a car chase between her and papparazi is a stark example of the various facets the media can play. Similarly, the portrayal of Blacks, Arabs or the representations based on class and caste has raised the debates of media purporting the ideology of certain dominant class.

For *those* engaged in the promotion of particular ideas, including diverse groups such as politicians, corporations, citizen activists, and religious groups; media are among the primary contemporary battlegrounds. Media are in fact at the centre of what James Davison Hunter (1991) has called the "culture wars" in contemporary American society, in which fundamental issues of morality are being fought (Hunter and Wolfe, 2006). Hunter stresses the ways in which media—advertising, news, letters to the editor, and opinion commentary—provide the principal forms of public discourse by which cultural warfare is waged. The morality of abortion, homosexuality or capital punishment debated, is often in very polarized terms, in the mass media, as cultural conservative and cultural progressives alike use various media technologies to promote their positions (Croteau, *et al.*, 2011).

However, media in context of shaping ideologies should be rather understood as sites where cultural contests over meanings are waged, rather than providers of some univocal articulation of ideology.

The commercialism of media along with selling consumerism has further casted the role and impact of media in a negative light. The sophistication of advertising and marketing has created needs in places where none exists and has turned luxuries in necessities. Even young children are not being spared and are one of the most lucrative businesses when it comes to selling consumerism. Through adverts, media doesn't just sell the product, they sell the idea. Like buying a certain brand of car makes one more powerful, wearing a certain cosmetic makes one more elegant and attractive. Furthermore, the ability of media to shape consumer trends through movies, television shows and now via social networking sites is adding the consumerist nature, which equates buying power with contentment and happiness.

All in all, one needs to understand that believing media is all powerful and audiences are helpless in front of media power, would be ridiculous. The need is to locate the growing influence of media within the changing scenarios around our environments. There is a need to not just study media content (which is mostly presumed to be media) but we need to develop a holistic way to understand media relationships with audiences, producers, economy and the social world beyond the media; if we are to completely understand the role of media in society, both of whom are continuously changing with changing times and working in tandem impacting and reflecting the changes in other.

References

David Croteau, William Hoynes and Stefania Milan (2011). *Media/Society Industries, Images, and Audiences*, fourth edition. Sage Publication.

Hakim Khalid Mehraj, Akhtar Neyaz Bhat and Hakeem Rameez Mehraj (2014). "Impacts of Media on Society: A Sociological Perspective". *International Journal of Humanities and Social Science Invention,* ISSN (Online): 2319 7722, ISSN (Print): 2319-7714.

Howard, Philip N., Duffy, Aiden, Freelon, Deen, Hussain, Muzammil, Mari, Wil and Mazaid, Marwa (2011). *Opening Closed Regimes: What Was the Role of Social Media During the Arab Spring?* (PDF). pitpi.org.

Investigative Journalism and the Watergate Scandal (n.d) History and Journalism. Retrieved from https://historyandjournalism.wordpress.com/journalism-and-watergate

Lyn Gorman, David McLean (2009). *Media and Society into the 21st Century: A Historical Introduction*, Wiley-Blackwell.

McQuail, D. (2005). *McQuail's Mass Communication Theory*. Fifth Edition. London: Sage.

Nordenstreng, Kaarle (n.d). *Media and Society, Department of Journalism and Mass Communication*, University of Tampere.

Salem, Fadi and Mourtada, Racha (May 2011). *Civil Movements: The Impact of Facebook and Twitter* (PDF).

19

Gender and Sexuality in Islam

An Interface of Patriarchy, Religion and Customary Practices

Sabiha Hussain

Introduction

Here I have tried to discuss some of the dominant discourses on women's body and sexuality along with other structural and institutional factors which impact on women's sexual rights and sexuality and the interplay between these factors and Islam. Also, I have tried to explain the way women's sexuality is constructed in Islam through various interpretations of the text and how the traditional customary practices trying to curb women's body and sexuality. Also, the challenges for women's movement in Muslim countries in raising the issue of women's sexuality and reproductive rights are highlighted in this chapter. These issues are important mainly for two reasons: the emergence of conservative forces using religion to curb women's rights and secondly, cultural or customary practices are overriding the textual Islam and thus, depriving women of their rights. The chapter is based on secondary sources.

In almost all religions of the world, women's body and sexuality is a subject of great debate especially in the discourse of feminist movement. It is true that like all major world religions, Islam has a strong patriarchal element, but the way it is practiced and experienced varies greatly across the Muslim countries, and is influenced by a number of factors other than religion (Hilsdon and Rosario, 2006, p.332). In Islam women's body and sexuality is often been represented as a dangerously disruptive force, and women have been urged or sometimes compel to veil themselves in order to protect men from distraction and temptation (Abdel-Halim, 2001, p.204). However, with the rise of patriarchy, many customs and traditions were developed and assimilated in the name of Islam that violates women's human rights and also goes against the teachings of Islam.

In the last decades, due to the adverse impacts of socio-economic and political developments, the issues around sexuality, sexual rights and women's bodies have increasingly become sites of political contestation in Muslim societies. While on the one hand rise of the Islamic conservative forces have given either no space or very little space for debating the issue of sexuality and women's reproductive and body rights. Further, a continuous effort by the conservative forces to maintain or reinforce the traditional mechanisms a new one in the name of religion to control over women's sexuality is depriving women of their rights.

Nevertheless, several factors such as the rise of new feminist and civil movements, globalization, the increasing influence of a global human rights discourse, and changing socio-economic conditions etc. have led to the emergence of new discourses and demands regarding sexuality and sexual rights of women. But the religious leaders have been advocating against any reforms in the laws related to marriage, adultery, divorce and inheritance and have started a global campaign against the concepts of sexual and reproductive rights as western agneda (Hulme, 2009, El Dawla, 2000).

Women's body and Sexuality in Islam: The Qur'an and the Hadith

In Islam both women and men are supposed to remain chaste until marriage, not just the women, and adultery consists of any married person engaging in sexual intercourse with someone other than the spouse. The punishment for adultery for both men and women is death by stoning. If a husband arbitrarily accuses his wife of being unfaithful, they both take an oath upon God, and if the wife swears that she is innocent and the husband swears that she is not, the marriage is irrevocably over and the woman is not considered an adulteress.

As far as Qur'an and hadith are concerned both these sources consider the nature of sexual relations as a means of attaining mutual satisfaction, closeness and compassion between a wife and husband. The Qur'an, in a basic manner, follows the understanding of equality, partnership and justice within the sexual relationship of men and women. This is expressed by the Qur'an itself with the use of a metaphor, 'They are your garments and ye are their garments" (al-Baqarah 187). Clothing or garments as mentioned here to create a symbol of a person's basic need for the other person.

It says, *"Permitted to you on the night of the Fasts is the approach to your wives. They are your garments and you are their garments."(2:187) Also, Muslims are advised to avoid sexual intercourse during menses so as not to cause discomfort to the woman (2:222).*

It is lawful for you to go in unto your wives during the night preceding the (day's) fast:-they are as a garment for you, and you are as a garment for them. God is aware that you would have deprived yourselves of this right, and so He has turned unto you in His mercy and removed this hardship from you. Now, then, you may lie with them skin to skin, and avail yourselves to that which God has ordained for (2:187).

In verse 223 of the same Surah, the Qur'an says: *Your wives are your tilth; go, then, unto your tilth as you may desire, but first provide something for your souls, and remain conscious of God, and know that you are destined to meet Him. And give glad tidings unto those who believe.*

When one looks at the sexual rights of the wife, one finds that several **hadith address** the issue of sexual satisfaction with reference to the wife's rights in this matter.

"Your body has a right over you, your eyes have a right over you and your wife has a right over you." (Bukhari, Vol. 7, No. 127) The wife's rights include a right to companionship from her husband and fulfillment of her sexual needs.

Hadiths that clearly reveals the importance of women's sexual and reproductive rights: When you intend to have sex with your wife, do not rush because the woman (also) has needs which should be fulfilled)." (*Wasa'il*, vol. 14, p. 40)

"..... cruel: a person who has sex with his wife before foreplay." (*Wasa'il*, vol. 14, p. 40)

"When anyone of you has sex with his wife, then he should not go to them like birds; instead he should be slow and delaying." (*Wasa'il*, Vol. 14, p. 82)

The Prophet said, "No one among you should have sex with his wife like animals; rather there should be a messenger between them." When asked about the messenger, he said, "It means kissing and talking." (*Tahzibu'l-Ihya*, vol. 3, p. 110)

Imam Ja'far as-Sadiq has been quoted as follows, "...there should be mutual foreplay between them because it is better for sex." (*Wasa'il*, vo. 14, p. 82)

In several hadith, the Prophet speaks about the importance of foreplay and speaking in loving terms during sexual relations. Hence, sexual dissatisfaction is considered legitimate grounds for divorce on the part of either wife or husband (An Islamic Perspective on Sexuality, Muslim Women League, 1996).

But at the same time destructive qualities of female sexuality have been quoted in many Hadith as well as in the writings of eminent Muslim scholars like Ghazali, Sha-wali-ullah etc. In all the books of Hadith and Fiqh, as well as in the interpretations of the Qur'an, one can easily find the chapters related to the destructive powers of women's sexuality which strongly support the physical mutilation of women i.e. circumcision. Though, Islam does not approve this practice, it provides the ideological justification for it.

Hence, to sum up there is no 'one definitive opinion' about gender and sexuality in Islam. Further, the interpretations of various school of Islamic jurisprudence make the issue even more complicated. In fact, there are a number of different scholarly opinions and even the Shariah is made up of a number of diverse opinions with regard to gender and sexuality in Islam. Similarly, there is no one universal way of understanding sexuality in Islamic societies due to a range of sexual ideals and beliefs. Moreover, the translation and interpretation of the *Qur'an* is done differently in different parts of the world by different schools of thought. Hence, defining sexuality or sexual behaviour in Islam seems to be a difficult task. ("http://www.safraproject.org/sgi-intro.htm")

Major Discourse on Women's Body and Sexuality: Conservative and Feminists

As far as issues around sexuality and women's bodies in Muslim societies are concerned, since the beginning of the 1990s, a growing number of NGOs in Muslim countries have started advocating for sexual and bodily rights, issues of eradication of customary practices such as honour killings, female genital mutilation[1] (FGM) or forced virginity tests to sex education and legal recognition of women's sexual autonomy in the penal codes.

However, when one looks into the discourse of the conservative forces, one finds that they are trying to reinforce traditional mechanisms to control women's sexuality in various ways by arguing; sexuality as a source of immorality, unrestrained sexuality is dangerous to morality and social order, women must abide by restrictive dress codes that signify asexuality, women must be segregated or secluded so as not to lure men, women's body requires 'modesty' that is expressed through the imposition of dress codes that signify asexuality and so on and hence, women's sexuality has to be curbed. For instance, in Sudan since the 1990s, a woman can be legally stopped and questioned by any man who feels she is not wearing appropriate attire.

On the contrary when it comes to the channelization of men's sexuality, it gives them more privilege and control over women. The conservative discourse gives men more means and avenues of satisfying desires—if heterosexual, Polygamy becomes an unchecked right for men—in some cases (like Nigeria) almost an obligation.

The right to marry girl children is defended and promoted as men's right and the prevention of immorality. Women's right to choose their partner is increasingly carved down or removed. (WLUML 1995, Sudan Woman and Law Project 1996).[2] The treatment of rape militates against women and so on.

In nutshell, the conservative discourse (like Christian and Hindu religious right groups—see WAF Journals) have been reconstructing and reinforcing the patriarchal control over women and their sexuality in the name of religion. The focus of control has been shifting from the micro unit of household patriarch to the macro level of the state control of women (and men), to state-sanctioned control of all women by all men. In words of Nazir, "the emergence of extremist Islamic forces stands as a threat to gains women have achieved as well as future possibilities for reform. Even where radical forces are not influential, the politicization of Islam seriously complicates the challenge of advocating for equal rights". (Nazir 2005:164)

As far as the feminists discourse on female sexuality is concerned Mernissi (1996) has identified the dominant attitude in Muslim societies towards male sexuality (male heterosexuality that is) as highly positive, while female sexuality has been conceptualised as 'implicit theory of female sexuality' and an 'explicit theory of female sexuality.' Though both the theories co-exist but are contradictory to each other. The concept of explicit female sexuality in Islamic thought consider female sexuality to be naturally passive and views women's submission to men as integral to their sexual pleasure. Men are seen as the active hunters and women as the passive prey. The implicit theory conceptualises women's sexuality as active and dangerous, and as posing a threat to men. Hence, women are seen as the aggressors and the hunters, and men are seen as the prey to women who are seductresses and manipulators, using their sexual charm to control men. Looking at these two competing and co-existing notions of female sexuality, it is often argued and understood that women need to be protected from men, and also need to control their own sexuality for the good of society.

Some of the feminist scholars opine that the male notions of sexuality include the idea that if it is not controlled, could result in social chaos and social disorder (fitna) (Dunne, 1998 Mernissi **Women's Rebellion and The Islamic Memory** Fatima Mernissi (1996), Wadud, www.safraproject.org/sgi-women sexuality in Islam accessed on 14th July, 2015). Some feminist scholars have pointed out that this so-called 'positive' or 'affirmative' Islamic approach to sexuality, is mostly confirm masculine sexual experience (Wadud, 1998).

For example, verses affirming men's rights to sexual satisfaction, allowing polygamy and allowing temporary marriage, as well as certain supposedly sexual references to the pleasures in paradise etc. This emphasis on male sexuality is also reflected in Muslim laws and the way they are used in society (Wadudwww.safraproject.org/sgi-women sexuality in Islam accessed on 14th July, 2016)

Contrary to men's sexuality, women's sexuality in Muslim laws and societies is limited to monogamous heterosexual marriage that is believed to be preserving a 'sexual purity' and requires male control over women's sexuality. In some cases where a woman is considered to have violated the codes of her family's 'sexual purity', her identity or behaviour can lead to violence, forced marriage and even killed. (www.soas.ac.uk accessed on 14th July, 2015).

Looking at these customary notion and conceptualization of women's body and sexuality, a few feminists have strongly argued that male control of women's sexuality is not mentioned in the Qur'an and have been trying to challenge the prevailing idea of fixed gender roles in Islam that hinder women from controlling their own sexuality (Wadud 1998, Barlas 2000, Yamani 1996). Further, these scholars have been making a continuous efforts to unravel different views on sexuality within the frameworks of progressive Islam, e.g. women's rights in family laws (An-Naim, WLUML) women's control over their own reproduction (WWHR), violence against women including honour crimes etc. (www.wwhr.org; www.wluml.org; www.SOAS.ac.uk/honour killing; Wadud 1998; Esack, 2000).

Women's Right to their Body and Sexuality: Customary Practices Vs. Religious Prescriptions

Having said about the religious text and discourses, now I would like to detail how customary practices try to control women's sexuality through patriarchy. For instance, customs like virginity test, genital mutilation, honour killings and forced marriage which has no sanctioned in Islam yet practiced as custom and often being justified in the name of Islam.

Two cases one of forced marriage and another virginity test from Pakistan (Saima Waheed) and Afghanistan (Raela) is worth mentioning to highlight how women's body and sexuality are seen as the bearers and reproducers of patriarchy and customary tradition than the rights (reproductive and sexual) given to them in Islam.

The case of Saima of Pakistan[3] married against the wishes of her parents to an ordinary teacher brings out the fact that despite ubiquitous references to 'Islam,' it was the patriarchies—that were at issue. The discourse around the case abounds in the established and familiar post-colonial binaries of East/West, tradition/modernity, public/private, sacred/profane. In this larger discourse, invariably women's bodies become sites for the cultural politics and the class struggles regardless of the kind of state/society. The regulation of women and their sexuality thus, became the key hegemonic move for securing the consent of social classes across the society.

In case of Raela, who was forcefully taken for medical examination on her wedding night after her husband accused her of not being a virgin and was beaten by her husband. The examination showed she had lost her virginity long before the marriage and the 22-year-old was handed over to the judiciary for prosecution on charges of adultery. The family had to pay back almost US$10,000 to their former son-in-law, that was allegedly spent on the wedding ceremony. Though virginity is not mentioned in the country's penal system and other laws, hundreds of women like Raela unfairly face serious formal and informal penalties for the alleged illicit loss of this cultural requirement.

Hence, I argue that religion is not the predominant factor related to women's sexuality and sexual rights within Muslim societies rather it is the convenience and inconvenience argument of the state and the society, the selective patriarchal interpretations of Islamic text that is adopted and rejected when it comes to women's rights especially in private domain. Even codified Islamic laws are precisely sidelined, ignored or overlooked when it appears as inconvenient. For example, honour killings are often justified to 'tradition' and 'custom' and not through recourse to *Islam*, as it was witnessed in 1999 in the Pakistani Senate.

Further, I would like to argue that women's bodies are often seen as belonging to society and the family. Bearers and reproducers of cultural identity and tradition are given more importance, than a person who has rights over their body and soul. Since, the collective and the community are emphasized as the Centre of moral authority and value in Islam (Obermeyer, 1995, p.371), 'the control of women can come to symbolize the means to cure a whole range of society's political, economic and cultural problems' (Feldman and Clark, 1996, p.16). The conservative forces often not only try to gain control over women's bodies but also try to fix a dress code for women, their sexuality and their reproductive capacities and choices (Berer and Sundari-Ravindran, 1996, p.7). Hence, largely puts a limit on women's control over their own bodies which creates hurdle for women in exercising their sexual and reproductive rights. (Amado, 2003, p. 6)

Women's Movement and Challenges: Reproductive Rights and Sexuality

In this given scenario, women's movement has numerous challenges in debating the issue of social construction of gender and sexuality in Islam and its impact on the rights of women. There are innumerable challenges that need to be taken by the women's movement across the globe and in particular by the Muslim feminists. First of all contextualizing the issue of sexuality in the present context from a gender and human rights perspective is essential. Why, because dealing with Muslim women's oppression in sexual matters solely in terms of the Quran and/or other Islamic sources largely leave out the context in which Quranic revelations occurred along with the context in which various interpretations of the sacred text were given. Further, it is also essential to evolve a common strategy at global level and regional level to combat the political use of religion and culture/tradition in private life along with the laws, policies and practices that intends to control women's sexual and reproductive freedom given to them in the Qur'anic text. Women's movement also need to expedite further the strategy to bring women's sexual and reproductive rights agenda on the political programme of the conservative forces who fanatically concentrate on the control of women particularly their body and sexuality. In almost all cultural traditions and interpretations of religion, it is the worst practices against women, which is chosen and promoted in the name of Islam. The challenge is how to deal with the pick and chose process adopted by the interpreters.

Therefore, the Muslim feminists movement in association with the global feminists movement need to work together to contextualize religious right discourses on sexual rights and sexuality at different level i.e. the contexts in which Muslim religious rights groups operate, the ideological-political state in which it is practiced and the content of hegemony in each community that deprives women of their rights.

One of the greatest challenges is look into the concept of sexuality as shaped by the combination of factors such as the law, customary practices and traditions, religious and cultural construction of sexuality, sexual rights needs to be deconstructed. This is important as the conservative forces are continuously making an effort to reconstruct and reestablish various social mechanisms to control women's bodies and sexuality for enhancing their power to maintain the patriarchal social order.

Conclusion

Looking at the various discourse and debates one could submit that virtually in almost all Muslim societies, women and their sexual purity (variously defined) have been attached with the honour of men and families i.e. patriarchal set up which is often been explained and perceived as Islamic. Hence, it is important to understand the role of Islam with regard to women's sexual rights and sexuality in a historical and sociological context. Such a framework rules out the idea that something static and immutable called 'Islam' exists anywhere. Further, any association of Islamic text with customary practices varies across the Muslim society and becomes complex, and sometimes even contradictory.

The above discussion clearly indicates that Islam takes a different approach and does not renounce sexuality as such. Sexuality itself is not dangerous (Sabbah, 1984) but some interpretations of it, are unfavourable to women. Hence, male control of women's sexuality is not envisaged by the Qur'an but male interpretations of the Qur'an and Hadith and the formulation of Shariah has led to the patriarchal practices in Muslim societies particularly related to sexuality and reproduction.

Further, the historical and exclusive interpretation of the Qur'an and Hadiths about women's sexuality is not universally accepted by all Muslims in the same manner and degree. For instance, the sexual offences laws, sexual segregation and compulsory hijab to 'control' women's sexuality are not Islamic vision of women's sexuality and hence, vary.

Male control of women's sexuality as a justification for maintaining identity and social order is an outcome of a whole range of the social, economic and political structure of early Islam. So, women's sexuality must be contested in a given context, political ideology of the state, the economy of the state, the pressure of the national and international forces and so on. Similarly, sexual patterns, to a large extent, influenced by the nature of function of the state, political economy and the cultural practices, connection between political systems and conservative religious groups than the Islamic text. The scope of the debate further decreases due to the stigmatization of those raising the issues related to sexual rights and sexuality.

These are some of the factors that complicate the debate on sexual rights and sexuality and provide conservative forces excuses to create extreme forms of control over women and their sexuality by incorporating and universalizing customary practices in the name of religion and patriarchy.

Notes

1. Female genital mutilation (FGM), also known as female genital cutting and female circumcision is the ritual cutting or removal of some or all of the external female genitalia. The practice is found in Africa, Asia and the Middle East, and within communities from countries in which FGM is common. It's often seen by practicing communities as a ceremony of purification, to prepare daughters for marriage.
2. Sudan Women and Law Project 1996 Interim Report (mimeo) In Sudan where there has been a shift from allowing women to make the choice to enabling her waliyi (guardian, always male) to enforce his choice on her. There is increasingly a lack of concern for the consent of the bride to marriage. Mut'a (temporary marriage permitted in Shiite Sharia) is on the increase, including in Sunni communities where it was previously unknown.
3. The case of Ms. Saima Waheed, an adult Muslim woman and a fourth year student at the Lahore Government College for Women, was widely publicized in the international press in the beginning of this year. Ms Waheed had, with neither the approval nor the knowledge of her parents, married her brother's tutor at the beginning of 1996, though she continued to live with her parents after the clandestine marriage. The events could have been taken straight out of the plot of a Hindi movie drama and, perhaps inevitably, her father eventually found out and strongly disapproved: he returned die nikahnama, i.e. die marriage certificate, to her husband's equally surprised family and

purported to cancel it. in complete defiance of her family's wishes, disappeared from her parent's home, only to surface again in a women's refugee managed by a non-governmental organization. The father immediately filed criminal charges against the hostel, alleging that his daughter had been abducted and argued that daughter's marriage was void ab initial, since he had not given his consent. The daughter, in turn, petitioned the court for a declaration that she had been validly married and was free to live with her husband.

References

Abdel-Halim, A. (2001). "Reconciling the Opposites: Equal but Subordinate", In Howland, C.W., (Ed.), 2001, *Religious Fundamentalisms and the Human Rights of Women,* New York, USA: Palgrave.

Afkhami, M. (2001). "Gender Apartheid and the Discourse of Relativity of Rights in Muslim Societies", In Howland, C.W. (Ed.), *Religious Fundamentalisms and the Human Rights of Women,* New York, USA: Palgrave.

Amado, L. (2003). "Sexual and Bodily Rights as Human Rights in The Middle East and North Africa", *Workshop Report,* Istanbul, Turkey: Women for Women's Human Rights—New Ways.

BarlasAsma (2002). "Believing Women in Islam: Unreading Patriarchal Interpretations of the Quran". University of Texas Press.

Bartelink, B. and Buitelaar, M. (2006). "The Challenges of incorporating Muslim women's views into development policy: Analysis of a Dutch action research project in Yemen", In *Gender and Development, 14(3),* UK: Routledge.

Berer, M. and Sundari-Ravindran, T.K. (1996). "Fundamentalism, Women's Empowerment and Reproductive Rights", In *Reproductive Health Matters, 4(8),* London, UK: Reproductive Health Matters.

Boland, R. and Katzive, L. (2008). "Developments in Laws on Induced Abortion: 1998-2007", In *International Family Planning Perspectives, 34(3),* The Guttmacher Institute.

Boonstra, H. (2001). "Islam, Women and Family Planning: A Primer", In *The Guttmacher Report on Public Policy, 4(6),* The Guttmacher Institute.

Bowen, D. (2003). "Contemporary Muslim Ethics of Abortion", In Brockopp, J.E. (Ed.), *Islamic Ethics of Life: Abortion, War and Euthanasia,* USA: University of South Carolina Press.

Casanova, J. and Phillips, A. (2009). "A Debate on the Public Role of Religion and its Social and Gender Implications", *Gender and Development Programme Paper Number 5,* (UNRISD).

Coalition for Sexual and Bodily Rights in Muslim Societies (CSBR), (2011). "Sexuality in Muslim Societies", In *CSBR NEWS, 4(2),* Istanbul, Turkey: Women for Women's Human Rights—New Ways.

Corrêa, S.; Petchesky, R.P. and Parker, R. (2008). *Sexuality, Health and Human Rights,* Oxon, UK: Routledge.

DeJong, J., Jawad, R., Mortagy, I. and Shepard, B. (2005). "The Sexual and Reproductive Health of Young People in the Arab Countries and Iran", In *Reproductive Health Matters,* Vol. 13(25), London, UK: Reproductive Health Matters.

Douki, S., Zineb, B., Nacef, F. and Halbreich, U. (2007). "Women's mental health in the Muslim world: Cultural, religious and social issues", In *Journal of Affective Disorders*, 102(1), International Society for Affective Disorders/ Elsevier.

Dunne, B. (1998). "Power and Sexuality in the Middle East", In The Middle East Report (Spring 1998).

El Dawla, A.S. (2000). "Reproductive Rights of Egyptian Women: Issues for Debate", In *Reproductive Health Matters*, Vol. 8(16), London, UK: Reproductive Health Matters.

El Dawla, A.S., Abdel-Hadi, A. and Abdel-Wahab, N. (1998). "Women's Wit Over Men's: Trade-offs and Strategic Accommodations in Egyptian Women's Reproductive Lives", In Petchesky, R.P., Judd, K., (Eds.), *Negotiating Reproductive Rights: Women's Perspectives Across Countries and Cultures,* London, UK: Zed Books.

El Hamri, N. (2010). "Approaches to family planning in Muslim communities", In *Journal of Family Planning and Reproductive Health Care,* 36(1), London, UK: BMJ Publications.

Farid Esack (2003). Sex: The Awkward Gift from God, Paper presented at 2nd International Muslim Leaders Consultation on HIV and Aids.

Farid Esack Farid (2000). Islam and Sexual Otherness, presented at Yoesuf Foundation Conference on Islam in the West and Homosexuality — Strategies for Action.

Feldman, R. and Clark, K. (1996). "Women, Religious Fundamentalism and Reproductive Rights", In *Reproductive Health Matters*, 4(8), London, UK: Reproductive Health Matters.

Hélie-Lucas, M. (2001). "What is your tribe?: Women's Struggles and the Construction of Muslimness", In Howland, C.W., (Ed.), *Religious Fundamentalisms and the Human Rights of Women,* New York, USA: Palgrave.

Hessini, L. (2005). "Global Progress in Abortion Advocacy and Policy: An Assessment of the Decade since ICPD", In *Reproductive Health Matters,* Vol. 13(25), London, UK: Reproductive Health Matters.

Hessini, L. (2007). "Abortion and Islam: Policies and Practice in the Middle East and North Africa", In *Reproductive Health Matters,* Vol. 15(29), London, UK: Reproductive Health Matters.

Hessini, L. (2008). "Islam and Abortion: The Diversity of Discourses and Practices", In *IDS Bulletin,* 39(3), Sussex, UK: Institute of Development Studies.

Hilsdon, A. and Rozario, S. (2006). "Islam, gender and human rights", In *Women Studies International Forum,* Vol. 29, USA: Pergamon Press.

Mahmood, S. (2005). *Politics of Piety: The Islamic Revival and the Feminist Subject,* (USA: Princeton University Press.

Malik Faris (undated) *Queer Sexuality and Identity In The Qur'an and the Hadith,* http://www.well.com/user/aquarius/Qurannotes.htm

Marcotte, R.D. (2003), "How Far Have Reforms Gone In Islam?", In *Women Studies International Forum,* Vol. 26(2), USA: Pergamon Press.

Mehryar, A., Ahmad-Nia, S. and Kazemipour, S. (2007). "Reproductive Health in Iran: Pragmatic Achievements, Unmet Needs, and Ethical Challenges in a Theocratic System", In *Studies in Family Planning,* Vol. 38(4) Wiley-Blackwell/The Population Council Mernissi, Fatima (1996) Women's Rebellion and The Islamic Memory.

Nazir, S. (2005). "Challenging Inequality: Obstacles and Opportunities Towards Women's Rights in the Middle East and North Africa", In *Journal of the Institute of Justice and International Studies*, Washington, USA: Freedom House.

Obermeyer, C.M. (1994). "Reproductive Choice in Islam: Gender and State in Iran and Tunisia", In *Studies in Family Planning,* 25(1), Wiley-Blackwell/ The Population Council.

Obermeyer, C.M. (1995). "A Cross-Cultural Perspective on Reproductive Rights", In *Human Rights Quarterly,* 17(2), Maryland, USA: John Hopkins University Press.

Riffat Hassan (2003). Women and Sexuality—Normative Islam versus Muslim Practice Paper presented at 2nd International Muslim Leaders Consultation on HIV and Aids.

Yamani, M. (1996). Feminism and Islam: Legal and Literary Perspectives, http://bit.ly/z1pttC

Zaidi, S., Ramarjan, A., Qui, R., Raucher, M., Chadwick, R. and Nossier, A. (2009). "Sexual rights and gender roles in a religious context", In *International Journal of Gynecology and Obstetrics,* Vol. 106, International Federation of Gynaecology and Obstetrics.

20

Cyber Crimes in India with Special Reference to Women in the Information Era*

Ghulam Yazdani

Introduction

The advantages of use of computers/any such devices along with internet are immense in the modern business and social life. The Science of Information technology has extensively developed over the last two decades and has turned out to be the nucleus of today's global and technological development. The worldwide network provides every user known as Netizen all the required information fastest beyond imagination. Information communication and its sharing with the help of tools making is possible in a friction of second's easily available as being precious source of information. With the advancement of internet, the occurrence of crime in the society by via internet has also broadened its roots in all directions. Factually commission of crime in cyber space is a constantly increasing phenomenon which is not only in India but all over the world. In a democratic country like India, the Internet has become a popular and integral feature of India's socio-political-cultural ethos. Long established traditional Newspapers, various public and private institutions/

* see, Ghulam Yazdani on Cyber Crimes against Women in National and International Perspective: Need for Effective Laws, Paper published in the Lex-Warrier-online Journal of Law, available at http://lex-warrier.in/2014/11/crimes-against-women-in-cyber-space-internet-crimes/#identifier_0_6707.

organizations and all political parties all maintain websites that serve as another medium through to attract, interact readers, members, volunteers, chat rooms, message boards and instant messaging programmes offer immediate and sometimes anonymous methods of communication with people all over the world. More recently, blogs or weblogs have become a pervasive feature of the cyber-world. The number of blogs increased exponentially after easy-to-use blog software became available free of charge in 1999.[1] Cyber crimes is a growing field of crime targeting everyone including the Institutions, Governments, non-State entities and individuals causing great damage to the social, economic, political and public and private life of the victims. The anonymous and the trans-national nature of the internet make it an easy weapon in the hands of the wrongdoer in the society. It is frightening to know that now a days even terrorists plot terror acts over the internet. Among others Women and Children are the most vulnerable to cyber crimes and they are habitually victimized. Internet provides an important platform in today's time to learn, discover, cultivate, advance and entertain oneself. All over the world individuals including women have been greatly emancipated by the use of internet technology by acquiring knowledge, learning new skills, opening up earning opportunities and a benevolent platform to express and entertain. While the internet has been a boon to women giving them an important means to communicate, it has also often been a bane for women who had been unfortunate victims of cyber crime.

It is true that cyber crime affects women in ways which are different from men. Cyber crimes against women which are usually sexual and implicit attack on the victim, apart from leading to a sense of insecurity and fear can severely impact the economic avenue open to the women, as it can drive women to move away from the use of internet technology, thereby snatching away all the benefits of internet which she is ideally suppose to enjoy as an individual member of the society.[2]

In this new era of technology it is matter of great concern to all of us to make sure so that women should not be deprived of using the cyber space due to fear of such targets by the man's world. The growing menace of cyber crimes and absence of legal mechanism, Policy makers and Legislators all over the globe have recognized the need to regulate the use of technology by everyone without any discrimination based on gender or otherwise. Laws have been enacted worldover to protect the governments, institutions and individuals from being victimized. Globally the initial attempts for legislative processes to make laws started slowly and they focused more upon the e-commerce aspect of cyber space dealing with the trade and commerce rather than focusing on preventing and punishing the offenders of such cyber offences.

The internet and its increased attraction bring opportunities and challenges simultaneously particularly to younger generation. Policy makers, legislators regulators, Judicial Officers, lawyers and teachers, NGOs, and individuals all grapple with how to address the many social and legal issues involved. Although there are many interesting issues, this chapter will only explore ideas on how to keep women, safe from sexual predators in the cyberspace using internet.

Nature and Meaning of Cyber Crimes: Present day, a wide range of adjectives are used to describe computer crime — virtual, online, cyber-digital, high-tech, computer-related, Internet-related, telecommunications-related, computer-assisted, electronic, and 'e-' (as in 'e-crime'). The concept of e-crime or cyber crime is not completely different from the concept of conventional crime. Both include conduct whether act or omission, which cause breach of rules of law counterbalanced by the sanction of the state. Computer crime or cyber crime refers to any crime that involves a computer and a network.[3] The computer may have been used in the commission of a crime, or it may be the target.[4] Cyber Crime is criminal activity done using computers and the Internet including downloading prohibited music records to thieving millions of dollars from online bank accounts. Cyber Crime also includes non-monetary offences, such as creating and distributing viruses on other computer or posting classified/confidential business or trade information on the Internet. The computer or such device may however be a target for unlawful acts in the following cases—unauthorized access to computer/computer system/ computer networks, theft of information contained in electronic form, e-mail bombing, data diddling, salami attacks, logic bombs, Trojan attacks, internet time thefts, web jacking, theft of computer system, physically damaging the computer system.[5]

It is an offence that is committed against individuals or groups of individuals with a criminal motive to intentionally harm the reputation of the sufferer or cause physical or mental harm to the victim directly or indirectly, using such system which is capable of transmitting the information from one place to other using modern communication networks.

Prior to this women are generally not yet get rid of different kinds of violence committed against her, new problem in the form of cyber crimes against women has posed the biggest challenge to whole world. Acknowledging the fact and looking into the domain of internet at international level, the UN Congress on Prevention of Cyber Crime and

Treatment of Offenders[6] defined Cyber Crime which comprises two categories a follows:

1. Cyber crimes in a narrow sense connotes a computer crime and includes any illegal behaviour directed by means of electronic operations that targets the security of the computer systems and the data processed by them.
2. Cyber crime in broader sense includes all computer related crimes and consists of any illegal behaviour committed by means of, or in relation to, a computer system or network, including such crimes as illegal possession and offering or distributing information by means of a computer system or network.

In the Indian context, cyber crime may be defined as a voluntary and willful act or omission that adversely affects a person or property or a person's computer systems. The term is a general term that covers crimes like phishing, credit card frauds, bank robbery, illegal downloading, industrial espionage, child pornography, kidnapping children via chat rooms, scams, cyber terrorism, creation and/or distribution of viruses, Spam and so on. Accordingly made punishable under the Information Technology Act, 2000 or liable to penal consequences under the Indian Penal Code.[7]

Different Kinds of Cyber Crimes: The following are the different kinds of cyber crimes:

1. **Unauthorized Access and Hacking:** Unauthorized access means any kind of access without the permission of either of the rightful person or person in-charge of the computer, computer system or computer network. Hacking means an illegal act of intrusion or breaking into a computer system and/or network with a desire to destruct the system to get personal monetary gains.
2. **Web Hijacking:** Web hijacking means taking forceful control of another person's website. In this case the owner of the website loses control over his website and its content.
3. **Pornography:** Pornography means showing sexual acts in order to cause sexual excitement. The definition of pornography also includes pornographic websites, pornographic magazines produced using computer and the internet pornography delivered over mobile phones. In Child Pornography on the internet, the Pedophiles start personal interaction with the children and then lure them to meet them. The children are then sexually exploited either by being used as sexual objects or by misusing their pornographic pictures for sale over the internet.

4. **Cyber Terrorism**: Targeted attacks involve target such as military installations, power plants, air traffic control, banks, trail traffic control, telecommunication networks. It also includes police, medical, fire and rescue systems etc. Cyber terrorism has become an attractive option for modern terrorists. The list of offenses given above is not exhaustive.
5. **Cyber Stalking**: Cyber Stalking means repeated acts of harassment or threatening conduct of the cyber criminal towards the victim by using internet services with a desire to control the victims life. It may include the acts like following the victim, making harassing phone calls, killing the victims pet, vandalizing victim's property, leaving written messages or objects etc.
6. **Denial of Service Attack:** This is an attack in which the criminal floods the bandwidth of the victim's network or fills his e-mail box with spam mail depriving him of the services he is entitled to access or provide. This kind of attack is designed to bring the network to crash by flooding it with useless traffic.
7. **Virus attacks:** Viruses are the programmes that have the capability to infect other programmes and make copies of itself and spread into other programme. Programmes that multiply like viruses but spread from computer to computer are called as worms. These are malicious software that attaches them to other software. For example: Virus, Worms, Trojan Horse, Time bomb, Logic Bomb, Rabbit and Bacterium.
8. **Software Piracy:** Software piracy refers to the illegal copying of genuine programmes or the counterfeiting and distribution of products intended to pass for the original. For example: copyright infringement, trademarks violations, theft of computer source code, patent violations.
9. **Salami attacks:** These attacks are used for the commission of financial crimes by making the alteration so insignificant that in a single case it would go completely unnoticed.
10. **Phishing:** Phishing is the act of sending an e-mail to a user falsely claiming to be an established legitimate enterprise in an attempt to scam the user into surrendering private information that will be used for identity theft.
11. **Sale of Illegal articles:** This category of cyber crimes includes sale of narcotics, weapons and wildlife etc., by posting information on websites, auction websites, and bulletin boards or simply by using e-mail communication.

12. **Online Gambling:** There are millions of websites; all hosted on servers abroad, that offer online gambling. In fact, it is believed that many of these websites are actually fronts for money laundering such as in case of Hawala Transactions.
13. **Email Spoofing:** Email spoofing refers to email that appears to originate from one source but actually has been sent from another source. Email spoofing can also cause monetary damage.
14. **Cyber Defamation:** When a person publishes defamatory matter about someone on a website or sends e-mails containing defamatory information to all of that person's friends, it is termed as cyber defamation.
15. **Forgery**: Computers, printers and scanners are used to forge counterfeit currency notes, postage and revenue stamps, mark sheets etc. These are made using computers, and high quality scanners and printers.
16. **Theft of information contained in Electronic form:** This includes theft of information stored in computer hard disks, removable storage media etc.
17. **Email Bombing:** Email bombing refers to sending a large number of emails to the victim resulting in the victim's email account (in case of an individual) or mail servers (in case of a company or an email service provider) crashing.
18. **Data Diddling:** This kind of an attack involves altering raw data just before it is processed by a computer and then changing it back after the processing is completed.
19. **Internet time theft:** Internet time refers to usage by an unauthorized person of the Internet hours paid for by another person.
20. **Theft of computer system:** This type of offence involves the theft of a computer, some part(s) of a computer or a peripheral attached to the computer.
21. **Physically damaging a computer system:** This crime is committed by physically damaging a computer or its peripherals.
22. **Breach of Privacy and Confidentiality**: Privacy refers to the right of an individual/s to determine when, how and to what extent his or her personal data will be shared with others. Breach of privacy means unauthorized use or distribution or disclosure of personal information. Confidentiality means non-disclosure of information to unauthorized or unwanted persons. For example Aadhar Card.

23. **Data diddling:** Data diddling involves changing data prior or during input into a computer. It includes automatic changing the financial information for some time before processing and then restoring original information.
24. **E-commerce/Investment Frauds**: It is an offering that uses false or fraudulent claims to solicit investments or loans, or that provides for the purchase, use, or trade of forged or counterfeit securities.

The following are the Cyber crimes under the Information Technology Act, 2000:

1. **Cyber crimes under the Information Technology Act, 2000**:
   - Tampering with Computer source documents—Sec.65
   - Hacking with Computer systems, Data alteration—Sec.66
   - Publishing obscene information—Sec.67
   - Un-authorized access to protected system Sec.70
   - Breach of Confidentiality and Privacy—Sec.72
   - Publishing false digital signature certificates—Sec.73
2. **Cyber Crimes under Indian Penal Code and Special Laws:**
   - Sending threatening messages by email—Sec. 503 IPC
   - Sending defamatory messages by email—Sec. 499 IPC
   - Forgery of electronic records—Sec. 463 IPC
   - Bogus websites, cyber frauds—Sec. 420 IPC
   - Email spoofing—Sec. 463 IPC
   - Web-Jacking—Sec. 383 IPC
   - E-Mail Abuse—Sec.500 IPC
3. **Cyber Crimes under the Special Acts**:
   - Online sale of Drugs under Narcotic Drugs and Psychotropic Substances Act
   - Online Sale of Arms under Arms Act

Cyber Violence against Women

Cyber crimes are committed against individuals as well as nations. Where in cyber crimes against individuals targets individual persons and it has been largely observed that women and children are more vulnerable to be victims of cyber crimes. They are easily targeted. In the men's world millions of women and girls are subjected to purposeful violence because of their being feminine. Violence against women and girls knows no boundaries/limits, cutting across borders, race, culture and income groups, extremely harming victims, people around them, and society as a whole. The International Community has urged governments and industry to work harder and more effectively together to better protect the growing number of women and girls who are victims of online threats and harassment.

The State should take necessary steps towards the sudden increase in the number of cyber crimes. Because, there is a different and additional disturbing statistic that goes on to suggest that nearly 13 per cent of the cases are targeted against outraging of modesty or blackmailing a woman. Over the years, the cyber crimes reported have risen by nearly 63.7 per cent.

If we really need to do something on the matter then we should stop the culture of denial and victim-blaming. Even the National Commission for Women had organized a consultation on "Ways and means to safeguard women from cyber crime in India" on 23rd July, 2014.[8] In a statement released after a day-long consultation on cyber crimes against women, the NCW called for sensitizing police regarding cyber crimes. The panelists called the government to provide proper guidelines for intermediaries to pull down any content offensive to women. Other suggestions called for an awareness training programme as part of curriculum in laws, and proper implementation of the Information Technology Act.[9]

Types of Cyber Offences against Women

Though, the life of women never was smooth in every period. The occurrence and the frequency of wrongs/crimes caused, are countless in her way amongst the various cyber crimes committed against women. Main crimes can be identified which are notorious and detrimental to her dignity and freedom are listed as under:

(A) Cyber Harassment: It is a repetitive behaviour intended to disturb or up rest a person through use of internet. The medium of emails and social networking sites are generally used to target women for harassment by way of blackmailing, threatening, bullying, cheating, impersonation etc. Section 67-A[10], 67-B[11] of the Information Technology Act provide Sexual harassment in respect of offences of publishing or transmitting of material containing sexually explicit act and child pornography in electronic form.

(B) Cyber Stalking: 'Stalking' in general means a harassing or threatening behaviour which an individual exhibits towards the other. "Stalking is a unique crime in that it is composed of a series of otherwise legal acts. Cyber stalking in particular is composed of words alone and therefore stands more distinctly as apart as a crime of accumulation. As one sociologist described it, "the separated acts that make up the intrusion cannot by themselves cause the mental abuse, but do taken together (cumulative effect)."[12] Cyber stalking, which is simply an extension of the physical form of stalking is where the electronic mediums such as internet are used to pursue, harass or contact another in unsolicited fashion.[13]

It is pertinent to know that Cyber Stalking is a behaviour wherein an individual willfully and repeatedly engages in a knowing course of harassing conduct directed at another person which reasonably and seriously alarms, torments, or terrorizes that person. Cyber Stalking usually occurs with women, who are stalked by men, or children who are stalked by adult predators or pedophiles. The motives behind cyber stalking have been divided into four reasons, namely, for sexual harassment, for obsession for love, for revenge and hate and for ego and power trips. The availability of free email and website space, as well as the anonymity provided by these chat rooms and forums, has contributed to the increase of cyber stalking as a form of harassment.[14] Why not the access of internet is being made based on identity of user strictly without any delay?

(C) Cyber Pornography: The word *porné* stands for *prostitute*, and *graphein* stands for *documentary*. Pornography literally means "Documenting a Prostitute" or "Depictions of acts of Prostitutes". Pornography in the eyes of law is not necessarily obscene. Today, the largest industry of Internet is Adult Entertainment. There are millions of individually owned pornographic websites. Research shows that 50 per cent of the web-sites containing potentially illegal contents relating to child abuse were 'Pay-Per-View'. This indicates that abusive images of children over Internet have been highly commercialized. Currently, there is no law against viewing pornography. The Indian Penal Code and the recent IT Act both prohibit the production and transmission of "obscene material". The IT Act stipulates three years in jail for publishing and transmitting obscene material electronically.[15]

Cyber Pornography is pornography that is distributed via the internet, primarily via websites, peer to peer file sharing, or Usenet newsgroup. Internet has provided a medium for the facilitation of crimes like pornography.[16] Child abuse, sexual violence against women, juvenile delinquency and other sexual crimes are the direct effect of pornographic images. Due to easy access to worldwide web through new multi-media technology, cyber pornography and other cyber crimes are increasing every second.

The Information Technology has built up the nature of the crime of cyber pornography in such a way that it has made it much easier to create and distribute pornographic material through internet. Such material could be transmitted all over the world in matter of seconds. Moreover, the social and moral deterrence of buying a porn magazine from a bus stand/ Railway stations or shop is no more there as anyone can now easily access pornographic material online with complete anonymity. Further child pornography, which is aggravated form of pornography is a much serious offence and consequently demands more stringent measures. The present Information Technology law enables the law enforcement agencies to take strict action against that seeking child pornography and its violation can lead to seven year term in jail and up to ten lac rupees fine.[17]

(D) Cyber Defamation: Cyber tort is a willful act done by a person on internet that may cause legal injuries to virtual identity or virtual property of a person in cyberspace. Cyber tort including libel and defamation is another common crime against women in the net. This occurs when defamation takes place with the help of computers and or the Internet. E.g. someone publishes defamatory matter about someone on a website or sends e-mails containing defamatory information to all of that person's friends.[18]

(E) Morphing: Morphing is editing the original picture so as to make it look completely or largely different. Often criminally minded elements of the cyber world download pictures of girls from websites such as Face book and then morph it with another picture in compromising situation so as to represent that those women were indulging in such acts. Often the next step after this is to blackmail those women through the threat of releasing the morphed images and diminishing the status of those women in society. Such acts can be penalized under I.T. Act, 2000 and attracts Sections 43[19] and 66[20] of the same. The violator of such crime can also be booked under Indian Penal Code of Sec. 509. For the purposes of this section, the word 'dishonestly' and 'fraudulently' shall have the meaning assigned to it in sections 24 and 25 of the Indian Penal Code, of 1860.

(F) Email Spoofing: E-mail spoofing is a term used to describe fraudulent email activity in which the sender address and other parts of the email header are altered to appear as though the email originated from a different source; it is done by properties of the email, such as the From, Return-Path and Reply-To fields, ill-intentioned users can make the email appear to be from someone other than the actual sender.

Position of Women in India

The Information Technology Act, 2000

In 1999, Indian Government, formed the Ministry of Information Technology. India was on the path to making India IT superpower. The impact of Glabalisation in the country was so imminent that in less than a year, India has made the enactment of its first statute relating to Information Technology on the pattern of Model Law on Electronic Commerce, 1996, adopted by the United Nations Commission on International Trade Law (UNCITRAL). The Electronic Transaction Act of 1998 of Singapore also significantly guided the framing of the Indian Act. The Information Technology Act, 2000 was passed by the Parliament on May 15, 2000, approved by the President on June 9, 2000 and notified to come into force on October 17, 2000. The Act, seeks to protect this advancement in technology by defining crimes, prescribing punishments, laying down procedures for investigation and forming regulatory authorities.[21]

The Information Technology Act, 2000 initially consisted of XIII Chapters and 4 Schedules and 94 Sections. Two schedules have been deleted by the Information Technology (Amendment) Act, 2008. At present it has 2 Schedules. Chapters IX and XI covers up offences and penalties. The Information Technology Act, 2000 nor defines 'cyber crimes' neither uses this expression, but only provides the definition and punishment for certain offences. It can be concluded that Information Technology Act, 2000 provides punishment for only certain offences and is not exhaustive of all cyber crimes.

The Information Technology (Amendment) Act, 2008 also added Section 66A which prohibited the sending of offensive messages through a communication device (i.e. through an online medium). The types of information covered were offensive messages of a menacing character, or a message that the sender knows to be false but is sent for the purpose of 'causing annoyance, inconvenience, danger, obstruction, insult, injury, criminal intimidation, enmity, hatred, or ill will'. However, the provision was challenged on the ground of vagueness, arbitrariness and misuse and was ultimately struck down by the Supreme Court in the case of Shreya Singhal.[22] In light of the sexual harassment, abuse and intimidation faced by women on the internet, the section could have provided for a proper remedy.

The crucial problems, which are confronted with Cyber-Crimes in general, are Jurisdictional issues, Loss of evidence, Lack of Cyber Cops, Army and Cyber savvy Judges who are the need of the day. Judiciary plays a vital role in shaping and interpreting the provisions of the enactment according to regulate and to suppress the mischief. The IT Act 2000 does not mention the typical cyber crimes like cyber stalking, morphing and email spoofing as offences. The Indian law is still unequipped to deal with various cyber offences against women such as revenge porn.[23]

Conclusion

In the contemporary era there is abundance of knowledge in every sphere of life. The world has become very small and has come to be known as global village. The means of communication have become very fast. Any kind of Information from any corner and from unknown place of the world can be obtained within minutes with the help of the Internet. Strict privacy and safety measures should be the utmost concern by the law-makers in order to deal with the cyber crimes against women. Every now and then we believe that we are making some development but every single time the visible progress is speedily followed by a return to the status quo. As the Internet is a not having boundaries known as borderless medium which allows instantaneous and anonymous distribution of one's message, and the follower/stalker has the protection of the "veil of anonymity. Creating awareness about the possible harms of the online world along with education to curb the interaction/access of illegal and immoral elements in the society by way of privacy features can go a long way in protecting women. It is fact that laws play an important role in combating crimes in any society, indisputably, over the years, India has witnessed huge developments as far as law and policy making for the protection of women and children. The recent Criminal Law Amendment Act, 2013 provides some respite with section 354 (B) that takes cognizance of online stalking, voyeurism and releasing of private moments in compromising situations online. However, our laws are inadequate to handle cases of cyber violence.

To keep away from the cyber-crime we should desist from making conversation with people we don't know. People on the other end of the computer may not be who they claim to be. We must keep our passwords protected and do not keep sensitive material on the computer as that can be accessed by the hacker. If anything seems out of place or wrong, contact law enforcement immediately without any delay to nearest cyber Police Stations.

For women, violence online and offline is supplementary and complimentary to each other. Abuse may be confined to networked technologies or may be supplemented with offline harassment including vandalism, phone calls and physical assault. It is pertinent to mention that measures such as skill training and sensitizing the police, conducting awareness programmes at the grassroots level, proper implementation of the IT Act, 2000. As per the guidelines to pull down offensive material should be done fully. To effectively combat cyber violence against women both the restructuring of laws and creating awareness to avoid victimization and to take proper steps for redress are important. At the end to achieve a place of joy in the digital era while searching safe and secure root for the Internet citizens will have to be articulate and choose a coherent set of values to live by online and feel happy. As time passes, one aspect of governance should be clear and visible, the will of government to be "seen and felt" on the Internet the issues of women.

Notes

1. See, Melissa Y. Lerner (2010). "Connecting the Actual with the Virtual: The Internet and Social Movement Theory in the Muslim World—The Cases of Iran and Egypt", In *Journal of Muslim Minority Affairs*, 30(4): 555.
2. Danielle Keats Citron, *Law's Expressive Value in Combating Cyber Gender Harassment*, available at http://digitalcommons.law.umaryland.edu/cgi/viewcontent.cgi?article=1687&context=fac_pubs
3. Moore, R. (2005). *Cyber crime: Investigating High-Technology Computer Crime*, Cleveland, Mississippi: Anderson Publishing.
4. Warren G. Kruse and Jay G. Heiser (2002). *Computer forensics: Incident Response Essentials 392* (Addison-Wesley Longman Publishing Co., Inc. Boston, MA, USA © 2002.
5. Dr. Atul Bamrara (2012). "The Challenge of Cyber Crime in India: The Role of Government", *Pakistan Journal of Criminology*, 3: 127-134.
6. See, Tenth UN Congress on Prevention of Crime & Treatment of Offenders was held in Vienna on April 10-17, 2000.
7. See, Rodney, D. Ryder, *Introduction to Internet Law & Policy*, 1st Edition, 2007, Wadhwa & Company, Nagpur. Also see, Dr. Vishwanath Paranjape, *Legal Dimensions of Cyber Crimes and Preventive Laws*, Central Law Agency, Allahabad.
8. http://ncw.nic.in/Pressrelease23072014.pdf (last visited on October 10, 2014)
9. http://www.business-standard.com/article/news-ians/ncw-seeks-guidelines-on-online-content-offensive-to-women-114072401659_1.html (last visited on October 15, 2014)

10. Section 67A. Punishment for publishing or transmitting of material containing sexually explicit act, etc., in electronic form—Whoever publishes or transmits or causes to be published or transmitted in the electronic form any material which contains sexually explicit act or conduct shall be punished on first conviction with imprisonment of either description for a term which may extend to five years and with fine which may extend to ten lakh rupees and in the event of second or subsequent conviction with imprisonment of either description for a term which may extend to seven years and also with fine which may extend to ten lakh rupees.
11. See, Section 67B. Punishment for publishing or transmitting of material depicting children in sexually explicit act, etc. in electronic form. Whoever,—
    (a) publishes or transmits or causes to be published or transmitted material in any electronic form which depicts children engaged in sexually explicit act or conduct or
    (b) creates text or digital images, collects, seeks, browses, downloads, advertises, promotes, exchanges or distributes material in any electronic form depicting children in obscene or indecent or sexually explicit manner or
    (c) cultivates, entices or induces children to online relationship with one or more children for and on sexually explicit act or in a manner that may offend a reasonable adult on the computer resource or
    (d) facilitates abusing children online or
    (e) records in any electronic form own abuse or that of others pertaining to sexually explicit act with children, shall be punished on first conviction with imprisonment of either description for a term which may extend to five years and with a fine which may extend to ten lakh rupees and in the event of second or subsequent conviction with imprisonment of either description for a term which may extend to seven years and also with fine which may extend to ten lakh rupees:
    Provided that the provisions of section 67, section 67A and this section does not extend to any book, pamphlet, paper, writing, drawing, painting, representation or figure in electronic form—
    (i) The publication of which is proved to be justified as being for the public good on the ground that such book, pamphlet, paper writing, drawing, painting, representation or figure is in the interest of science, literature, art or learning or other objects of general concern; or
    (ii) which is kept or used for bonafide heritage or religious purposes.
    Explanation: For the purposes of this section, "children" means a person who has not completed the age of 18 years.
12. Lambèr Royakkers, Cyberstalking: menaced on the internet, cited in West's Encyclopedia of American Law, available at http://www.sociosite.org/cyberstalking_en.php as cited by Merritt Baer, Cyberstalking and the Internet Landscape We Have Constructed in Virginia Journal of Law & Technology Fall 2010, University of Virginia Vol. 15, No. 154.

13. Wayne Pethererick, "Cyber-Stalking: Obsessional Pursuit and the Digital Criminal". CrimeLibrary.com. as quoted in Chapter 5.
14. Debarati Halder, "Cyber Crimes Against Women in India", http://www.cyberlawtimes.com/articles/103.html (last visited on November 17, 2014). For further detail see *Cyber Crimes against Women in India* by Debarati Halder and K. Jaishankarapa (American Psychological Assoc.) *Cyber Crimes Against Women in India*, 2016, Sage Publications Pvt. Ltd.
15. http://www.livemint.com/Politics/3MpSaU1JOWj0I23Tm521NL/PIL-in-Supreme-Court-seeks-ban-on-Internet-pornography.html/(last visited on April 16, 2013).
16. See, Mohit Mittal, "Issue of Jurisdiction in Combating Cyber Crimes: Issues and Challenges Pornography and Indian Jurisdiction" Available at http://www.legalservicesindia.com/article/print.php?art_id=1386
17. See, Charandeep Singh Samrao (2013). *Cyber Crimes*, Delhi: Random Publications.
18. Available at http://dictionary.reverso.net/english-definition/Cybertort (last visited on September 17, 2014).
19. Section 43 of the Information Technology Act, 2000: Penalty and compensation for damage to computer, computer system, etc.
    If any person without permission of the owner or any other person who is in charge of a computer, computer system or computer network, or computer resource—
    1. accesses or secures access to such computer, computer system or computer network;
    2. downloads, copies or extracts any data, computer data base or information from such computer, computer system or computer network including information or data held or stored in any removable storage medium;
    3. introduces or causes to be introduced any computer contaminant or computer virus into any computer, computer system or computer network;
    4. damages or causes to be damaged any computer, computer system or computer network, data, computer data base or any other programmes residing in such computer, computer system or computer network;
    5. disrupts or causes disruption of any computer, computer system or computer network;
    6. denies or causes the denial of access to any person authorised to access any computer, computer system or computer network by any means; (g) provides any assistance to any person to facilitate access to a computer, computer system or computer network in contravention of the provisions of this Act, rules or regulations made thereunder;
    7. charges the services availed of by a person to the account of another person by tampering with or manipulating any computer, computer system, or computer network, he shall be liable to pay damages by way of compensation to the person so affected.
    8. destroys, deletes or alters any information residing in a computer resource or diminishes its value or utility or affects it injuriously by any means;

9. steel, conceals, destroys or alters or causes any person to steal, conceal, destroy or alter any computer source code used for a computer resource with an intention to cause damage.
20. see, Section 66 Computer related offences. —If any person, dishonestly or fraudulently, does any act referred to in section 43, he shall be punishable with imprisonment for a term which may extend to three years or with fine which may extend to five lakh rupees or with both.
21. K.P. Malik (2010). *Computer and Information Technology Law*, Allahabad Law Agency.
22. *Shreya Singhal v. Union of India*, (2013) 12 SCC 73.
23. Debarati Halder and K. Jaishankar (2008). "Cyber crimes against women in india", *TMC Academy Journal*, Singapore, 3(1): 48-62.

SECTION-IV
Growth, Governance and Development

21
Inclusive Growth and Sustainable Development

Suresh Prasad Singh

Introduction

The main objective of public policies in India is to propel the country to a global leadership position while ensuring that no Indian is left behind. It is intended to leverage talent, entrepreneurship and energy to catapult the country to the status of a developed nation. The concept of Inclusive Growth ensures that every citizen is included in the growth regardless of his caste, creed, gender, sex, economic class and religion, focusing on productive employment rather than merely direct income redistribution as a means of increasing income for an excluded group. It does not propose a faster growth but a growth that ensures broad based improvement in the quality of life of every citizen especially the poor and downtrodden persons of the society. Equal opportunities should be provided to all. The main concept of Inclusive Growth is the type of inclusion of the excluded group of the society into the mainstream of the society so that they are able to enjoy the benefits of faster economic growth. This concept expands upon the traditional economic growth models to include equity of health, social protection, food security, human capital, environmental quality and other basic needs which are essential for survival. The goals of Inclusive Growth cannot be achieved unless we have a new society with equity at all levels—social, economic, political and cultural.

If the evils of poverty and hunger, inequalities and deficiencies exist in any part of the society there can be no Inclusive Growth. Social and economic equity is the essential condition for the human development. If the rich get richer and poor becomes more in number, the growth cannot be perceived as inclusive. Generation of employment of livelihood opportunities, removal of regional and social disparities, poverty alleviation, agricultural and industrial growth and environmental sustainability are the key factors of inclusive growth. It is a strategy where the growth will be achieved through certain instrumentalists so that the benefits reach the every person of the society.

Detailed Explanation

In developing countries like India, Inclusive Growth means serious governmental schemes and support to get the desired rate of economic growth and human development. The challenge in India is to foster Economic Growth, wealth distribution, development of the underprivileged and downtrodden by providing quality education for all, increasing agricultural production, adopting post-harvest technologies and industrial development and skill development. It also encompasses a growth process that is eco-friendly aims for good governance and helps in creating a gender sensitive society. Serious efforts should be made to increase employment opportunities which are necessary condition for improvement in the standard of living of the people. The Government of India has launched various programmers for the improvement in the domain of education, health, infrastructure etc. e.g. Mahatma Gandhi National Rural Employment Guarantee Act (MGNREGA), Sarva Seva Abhiyan (SSA), National Rural Health Mission (NRHM), Bharat Nirman etc. These projects have definitely alleviated the poverty and raised the standard of living of the masses but still a lot has to be done to completely eradicate the poverty.

Table 21.1: Average GDP Growth per Year

1947-77	3.5
1980	5.6
1990	5.8
2005-10	8.5
2011	7.6
2013-15	7.5
2016-17	7.3

The GDP Annual Growth Rate in India averaged 6.08 per cent from 1951 until 2016, reaching an all time high of 11.40 per cent in the first quarter of 2010 and a record low of – 5.20 per cent in the fourth quarter of 1979. There has been phenomenal improvement in economic growth and social development of India since Independence. After the post-reform period India has done extremely well in some of the Indicators like Balance of payment resilience to shock and growth of service sector. There has been significant growth of IT sector, improvement in Telecommunication, accumulation of foreign exchange reserves and increasing investment and saving rates. But the average Unemployment rate has gone down by 9 per cent from 1983 to 2011.

Poverty is an important issue in India despite having one of the fastest growing economics in the world at the growth rate of 7.3 per cent in 2016. If current trends continues India's share of world GDP will increase from 7.3 per cent in 2016 to 8.5 per cent by 2020. According to Millennium Development Programme (MDG) programme 270m. or 21.9 per cent people out of 1.23 b of Indian lived below poverty line of $.25 in 2011-12. The World Bank revised poverty calculation methodology and purchases power parity (PPP). According to this world had 872.3 m. below the new poverty line of which 179.6 m people lived in India. Some of the main causes of poverty in India are lack of education, overpopulation, epidemic diseases, environmental problems and reduction of agricultural production due to poor water resource management. However, it is a matter of pleasure that World Bank's Global Monitoring Report for 2014-15 on the MDG advocates that India has been the single largest contributor to poverty reduction in the recent years.

The performance of Agriculture sector in India during the recent years has declined due to the following main factors:

(a) Inefficient use of resources.
(b) Increased Non-agricultural demand, due to higher GDP growth and urbanization.
(c) Frequent changing of world commodity prices.
(d) Fall in agricultural growth.

The agriculture growth in India is low due to:

(a) Low literacy rate
(b) Malnutrition
(c) Lack of employment skills
(d) High dropout rate in education
(e) High expenditure on health care in rural population.

The Inclusive Growth reemphasizes economic growth which is the main factor for poverty alleviation. It adopts a long-term perspective and is concerned about inequalities and exclusion. Late honourable president Dr. A.P.J. Abdul Kalam has advocated the following concept for the Inclusive Growth and profile of a globally competitive nation:

1. A nation where the rural and urban divide has reduced to a thin line.
2. A nation where there is an equitable distribution and access to energy and quality water.
3. A nation where agriculture, industry and service sector work together in symphony, absorbing technology thereby resulting in sustained wealth-generation leading to greater high value employment opportunities.
4. A nation where education is not denied to any meritorious candidates because of societal or economic discrimination or because of constraints of rules.
5. A nation which is the best destination for the most talented scholars, scientists, and investors from all-over the world.
6. A nation where the best of healthcare is available to all and the communicable diseases like AIDS/TB, water and vector borne diseases and other stress diseases, cardiac diseases, cancer and diabetes are brought down.
7. A nation where the governance uses the best of the technologies to be responsive, transparent, fully connected in a high bandwidth e-governance grid, easily accessible and also simple in rules, thereby corruption free.
8. A nation where poverty has been totally eradicated, illiteracy removed and crimes against women are absent and none in the society feels unalienated.
9. A nation that is prosperous, healthy, secure, peaceful and happy and continues with a sustainable growth path.
10. A nation that is one of the best places to live in on the earth and brings smiles on the one billion-plus faces.

Role of Education in Inclusive Growth

It is the education which is the backdrop of all the developmental process whether it is social, political, economical or spiritual. At present the higher education system comprises of about 17 m. students in 634 Universities

(UGC 2012) as compared to 0.2 m. students and 20 universities during 1950-51. The country is the third largest system in the word after China and USA in terms of enrolment and largest in the world in terms of number of higher education institutions. Now here the question arises — Is the education system imparting quality education? Is it playing its important role in Inclusive Growth and development process of the masses? But the fact is millions of unemployable graduates have been produced, who have little practical knowledge and skills and thus not capable of earning a living commensurate with their qualification.

Quality has been casualty in the wake of unconsolidated expansion in the field of higher education. The phenomenal rise in the number of colleges and universities may be attributed to social needs and aspirations of the Indian society to have access to them. This expansion would not have marred quality, had it been accompanied by sincere measures of consolidation and conformation of minimum standards and also by a perspective plan of linking universities with production units for ensuring growth target.

A good system of Education can be judged by these indicators:

(A) What does it do for the society or the nation—

- Is the society growing richer?
- Is there enough material production and materialistic gains?
- Does the socio-economic system permit equitable distribution of wealth and production?
- Is there a reduction in the drudgery of the common man?
- Does the system permit pursuit of excellence?
- Does the system permit inculcation and establishment of ethical and personal values along with pursuit of justice, Freedom, Compassion and Fearlessness?
- Do the people have a sense of commitment towards:
  - (a) The society,
  - (b) The cultural and philosophical heritage,
  - (c) The Nation,
- Do people regard contentedness as a cherished value?
- Does the society uphold truth as the ultimate goal?

(B) What does it do for the Individual:

The education for an individual,

- Must make her to the pursuit of excellence.
- Must encourage her to the pursuit of excellence.
- Must build up the sense of compassion and friendliness towards others.

- Must build up the sense belonging towards the society and nation.
- Must bring in appreciation of social harmony.
- Must inculcate dignity of human life and human labour.

The present education lacks in many ways and a listing of the same also suggests the remedial action that can be taken urgently.

- Too costly—Not affordable to a vast majority.
- Too discriminatory — promotes cliches and division in society among the haves and have-nots, among the elite and the common and to some extent between man and woman.
- Does not teach quest of knowledge or Rigour of Experimentation. The country's capabilities for research are at low ebb.
- Does not teach to question the veracity of basic assumption. This leads to non-development of a philosophical perspective.
- Vocation and skill training is missing — The budget, facilities and innovative ideas for vocational training are lacking even at a concept level.
- Too much emphasis on form and procedure such as compulsory attendance.
- Poor sense of dedication and self-respect among teachers—no teaching through heart.
- Poor quality of teaching — mushrooming coaching classes must be seen as its index.
- Lack of facilities to develop the attitude and skills for Sports, Art and Theater.
- A wall of impregnability between them. A smooth transition is a needed input to upgrade their training, skills and knowledge. Women are affected must more by this because they learn many skills informally.
- Promotes rat-race and a philosophy of dissatisfaction, frustration and non-compassion.
- No recognition or provision for the End-of-Spectrum students — neither for the genius nor for the handicapped.
- No recognition for experience and expertise obtained through life-experience.
- No proper methodology for Value education—Values are inculcated amongst individuals through their Role Models. In the society values are inculcated through long standing traditions.

Both the role models and the traditions have to be re-emphasized through their dynamic interpretation relevant to the contemporary psych.

- Utterly moved away from a lifestyle compatible for a country that boasts for being 75 per cent agricultural in occupation and geographically needs to keep the agricultural emphasis.

Low Carbon Inclusive Growth Key to Sustainable Development

Inclusive Growth encompasses a growth process that is environment friendly growth. India's effort in this regard is praiseworthy as it is one of the lowest Green-House Gas (GHG) emitters in the world. Low carbon Inclusive Growth is the priority in 12th Five Years Plan. India can reduce its emission intensity by 25 per cent by 2020 as proposed by India at Copenhagen, with a more aggressive effect even 35 per cent reduction is possible even with 8 or 9 per cent growth. Energy efficient appliances, Vehicles, buildings and Industrial processes are needed. Solar, wind and Nuclear Technology required for electricity generation sector in future.

India's emissions in 2008 were 1.3 tonnes/capita. Global average per capita emissions were more than 3 times; china 4 times, the US 14 times and EU 6 times as much as India's. Taking into account growth since 2008 and other GHG, India's emissions per capita are probably around 2 tonnes CO_2e (CO_2 equivalent). Annual Global emissions are close to 506 tonnes CO_2e/annum. This must be reduced to less than 35b. tonnes in 2030 and less than 20b. tonnes in 2030, if we want temperature does not increase to 2 degree Celsius above the 19th Century level which was internationally agreed in Cancum in 2010. India total emission are now around 2.5 b. tonnes CO_2e and likely to be doubled in the next 10 yrs towards 5b. tonnes that is still below the emission level of rich and developed countries.

India has already taken a number of measures. These include a tax of Rs. 50/tonne of coal to promote renewable energy; various incentives for the promotion of wind power and solar energy; the Green India Mission, the Energy efficiency mission, Encouragement of Energy effective building, development of dedicated freight train corridors to shift the movement of goods from trucks to trains and development of public transport systems in cities.

Technology is the most important strategy to mitigate climate change with the participation by common people. Reduction of Carbon footprints from Industries and other sectors improves the environmental sustainability. Growth of Industry and agriculture will undoubtedly uplift the GDP of the country and GDP is directly linked with Carbon emission. It is a fact that a higher GDP will lead to higher income generation and higher living standard of people, who will be more and more dependent on energy efficient machinery which in turn will increase the total emission of the country. But appropriate climate-responsive technologies can balance the conflict between Inclusive Growth and sustainable development. Appropriate technology is the key enabler to achieve sustainable livelihood, reduction poverty and improvement of quality of life for the downtrodden, at a lower cost and with less impact on environment. With the larger participation of the excluded section of the society, they are sensitized about eco-friendly technologies and renewable energy sources.

Low Carbon Emission by Recent Technological Development

Technological developments in the past decades and especially after the 1980s have delivered spectacular improvements in the environmental quality, cleaner air and water low emissions automobiles, less toxic and hazards wastes, water and energy efficient homes and appliances etc.

Some of the recent technological achievements which emit low carbon are as follows:

- A significant reduction in the air borne lead (Pb) has been achieved by developing 'lead free' petrol and use of natural gas and ethanol as auto-fuel.
- More fuel efficient, quieter and less polluting automobiles driven on environmentally benign auto-fuels like compressed natural gas (CNG), liquified petroleum gas (LPG) and ethanol, less body and wheel weight and aerodynamic bodies to introduce less resistance to wind.
- More energy efficient electrical appliances and instruments such as automatic lighting control system (ALCS), compact fluorescent light bulbs, low voltage tungsten halogen and sodium lamps etc. they save electricity from 70-80 per cent.
- The 'flue gas desulfurization technology' (FGDT) in coal power plants have led to significant reduction in sulfur dioxide (SO_2) emission and acid rains.
- The 'coal gasification technology' (CGT) in coal power plants

has led to significant reduction in the greenhouse gas carbon dioxide (CO_2).

- The 'solar photo voltaic cell technology' (SPVCT) has brought a new era in economic lighting and heating devices and reduction in greenhouse gas (CO_2).
- Partial plugging of the 'ozone hole' in the stratosphere has been achieved by developing lesser evil substitute Hydro Chloro Fluro Carbon (HCFC) which has 30 per cent less ODP than CFC.
- A significant reduction in the waste of portable water has been achieved by developing 'automatic closing taps', 'water efficient showers', and 'dual-flushing cisterns' in the bathrooms and toilets and development of 'sprinkler and drip' irrigation system in the agriculture.

Sustainable Development

In 1987, the world commission on Environment and Development of the United Nations (UNCED) was established. This commission published famous Burndt Land Report which defined sustainable development as 'development that meets the needs of the present without compromising the ability of future generations to meet their own needs'. This has been interpreted as meaning that each generation must rely on the use of renewable resources, and to reuse and recycle waste materials before considering taking 'virgin' resources from the earth which cannot be replaced. In this way we must adopt a way of life which passes on the earth's resources undiminished to the next generation. This encompasses the concepts of 'stewardship' of the earth, and living within its 'carrying capacity'.

The key objectives of sustainability include:

- Reviving economic growth so that it has a reduced impact on the environment by using less materials and energy;
- Meeting essential needs for jobs, food, energy, water and sanitation;
- Ensuring a sustainable level of population;
- Conserving and enhancing our natural resource base;
- Reorienting technology and managing risk;
- Merging ecological and economic considerations in decision-making.

The key to growing sustainable is not to produce less but to produce differently in a way which is environment friendly and compatible i.e. by embracing the philosophy of 'Cleaner Production'; not to consume less but to consume judiciously and efficiently within the regenerative capacity of the Earth ecosystems and with minimum waste generation.

The local concerns are air, water and noise pollution, declining groundwater table and increasing shortage of potable water, chemical spills and contaminated sites (land), acid sulfate soil, indoor air. The regional concerns are rural decline, declining rain and depleting natural water resources, increasing soil salinity, increasing natural and man-made disasters, disposal of chemical and radioactive wastes, ocean oil spills and marine pollution, degrading coastal ecosystems, acid rains etc. The global environmental concerns are threat of global warming and climate change, stratospheric ozone depletion, deforestation and biodiversity erosion, overpopulation and resource depletion specially in poor developing countries. Stockholm Conference (1972) was a landmark towards the development of global consensus on the need of environmental protection leading to sustainable development. The world leaders declared—Man is both creature and moulder of his environment, which gives him physical sustenance and affords him the opportunity for intellectual, moral, social and spiritual growth. Both aspects of man's environment the natural and man-made are essential to his well-being and to the enjoyment of basic human rights the right to life itself.

Bruntd Land Commission Report on Sustainable Development (1987) was a system of socio-economic development to meet the 'needs' (but not the 'greed') of the present generation without compromising with the abilities of the future generations to meet their own needs. A system of stable socio-economic and ecological development that should improve the total quality of all life. (Human beings, plants and animals) on Earth now and in the future too, while maintaining the social and ecological integrity of the earth upon which all life depends. A system of socio-economic development which can provide good quality of life to all the people.

UN Conference on Environment and Development

The Agenda 21 (agenda for 21st century) was adopted at UNCED. It was the blueprint for global sustainable development. In the opening lines of Agenda 21, the nations of the world pronounced that—'Humanity stands at defining moment in history. We are confronted with a perpetuation of disparities between and within nations, a worsening of poverty, ill health and illiteracy, and the continuing deterioration of natural ecosystems on which we depend for our well- being. However, integration of environment and development concerns and greater attention to them will lead to the fulfilment of basic needs, improved living standards for all, better protected and managed ecosystems and a safer more prosperous future. No nation can achieve this on its own, but together we can—in a global partnership for sustainable development."

3rd World Summit on Sustainable Development (WSSD), Johannesburg, S.A., 2002

These are some of the disheartening episodes of the efforts made towards achieving global human sustainability—

- (Piling waste), lurched from bad to worse. On the socio-economic front, the rich and the powerful got richer and more powerful while the poor became poorer and weaker. The concept of 'sustainable development' and the much lauded movement sustainability remained on paper.
- In the 10 years between Rio (1992) and Johannesburg (2002), critical environmental problems such as greenhouse gas emission (global warming), loss of old growth and primary forests (biodiversity erosion), ocean plunder and waste of resources.
- Two billion people currently do not have access to modern energy services.
- About 1.1 billion people globally do not have access to safe drinking water. It is predicted that water supply will be the major constrains on sustainable development in the 21st century.
- About 2.4 billion people lack adequate and improved sanitation.
- More than 1.2 billion people still live on less than 1 dollar a day.
- More than 3 million people die of air pollution, and the same number dies from diseases caused by unsafe and polluted water. The same number dies from diseases caused by unsafe and polluted water. The target of 'Health for All by the Year 2000' never became a reality.
- 'New highly toxic chemicals'e.g. N-nitrosodimethylamine (a principal ingredient in rocket fuel), methyl tertiary butyl ether (a gasoline additive), and acrylonitrile (used in textile industry) have appeared in surface and ground water.

- Half of the tropical rainforests and mangroves (treasure of pristine biodiversity) have already been lost.
- About 75 per cent of the marine fisheries have been fished to capacity.
- In September 2000, the ozone hole over Antarctica covered more than 28 million square kilometers.
- Some 75 billion tonnes of 'top soil' (the fertile layer) are eroding every year. Around 2 billion hectares of soil—15 per cent of Earth's land is now classed as degraded.

The Strategies for Sustainable Development

Sustainable development will deliver social, economic and ecological benefits, for it will conserve resources, reduce waste, prevent loss of energy and protect human health. The new paradigm of development is not the game of economics alone. All issues—economic, ecological, social (health), cultural (educational), legal (legislative), political and technology have to be merged into a collective decision making for sustainable development. Earlier economy was at the centre of decision-making. This assumed that all environmental problem could be solved if economy was sound. This has now become an obsolete theory. Now ecology has to be at the centre. We have to integrate ecological thinking into social and economic planning. The developmental activities have to be 'economically viable', 'ecologically compatible', 'socially equitable', 'culturally acceptable' and 'politically justifiable'. Then only it can be environmentally sustainable. This will require giving up the 'culture of consumerism', 'producing less consumers' that the Earth can sustain and also achieving 'equity in resource use and consumption' across the world. Over- consumerism and too much of prosperity in one part of the world, or overpopulation and poverty in other part, would thwart the spirit of sustainable development.

Conclusion

Mankind will perish if the protection of the environment does not become an integral part of all technological development, planning and management. We must seek lessons from history. The flourishing civilizations of the past perished not at all hands of any cruel enemy, by due to human's own activity, clearing of forest, overuse of soil and lack of awareness for development compatible with the environment. Making economic development programmes less dependent upon the 'fossil fuels' and more dependent on renewable energy sources, less energy and material intensive and more equitable in its social and economic impact on global level is the need of the hour.

References

Asian Development Bank (2011). "Framework of Inclusive Growth Indicators".

Gupte, Medha (2015). "Inclusive Growth for Sustainable Development in India—The need of the hour", *Sai Om Journal of Commerce and Management*.

Mehendle, L. (2013). "Women Education", Approach Paper—National Conference of VC on Swami Vivekananda on Education, 16-17 Nov. 2013, New Delhi.

Sanyal, S. (2015). "Sustainable and Inclusive Growth in India and Role of Engineers", Chennai 36 Transcending Time.

Sinha, R.K. (2007). *Sustainable Development*, Pointer Publication, Jaipur, India.

22

Good Governance and Human Development

A Conceptual Analysis

Niharika Tiwari

Introduction

Since the 1990s notions of good governance and human development have emerged as two very important discourses in the realm of development literature. Both the concepts reciprocate each other. The idea of governance has two broader classifications 'good governance' as well as 'bad governance', and the attainment of a better level of human development hinges upon the good governance to a large extent and at the same time it is necessary for good governance. It is well known that the notion of good governance was first introduced by World Bank (WB) in its report on sub-Saharan Africa in 1989. In this report, the Bank pointed out that the development oriented structural adjustment programmes were being ineffective because of the crisis of governance and the weaknesses on the side of the state. Since then the notion of good governance has emerged as a crucial instrument of human development. The key point is that the success of a socio-economic planning is inevitably dependent on certain political and administrative prerequisites to a large extent.

Once this linkage became evident, it naturally assumed a central position among the think-tanks of the multilateral donors, including the World Bank and International Monetary Fund (IMF) who have traditionally believed in no direct interference in the politico-administrative functioning of the client-countries.

To continue with their traditional policy methods would have amounted to them constant failure in eradication of the real causes of the problems of continued poverty and underdevelopment across the world.

Human Development is cornerstone for United Nations Development Programmes (UNDP). It considers the individual both means and end of development. This perspective depends on the richness of human potentiality and people are always at the centre of all activities and decisions. According to HDR (2015), "if the potential of all people is harnessed through appropriate strategies and proper policies, human progress would be accelerated and human development deficits would be reduced"(UNDP, HDR, 2015).

The idea of human development implies that the human beings should be empowered so much that they can realize their full human potentials. It goes beyond the growth of national or even per capita income to critical aspects of well-being like—*education, longevity and quality of life*. It enables the individuals to realize his or her full potential with the help of the government and civil society organizations.

In order to understand the linkages between the two concepts, the detailed analysis of both the concepts are discussed as follows:

The Concept of Governance

Governance is the process through which good or bad intentions of the ruler (democratic or authoritarian) reach to the people. Whenever establishment is against the people revolutions occur. For instance, behind the recent uprisings in several Arabian countries the problem of governance has been one of the causes of revolution. According to Chakrabarty and Bhattacharya (2008), the notion of governance has several perspectives and definitions given by the leading world institutions and scholars whereby, governance means—the act or process of governing, especially authoritative direction and control. To be more precise, governance can be defined as the political direction and control exercised over the actions of the members, citizens or inhabitants of communities, societies and states. The widest definition of governance is given in the Report of the Commission on Global Governance (Chapter one, page 1, 2: 1995).[1]

> "Governance is the sum of the many ways individuals and institutions, public and private, manage their common affairs. It is a continuing process through which conflicting or diverse interests may be accommodated and co-operative action may

> be taken. It includes formal institutions and regimes empowered to enforce compliance, as well as informal arrangements that people and institutions either have agreed to or perceive to be in their interest. At both the practical and theoretical levels, the concept continues to mean different things to different people".

Etymologically, the word governance derives from the Greek verb —Kybenan and noun—Kybernet as which means 'to steer' and 'pilot or helmsman' respectively. The meaning ranges from adopting liberal economic policies, to strengthening and reforming market institutions, building capacities of public institutions to perform, encouraging democratic participation through strengthening autonomous civil society institutions etc. The concept of "governance" is not new. It is as old as human civilization. Simply put "governance" means: the process of decision-making and the process by which decisions are implemented (or not implemented). Governance can be used in several contexts such as corporate governance, international governance, national governance and local governance. Since governance is the process of decision-making and the process by which decisions are implemented, an analysis of governance focuses on the formal and informal actors involved in decision-making and implementing the decisions made and the formal and informal structures that have been set in place to arrive at and implement the decision (UNDP, 2002).

Government is one of the actors in governance. Other actors involved in governance vary depending on the level of government that is under discussion. In rural areas, for example, other actors may include influential landlords, associations of peasant farmers, cooperatives, NGOs, research institutes, religious leaders, finance institutions, political parties, the military etc. The situation in urban areas is much more complex.

> "The interconnections between actors involved in urban governance, at the national level, in addition to the above actors, media, lobbyists, international donors, multi-national corporations, etc. may play a role in decision-making or in improving the delivery of public and collective services, will require closer partnerships with the private sector and civil society. Such partnerships should be encouraged, especially when the links between the state and civil society are underdeveloped" (WDR, 1997:162).

Therefore, the responsibility of the institutions of governance is greater in the underdeveloped and developing countries in order to take the governance to the level of good governance. While government refers to the machinery and institutional arrangements for the exercise of sovereign power for serving the internal and external interests of the political community; governance means the process of decision-making and the process by which decisions are either implemented or not implemented.

Governance is a broader notion than government, state, and regime and stands for the interaction between formal institutions (state), those in the civil society (NGOs, social activists, common people) and the market. Thus it includes political, economic and social aspects.

The World Bank is more concerned with the reform of economic and social resource control in order to improve a country's process of governance. In many reports World Bank emphasized three aspects of society which affect the nature of a country's governance. These are:

1. Type of political regime;
2. Process by which authority is exercised in the management of the economic and social resources, with a view to development; and
3. Capacity of governments to formulate policies and have them effectively implemented.

In recent times, the term good governance is being increasingly used in development literature, as bad governance is considered one of the root cause of all problems within our societies. Therefore, major international financial institutions are increasingly giving aid and loans on the condition to ensure good governance.

1.1.1 *There are several definitions of good governance given by major international institutions in the development arena.*

According to World Bank, Good governance is epitomized by predictable, open and enlightened policy making (i.e. transparent); a bureaucracy imbued with a professional ethos; an executive arm of government accountable for its actions and a strong civil society participating in public affairs; and all behaving under the rule of law.

United Nation defines good governance as, Consensus Oriented, Participatory, following The Rule of Law, Effective and Efficient, Accountable, Transparent, Responsive, Equitable and Inclusive governance.

The International Monetary Fund (IMF) declared in 1996, that Promoting good governance in all its aspects includes ensuring the rule of law, improving the efficiency and accountability of the public sector and tackling corruption are essential elements of a framework within which economies can prosper.

According to OECD, Good governance is characterized by participation, transparency, accountability, rule of law, effectiveness, equity, etc.

The words 'Governance', 'Good-governance', and 'Government' are related to same realm but have different meanings. The word governance deals with the process through which government executes the laws and rules made by the legislature of the country, whereas, good governance stands for a process of governance which is able to address the problems of the marginalized sections of the society. The government is the agency of the state through which it not only enunciates the legislations, it executes and adjudicates as well. Thus, there are three branches of the government i.e.—executive, legislature and judiciary. These are the branches which perform the process of governance.

The definition of good governance given by the World Bank is more comprehensive definition taking into account social, economic and political dimensions of governance. For instance, it discusses rule of law, control of corruption, government effectiveness, political stability, regulatory quality, voice and accountability, absence of violence etc. and analyses almost all the relevant factors helpful for good governance. Further, based on this definition, the WB provides the worldwide governance indicators with relatively more accurate database for measuring the level of good governance, on a consistent basis, worldwide. The other major international institution International Monetary Fund (IMF) has also judged the notion of good governance on the criteria of good political and economic growth, whereas, the UN's definition focuses on human development through political institutions' reforms.

World Wide Governance Indicators (WWGI): There are 'six' indicators[2] of good governance as identified by World Bank. This reports aggregate and individual governance indicators for 215 economies over the period 1996–2015, for six dimensions of governance. This conceives governance as, the traditions and institutions by which authority in a country is exercised. This includes the process by which governments are selected, monitored and replaced; the capacity of the government to effectively formulate and implement sound policies; and the respect of citizens and the state for the institutions that govern economic and social interactions among them. These indicators are as follows—

Voice and accountability: Reflects perceptions of the extent to which a country's citizens are able to participate in selecting their government, as well as freedom of expression, freedom of association, and a free media.

Political Stability, No Violence: It Reflects perceptions of the likelihood that the government will be destabilized or overthrown by unconstitutional or violent means, including politically-motivated violence and terrorism.

Government Effectiveness: It is an indicator of the quality of public services, the quality of civil services, and the degree of its independence from political pressures, the quality of policy formulation and implementation and the credibility of government's commitment to such policies.

Regulatory Quality: It reflects the ability of the government to formulate and implement sound policies and regulations that permit and promote private sector development.

Rule of law: Reflects perceptions of the extent to which agents have confidence in and abide by the rules of society, and in particular the quality of contract enforcement, property rights, the police, and the courts, as well as the likelihood of crime and violence.

Control of Corruption: This WWGI illustrates the extent to which public power is exercised for private gain, including both petty and grand forms of corruption, as well as capture of the state by elites and private interests.

According to UNDP, governance is the exercise of economic, political and administrative authority to manage a country's affairs at all levels. It comprises mechanism, processes and institutions through which citizens and groups articulate their interests, exercise their legal rights, meet their legal obligations and mediate their differences. In addition to this, ESCAPE[3] has also identified eight characteristics of good governance, such as:

1. Participatory in nature
2. Consensual in orientation
3. Accountable
4. Transparent
5. Responsive
6. Effective and Efficient
7. Equitable and Inclusive
8. Rule of Law

The Concept of Human Development

In a broader perspective, Human Development not only emphasizes the development of human being but also focuses on creating the economic opportunities and ensuring the participation of people in it. Thus, Human Development encompasses these aspects of development *viz.* economic growth, economic opportunities and people's participation. UNDP added some new dimensions i.e. development, security and sustainability, gender empowerment and cultural liberties. This description of Human Development reflects that it is multidimensional and dynamic concept. Human development is a process of enlarging people's choices. The most critical ones are to lead a long and healthy life, to be educated and to enjoy a decent standard of living. Additional choices include political freedom, guaranteed human rights and self respect—what Adam Smith called the ability to mix with others without being ashamed to appear in public (HDR, 1990:10).

The concept of human development has also been enriched by noble laureate Amartya Sen by his *'Capability Approach'*. According to him, *the goal of human development should be to expand the capability that people have to enjoy as valuable being and doings.* This includes access to positive resources they need to have these capabilities, able to make choices and social arrangements should be evaluated in terms of freedom they promote. Therefore unless the dream of the strengthening the individual is achieved human development remains incomplete. The concept of human development is different from other similar concepts: like basic needs concept which unlike human development approach focuses on the fulfilment of the basic need of the people only. Similarly, Human resource development focuses on investment in the education and health of people as a means of accelerating growth. Human development is a broader concept, it does not regard people as passive beneficiaries of services given to fulfil basic needs, nor does it focus on the expansion of the skill and health of the people to increase economic growth. Instead people are seen as active agents of change.

> "Human development encompasses all aspects of human existence. It is generally accepted that its scope includes political and social rights as well as economic ones but the different rights are not always given the same weight. For example, some people still claim humanitarian aid and economic assistance cannot wait for political and social progress. This insidious idea creates dissonance between complementary requirements. If the people that aid targets are not empowered, it cannot achieve more than a very limited, very short-term alleviation of problems rooted in long-standing social and political ills. After all, human development is not intended to produce impotent objects of charity" (HDR, 2002:52).

Ironically, the human development approach to development has fallen victim to the success of its human development index (HDI). The

HDI has reinforced the narrow, over simplified interpretation of the human development concept as being only about expanding *education, health and decent living standards*.

This has obscured the broader, more complex concept of human development as the expansion of capabilities that widen people's choices to lead lives that they value. Despite careful efforts to explain that the concept is broader than the measure, human development, continues to be identified with the HDI—while political freedoms, participating in the life of one's community and physical security are often overlooked. But such capabilities are as universal and fundamental as being able to read or to enjoy good health. They are valued by all people—and without them, other choices are foreclosed. They are not included in the HDI because they are difficult to measure appropriately, not because they are any less important to human development. The notion of human development asserts that the People are the real wealth of nations. People are not only the beneficiaries of economic and social progress; they are also its agents, both as individuals and by making common causes with others. That is one reason strategies for promoting human development have traditionally emphasized investing in education and health and promoting equitable economic growth.

Moreover, the HDR-2002 has added a new pillar of human development i.e. promoting participation through democratic governance. Basically, participation promotes collective as well as individual aspects. For example, collective action through social and political movements has often been a motor of progress for issues central to human development: protecting the environment, promoting gender equality, fostering human rights. In addition, participation and other human development gains can be mutually reinforcing. Political freedom empowers people to claim their economic and social rights, while education increases their ability to demand economic and social policies that respond to their priorities.

Definitions of Human Development

Aristotle argued for seeing "the difference between a good political arrangement and a bad one" in terms of its successes and failures in facilitating people's ability to lead "flourishing lives". Human being as the real end of all activities was a recurring theme in the writings of most of the early philosophers. Emmanuel Kant observed:

> "So act as to treat humanity, whether in their own person or in

that of any other, in every case a. an end withal, never as means only."

The same motivating concern can be found in the writings of the early leaders of quantification in economics—William Petty, Gregory King, Francois Quesnay, Antoine Lavoisier and Joseph Lagrange, the grandparents of GNP and GDP. It is also clear in the writings of the leading political economists—Adam Smith, David Ricardo, Robert Malthus, Karl Marx and John Stuart Mill.

Human development brings together the production and distribution of commodities and the expansion and use of human capabilities. It also focuses on choices—on what people should have, be and do to be able to ensure their own livelihood. Human development is, moreover, concerned not only with basic needs satisfaction but also with human development as a participatory and dynamic process. It applies equally to less developed and highly developed countries[2].

All the three can be realized only when everyone is given opportunity to realize his/her freedom within the process of allocation of resources. Moreover, the freedom in the process of distribution must be based upon socio-economic and political justice. Different countries, communities and individuals will emphasize different dimensions and principles. Human development carries the melody of their culture, values and current priorities in a way that reflects inclusive democratic choices. Many people activists, leaders, intellectuals and many others—help articulate human development in diverse contexts, as with the local and national HDRs, offering people more opportunities while fostering their ability to shape their lives and advance justice across society, now and into the future (HDR:2010).

Measuring Human Development, focuses on the three essential elements of human life—longevity, knowledge and decent living standards. These elements have their own limitations as well. These limitations along with the utility of the elements are mentioned here; *For the first component*, longevity life expectancy at birth is the indicator. The importance of life expectancy lies in the common belief that a long life is valuable in itself and in the fact that various indirect benefits (such as adequate nutrition and good health) are closely associated with higher life expectancy. This association makes life expectancy an important indicator of human development, especially in view of the present lack of comprehensive information about people's health and nutritional status.

For the second key component, knowledge—literacy figures are only a crude reflection of access to education, particularly to the good quality education so necessary for productive life in modern society. But literacy is a person's first step in learning and knowledge-building, so literacy figures are essential in any measurement of human development. In a more varied set of indicators, importance would also have to be attached to the outputs of higher levels of education. But for basic human development, literacy deserves the clearest emphasis.

The third key component, of human development—command over resources needed for a decent living—is perhaps the most difficult to measure simply. It requires data on access to land, credit, income and other resources. But given the scarce data on many of these variables, we must for the time being make the best use of an income indicator. The most readily available income indicator—per capita income — has wide national coverage. But the presence of non-tradable goods and services and the distortions from exchange rate anomalies, tariffs and taxes make per capita income data in nominal prices not very useful for international comparisons. Such data can, however, be improved by using purchasing power-adjusted real GDP per capita figures, which provide better approximations of the relative power to buy commodities and to gain command over resources for a decent living standard. Basically, there are so many other factors related to these basic elements of human development which influence these elements in a significant manner such as, gender equality, poverty alleviation etc. But the idea of human development index although provides us a well demarcated criteria to map human development, seems to have a lop-sided view of the concept. As, other factors are not the main part of HDI. Nevertheless, the concept of Human Development has been enlarged over a period of time in the following manner and has incorporated more issues. Enlarged conception of Human Development[4] is as follows:

1. The HDI itself, which includes health, education and a measure of income
2. Mental well-being — an individual's psychological state
3. Empowerment
4. Political freedom
5. Social relations
6. Community well-being
7. Inequalities
8. Work conditions
9. Leisure conditions

10. Political security — freedom from political violence or instability
11. Economic security — freedom from economic fluctuations
12. Environmental conditions (UNDP IPC 2006: 12)

Formula to Calculate Human Development Index (HDI) is a summary measure of human development. It measures the average achievements in a country in three basic dimensions of human development. Before the HDI itself is calculated, an index needs to be created for each of these dimensions. To calculate these indices—the life expectancy, education and GDP indices—minimum and maximum values (goalposts) are chosen for each underlying indicator. Performance in each dimension is expressed as a value between 0 and 1 by applying the following general formula:

$$\text{Dimension index} = \frac{\text{Actual value} - \text{minimum value}}{\text{Maximum value} - \text{minimum value}}$$

The HDI is then calculated as a simple average of the dimension indices. There are other important dimensions as part of human development that has been added recently. Human Development Report 2010 provides this newly created HDI which is more comprehensive. This 2010 HDR makes the HDI more specific and inclusive. There are four human development indices for calculating HDI graphically presented as follows:

Human Development Index Components (HDR, 2010)

Human Development Index Dimensions Long and healthy life, Knowledge, A decent standard of living.

Indicators Life expectancy at birth, Mean years of schooling and expected years of Schooling GNI per capita (PPP US$).

Dimension Index Life expectancy index, Education index, GNI index.

Human Development Index Human Development Index (HDI) is a composite index measuring average achievement in three basic dimensions of human development —a long and healthy life, knowledge and a decent standard of living.

Inequality-Adjusted Human Development Index Components

Inequality-Adjusted Human Development Index Dimensions Long and healthy life, Knowledge, A decent standard of living.

Indicators Life expectancy at birth, Mean years of schooling and expected years of schooling GNI per capita (PPP US$)

Dimension Index Life expectancy, Years of schooling, Income/ Consumption

Inequality-Adjusted Index Inequality adjusted Life expectancy index, Inequality adjusted Education index, Inequality-adjusted income index.

Human Development Index, in terms of Inequality-adjusted Human development index where value is adjusted for inequalities in the three basic dimensions of human development.

Gender Inequality Index (GII)

Gender Inequality Index (GII) Dimensions Health, Empowerment, Labour, Market.

Indicators, Maternal mortality rate and adolescent fertility rate female and male population with at least secondary education female and male shares of parliamentary seats Female and male labour force participation rates

Dimension Index Female reproductive health index Female and male empowerment index Female and male labour market index.

Female Gender Index and Male Gender Index

Gender Inequality Index (GII)

Gender Inequality Index is a composite index measuring loss in achievements in three dimensions of human development—reproductive health, empowerment and labour market, due to inequality between genders.

Multi-dimensional Poverty Index (MPI)

MPI Dimensions Health Education Standard of living Indicators Nutrition Child mortality Years of Schooling Children enrolled Cooking fuel Toilet Water Electricity Floor Assets Poverty measures Intensity of Poverty and Head Count Ratio.

Multidimensional Poverty Index is the share of the population that is multidimensionally poor adjusted by the intensity of the deprivations.

Interlinkages between Good Governance and Human Development

The above concepts of good governance and human development have crucial interlinkages. Human development is also linked to political structures and forms of governance of nation states. Since there is a clear recognition of the state's responsibility to provide basic conditions that enable people to enjoy their right to life with dignity, it is crucial to put existing state structures under scrutiny. Some of these structures are inherently exclusionist. Correcting the exclusionist nature of state structures is important because human rights and human development are interconnected.

Good governance is a mean through which available resources of a state reach to its people in the form of good education, health facilities and other social, economic and political securities, promoting better human development. On the other, better level of human development helps in creating well informed citizens through better education, health, and proper living conditions, promoting good governance in true sense of terms. Moreover, well educated and physically as well as mentally healthy people can raise their voice against bad governance leading to a transparent system based upon rule of law. Both are interdependent and provide support to each other. As in the absence of a transparent state apparatus and people oriented policies human development will remain elusive in the same way people surrounded with illiteracy, poverty, unemployment, and structural violence cannot convert governance into good governance as what distinguishes good governance from traditional notion of governance is the centrality of the citizens in the institutions and processes of governance.

Even after facing the strong erosive forces of globalization the state establishment is still very much relevant particularly in developing and underdeveloped countries. Here society is facing a transition phase where on the one hand democratic values are instilled in the socio-economic and political institutions, and on the other traditional and fundamentalist forces are opposing their eradication to maintain hierarchical system which benefits a few. Here a positive and progressive inter-linkage between these two notions is imperative because human development promotes empowerment in its optimum point. Empowerment cannot be achieved without good governance. Empowerment has been recognized since the inception of the Human Development Report (HDR). The overview to the 1990 HDR states: Human freedom is vital for human development. People must be free to exercise their choices in properly Functioning markets, and they must have a decisive voice in shaping their political frameworks. It pointed to the need to measure political freedoms, because the valuation given to similar human development achievements is quite different depending on whether they were accomplished in a democratic or an authoritarian Framework.

The 1993 HDR on participation was the first to directly address empowerment, which also underpinned the 2000 HDR on human rights, the 2002 HDR on democracy and the 2004 HDR on cultural liberties (HDR, 2010:67). UNDP envisages a versatile role for the state. It believes that the state is critical for creating the economic environment conducive to sustainable human development.

The state should protect the vulnerable, improving governance efficiency and responsiveness, empower people and democratize the political system. These objectives can be achieved only by the state through decentralization, reducing the gap between rich and poor, by encouraging cultural diversity and social integration, and protecting the environment.

Conclusion

Linkage between good governance and human development is a two way process. Both depend on each other because only well educated prosperous and healthy citizens can understand and incorporate in their life the values of democracy in true sense of terms. For instance, in countries like India and Pakistan, the values of democracy i.e. equality, liberty and fraternity could not get accomplished in a substantial manner due to the malpractices such as, rigging of elections use of money-muscle power etc. Demagogues are able to allure the voters in these countries because of abject poverty, illiteracy and absence of functional literacy leading to conservative attitude, and unemployment etc. Thus, to take assertive part in the allocation of available resources human development is necessary. Similarly, in the absence of free and fair authority controlled by the people judicious allocation of available resources will not be possible. Therefore, it seems that a crucial interlinkage between the good governance and human development is necessary for the sustainable and just development of the citizens. As scholars have pointed out:

> "Well-institutionalized democracies are more likely to produce, over the long run, effective, efficient and sustainable economic and social policies, because they provide effective and stable institutional and procedural mechanisms to represent interests, arbitrate disputes, provide checks and balances, and negotiate change. According to Dani Rodrik (2000), political institutions matter for economic development because of the propensity of democracies to moderate social conflict and induce compromise.

> Jonathan Isham Daniel Kaufman and Lant Pritchett (1997) find that effective citizen voice and public accountability often leads to greater efficacy in government action and a more efficient allocation of resources. More fundamentally, open governance systems are more likely to generate responsible and responsive government and thus adopt pro-poor public policies. Daniel Kaufmann, Aart Kraay and Pablo Zoido Lobaton (1999) show that these various aspects of good governance are significantly associated with income levels in the expected manner. Effective democratic institutions, rather than their mere formal existence, are thus key" (Santiso, 2001, 07).

The need of the hour is that upward economic growth of the countries, particularly of those who have adopted the structural adjustment programme, must be based upon the objective of human development. This will not only eradicate the miseries of the people, it would also create a conducive environment for good governance as envisaged by the people and the institutions advocating good governance as a key for development. The inter-linkages between the good governance and human development are also recognized by the World Bank in World Development Report, 1997:

> "The state's unique strengths are its powers to tax, to prohibit, to punish, and to require participation. The state's power to tax enables it to finance the provision of public goods. Its power to prohibit and punish enables it to protect personal safety and property rights. And its power to require participation enables it to minimize free riding: those who would reap the benefits of public goods can be made to pay their share of the costs. The same power can help resolve problems of collective action that would otherwise reduce the social benefits of insurance markets, or prevent mutually complementary private investments from being made, to take just two examples" (WDR 1997: 25).

Although the idea of good governance goes beyond the state authority, in case of underdeveloped and developing countries state plays very crucial role as the civil society organizations are still in the process of emergence. If achieved by the countries the reciprocity between good governance and human development can make people the real and active agents of dynamic changes in the society.

NOTES

1. Our Global Neighbourhood Report of the Commission on Global Governance (ISBN 0-19-827998-1; Published by Oxford University Press, 1995)
2. See, http://info.worldbank.org/governance/wgi/
3. https://www.unescap.org/sites/default/files/good-governance.pdf
4. https://ipcig.org/pub/IPCPovertyInFocus9.pdf, page-12

References

Alkire, Sabina (2002). *Valuing Freedoms, Sen's Capability Approach and Poverty Reduction*, New Delhi: Oxford University Press.

Chakrabarty, Bidyut and Mohit Bhattacharya (eds.) (2008). *The Governance Discourse: A Reader*, Oxford.

Santiso, Carlos (2001). "Good Governance and Aid Effectiveness: The World Bank and Conditionality", *The Georgetown Public Policy Review*, Vol. 7 No. 1 Fall 2001, [Online: web] Accessed 12 Aug 2013 URL: http://www.sti.ch/

UNDP (1990). "Concept and Measurement of Human Development", *Human Development Report*, Oxford University Press, New York.

UNDP (1993). People's Participation, Human Development Report, Oxford.

UNDP (2006). *Poverty in Focus,* International Poverty Centre, [Online: web] Accessed on 13 Aug 2013URL: http://www.ipcundp. org/pub/IPCPovertyInFocus9.pdf.

UNDP (2010). "The Real Wealth of Nations: Pathways to Human Development", *Human Development Report*, Macmillan, New York.

UNDP (2015). *Work for Human Development*, Human Development Report, UNDP, New York.

World Bank (1989). *Sub-Saharan Africa, From Crisis to Sustainable Growth: A Long Term Perspective Study,* Washington.

World Bank (1997). *The State in a Changing World*, World Development Report, Washington.

23

Introducing Islamic Banking in India for Economic Growth and Social Welfare

Sana Beg

Introduction

Islamic banking is a banking system that is primarily based on the Islamic 'Shariah' law. Islamic banking is a banking system that takes inspiration from the Quran and the Sunnah, that are the verbatim word of Allah (swt) and the traditions of the Prophet Mohammad (saw) respectively. The need for Islamic finance arises from the desire of many Muslims to regulate their finances in accordance with the requirements of their faith, as Islam is a total way of life and not just a relation between man and the Almighty. The main reason for the existence of Islamic banking is the divine prohibition of taking and giving interest. Besides, Islamic finance also prohibits *gharar* which is selling something that one does not own, investments in industries related to pork, alcohol and entertainment as well as transactions involving speculation and/or gambling. Although Islamic finance has always existed but the modern Islamic banking is only about five decades old but has become one of the fastest growing segments of the international banking and capital markets. Throughout the world it is being recognized as a viable alternative to the conventional banking system. In a short period, it has spread to almost all parts of the world. Although it initially emerged in the Muslim-majority countries like Egypt, Malaysia and the Middle-East, but today has spread far and wide to even countries like United States of America, United Kingdom,

Singapore and Japan. Today, Islamic banking has presence in over 100 countries, many of them being IMF member countries. Seeing the potential of Islamic banking, the IMF too appears to be promoting it and was instrumental in the establishment of many international Islamic financial institutions. Countries are embracing it because of the potential and the benefits that it brings with it. India, however, has so far shied away from allowing Islamic banking although few Islamic financial institutions exists as Non-Banking Financial Institutions.

Importance of Economic Growth and Social Welfare in Islamic Economics

Islamic economics forms the basis for the Islamic banking and finance. It acts as the foundations on which the Islamic banking and finance is developed. Islam lays great emphasis on growth and development in an economy while simultaneously encouraging equity and justice — both social and economic.

The following verses from the Quran and the sunnah can be called as the guiding lights for Islamic Economics, Banking and Finance specially w.r.t. economic growth and social welfare:

- Islam emphasizes on efficient use of wealth as it looks at wealth to be life sustaining.
- "Give not unto the foolish your wealth which Allah has made a means of support for you". (Quran, 4:4).
- Private ownership is affirmed but viewed as a trust according to the Quran:
  "Believe in Allah and His messenger, and spend of that whereof He hath made you trustees." (Quran, 57:7).
- Islam encourages enterprise and efforts to create wealth, which has been characterized as Almighty's bounty:
  "And when prayer is ended, then disperse in the land and seek Allah's Bounty". (Quran, 62:10).
- Muslims are obligated to fulfill contracts and keep their promises:
  "O you who believe fulfill your undertakings". (Quran, 5:1)
  "...And be true to every promise, for, verily, (on judgment day) you will be called to account for every promise you made". (Quran, 17:34)
- All exchange should be with willing consent of the parties concerned:

"O you who believe squander not your wealth among yourself in vanity except it be a trade by mutual consent". (Quran, 4:29)

- Use of wealth and exercise of freedom of enterprise is constrained by the obligation not to harm others. The Prophet ruled:
  "No injury, and no inflicting of injury". (Ibn Maja, *Sunan*: chapter on Ahkam)

This has to be seen in the perspective of the positive obligation to care for others and share with them. This is symbolized by the well-known duty of paying *Zakat* or religious tax. But that is not all, the important thing is the spirit of a cooperative, helpful behaviour as mandated by the Islamic view on life being a test:

"Who hath created life and death that He may try you, which of you is best in conduct". (Quran, 67:2).

- Racism is not allowed in Islam, for the Quran speaks of human equality in the following terms:
  "O mankind, We have created you from a male and a female and have made you into nations and tribes for you to know one another. Truly, the noblest of you with Allah is the most pious. Truly, Allah is All-Knowing, All-Aware." (Quran, 49:13)
- Islam is a religion of justice, as described in the Quran:
  "Truly Allah commands you to give back trusts to those to whom they are due, and when you judge between people, to judge with justice...." (Quran, 4:58)

The above mentioned texts clearly provide a sound basis for a positive attitude towards wealth creation, economic activity and social welfare.

The paradigm shift advocated by the Islamic economic systems in its teachings challenges the conventional thinking in several areas, such as following:

Without doubt the foremost priority of Islam and its teachings on economics is about "Justice and Equity". The notion of justice and equity is embedded deep in the system. As an aspect of justice, social justice in Islam consists of the creation and provision of equal opportunities and the removal of obstacles equally for every member of the society. Legal justice, too, can be interpreted as meaning that all members of the society have

1. equal status before the Law, equal protection of the Law and equal opportunity under the Law. The notion of economic justice, and its attendant concept of distributive justice, as an aspect of the overall principle of justice in Islam, is particularly important as an identifying characteristic of the Islamic economic system, because the latter's rules governing permissible and forbidden economic behaviour on the part of the consumers, producers and government, as well as questions of property rights and of production and distribution of wealth, are all based on the fundamental principle of justice in Islam.
2. The Islamic paradigm incorporates a spiritual and moral framework that values human relations above material possessions. In this way, it is concerned about not only the material needs but also about establishing a balance between material and spiritual fulfilment of the human being.
3. The Islamic system creates a balanced relationship between the individual and the society. Self-interest and private gains of the individual are not denied, but they are regulated for the larger betterment of the society.
4. The individual's pursuit of maximum profit in enterprise and maximum satisfaction in consumption are not the sole objectives of society and any wasteful consumption is discouraged.
5. Recognition and the perfection of property rights of all members of the society is the foundation of a stakeholder-oriented society, preserving the rights of all and reminding them of their responsibilities.

Government of India's Initiatives for Economic Growth and Social Welfare

Since independence Indian Government has continuously worked to foster economic growth in the country. All five-year plans were made and implemented to achieve the target of economic growth for all, especially for the deprived section of the society. Widespread social inequity was largely the result of economic inequity. Having realised this, the government took upon itself to improve economically the conditions of the people at the lowest strata of the economy. For this it was realised that sound financial infrastructure is a necessity. Banking has a long history of about 300 years in India. During this long period, the banking sector has undergone several changes in the structure to improve and bring in greater efficiency. At the time of independence, the commercial banks were under private sectors and were more businessmen friendly. Although agriculture was the backbone of the Indian economy but it did not get the required financial empathy.

As part of the economic development plan, the Indian Government nationalised 14 commercial banks in the year 1969. Another nationalisation phase was in the year 1980. Nationalization meant the government had greater control over whom to lend money and oversee the use of these funds, which was in sync with India's aim of socialism and the central bank, Reserve Bank of India, was in a better position to regulate the nationalised banks.

RBI has identified certain sectors as priority sectors for advances. In fact it was in 1968, when in a meeting of the National Credit Council it was emphasised that commercial banks should increase their involvement in the financing of priority sectors *viz.*, agriculture and small scale industries. The description of the priority sectors was formalised in 1972 by the RBI. It had prescribed a modified return for reporting priority sector advances and guidelines were issued indicating the scope of items to be included under the various categories of priority sector. In 1974, for the first time the banks were advised to raise the share of these sectors in their aggregate advances to the level of 33.33 per cent by 1979. This has been revised from time to time depending on the need of the time. In 2005, it was decided that the priority sectors would be included in the priority sector that impact large sections of the population, the weaker sections and the sectors which are employment-intensive such as agriculture, and tiny and small enterprises. Interest rates for loans to these sectors are as per RBI's directives. According to present priority sector norms, scheduled commercial banks have to give 40 per cent of their loans (measured in terms of Adjusted Net Bank Credit or ANBC) to the identified priority sectors in accordance with the RBI regulations. In April 2016, RBI has introduced Priority Sector Lending Certificates so that banks can trade the loan certificates given to the different sectors to meet their targets. The new regulations stipulate that banks should give 10 per cent of their loans to the weaker sections. Weaker sections include: Small Marginal Farmers, artisans, village and cottage industries with a credit limit up to Rs. 1 lakh, beneficiaries of certain government sponsored schemes, SC/STs, SHGs, persons with disabilities, overdrafts up to Rs. 5000 under PMJDY, distressed persons, individual women beneficiaries up to Rs. 1 lakh, beneficiaries of differential interest rate regime.

Cooperative banks serve an important role in the Indian economy, especially in rural areas. In urban areas they mainly serve small industry and self-employed workers. They are regulated by the RBI under the Banking Regulation Act, 1949 and Banking Laws Act, 1965 (Application to Co-operative Societies). Urban Co-operative Banks (UCBs) refer to primary co-operative banks located in urban and semi-urban areas. They essentially lent to small borrowers and businesses. However, today their scope of operations has widened considerably.

The RBI is trying to take all possible steps to bring in greater financial inclusion. This has led to licensing of new banks, opening of new bank branches, easier KYC (know your customer) norms for smaller customers, expansion of ATM network and financial literacy initiatives and even license to niche banks.

The above arguments basically point that there is room for introduction of Islamic banking in India as one of the ways to cater to the needs of a section of the society. It is a fact that the current Banking Regulations demand that all banks have to necessarily transact on the basis of interests. However, this is also true that seeing the need of the time many amendments have been made and exceptions have been granted for the overall benefit of the country and its people. Special provisions are given to Non-banking finance companies (NBFCs), Self-Help Groups (SHGs), Non-Governmental Organisations (NGOs) and MSME lending. Similarly, necessary amendments can be brought about to accommodate interest-free banking as well.

Possible Benefits of Introducing Islamic Banking in India

India is home to the second highest population of Muslims in a single country, Indonesia having the highest. According to the 2011 census, the Muslim population is a little over 172 million and is over 14 per cent of the total population of the country. The financial system adopted by the Reserve Bank of India for banking and financial services in India is interest-based and Islam prohibits Muslims to give or take interest. Thus in a way, it is conflicting with the fundamental right to and grow businesses rather than the one with more means but an average or less profitable project. This provides a level-playing field to everyone in an economy. Another great benefit that the Islamic Banking offers to the economy is that it is less inflationary than the conventional banking since interest payments are linked with real profits and are not to be paid at pre-defined regular intervals. Inability to pay interest obligations, leads to instability in the conventional system. Money expansion is linked with the growth in real assets, i.e. such a system is asset-backed and not debt-backed and is thus less inflationary. Islamic micro-finance can also prove to be more successful than the conventional micro-finance as it is free of the disadvantages that are in the conventional system.

India needs to no longer ignore Islamic banking and finance. Many high level committees have recommended introduction of interest-free banking in India primarily to increase financial inclusion, like the Raghuram Rajan Committee Report of 2009, Deepak Mohanty Report in 2015 and the very latest Annual Report of the RBI for the year ending June 2016. If India wishes to become a global financial services centre in the region, it should embrace Islamic finance. India is very strategically located in the vicinity of the Middle-East and the other Arab nations. These countries are looking for investment especially in the developing world that would give a higher return, provided these investment opportunities are Shariah-compliant. India's attractiveness as a financial centre is supported by a sizeable domestic economy and financial market. The absence of Islamic banking in India is resulting in losses in terms of investments from these surplus countries. Seeing this immense potential of attracting investments, China and Hong Kong are already opening its doors to Islamic banking and finance. China is fast becoming an important centre of Islamic financial market. China also became a member of IFSB in 2009. Since then number of contracts have been signed between Chinese banks and financial institutions and the Islamic Financial institutions of Gulf Cooperation Council and South-east Asia.

Conclusion

The Islamic law ensures economic justice along with economic growth through rules regarding resource allocation, production, exchange and the distribution of resulting income and wealth. Islam firmly believes that the returns from the use of various resources by the more able must be shared with the less able, who have equal rights on them. Islam places great emphasis on redistribution of income and wealth and thus legislate institutions for this purpose such as Zakat, Sadaqah, and Qard-al-hasan. These instruments are envisaged to enhance access to financing while addressing equity and contributing to poverty alleviation. The Zakat and the Sadaqah are gifts but Qard-al-hasan is a loan without interest for a needy.

Thus it can be said that Islamic-Banking has products that are better placed to serve the objectives of promoting economic growth, financial inclusion and social well-being of all. This is one of the reasons of spread of Islamic banking. Besides, Islamic banks and windows were found to be less vulnerable than their conventional counterparts during the financial crisis of the previous decade that increased the confidence in Islamic banking and finance. The spread of Islamic banking resulted in the need of appropriate regulations and supervision so that the faith of customers is not shaken. Many organisations emerged and formalised this banking system across various countries. Most of the Islamic banks fulfil the Shariah regulations as well as the regulations laid down for the conventional banks.

The functions and objectives of Islamic banks are similar to those of conventional banks. Islamic banks also need the legal, regulatory and supervisory frameworks as much as the conventional banks, in order to mitigate the risks and safeguard the interests of their clients. What is desired is that a level-playing field should be made available to the Islamic banks in order to have a healthy competition with their conventional counterparts. There could be a unified core set of banking framework for both types of banking or separate framework and regulations for the Islamic banks and the conventional banks. A single set avoids the duplication but the advantage with separate sets is that it increases transparency.

There is little doubt that India too would gain a lot once Islamic banking is introduced. With many recommendations already in favour, India needs to make little amendments in the banking regulations to make room for Islamic-Banking. India should introduce Islamic banking in a gradual manner, starting with opening of Islamic windows in the conventional banks and then gradually increasing the other Islamic banking products and services.

References

"A Hundred Small Steps", *Report of Committee on Financial Sector Reforms*, 2008.

Ahmad, A. (1995). "The Evolution of Islamic Banking", *Encyclopedia of Islamic Banking and Insurance*, London: Institute of Islamic Banking and Insurance.

Ariff, M. and Iqbal, M. (2011). *The Foundations of Islamic Banking: Theory, Practice and Education*, Edward Elgar.

Asli Demirguc-Kunt, Leora Klapper, Dorothe Singer, Peter Van Oudheusden, "The Global Findex Database 2014: Measuring Financial Inclusion around the World", Policy Research Working Paper 7255, The World Bank, April 2015.

Asli Demirguc-Kunt, Leora Klapper and Douglas Randall, "Islamic Finance and Financial Inclusion: Measuring Use of and Demand for Formal Financial Services among Muslim Adults", Policy Research Working Paper 6642, The World Bank, October 2013.

Askari, H., Iqbal, Z., Krichne, N. and Mirakhor, A. (2011). *Risk Sharing in Finance: The Islamic Finance Alternative*, John Wiley, Singapore.

Askari, H. Iqbal, Z. and Mirakhor A. (2015). *Introduction to Islamic Economics*, Wiley Finance Series.

Beg, S. (2016). "Islamic Economics: An Alternate Economic System for the Third Millennium", *International Journal of Business and General Management*, 5(5).

Beg, S. (2016). "Prospects, Problems and Potential of Islamic Banking in India", *International Journal of Accounting and Financial Management Research*, 6(3).

Bellalah M. and Masood O. (2013). *Islamic Banking and Finance*, Cambridge Scholars Publishing.

Chapra, M.U. (1995). Islam and the Economic Challenge, *Islamic Economic Series-17*, The Islamic Foundation and the International Institute of Islamic Thought.

Chapra, M.U. (2000). *The Future of Economics — An Islamic Perspective*, Leicester, UK: The Islamic Foundation.

Chapra, M.U. (2005). *Prohibition of Interest: Does it make sense?*, Markazi Maktaba Islami Publishers.

Di Vanna J. and Sreih A. (2009). *A New Financial Dawn: The Rise of Islamic Finance*, Leonardo and Francis Press Ltd., Cambridge, UK.

Dusuki, A.W. (2008). "Banking for the poor: the role of Islamic Banking in microfinance initiatives", *Humanomics*, 24(1).

Earnst & Young's, "World Islamic Banking Competitiveness Report 2014-15"; Participation Banking 2.0.

El-Galfy A. and Khiyar A.K. (2012). "Islamic Banking and Economic Growth: A Review", *The Journal of Applied Business Research*, 28(5).

Faridi, F.R. (1994). "A Case for Islamic Economics: An Indian Perspective", *Journal of Objective Studies*, 6(I).

Hassan K. and Lewis M. (2007). *Handbook of Islamic Banking*, Edward Elgar.

Kammer A. and Norat M. *et al.*, "Islamic Finance: Opportunities, Challenges and Policy Options", IMF Staff Discussion Note, April 2015.

Khan M.M. and Bhatti M.I. (2008). "Islamic Banking and finance: on its way to globalization", *Managerial Finance*, 34(10).

Mirakhor, A. and Askari, H. (2010). *Islam and the Path to Human and Economic Development*, New York: Palgrave Macmillan US.

Mohieldin, M. (2012). "Realising the Potential of Islamic Finance", *World Economics*, 13(3).

Rosly, S.A. (2008). *Critical Issues on Islamic Banking and Financial Markets: Islamic Economy, Banking and Finance, Investments, Takaful and Financial Planning*, Author House UK.

Samad, M.A. (2014). "Islamic microfinance: tool for economic stability and social change", *Humanomics*, 30(3).

Siddiqui, M.N. (2005). *Riba, Bank Interest and Rationale of Its Prohibition*, New Delhi: Markazi Maktaba Islami.

Wilson, R. (2008). *History of Islamic Economics*, Leiden: E.J. Brill.

24

Development Communication

Case Study of the Pulse Polio Campaign

Sadhna Shanker

Introduction

These days in every corner of India, one campaign that hits the eye constantly is of "Swachh Bharat", drawing people's attention towards cleanliness. It is a visible and proactive development communication campaign.

What do we mean by the term 'Development Communication'? Simply put it can be defined as the *use of communication* to *promote development*. More specifically, it refers to the practice of systematically applying the processes, strategies, and principles of communication to bring about *positive social change*. "Development communication, as an interdisciplinary field, is based on empirical research that helps to build consensus while it facilitates the sharing of knowledge to achieve a positive change in the development initiative. It is not only about effective dissemination of information but also about using empirical research and two-way communications among stakeholders."[1]

This chapter will emphasise on the use of development communication in the public sector, with the Pulse Polio campaign as the main example.

Soon after the Second World War, the importance of mass media in spreading information and ideas about progress and development began to gain ground. Effective reporting of the war and its propaganda through mass media opened the gates for the use of such media in other public spheres as well. When applied in the context of developing countries, some Western thinkers were of the view that development meant the process by which these societies could "catch up" with developed societies as measured in terms of political system, economic growth, and educational levels. The role of communication in this, was meant to be spread information.

The Dominant paradigm of development envisaged a transition from traditionalism to modernization in a unidirectional way. This mindset led to an approach to communication for development that was "vertical in nature, authority-based, top down, expert driven non-negotiable, well-intentioned and exhorting people to adopt new attitudes and behaviours that held promise of a much better future"[2]. Communication in this era was the SMCR model

(S) Source > (M) Message > (C) Channel > (R) Receiver, primarily a linear and one way transmission

The family planning campaign of the early seventies, adopting the 'cafeteria approach', concentrated on informing people about the various methods of contraception available did not take into account the socio-economic conditions of the target audience. Often messages put out were not backed by services at the field level, and the desired result of smaller families did not resonate with the rural realities of high infant mortality, and the need for additional hands as farm labour.

The dominant paradigm of development had started being questioned. The top down approach to planning and development had failed to answer the needs of the people and fulfil their aspirations. As the importance of a bottom-up approach to development came into vogue, communication for the same also saw a change. From the SMCR linear model, feedback in communication became a vital ingredient.

In this new approach to development that sought a more direct participation of the people, there was an emphasis on dialogue and the symbolic communication process looked like this

I (interlocutor) ↔ Media ↔ I (interlocutor)[3]

Apart from mass media, communicators used interpersonal dialogue, folk, and small group discussions to share knowledge and skills. This change in communication methods brought in alterations in the manner in which communication was planned. Communication began to be planned strategically:

- Use of data to set goals and strategies.
- Define target audiences.
- Research barriers, benefits and perceptions.
- Decide on channels and strategy.

Much like in the private sector for development communication, too strategic planning became essential. In 1982, the Johns Hopkins University came up with the P Process. It is a tool for planning strategic, evidence-based health communication programmes.[4]

The P Process acknowledges the real-time, dynamic nature of the strategic process as well as new technologies and the constantly changing nature of communication, social norms and individual behaviour and decision making. The five step process involves a process of inquiry, design a strategy as a result of the analysis, create and test the communication interventions, implement the campaign and monitor it, evaluate and then evolve by using the leaning from evaluation to alter or tweak. Ensuring participation and building capacity of the planners and other stakeholders in the process is a continuous part. This tool is dynamic as it takes into account evaluation results in the planning process.

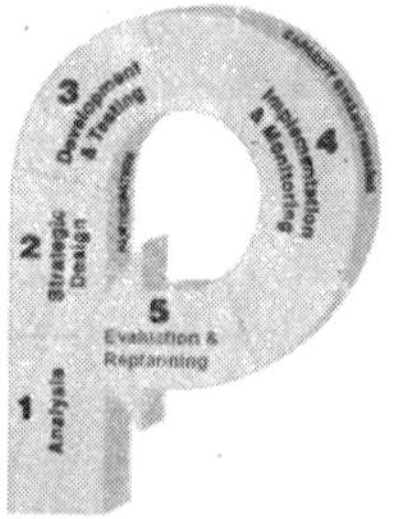

Fig. 24.1: Steps in Strategic Communication.

The use of strategic communication has been evident in public health campaigns in the recent past in areas such as NSV, HIV/AIDS and of course polio.

The main aim of all these campaigns is to change behaviour for a desired outcome. Strategic and systematic communication is aimed at some change of behaviour. In communication literature, the steps towards behaviour change are as follows —

- Knowledge: Recall and understanding
- Approval: Respond, think, approval
- Intention: Recognizes and intends to practice

Fig. 24.2: Johns Hopkins Centre for Communication Programmes (CCP). (2007)

- Practice: Chooses and continues
- Advocacy: Supports and advocates to others

A change of behaviour is complete when the target individual or group becomes an advocate for the cause. The aim of communication campaigns is a long and iterative process, which requires constant monitoring, feedback and evaluation.

The Pulse Polio Campaign

A key success in the arena of public health is the Pulse polio programme in India. In 2014, the South East Asia Region (SEARO) of the World Health Organization (of which India is a part) was declared polio free. This was the culmination of a long journey that began in the early nineties. Polio drops were given on national immunization days and followed up by a house to house outreach for the next three days. On an average 770 million children of 0 to 5 age group were covered in one such round. The scale of the programme was stupendous, and a huge communication effort backed the programme.

The campaign for polio was handled by two committees at the central level, which met every week. They assessed the data and feedback coming in, and made necessary changes in strategy and messaging. For example when the questions of why again and again started coming in, celebrity endorsement in the form of the Bollywood legend Mr. Amitabh Bachchan was roped in to answer the questions. TV spots addressing concerns coming in through the data were prepared and broadcast. When certain regions and communities were beset with rumours about the vaccine, the Imam of Jama Masjid was called into spread the message towards acceptability of the programme.

When large parts of the country were polio free and only some districts of UP and Bihar remained as high risk, the communication strategy was modified into two. An intensive approach was planned for the high risk districts, and one for the rest of the country. In high risk areas health camps were held, vaccination teams had local people, vaccinators were trained to handle issues being raised and religious leaders were involved in promoting the programme. For the rest of the country mass media, intensified miking efforts, banners, hoardings etc. were the key interventions.

The experience in the polio programme clearly brought out the importance of interpersonal communication in getting people to change behaviours. It also brought out that there is no one channel which makes for a successful strategy. Mass media, innovative ideas like miking and drum beating, were all necessary to create an enabling environment for the interpersonal communication to succeed. The importance of advocacy at the highest level was also amply demonstrated.

Fig. 24.3: Development communication campaigns are being used extensively these days too.

Conclusion

Be it "Swachh Bharat", "Namami Ganga" or "jahan soch vahan

shouchalya", all these important programmes are being planned and targeted as behaviour change communication programmes.

The experience in development communication clearly brings out that strategic planning is key. However, equally important is that communication campaigns need to be backed by service delivery. Much like any commercial product, unless the services are available on the ground level, there develops a trust deficit.

The communication strategy needs to be localized and contextualized keeping in mind the ground realities. It needs to be reworked and tweaked based on inputs received. The Ministry of Overseas Indian Affairs had produced some TV spots regarding precautions to be taken while proceeding for a job abroad. Feedback was received that since the actors in the TV spots were all north Indians, they did not evoke a connect in the South, despite dubbing in regional languages. The spots were then remade.

One of the key challenges that face communication efforts is the difficulty in measuring the short-term and long-term impact of communication. This leads to problems of replication and scaling up. Another challenge is that there will always be a core "hard to reach" and "hard to convince" audience. Intensive strategies and efforts have to be tailored for such groups. Increasingly, integrating new information technologies in development communication is both an opportunity and a challenge. Finally, we all need to on the same page and have a shared vision and understanding of development for bringing about positive social change.

Notes

1. http://www.devalt.org/newsletter/nov09/of_6.htm
2. Communication Technology and Human Development, Avik Ghosh, 2006, Sage Publications
3. *Ibid.*
4. Health Communication Capacity Collaborative (November 2013). The P Process. Five Steps to Strategic Communication. Baltimore: Johns Hopkins Bloomberg School of Public Health Center for Communication Programs.
5. *Ibid.*

25

Indian Diaspora

A Factor for Development and Global Image

Anisur Rahman

Introduction

Globalisation has lead to a staggering movement of people and a resultant rise in the diaspora population. This also meant a change in the idea and imagination of diaspora which etymologically is associated with the dispersion of Jews following the Exodus. According to the United Nations, Department of Social and Economic Affairs, Population Division, in 2013, 232 million people, or 3.2 per cent of the world's population, were international migrants, compared with 175 million in 2000 and 154 million in 1990. Globally, women account for 48 per cent of all international migrants. According to International Organisation of Migrations, World Migration Report 2013, India is among the top four migrant 'sending and receiving' countries after the United States, the Russian Federation and Ukraine.

The modern Indian Diaspora is considered to be about 200 years old which is in fact, the creation of British colonialism. Demographically, the Indian Diaspora is the second largest in the world after the Chinese Diaspora. Currently, the total number of overseas Indians is more than five million, who are settled in more than 110 countries, including US, Canada, UK, European countries, Australia, West Asian Countries, South-east and Far Eastern countries (Rehman and Naweed, 2020).

The Indian Diaspora can broadly be classified into two categories: NRIs (Non-Resident Indians) and PIOs (Persons of Indian Origin). The genesis of Indian Diaspora is traced to the labour migration to different parts of the World for multiple reasons under various circumstances. There have various patterns of migration which lead to the formation of Indian diaspora. Historically, these patterns of emigration could be divided into broad five categories out of which Indenture, Kangani and Passage emigration can be identified as colonial phenomena. The formation of Diaspora communities is in fact the result of different waves of migration over hundreds of years under colonial regimes. The other two patterns of contemporary migrations flows of post-independence highly skilled professionals, workers and students with higher educational qualifications migrating to developed countries and unskilled and semi-skilled workers moving mostly to the Gulf countries.

Emigration and Patterns of Migrant Formations

In order to understand successions of migrations one needs to have the following categories in mind:

Indentured Labour Migration

The migration of Indian indentured labour began in 1834 and officially ended in 1920. The major importing countries of Indian labour were the West Indian colonies, Fiji, South Africa, Mauritius, Malaysia and Ceylon (now Sri Lanka) and also to East African countries such as Kenya, Uganda, Tanzania, etc. The majority of emigrants were recruited from the 'hill coolie' district of Chota Nagpur division and the Bankura, Birbhum and Burdwan districts of Bengal Presidency. Bihar and Eastern Uttar Pradesh were the leading areas in the Northern region. In South India, Trichinopoly, Madurai, Salem and Tanjore were the main recruiting districts. From West India, in Bombay Presidency, Ahmadnagar district was the main area of recruitment.

The export of indentured labour happened mainly due to the abolition of slavery in the British Empire. Labour was nevertheless needed to work on plantations in various British colonies. Indenture was, in fact a contract by which the emigrant was bound to work for a given employer for a three to five year term, performing the task assigned to him for a specified wage. It was bonded labour under contract to work for an employer for a specific amount of time to pay off his passage to a new country. In the 19th century, hundreds of thousands of Indian and Chinese labourers worked on plantations, in mines and road or railway construction projects around the world. Most settled there when they were provided a piece of land. By sheer virtue of their hard work they established themselves and progressed in those colonies.

Today, Indian communities have become immensely diversified in terms of occupations. They also have visible share in the power and politics of many of the host countries. In Mauritius where the Indians constitute about 70 per cent of the total population of the country, they have had a visible domination for long time. In the recent past in Guyana, Fiji and Trinidad and Tobago, government heads are persons of Indian origin. This has lead to an image making of Indians as diligent and sincere. Though they may be second or third generations, Indians around the world are now in a position not only to project the country's image but also have partnership with India for growth and development.

Kangani/Maistry System

The *Kangani* system of recruitment was used to supply labour from South India to Malaysia and Sri Lanka and the *maistry* to Burma. The word *Kangani* is the anglicised version of the Tamil word *Kankani* meaning overseer and foreman. Under this system, a *Kangani* used to recruit the coolies in India paying them in advance for expenses. The *maistry* system was more or less similar to the *Kangani* system except that the former was characterised by gradation of middlemen employers. As compared to indentured system, coolies under this system were legally free. There was no contract and no fixed period of service.

The *Kangani* system began in the first quarter of the nineteenth century and continued until its abolition in 1938. The *maistry* system began sometime in the third quarter of the nineteenth century. The exact number of migrants under these systems is not known. In all, probably 10 million Indians moved back and forth between India and Burma, Ceylon and Malaysia. The majority of Indian immigrants were Tamil — speaking Hindus, the remaining being Muslims, Christians and Sikhs.

Indian immigration to South-east Asia also consisted of such groups as traders, shopkeepers, entrepreneurs, salesman, clericals and professionals. In Malaysia, until 1957 this constituted about one-third of the total immigration. A similar dynamics existed in Burma, though in the case of Ceylon non-labour Indian immigration was substantially less. South Indian Chettiar Hindus were the leading commercial and business community in Burma and Malaysia.

Free Passage Emigration

The third form of Indian migration within the British Empire was the 'passage of free' emigration, or emigration of trading castes and classes. Passage emigration was predominant in South Africa as well as in the East African countries of Kenya, Tanzania and Uganda. Gujaratis and Punjabis immigrated to East Africa following the 'opening up' of East Africa by the British and other European powers. The completion of the Ugandan railway offered new economic opportunities in the hinterland as well as along the railway route. Indians, mainly Gujaratis, soon established themselves as shopkeepers. Subsequently, they monopolized trade and commercial activities in cities and towns. The Indians were merchants in native produce, carters and teamsters, small contractors, moneylenders, quarry-masters, dealers in limc, sand, stone and domestic firewood, barbers, saddlers, boot makers, nurseryman, tailors, etc. Some businessmen successfully rose to prominence.

The success of the diasporic communities, on occasions, led to conflict with local populations. A large number of Indians from East Africa migrated to Britain, Canada and US, who subsequently were aptly described as 'twice migrants', and many of them are now well settled in these countries. The remaining Indians in East Africa continue to thrive in businesses and other professions.

Voluntary Emigration to Western Societies

Large-scale Indian immigration to advanced industrial societies of Europe and North America began in the sixties, though the history of Indian immigration goes back to the early years of the twentieth century in North America and the nineteenth century in Britain. The migrants were either highly educated professionals or skilled and semi-skilled industrial workers. Early Indian migrants who went to settle down in Britain and North America were mainly Sikhs, who still constitute the single largest ethnic group in Britain, Canada and the US.

Today, there are about 5 million people of Indian origin in Europe, North America and Oceania. In the US, the majority of Indians are educated professionals — scientists, engineers, doctors, teachers, etc. In Britain and Canada, Indian communities are occupationally more diversified and relatively less well off.

Racial discrimination and prejudices against the migrants in the western societies is a known phenomenon. One possible explanation could be that when a group attains a palpable visibility, it incurs some sort of resistance from the host culture in the form of discrimination or prejudices that could manifest in the form of competition for jobs and resources, especially during economic crises. Indians in the Europe and the North America have been victims of such discrimination time and again.

Also, Indians communities in all these countries have begun to exert political influence in varying degrees. In the UK, four members of the House of Commons and eleven members of the House of Lords are of Indian origin, and in Canada, Ujjal Singh Dosanjh rose to become the Premier of British Columbia. Indians settled in these countries are very conscious of their distinct identity and try to preserve it.

Indian Labour Diaspora in West Asia

The fifth and final pattern consists of Indian labour migration to West Asia. This migration pattern differs from the previous once in that all the migrants are generally 'contract' workers are not allowed to settle permanently in the countries of their destination. But this was not always the case, as will be clear from the following.

India has had trade and cultural relations with the Persian Gulf region since antiquity. However, there is evidence of Indian settlement in the region only since the sixteenth century. Small communities of Indian traders called *baniyas* in Hindi, in present-day Iraq, Iran, Oman, Yemen and Saudi Arabia in the seventeenth and eighteenth centuries. When the region came under British influence in the nineteenth century, Indian merchant communities flourished in a number of towns in the Gulf countries. Indians served as bankers, importers and exporters, customs farmers, agents for local merchants, government contractors, financiers, etc.

In the early, 1970s, due to the spurt in oil prices, some oil producing countries of the West Asia started investing in infrastructure development that created a huge demand for labour. As a result migrant workers from South Asia joined the labour market predominantly in the Gulf countries such as Saudi Arabia, UAE, Kuwait, etc.

Since mid-1980s, it was noticed that horizon of migration was expanded and migrant workers began to migrate to the newly industrialised countries in South-east Asia and East Asia, such as the Republic of Korea, Malaysia, and Singapore. It was noted that they faced a shortage of labour and local workers were reluctant to take up the so-called 3D jobs — dangerous, dirty and degraded.

The number of migrant workers showed an increase after 1990, following the liberalisation of overseas travel by the government. The majority of migrant workers from South Asia constitute semi-skilled and unskilled manpower (Ahn, 2004, p. 3). It is also observed that overwhelming majority of migrant workers are found to be males from India, Pakistan, Bangladesh, and Nepal, while only in case of Sri Lanka, women migrant workers constitute majority. Women are found to be more vulnerable to all kinds of exploitation in comparison to their male counterparts. Their human rights need to be protected along with their male counterparts.

Growing Composition of Labour Diaspora in the Gulf

It was noted that the percentage of expatriate workers in the GCC countries grew from 22.9 per cent in 1975 to 38.5 per cent in 2002 and then to 48.1 per cent of the total population of 48.1 million GCC residents. Reliance on foreign labour has resulted in expatriates currently constituting 88 per cent of the workforce in the UAE, 83 per cent in Qatar, 81 per cent in Kuwait, 72 per cent in Saudi Arabia, 55 per cent in Bahrain, and 54 per cent in Oman. However, the composition of expatriate workers has changed periodically. If the current trend continues, it is projected that the number of migrant workers would grow by another 1 million. It is equally likely that the number of non-Gulf Arab workers in the GCC states will diminish, the presence of Asian workers would likely to grow further. The proportion of non-citizens in the Gulf has steadily increased during the last four decades which is contrary to the plans and desires of the Gulf countries. It is revealed by the data that the proportion of non-nationals vary from country to country, ranging from 32.0 per cent in Saudi Arabia to 88.5 per cent in the United Arab Emirates (Rehman and Naveed, 2020).

Diaspora Investment Policy

The Indian Government was unable to realise the potential of Indian diaspora in the early years of independence. It was during the 1970s that the NRIs' contribution in the development of India was realised. Consequently, the Indian Government began adopting policies and introducing schemes for increased NRI involvement in India. As rightly stated by C.S. Bhat, it was the liberalisation and the new industrial policy in 1970s that sought involvement of overseas Indians in investing both in terms of capital and technology. NRIs were encouraged to invest in India through certain attractive schemes such as Resurgent India Bond (RIB) and they were welcomed to launch industrial enterprises along with transfer of technology. There is hardly any evidence that the government reached out to the majority of the People of Indian Origin, till the announcement of the new scheme of *PIO Card* was announced during the early 1999. The overseas Indian holders of the card could visit India without a visa, and also had other facilities in India regarding acquisition of properties etc.

Besides engaging the NRIs and PIOs to understand their sentiments about India, special measures were devised to facilitate the involvement of the Indian Diaspora in the investment sector in major cities in India (ITES) sectors in India. It is evident that NRIs and PIOs have transferred knowledge and expertise that resulted in positive change in several sectors. On account of India's foreign exchange reserves and the massive entrepreneurial energy has also led to the rise of India's Information Technology (IT) and IT Enabled Services, Omni Solutions Information Technologies (OSIT) worth $513 million.

The Indian Diaspora has always played an important role in adding India's national income and wealth, thereby being actively involved in the country's development and strategic decision making. The Indian Government has realised the significance of its diaspora, and is taking steps to tap productive investments from the overseas Indians in order to engage them as long-term partners in India's growth process. These flows and investment in fact play a significant role for national growth and development in our country.

The current Government at the Centre has recently revised diaspora policy with the objective to tap the technical expertise from the Indian Diaspora for India's growth and development. Their involvement in India's signature programmes including cleaning of Ganga River, Swachch Bharat etc. are considered to be vital for the progress of their homeland. The new policy is in fact looking at the Indian Diaspora in a new perspective. It is realised that their contribution in terms of time, expertise and investment in all the sectors of Indian economy and society are crucial for India. It is evident that the Diasporas provide important bridge between home and host societies by building transnational networks. These networks can serve the purpose of not only emotional and familial ties for Diaspora, but also cultural, social and economic interests of India.

Diaspora and Financial Flows

The flow of funds from migrant workers to their families in their home country is an important source of income in many developing economies. International migration from developing countries has increased significantly during the last two decades. Remittances sent by migrant workers contribute significantly in foreign exchange earnings and GDP growth of nations. They also enhance economic betterment of migrants' families and are considered to be the engine of economic growth for many developing countries like India. Remittances sent through informal channels are considerable in many developing countries such as Pakistan, India, Bangladesh, the Philippines and Sudan. The actual value of remittances is likely to be much higher as only a portion of total remittance flow through official channels.

Migration empowers migrant workers in terms of economic independence and higher self-esteem. Migration has made a significant contribution in terms of earning foreign exchange, enhancing migrants' skills, and reducing unemployment and underemployment in labour sending countries like India, Pakistan, Bangladesh, Nepal, and Sri Lanka. In 2010, the flow of international remittances to developing countries stood at US $325 billion that rose to $406 billion in 2012, a growth of 6.5 per cent over the previous year. These flows rose 8 per cent in 2013 and 10 per cent in 2014 and are expected to reach $534 billion in 2015. (World Bank Report, 2015).

India is the world's largest remittance recipient country in the World. According to latest information, it was estimated to be around $ US71 billion. (A global share of about 20%). It was estimated to be less than $2 million in 1970-71 which rose to more than $2 billion in 1980-81. (World Bank Report) Throughout 1980s, annual inflows remained more than $2 billion. But in 1990s, a considerable rise in the annual inflows of remittances.

At the turn of the century, remittances rose to more than $12 billion in 2000-01. Remittances further went up to $ 55 billion in 2009-2010 and it finally rose to US $80 billion in 2018 (World Bank Report, 2018). There is a substantial growth in remittance flows during the last two decades. Due to this huge inflow of the remittance, a lot of developmental activities are going on in India. This could be observed both at micro as well macro levels.

Economic and Social Benefits of Diaspora

Diaspora from India is not only helping to reduce the situation of unemployment but also earn foreign exchange. Migration has reduced poverty and bought prosperity in migrating regions. Gulf money has improved the income level of the migrants' households considerably. It has improved the consumption, investment and saving patterns in the migrating areas. Work experience has made the migrants more skilled economic assets. Expatriate workers are also the backbone of the Gulf Economy and society.

Gulf is one of the regions from where the huge amount of remittance comes to India every year.

Kerala is one of the Indian States that receives substantial amount of remittances. India has still maintained the first position in the world in terms of receiving remittances from abroad. The effects of financial inflow and remittances in all labour sending countries are noticeable in terms of reducing poverty, unemployment, etc. In order to channelize the interests of Indians abroad a new Ministry, named Ministry of Overseas Indian Affairs, was created in 2004. It works to address the issues pertaining to diasporic community. One of the other functions of this Ministry is to engage them for their mutual benefit and interests. It is now very important to protect their rights so that they could become economically, socially and strategically, crucial for both (home and host) countries. The diaspora provides important links between home and host societies by building transnational networks which transact not only emotional and familial bonds, but also cultural, social and economic interests.

In addition to economic remittances, they also bring social remittance to the home land. There is a visible change in their attitude towards education and social mobility in migrants' families. This also lead to social acceptance of the migrants in the home country. A family that was looked down in the past began to be welcomed in social functions. Similarly, poverty stricken villages are becoming prosperous. A sizeable proportion of houseless population could now have a house of their own. These observations are made on the basis of common findings from the studies conducted by independent researchers.

Diaspora and Human Rights

In spite of the fact that the diaspora have made a significant contribution to the welfare of both host and home countries, their rights have been violated from time to time. The situation is worse in countries that have a non-democratic set-up. Incidents of racial discrimination and human right violation against members of the Indian community are often reported. Their rights to conserve or practice their own culture have been challenged if not denied. They are being denied the basic human right of equality, social justice and human dignity in places like Fiji, Malaysia, the Caribbean, Gulf countries and even in some Western countries.

The grievances of the members of the diaspora are not addressed either by the legal framework or by trade unions, and their welfare is not sufficiently secured in the societies they are a part of. In contrast to the fact that none of the governments in South Asian countries has ratified ILO (International Labour Organization) Conventions. Individual States have taken alternative measures, such as bilateral agreements, implementation of model contracts and establishing institutions to defend even partially migrant workers rights. Moreover, the 1990 Convention on the rights of Migrant Workers has not been ratified by any major countries of the World. An early ratification of these Conventions by these countries will represent an initial step towards the improvement of the situation of diaspora workers and their rights. This would not only be in the interest of labour, but also in the interest of the both (home and host) countries as they would then amount to a more productive and motivated human capital.

In India, the migratory flows of the both skilled and the unskilled, have undergone changes due to the pervasive economic restructuring under globalisation that creates opportunities as well as challenges. In the case of unskilled migrants the policy responses from public administration, both in the countries of origin and destination towards safe and adequate legal protection to the migrants, continue to maintain its salience. At the same time, limiting the scope of irregular migration primarily by ensuring transparent systems and regulation for the transnational movement of people continues. Even amongst moderates, the issue of integration and assimilation of the overseas community with the host society continues to be a concern. The truth is that migrants of all skill levels considerably contribute to societies. They spawn creativity, nourish the human spirit and spur economic growth. They bring diversity, provide innovation and bring about economic development and growth in the host societies.

It is in this context that MOIA (Ministry of Overseas Indian Affairs) engages with a wide range of academia to collaborate on empirical and analytical work to enable evidence-based policy-making. There is a need to foster international cooperation amongst countries of origin and destination, and for greater policy coherence amongst various departments of government, to enhance our ability to manage migration in a better way. The approach is to work towards building a consensus that can transform migration into an orderly and mutually beneficial economic process that is a win-all for all stakeholders in both the countries of origin and destination. India is well placed to contribute to developing a robust, harmonious and efficient migration framework. The primary motivation for migration is economic and at the heart of migration management, is the imperative to maximise the development impact of international migration for all. The scale and spread of the Indian experience of managing migration as well as development, and the intimate interplay of these two complex processes, is substantial. With the second-largest overseas population, its status as the country that receives amongst the highest remittances, its experience in effectively addressing the problems of poverty, inequality and unemployment in an unfailingly democratic manner, India can provide the much needed impetus to meaningfully reinforce the symbiotic development-migration paradigm.

Conclusion

Being the second largest in terms of the number and enormously diverse in terms of religious, ethnic as well as occupational background, the Indian diaspora becomes an important case of analysis. Indian diaspora communities not only become the ambassadors of India in the outside but also bring back both culture and capital from the host country. It is also witnessed that India gets economic and strategic benefits due to the enormous presence of its diaspora worldwide. Though the significance of remittances has been realised by the Indian Government and it has been taking steps towards channelising the potential of the Indian diaspora by making them invest in schemes back home that are mutually beneficial, more steps need to be taken to safeguard the economic position as well as basic rights of the Indian diaspora abroad.

References

Anisur Rahman (2001). *Indian Labour Migration to the Gulf: A Socio-economic Analysis*, New Delhi: Rajat Publications.

Anisur Rahman and Naziya Naweed (2020). "Indian Diaspora as a factor in Indo-Gulf Relations", in *India's Foreign Policy Modi 2.0: Challenges and Opportunities*, ed. Sudhir Singh, New Delhi: Pentagon Press LLP..

Birks, J.S. and Sinclair, C.A. (1980). *International Migration and Development in the Arab Region*, Geneva: ILO.

Fargues P. and I. Brouwer (2012). "GCC Demography and Immigration:

Challenges and Policies", In *National Employment, Migration and Education in the GCC*, ed. S. Hertog, Cambridge: Gerlach Press.

Giovanna Tattolo, Arab Labour Migration to the GCC States, accessed through internet, http://jmobservatory.eco.uniroma1.it/home.html

Government of India, Ministry of Overseas Indian Affairs, Annual Reports (recent years) accessed through internet, http://moia.gov.in/writereaddata/pdf/Annual_Report_2014-15.pdf

Government of India, Report of the High Level Committee on Indian Diaspora, 2001 accessed through internet, http://moia.gov.in/services.aspx?ID1=63&id=m10&idp=59&mainid=23

Indentured Labour Migration from India, accessed through internet, http://www.zahie.com/categories/details/history/indentured-labour-migration-from-india.html

Jain, Prakash C. (1989). "Emigration and Settlement of Indians Abroad", *Sociology Bulletin*, 38(1): 155-68.

Jain, Prakash C., *Indian Diaspora: An Overview*, Think India, New Delhi.

Kapiszewski, Andrzej, *Arab vs. Asian Migrant Workers in the GCC Countries*, accessed through internet, http://www.un.org/esa/population/meetings/EGM_Ittmig_Arab/P02_Kapiszewski.pdfhttp://www.un.org/esa/population/meetings/EGM_Ittmig_Arab/P02_Kapiszewski.pdf

Khadria, Binod (1999). *The Migration of Knowledge Workers: Second-Generation Effects of India's Brain Drain*, New Delhi: Sage Publications.

Nasra, M. Shah (2005). *Restrictive Labour Immigration Policies in the Oil Rich Gulf: Implications for Asian Countries*, Accessed through internet, http://iussp 2005.princeton.edu/download.aspx?submissionId=50842

Patrick Seale (2005). *The Challenges Facing Arab Gulf States*, accessed through internet http://www.genceglobal.com

Pong-Sul Ahn (ed.) (2004). *Migrant Workers and Human Rights: Out-Migration from South Asia*. ILO, Subregional Office for South Asia, New Delhi.

Sheffer, Gabriel (ed.) (1986). *Modern Diasporas in International Politics*, London: Croom Helm.

Special Report, *Promoting Investments from the Indian Diaspora: A New Beginning*, An OIFC Publication, accessed through internet, http://www.oifc.in/Uploads/MediaTypes/Documents/PromotingInvestmentsFromTheIndianDiaspora.pdf

Tinker, Hugh (1974). *A New System of Slavery: The Expert of Indian Labour Oversea, 1830-1920*, London: Oxford University Press.

Tinker, Hugh (1977). *The Banyan Tree: Overseas Emigrants from India, Pakistan and Bangladesh*, Oxford University Press.

Weiner, Myron (1982). "International Migration and Development: Indians in the Pakistan Gulf", *Population and Development Review*, 9(1): 1-36.

SECTION-V
Environment, Technology and Sustainable Development

26

Climate Change and its Impact

Issues and Concern

Atiqur Rahman

Introduction

Climate change is one of the most important global environmental challenges, with implications for food production, loss in water supply, surface water bodies and water pollution, coastal submergence, forest ecosystems, health impacts, energy, etc. The climate of the earth is dynamic and always changing; in the past few million years there have been spells of ice age and warm periods. Climate change is preferred phrase for 'Global Warming' as it helps convey that there are changes in addition to rising temperature. The projected climate change under various scenarios is likely to have serious implications on the global environmental sustainability which is largely equated with the green house gases. The CO_2 accounted for about 60 per cent and methane 20 per cent of six major GHGs. Since 1750 atmospheric concentrations of carbon dioxide have increased by about 30 per cent and methane by 145 per cent etc. keeping in view the above facts and figures in this chapter an attempt has been made to assess and measure the various issues which cropped up because of urbanization and developmental activities and what are the challenges that may put a threat to the global environmental sustainability.

As per Intergovernmental Panel on Climate Change (IPCC) Report, (2007), earth's averaged surface temperature has increased by 0.74°C during (1901-2005) and projects that it may increase somewhat in between 2 to 4.5 °C if CO_2 emission gets double from the current rate. Consequent upon increase in temperature, glacier melt is most likely to happen. With the Himalayan glacier's melt it is projected to increase flooding, and will affect water resources within the next two to three decades. In India with 1 m rise in sea-level would affect 5,763 km^2 coastal land, 1,700 km^2 agricultural land and 4200 km of roads and will render 7.1 million people at risk. Freshwater availability in Central, South, East and South-East Asia, particularly in large river basins, is projected to decrease, and could adversely affect more than a billion people by the 2050s. This shows that the impact would be particularly severe in the tropical areas, which mainly consist of developing countries, including India.

Our earth is very dynamic and is changing constantly due to various natural and anthropogenic processes; global warming (GW) and climate change (CC) are one of them. CC is the study of how weather phenomenon and seasonal changes for a long period of time in the world. After industrial revolution in the world, human have contributed as a most active agent to CC through the emission of greenhouse gases (GHGs) and aerosols, and through changes in various other anthropogenic activities like land use/ land cover (LULC) changes, resulting increase global temperature (World Meteorological Organization, 2005). Climate model simulations of the effect of GHGs emission are compared against the observed climatic variation in the past and their possible outcomes on natural phenomena are done by Climatologists. There is debate going on since long time that whether climate change/global warming is a reality or a myth? This chapter tries to answer this question by taking certain aspects of global climate change as an example and by analysing long term historical data at the global level. There is strong evidence that the anthropogenic activities are mainly responsible for warming over the last 50 years and since mid-19th century average land and sea surface temperature has increased by 0.6±0.2°C globally where most of the change had occurred since 1976 (Fig. 26.1), Intergovernmental Panel on Climate Change (IPCC, 2001).

There is variation in rise in temperature on regional basis; it may be greater or lesser than the global average of rise in temperature (IPCC, 2001). For instance, warming in the United States is anticipated to be more than the global average and highest warming is expected over Arctic (Georgi *et al.*, 2001). The ten warmest years occurred between 1995 and 2005, since thermometer records became available in 1860 and after 1998, 2005 was the second hottest year on record, because of influence of El Nino in the Pacific Ocean which contribute into rise in temperature above than the average temperatures of the world (WMO, 2005). As per Intergovernmental Panel on Climate Change (IPCC), average global temperature is expected to increase by 2½ to 10 °F in the next century.

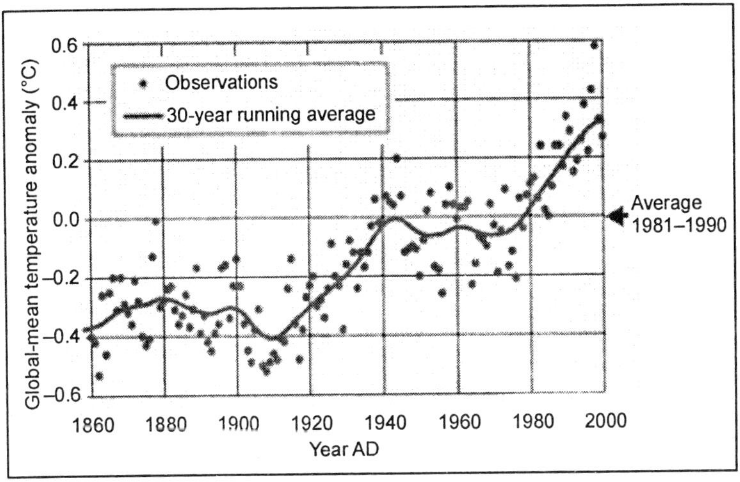

Fig. 26.1: Global average of land and sea surface temperature.

Source: IPCC, 2001.

All seven continents and five oceans are affected by warming but mid and high latitude area of the continent are most affected because of climate change. Precipitation becomes more erratic, arid and semi-arid areas are becoming drier, whereas other regions are becoming wetter and frequency of the heaviest precipitation events have increased (Karl and Knight 1998; Mason *et al.*, 1999). The little glimpse of climate change that has occurred so far has already had comprehensible effects on an extensive diversity of natural ecosystems (Walther *et al.*, 2002). The earth's climate is changing very fast and differently, these climate changes affect our lives socially, economically and physically and the outcome of climate change is more than a GW. The increase in average temperature in the single factor for massive changes which translates into extreme temperatures, flooding, storms, sea level rise expected 0.11 to 0.77 meters by 2100 (IPCC, 2001), drought, impact of agriculture or food production, and impact on health conditions etc. The atmospheric temperature of the earth has increased due to rise in GHGs emission, with the exact change differs regionally. The rate of emission of GHGs is responsible to increase the average surface temperature of the Earth which is about 0.2°C per decade.

Climate change can have impact on formation of storm by regulating the difference in temperature between the poles and the equator. There will be high risk of flood, droughts, and storms like tropical cyclones with devastating wind speeds, a wetter and erratic Asian monsoon, and, stronger mid-latitude storms (Pounds and Puschendorf, 2004). This difference in temperature provides the energy to mid-latitude storms which affect the most populated area over the Earth surface. Equator is already hot and humid so slight change in temperature does not matter very much as on the poles, because at the poles the air is cold and dry and a little additional heat and water vapour can increase temperatures substantially. Pattern of climate change can be observed worldwide and seen in latest natural disaster in Haiti by hurricane Mathew. It is the strongest storm which hit Haiti since hurricane Cleo in 1964. About 1.125 million people were affected and around 546 people were died according to Haitian government figure (Stewart, 2017). This can also be equated with the global climate change.

Greenhouse Gases and Global Climate Change

The incoming solar radiation is responsible to warm the earth's surface. The temperature at the outer surface of the sun i.e. at photosphere is about 5700 °K, which means the Earth's temperature should be approx. 6000/20 = 300 °K or 80 °F. Only 60 per cent of the energy is absorbed by the Earth comes from the Sun and rest of 40 per cent reflected back to atmosphere is called Earth's albedo. As per this equation the temperature of the Earth should be around 26 °F, well it is below freezing (The freezing point of water is 32° F and the boiling point of water is 212 °F). If that were true, the life on Earth is not possible but in reality it is not that cold, the average temperature of the Earth is 57°F. The extra warm temperature about 31°F comes from GHG effect (Muller, 2008).

The major greenhouse gases (GHGs) in Earth's atmosphere includes carbon dioxide (CO_2), methane (CH_4), nitrous oxide (N_2O), water vapour (H_2O), Chlorofluorocarbons (CFCs), Hydro-fluorocarbons (HFCs) and Ozone (O_3). Out of these seven GHGs gases CO_2 which is emitted mainly by the burning of fossil fuel, industrial activities, land use change and deforestation etc. is the primary source of GHGs and contributes about 55 per cent of the total GHGs. Methane (CH_4) contributes 16 per cent of GHGs which is mainly coming out of agricultural activities, waste management, energy use, and biomass burning etc. The share of nitrous oxide (N_2O) is 6 per cent of total GHGs which is mainly due to fertilizer use and fossil fuel combustion etc. (IPCC, 2014). The global averaged concentration of GHGs has increased several folds.

The climate change is affected by both natural (volcanic eruptions and aerosols etc.) and anthropogenic (vehicular and industrial pollution) factors. The influence of human beings on climate change is well-known and recent emissions of greenhouse gases (GHGs) by anthropogenic activities can be noticed more often. The impact of GHGs has been observed on human and natural system. Here, we quantify the concentration of global averaged GHGs like CO_2, CH_4 and N_2O during 1850 to 2011. The minimum concentration of CO_2 is approx 285 parts per million (ppm) recorded in the year 1850, while the maximum concentration of CO_2 is approx 390 ppm was recorded in 2011 (Fig. 26.2) (IPCC, 2014).

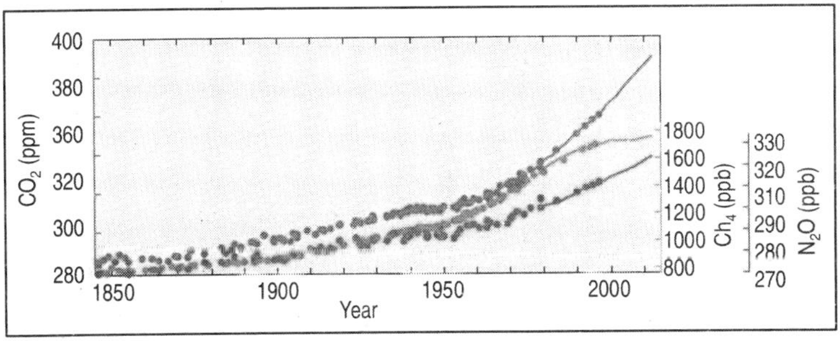

Fig. 26.2: Global averaged GHGs Concentration, Source: IPCC Synthesis Report, 2014.
Source: Boden *et al.* (2017).

The increased amount of water vapour in the atmosphere produces the greenhouse effect because GHG increases the capacity of atmosphere to hold more water vapour. The rate of increase in temperature by 1^0C globally results in approx 7 per cent increase in water vapour present in the atmosphere (Myhre, *et al.*, 2013). Aerosols comes from industrial emissions contribute about 26 per cent of greenhouse warming by trapping the solar radiation to reach earth's surface.

The chapter shows the global carbon emissions from fossil fuels have significantly increased since 1900. Its emission increased drastically from 1970, by about 90 per cent, where emissions from fossil fuel combustion and industrial activities contribute about 78 per cent of the total GHGs emissions during 1970 to 2011 and at the end of 2010 Global Carbon Emission from Fossil Fuel increased to about 10,000 million metric tons (Figure 26.3).

Global Warming and Climate Change

The term global warming used to quantify the amount of an increase in the average Earth's atmosphere temperature constantly to cause changes in the global climate. During the last couple of years, the consistently changes in the temperature of earth's surface, atmosphere and ocean was

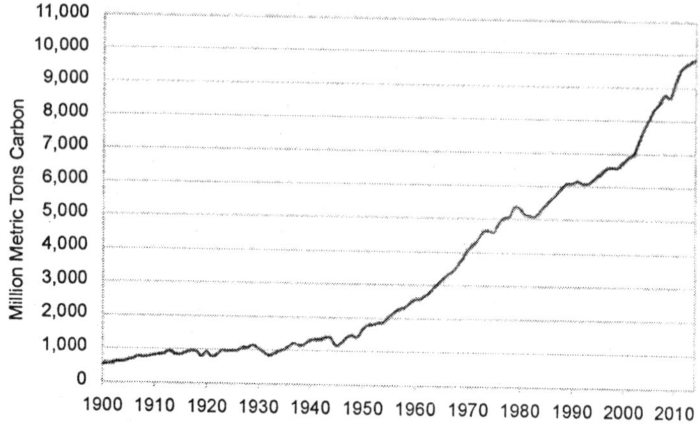

Fig. 26.3: Global Carbon Emission from Fossil Fuel during 1900 to 2014.
Source: Boden *et al.*, 2017.

a debate topic in the scientific and political community. The contribution of anthropogenic activities is more in global warming, primarily the burning of fossil fuels that emit the CO_2, CH_4 and greenhouse gases (GHGs) into the atmosphere (Bradford, 2014).

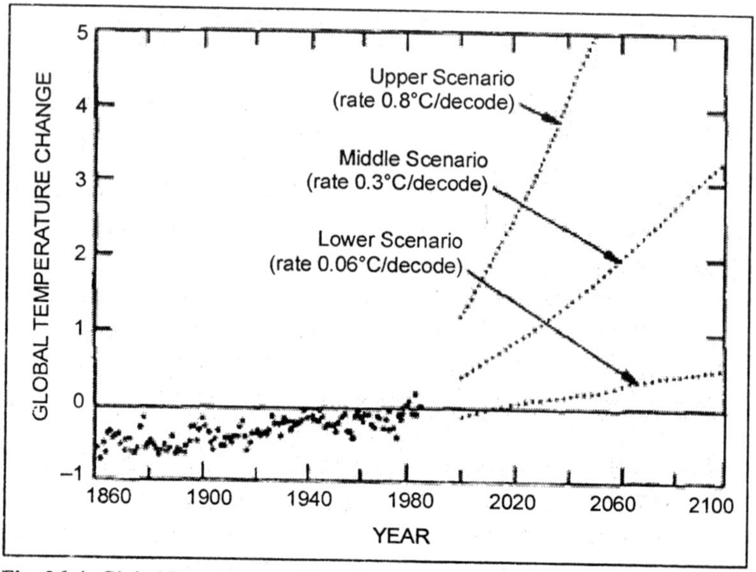

Fig. 26.4: Global Temperature Change.

The GHGs and particles present in the earth's atmosphere are responsible to trap the infrared radiation, and 25 per cent increased the atmospheric CO_2 level since 1850. The global average surface temperature will increase about 1.5 °C to 4.5 °C during the next century suggested by recent climatic model. An international group of scientists convened by the international council of scientific unions drawn global warming possibilities in 21st century. It shows the earth's surface temperature increased from 0.5 °C up to 5 °C or greater warming before the end of the coming next century, Fig. 26.4 (Jaeger, 1988).

Since 1900, global surface temperature show global warming between +0.8 °C and +1.0 °C (IPCC third assessment report, 2001). The measurement indicate warming trend of land only between +1.1 °C and +1.3 °C, as land surface temperature tend to respond more rapidly than ocean to the earth's changing climate. Fig. 26.3, shows the trend of global surface temperature during 1880 - 2014 (Hansen *et al.*, 2010).

Climate Change and Sea Level Rise

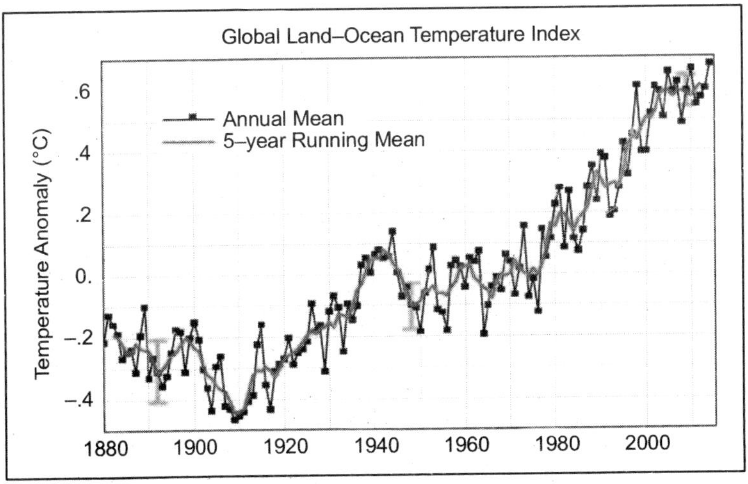

Fig. 26.5: Global Land and Ocean Temperature during (1880-2014).
Source: Hansen *et al.*, 2010.

Rising sea level is one of the most severe catastrophic effects of climate change. Most important reason behind the rise in sea level is because of melting of glacier and if sea level rising with same rates then by the end of the century it may be three feet higher than today (Levitus *et al.*, 2005). Communities living in low-lying coastal area are the major victims of the rising sea level. For instance in Bangladesh 17 per cent area of the country would be flooded or even submerged by just a one-meter rise in sea level (Anthoff *et al.*, 2010). South-east and mid-Atlantic coast of United States are the most vulnerable area from rising sea level and not only this, about 54 per cent of its population lives in close proximity to the ocean are also lives in risk of inundation. Some other area like North Carolina's Outer Banks, the Florida Coast, and much of southern California and Maldives are in risk (National Centre for Atmospheric Research, 2005). It is projected that Maldives will face rise in level of 1.5 feet (half a meter) and about 77 per cent of its land will submerged by 21st century (Woodworth, 2005 & Tol, 2007) and if sea levels rise by 3 feet (1 meter) then by about 2085 whole Maldives could be submerged in the ocean (Anthoff *et al.*, 2010).

Cause of sea level rise: Since the industrial revolution global warming is the main cause behind the sea level rise. Anthropogenic processes like burning coal and oil and deforestation of tropical forests increase the concentration of green house gases in the atmosphere which leads to the warming of the earth by 1.4°F since 1880 (Hansen *et al.* 2010). Ocean waters also get warm because of rising atmospheric temperature and 85 per cent of the excess heat of the atmosphere have been absorbed since 1880 (Levitus *et al.*, 2001; Levitus *et al.*, 2005; Levitus *et al.*, 2009; Cazenave and Llovel, 2010). Ocean water expands when gets heated so main cause of rising sea level for about 100 year after the beginning of the Industrial Revolution. Nonetheless, the contribution of thermal expansion in rising sea level has reduced in past few decades because of acceleration of melting of land ice (Lombard *et al.*, 2005; Cazenave & Llovel, 2010). Two-third of world fresh water is stored in the form of land ice glaciers, ice caps, and ice sheets and they are shrinking because of rise in atmospheric temperatures (Trenberth *et al.*, 2007). Indeed additional water cause rise in sea level (Kaser *et al.*, 2006; Meier *et al.*, 2007; Cogley, 2009; EPA, 2012). About one inch of water added into the sea from 1993 to 2008 from melting of glaciers, ice caps and ice sheets which accounts for more than half of the increase during said period (Church *et al.*, 2011).

Changes in regional ocean current because of submergence of land are another cause for sea level rise. These types of phenomena have effects on 'hot spots' that are experiencing local sea level rise more than the average, for example the East and Gulf coasts of the United States (Sallenger *et al.*, 2012; Milne, 2008). Global warming and climate change is the main culprit of rise in sea level. Since 1880, there is about eight inches rise in sea level. Long term rise in sea level is recorded by tide gauges since 1870 and these trends are also confirmed by satellite observations since 1993 (blue line) Fig. 26.6.

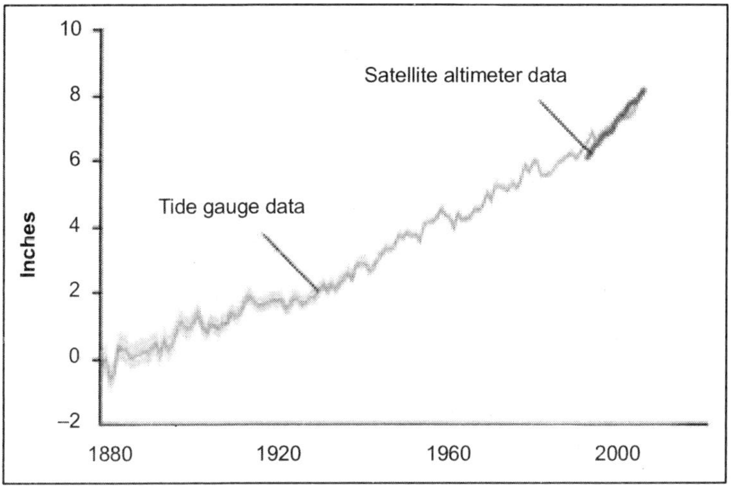

Fig. 26.6: Average Global Sea Level Rise.

Source: NRC, 2012; Church *et al.*, 2011, Cazenave and Llovel, 2010.

Another significant cause of sea level rise is the melting of land ice glaciers, ice caps, and ice sheets which contributes about 52 per cent of sea level rise between 1972 and 2008, whereas thermal expansion of oceans accounts for about 38 per cent and remaining 10 per cent rise in sea level are because of withdrawal of groundwater and other factors. Between 1880 to 2009 global sea level rise approximately eight inches from and decadal rise is about 0.8 inch from 1972 to 2008 (Church *et al.*, 2011). The coastal region between Nova Scotia to the Gulf of Mexico experience one of the rapid sea level rise in the twentieth century from 0.01 inch yearly in Boston to 0.38 inch yearly in Louisiana (NOAA, 2012) Fig. 26.7.

Average absolute sea level change refers to the height of the surface of the ocean without taking into account the rise and fall of the nearby land surface. GMSL data are collected from CSIRO (Commonwealth Scientist and Industrial Research Organisation, 2015) and NOAA (National Oceanic and Atmospheric Administration, 2015). Global

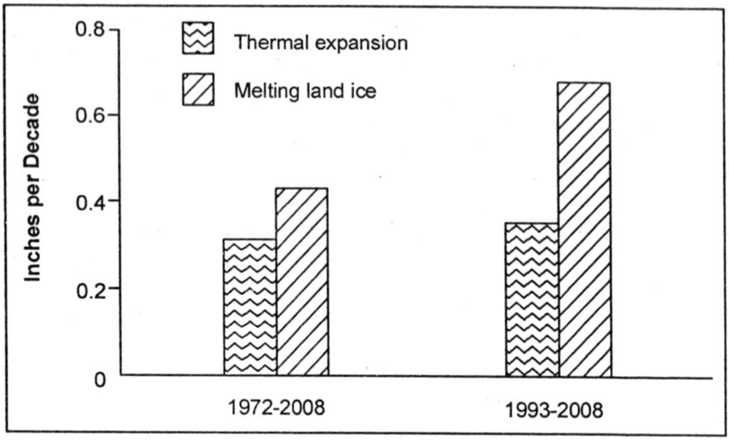

Fig. 26.7: Contribution of Climatic Phenomena in Sea Level Rise.

Source: NRC, 2012; Church *et al.*, 2011, Cazenave and Llovel, 2010.

average absolute sea level (GMSL) change between 1880 to 2010 is shown in Table 26.1. These data are showing cumulative change in global sea level since 1880. Long terms tide gauge measurement and data measured from satellite imageries are used in the calculation of the GMSL data. Between 1880 to 2014 GMSL value increase from to about 8.98 inches. Average decadal growth rate of GMSL is about 17.4 per cent and the highest 37.40 per cent GMSL change is recoded in between 1940 to 1950.

Regional sea level change: Changing wind field and associated change in ocean circulation are responsible for variation in regional sea level change (Kohl & Stammer, 2008). There is spatial variation in sea level rise in ocean. There is higher rate of rise in sea level in western tropical Pacific and decline in sea level in eastern Pacific between 1993 to 2010 and also about 5.4 ± 0.3 mm/year rise in the region between Japan and Korea, which is about two times higher than the GMSL trend (Kang *et al.*, 2005). Tide gauge measurement is used to show the observed and projected relative change in sea level for nine coastal regions since 1970. Shaded region is showing the projected range for 2006 to 2021. *In situ* relative sea level value and satellite record are almost similar in all region range between -0 to 0.2 m. Projected change in sea level is highest in New York between 0.3 to 0.9 m followed by Ijmuidin (port city in North Holland) 0.2 to 0.8 m (Fig. 26.8). At San Francisco the projected value is about 0.3 to 0.8 m and in Bay of Bengal

Table 26.1: Global Mean Sea Level Change (GMSL) between 1880-2013

S. No.	*Decade/ Year*	*Global Mean Sea Level (inches)*	*Decadal rate of change (%)*
1.	1880	—	—
2.	1890	0.44	0.44
3.	1900	1.12	154.54
4.	1910	1.27	13.39
5.	1920	1.90	49.60
6.	1930	2.06	8.42
7.	1940	2.62	27.18
8.	1950	3.60	37.40
9.	1960	4.50	25.00
10.	1970	4.68	4.00
11.	1980	5.60	19.65
12.	1990	6.23	11.25
13.	2000	7.06	13.32
14.	2010	8.90	26.06
15.	2011	8.96	—
16.	2012	9.32	—
17.	2013	8.98	—

Source: EPA (United States Environmental Protection Agency) & CSIRO (Commonwealth Scientific and Industrial Research Organisation), 2015.

it is 0.3 to 0.7 m. In Kanmen, China the projected range is also very high i.e. 0.3 to 0.8 m. In Brest (France) and Mar de Plata (Argentina) the projected range is 0.3 to 0.7 m and in Fremantle (Australia) and Pago Pago (main island of American Samoa) the projected range is between 0.3 to 0.8 m (Fig. 26.6).

Increased surface temperature of earth caused by climate change will make the water of seas and oceans expand due to melting of ice in the Antarctica and Greenland, it will also play an important role in sea level. The level of seas could rise approx. 25 - 50 cm by 21st century. The low lying coastal areas or countries like Netherland, Bangladesh and other millions of areas of land will be vanished and hugely affected due to greater rise in sea levels.

Melting of Glaciers: Impact of climate change is most visible on the glaciers and ice caps. Climate determines the mass balance of the glacier at the earth surface by the gain or loss of snow and ice in hydrological cycle. Air temperature determine the hydrological cycle where ice accumulated in winter and melted in summer. Most accumulation and ablation of ice in Himalayas occurs in summer itself (Fujita and Ageta, 2000), whereas in tropical region accumulation of ice is determined by

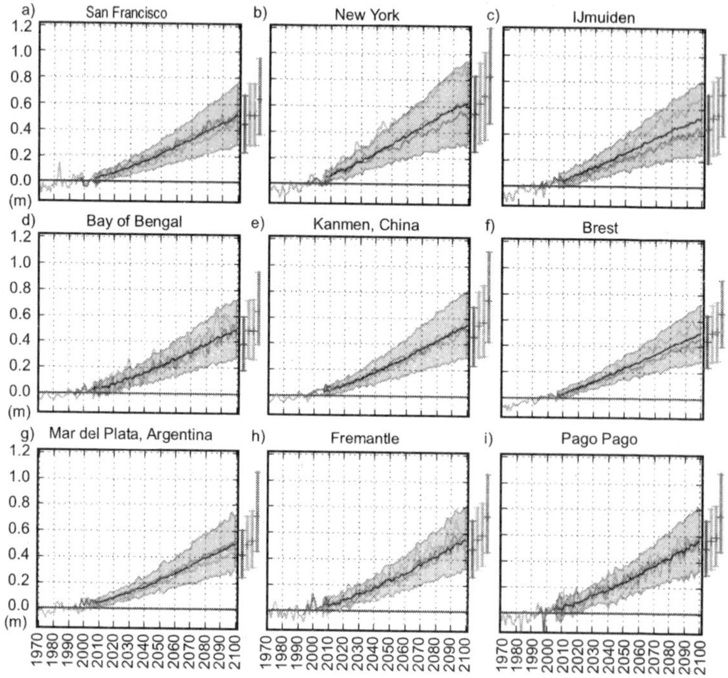

Fig. 26.8: Regional Sea Level Change.

Source: IPCC Report, 2013.

precipitation and ablation takes place throughout the year (Kaser and Osmaston, 2002). But the rate of accumulation and ablation of snow and also the duration of mass balance of snow is affected by the climate change. Glaciers cannot attain the static variability because of variability in climate. Variation in the area of glaciers because of change in climate is very small in steep and shallow glaciers of the tropical mountains (Kaser *et al.*, 2003) but climate change have very substantial impact on the ice caps of less slope and glaciers of large extent (Paterson, 2004). Main cause behind the loss or melting of glacier is the human influence, as it accounts for 25 per cent loss of glacier between 1851 and 2010 and it rose to about 69 per cent between 1991 and 2010. Recently, it was estimated that thawing of glacier and ice caps lag behind the change in climate, so this unbalance adjustment will leads to ablation of glaciers and ice caps which are equivalent to 18 cm of sea level. On the basis of current trend of warming there is ablation of glacier equivalent to 38 cm sea level by 2100 (Bahr *et al.*, 2009).

Besides climate change disturbance in atmospheric circulation pattern also have large effect on behaviour of glaciers of entire mountain range. For instance in 1976-77 there was acceleration in the ablation of glacier in the continental USA and south-west Canada because of alteration in atmospheric circulation. There is another example of effect of atmospheric circulation i.e. ENSO (El Niño-Southern Oscillation) effect on the glaciers of tropical Andes (Wagnon *et al.*, 2001; Francou *et al.*, 2004; Sicart *et al.*, 2005) and the North Atlantic Oscillation effect on glaciers in the European Alps and Scandinavia (Nesje *et al.*, 2000).

Ten per cent of the land surface is permanently covered with ice, out of which only a little extent falls in ice caps and glaciers besides Antarctica and Greenland. In the Northern Hemisphere 49 per cent area is under the snow cover in midwinter. Through the geological history there are alternate ice age periods. Each component of the cryosphere has its contribution in short-term change in climate, whereas permafrost, ice shelves and ice sheet play important role in longer-term changes also like the ice age cycles (Dyurgerov *et al.*, 2005).

Table 26.2 shows the annual minimum and maximum value of snow, sea ice and seasonally frozen ground, and the annual mean of the other components. The sea ice area is shown by the stretch (area covered by the sea ice edge). The values for glaciers and ice caps denote the smallest and largest estimates excluding glaciers and ice caps surrounding Greenland and Antarctica. Area under snow on land is highest i.e. 1.9 to 45.2 million sq kms followed by sea ice i.e. 19 to 27 million sq. kms and permafrost i.e. 22.8 million sq. kms.

Table 26.2: Area, Volume and Sea Level Equivalent (SLE) of Cryospheric Component

S. No.	*. Type of snow covered region*	*Area (10^6 km^2)*
1	Snow on land	1.9-45.2
2	Sea ice	19-27
3	**Glaciers and ice caps**	—
3.1	Smallest estimates	0.51
3.2	Largest estimates	0.54
4	Ice shelves	1.5
5	Ice sheets	14.0
6	Greenland	1.7
7	Antarctica	12.3
8	Seasonally frozen ground	5.9-48.1
9	Permafrost	22.8

Source: Lemke *et al.*, 2007.

Cumulative mass balance shown in Fig. 26.9 show the stability between accumulation of snow and thawing of glaciers, and it also examines how glaciers around the world have changed through time. Dark line is showing means of all glaciers and light line is showing mean of reference glaciers. Unit of value shown in the figure is msw (meters of water equivalent) that depict the variation in average width of glacier. Values are compared by taking 1945 as base year and value in minus shows net decrease in ice and snow. Between 1945 and 2005 about 60 years there is change in mass balance from 0 to -25 msw.

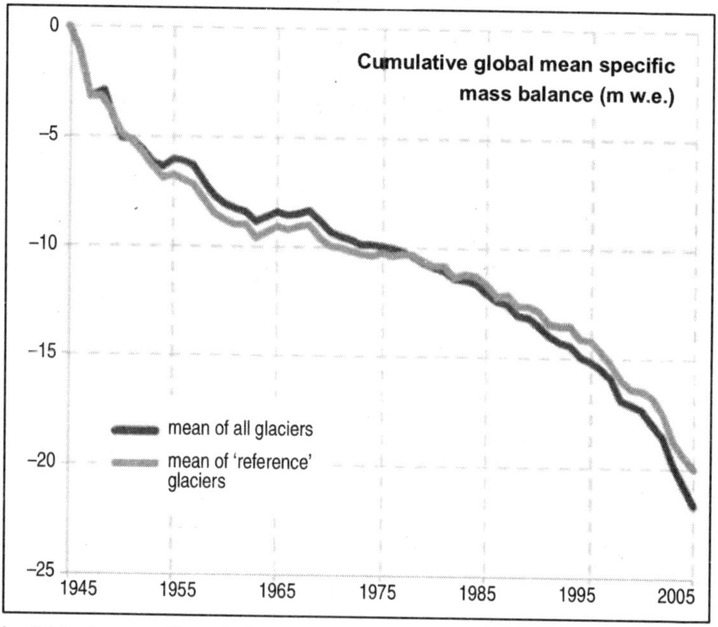

Fig. 26.9: Average Cumulative Mass Balance (1940-2015).
Source: WGMS, 2016.

Regional Change in Glaciers and Snow

Currently almost all glaciers of the globe are in a situation of thawing. High regional temperature and reduction in the accumulation of snow are the reason behind the retreats of the glacier. Above said factors are responsible for reducing the mass balance value of glacier into negative side (Debeer *et al.*, 2016). It means that there is not enough accumulation of snow at higher mountains and high latitude region which can replace the melting of snow at low altitude and low latitudinal region.

Cumulative mean specific mass balance (CMSMB) is shown in Fig. 26.9. In Patagonia, America and Canada cumulative mass balance is reducing at very high rate. In Patagonia CMSMB value reduced from 0 to –35 between just 40 years, followed by America i.e. 0 to –25. Incorporation of mean specific mass balances over the present glacier area is total mass balances. So as per the Fig. 26.10, the largest losses of the mass and aid to rise in sea level rise are from Alaska with 0.11 mm yr^{-1} SLE from 1960/1961 to 1989/1990 and 0.24 mm yr^{-1} SLE from 1990/1991 to 2002/2003, the Arctic (0.09 and 0.19), and the high mountains of Asia (0.08 and 0.10).

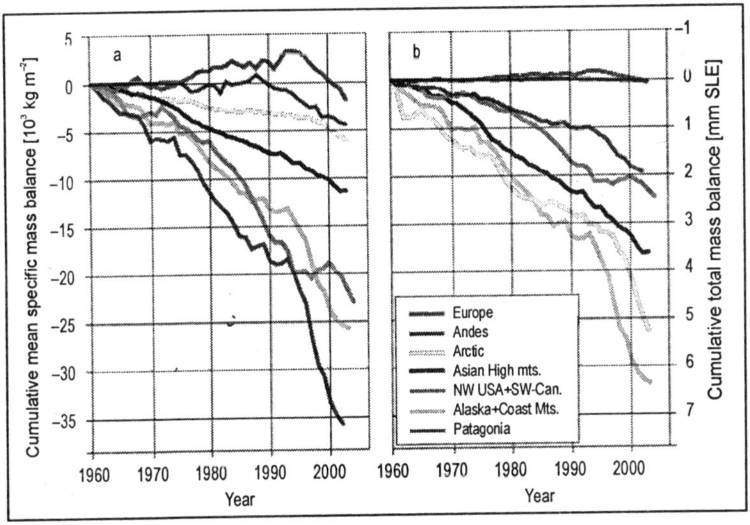

Fig. 26.10: Regional Cumulative Mass Balance.

Source: WGMS, 2016.

Large-scale regional mean length variations of glacier tongues are shown in Fig. 26.10, where 1950 is taken as base year to measure the change in mass of glaciers. After 1800 retreat of glacier was started as shown in Fig. 26.10. There is a slowdown in the retreat of glacier between about 1970 and 1990 and again in 1990s retreat was started with high rate. Retreat of glacier is highest in case of Atlantic and Southern Hemisphere.

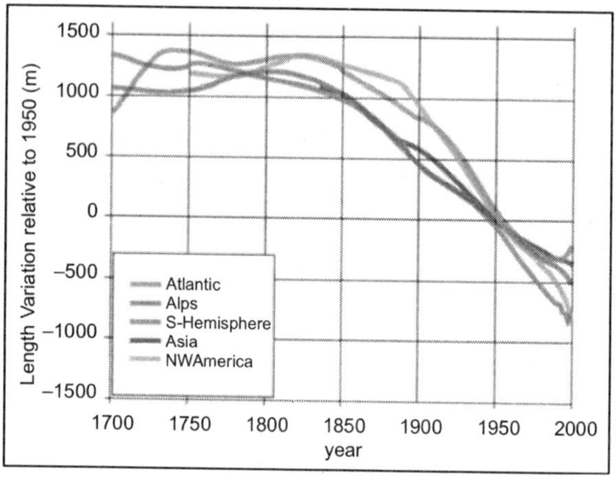

Fig. 26.11: Regional Mean Length Variation.
Source: IPCC, 2007.

Impact of Global Climatic Change

The potential impact of climatic change at the global level is observed on all aspects like environmental, social and economic etc. These climatic change impacts are mainly negative like rise in average global temperature, rise sea level and melting glacier etc. Due to these changes in climate people from countries such as Brazil, South-east Asia, Parts of Africa and China could be affected by hunger. The homes of various plants and animals will be affected by the climate change across the world. For example Polar bear and seals are affected by climate change, if the ice in the Antarctic and Antarctica melts they will have to find new land for hunting and living or these species could become wipe out. On the other hand sometime these impacts are positive e.g. increased in crop yield especially in the countries situated at the higher latitudes. During 1950 - 2010 Canada has reported increase in temperature by 1.5 °C (Warren *et al.*, 2014). The impact of changing weather, climate and rainfall pattern have shown positive impacts on many crops grown around the world. Wheat and rice crops grown well in high temperature, on the other hand crops such as maize and sugarcane have grown in cooler temperature.

Any change in the physical feature of the environment has cumulative impact on society and economy because welfare of human beings depends on the availability and quality of natural resources (SNIFFER, 2009). Proximity of place to coastal areas makes them most vulnerable because of climate change. Direct risk and impact of climate change depends upon density of human population and characteristics of settlement along the coastal area (Lemmen *et al.*, 2008). For example, the costs of damage because of storm and hurricane on coastal areas are very high, as evidenced in estimates for Hurricane Katrina, which was the most costly natural disaster in US history, which generated damage in excess of US$ 100 billion i.e. commercial structure damages of $ 21 billion, commercial equipment damages of $ 36 billion, residential structure and content damages of almost $ 75 billion, electric utility damages of $ 231 million, highway damages of $ 3 billion, sewer system damages of $ 1.2 billion and commercial revenue losses of $ 4.6 billion (Burton and Hicks, 2005). By comparison, in a less populated area the estimated costs of Hurricane Juan, which passed over Nova Scotia in 2003, amounted to CAD $ 200 million (Lemmen *et al.*, 2008).

Impact of Climate Change in India

Geographically India is located in warm zone but there is expectation of abnormal and record breaking spells of warm and dry weather which cover almost whole Indian subcontinent. The western coastal region and southern part of India are predicted to be shifted to the new high-temperature climatic regimes because of just 4 °C warming, which will have significant impacts on agriculture (IPCC, 2014). Nonetheless just 2 °C rise in the mean world temperatures, Indian summer monsoon become highly erratic and unpredictable. An enormously wet monsoon that occurs in 100 years till now is predicted to be occurred in every 10 years because of 4 °C warming in global means temperature. An unexpected alteration in the monsoon could bring crisis like situation. Like it can trigger more repeated flood and droughts in almost all parts of India. There will be higher than average rainfall in the north-western coastal region than the south-eastern coastal region. It is expected that dry year becomes drier and wet years becomes wetter (World Bank, 2013).

It is expected that there will be more frequent droughts in some region of India, particularly in north-western part of India like, Jharkhand, Orissa and Chhattisgarh. There will be unexpected and substantial fall in yield of crop because of extreme rise in atmospheric temperature by 2040s (Aggarwal, 2008). In India agriculture is highly dependent on groundwater for irrigation as more than 60 per cent of its agriculture is under rain-fed category. If we do not take into account the impact of climate change even though, 15 per cent of groundwater resource of India is overexploited (Kumar *et al.*, 2004).

North-western Himalayan glaciers and glaciers of Karakoram Range remain stable range for which westerly winter winds are the most important supply of moisture. In contrast, glaciers of Himalaya have been melting over the past centuries, for which Indian monsoon is the major supplier of moisture (IPCC, 2014). With 2.5 °C rise in temperature, there is reduction in snow cover and area under glacier in Himalayas because of thawing of snow. It lead to the reduction in stability in geology, environment and ecosystem in northern part of India and most importantly in Indus and the Brahmaputra river basin as they are glacier-fed rivers. Around 209 million people in the Indus basin, 478 million people in the Ganges basin, and 62 million people in the Brahmaputra basin are affected yearly because of change in the flows of the Indus, Ganges, and Brahmaputra rivers. Increased flow in these rivers also cause change in its morphometry which leads to the problem of geological disturbance and soil erosion and further impact on irrigation, production of food and livelihood of local people (Mondal & Mujumdar, 2015).

Besides this flood, droughts, erratic monsoon, rise in temperature and invasion of sea water would reduce the yields of crop and affect the food security of country. It was expected that there will be substantial decline in the yield of both rice and wheat in coming years and there will be a situation when India has to import more than twice of the amount of food grain by 2050s (Poornima, 2015). India is affected with increasing malnutrition and associated health problems like child stunting because of climate change, where poor are severely affected. By 2050s, case of child stunting projected to increase by 35 per cent as compared to present situation. Malaria and other vector-borne diseases, along with and diarrheal infections which are a major cause of child mortality, are likely to spread into areas which are not affected by vector-borne disease because of colder temperature. There is rise in death and injuries because of heat waves and other extremes weather events (Kumar *et al.*, 2007). Therefore, it can be seen that India is also going to be affected in many ways due to climate change.

Conclusion

Increase in average temperature translates into extreme temperatures, flooding, storms, sea level rise that is expected be somewhere in between 0.11 to 0.77 meters by 2100. The atmospheric temperature of the earth has increased due to rise in GHGs emission, with the exact change differs regionally. The rate of emission of GHGs is responsible to increase the average surface temperature of the Earth which is about 0.2 °C per decade.

Global warming is the main cause behind the sea level rise due to various anthropogenic activities like burning coal and oil and deforestation of tropical forests. Two-third of world fresh water is stored in the form of land ice glaciers, ice caps, and ice sheets and they are shrinking because of rise in atmospheric temperatures About one inch of water added into the sea from1993 to 2008 from melting of glaciers, ice caps and ice sheets which accounts for more than half of the increase during said period.

While taking the case of India and its impact of climate change it is expected that there will be more frequent droughts in some region, particularly in north-western part like, Jharkhand, Orissa and Chhattisgarh. Also there will be unexpected and substantial fall in yield of crop because of extreme rise in atmospheric temperature by 2040s due to climate change. In India agriculture is highly dependent on groundwater for irrigation as more than 60 per cent of its agriculture is under rain-fed category. If we do not take into account the impact of climate change even though, 15 per cent of groundwater resource of India is overexploited. The question that we propose in the beginning tends to positive that the global climate change is not a myth but it is a reality in the present day context be in India or other parts of the world.

References

Aggarwal P.K. (2008). "Global climate change and Indian agriculture: Impacts, adaptation and mitigation", *Indian Journal of Agricultural Sciences*, 78(10): 911-919.

Anthoff D., R.J. Nicholls and R.S.J. Tol (2010). "The economic impact of substantial sea-level rise", *Mitigation and Adaptation Strategies for Global Change*, 15:321-335.

Bahr, D.B., Dyurgerov, M. and Meier, M.F. (2009). "Sea-level rise from glaciers and ice caps: a lower bound", *Geophysical Research Letters,* 36, L03501, doi 10.1029/2008GL036309.

Boden, T.A., Marland, G. and Andres, R.J. (2017). *Global, Regional and National Fossil-Fuel CO2 Emissions*. Carbon Dioxide Information Analysis Centre, Oak Ridge National Laboratory.

Bradford, A. (2014). "Effects of Global Warming", Live Science Contributor.

Cazenave, A. and W. Llovel (2010). "Contemporary sea level rise", *Annual Review of Marine Science*, 2:145-173.

Church, J.A. and N.J. White (2011). Sea-level rise from the late 19th to early 21st century. Surveys in Geophysics doi:10.1007/s10712- 011-9119-1.

Church, J.A., P.U. Clark, A. Cazenave, J.M. Gregory, S. Jevrejeva, A. Levermann, M.A. Merrifield, G.A. Milne, R.S. Nerem, P.D. Nunn, A.J. Payne, W.T. Pfeffer,

D. Stammer and A.S. Unnikrishnan (2013). "Sea Level Change", In: Climate Change 2013: The Physical Science Basis. Contribution of Working Group I to the Fifth Assessment Report of the Intergovernmental Panel on Climate Change [Stocker, T.F., D. Qin, G.K. Plattner, M. Tignor, S.K. Allen, J. Boschung, A. Nauels, Y. Xia, V. Bex and P.M. Midgley (eds.)]. Cambridge University Press, Cambridge, United Kingdom and New York, NY, USA.

Climate Change (2014). Impacts, Adaptation and Vulnerability. Fifth Assessment Report, Intergovernmental Panel on Climate Change, Working Group II.

Cogley, J.G. (2009). "Geodetic and direct mass-balance measurements: Comparison and joint analysis", *Annals of Glaciology*, 50:96-100.

CSIRO (Commonwealth Scientific and Industrial Research Organisation). 2015 update to data originally published in: Church, J.A. and N.J. White (2011). "Sea-level rise from the late 19th to the early 21st century." *Surv. Geophys.* 32:585–602. www.cmar.csiro.au/sealevel/sl_data_cmar.html.

Deccan Herald, April 3, 2012, Greenhouse gases warm the Arctic, creating ripples, p. 11.

Dyurgerov, M. and M.F. Meier (2005). *Glaciers and the Changing Earth System: A 2004 Snapshot*. Occasional Paper 58, Institute of Arctic and Alpine Research, University of Colorado, Boulder, CO, p. 118.

Environmental Protection Agency (EPA) (2012). Climate change indicators in the United States, 2012. www.epa.gov/climate change/science/indicators/download.html.

Fujita, K. and Y. Ageta (2000). "Effect of summer accumulation on glacier mass balance on the Tibetan Plateau revealed by mass-balance model". *J. Glaciol*, 46(153), 244-252.

Giorgi, F., B. Hewitson, J. Christensen, M. Hulme, H. Von Storch, P. Whetton, R. Jones, L. Mearns, C. Fu. and 48 others (2001). "Regional Climate Information—Evaluation and Projections", In *Climate Change 2001: The Scientific Basis. Contribution of Working Group I to the Third Assessment Report of the Intergovernmental Panel on Climate Change*. J.T. Houghton, ed. Cambridge University Press, New York. Available from http://www.grida.no/climate/ipcc_tar/wg1/373.htm.

Hansen, J., R. Ruedy, M. Sato and K. Lo. (2010). "Global surface temperature change", *Reviews of Geophysics* 48: RG4004; doi:10.1029/2010RG000345.

http://www.worldbank.org/en/news/feature/2013/06/19/india-climate-change-impacts

Intergovernmental Panel on Climate Change (2001). "Climate Change 2001: Synthesis Report; Summary for Policymakers". See http://www.ipcc.ch/pub/un/syreng/spm.pdf.

IPCC (2001). Synthesis Report, Third Assessment Report. Cambridge University Press.

IPCC (2007). Fourth Assessment Report, https://www.ipcc.ch/pdf/assessment-report/ar4/wg3/ar4_wg3_full_report.pdf

IPCC (2013). "Summary for Policymakers". In *Climate Change 2013: The Physical Science Basis. Contribution of Working Group I to the Fifth*

Assessment Report of the Intergovernmental Panel on Climate Change [Stocker, T.F., D. Qin, G.-K. Plattner, M.

IPCC (2014). Climate Change 2014. Synthesis Report. Contribution of Working Groups I, II and III to the Fifth Assessment Report of the Intergovernmental Panel on Climate Change, R.K. Pachauri and L.A. Meyer (eds.). Switzerland.

IPCC (2014). *Climate Change 2014. Mitigation of Climate Change* Contribution of Working Group III to the Fifth Assessment Report of the Intergovernmental Panel on Climate Change, Edenhofer, O., R. Pichs-Madruga, Y. Sokona, E. Farahani, S. Kadner, K. Seyboth, A. Adler, I. Baum, S. Brunner, P. Eickemeier, B. Kriemann, J. Savolainen, S. Schlömer, C. von Stechow, T. Zwickel and J.C. Minx (eds.), Cambridge University Press, Cambridge, United Kingdom.

Jaeger, J. (1988). Developing policies for Responding to climatic Change: A Summary of the Discussions and Recommendations of the Workshops Held in Villach, 28 September to 2 October 1987, WCIP-1, WMO/TD-No. 2250.

Karl T.R. and Knight R.W. (1998). "Secular trends of precipitation amount, frequency, and intensity in the United States", *Bulletin of the American Meteorological Society*, 79:231–241.

Kaser, G. and H. Osmaston (2002). *Tropical Glaciers*, UNESCO International Hydrological Series. Cambridge University Press, Cambridge, UK, 207.

Kaser, G., *et al.* (2003). "The impact of glaciers on the runoff and the reconstruction of mass balance history from hydrological data in the tropical Cordillera Blanca", *Peru. J. Hydrol.*, 282: 130-144.

Kaser, G., J.G. Cogley, M.B. Dyurgerov, M.F. Meier and A. Ohmura (2006). Mass balance of glaciers and ice caps: Consensus estimates for 1961–2004. Geophysical Research Letters 33(L19501); doi:10.1029/2006GL027511.

Kumar A., Valecha N., Jain T., Dash A.P. (2007). "Burden of Malaria in India: Retrospective and Prospective view", *Am. J. Trop. Med. Hyg.* 77(6): 69-78.

Kumar K., Kumar R., Ashrit, Deshpande and Hansen. "Climate impacts on Indian agriculture". *International Journal of Climatology*, 24:1375ñ 1393, 2004. doi: 10.1002/joc.1081.

Lemke, P., J. Ren, R.B. Alley, I. Allison, J. Carrasco, G. Flato, Y. Fujii, G. Kaser, P. Mote, R.H. Thomas and T. Zhang (2007). Observations: Changes in Snow, Ice and Frozen Ground. In: *Climate Change 2007: The Physical Science Basis. Contribution of Working Group I to the Fourth Assessment Report of the Intergovernmental Panel on Climate Change* [Solomon, S., D. Qin, M. Manning, Z. Chen, M. Marquis, K.B. Averyt, M. Tignor and H.L. Miller (eds.). Cambridge University Press, Cambridge, United Kingdom and New York, NY, USA.

Lemmen D.S., Warren F.J., Lacroix J. and Bush E. (eds.) (2008). *From Impacts to Adaptation: Canada in a Changing Climate 2007*, Government of Canada, Ottawa, ON, p. 448.

Levitus S., J. Antonov and T. Boyer (2005). "Warming of the World Ocean, 1955-2003", *Geophys. Res. Lett.*, 32, L02604, doi:10.1029/2004GL021592.

Levitus, S., J.I. Antonov, J. Wang, T.L. Delworth, K.W. Dixon and A.J. Broccoli

(2001). "Anthropogenic warming of Earth's climate system". *Science,* 292:267 270.

Levitus, S., J.I. Antonov, T.P. Boyer, H.E. Garcia and R.A. Locarnini (2005). "Linear trends of zonally averaged thermosteric, halosteric and total steric sea level for individual ocean basins and the world ocean, (1955–1959)–(1994–1998)". *Geophysical Research Letters* 32 (L16601); doi:10.1029/2005GL023761.

Levitus, S., J.I. Antonov, T.P. Boyer, R.A. Locarnini, H.E. Garcia and A.V. Mishonov (2009). "Global ocean heat content 1955–2008 in light of recently revealed instrumentation problems". *Geophysical Research Letters* 36: L07608; doi:10.1029/2008GL037155.

Mason S.J., Waylen P.R., Mimmack G.M., Rajaratnam B. and Harrison J.M. (1999). "Changes in extreme rainfall events in South Africa". *Climatic Change*, 41:249–257.

Meier, M.F., M.B. Dyurgerov, U.K. Rick, S. O'Neel, W.T. Pfeffer, R.S. Anderson, S.P. Anderson and A.F. Glazovsky (2007). "Glaciers dominate eustatic sea-level rise in the 21st century". *Science,* 317:1064–1067; doi:10.1126/science.1143906.

Milne, G. (2008). "How the climate drives sea-level changes." 2007 Bullerwell lecture. *Astronomy and Geophysics* 49:2.24–2.28.

Mondal and Mujumdar (2015). Hydrological Sciences and Water Security: Past, Present and Future (Proceedings of the 11th Kovacs Colloquium, Paris, France, June 2014). IAHS Publ. 366, 2015.

Muller, R.A. (2008). Climate Change, Department of Physics, University of California at Berkeley.(http://muller.lbl.gov/teaching/Physics10/PffP_textbook/PffP-10- climate.pdf)

Myhre, G., D. Shindell, F.-M. Bréon, W. Collins, J. Fuglestvedt, J. Huang, D. Koch, J.-F. Lamarque, D. Lee, B. Mendoza, T. Nakajima, A. Robock, G. Stephens, T. Takemura and H. Zhang (2013). Anthropogenic and Natural Radiative Forcing. In: Climate Change 2013: The Physical Science Basis. Contribution of Working Group I to the Fifth Assessment Report of the Intergovernmental Panel on Climate Change [Stocker, T.F., D. Qin, G.-K. Plattner, M. Tignor, S.K. Allen, J. Boschung, A. Nauels, Y. Xia, V. Bex and P.M. Midgley (eds.)]. Cambridge University Press, Cambridge, United Kingdom and New York, NY, USA.

National Centre for Atmospheric Research. 2005. "Climate Change Inevitable in 21s Century Sea Level Rise to Outpace Temperature Increase" http://www.ucar.edu/news/ releases/2005/changes.html.

National Oceanic and Atmospheric Administration (NOAA). 2012b. Sea levels online. Online at *http://tidesandcurrents.noaa.gov/sltrends/ sltrends.shtml.*

Nesje, A., Lie, O. and Dahl, S.O. (2000). "Is the North Atlantic Oscillation reflected in Scandinavian glacier mass balance records?" *Journal of Quaternary Science* 15(6): 587–601.

NOAA (National Oceanic and Atmospheric Administration) (2015). Laboratory for Satellite Altimetry: Sea level rise. Accessed June 2015. www.star.nesdis.noaa.gov/sod/lsa/SeaLevelRise/LSA_SLR_ timeseries_ global.php.

Paterson, W.S.B. (2004). *The Physics of Glaciers*, Ed. 3.A, Elsevier, Oxford, UK, p. 496.

Pesch GG and Wells PG (2004). Tides of Change across the Gulf. Prepared for the Gulf of Maine Summit: Comitting to Change. Gulf of Maine Council and the Global Programme of Action Coalition for the Guf of Maine. 81p. www.gulfofmaine.org.

Poornima S. (2015). "Climate Change in India: Challenges and Solutions" *Mainstream*, Vol. LIII No. 50.

Pounds J.A. and R. Puschendorf (2004). "Clouded Futures". *Nature*, 427, 8 January 2004.

Sallenger, A.H., Jr., K.S. Doran and P.A. Howd (2012). Hotspot of accelerated sea-level rise on the Atlantic coast of North America. Nature Climate Change 2:884–888; doi:10.1038/nclimate1597.

SNIFFER (2009). Differential impacts of climate change in the UK. Scotland and Northern Ireland Forum for Environmental Research. Literature Review, Project UKCC22. 85pp. http://www.sniffer.org.uk

Stewart, Stacy R. (April 3, 2017). Tropical Cyclone Report: Hurricane Matthew 2016 (PDF) (Technical report). United States National Hurricane Centre, 5 April, 2017.

Tol, R.S.J. (2007). "The double trade-off between adaptation and mitigation for sea level rise: An application of fund." *Mitigation and Adaptation Strategies for Global Change*, 12:741–753.

Trenberth, K.E., L. Smith, T. Qian, A. Dai and J. Fasullo (2007). "Estimates of the global water budget and its annual cycle using observational and model data." *Journal of Hydrometeorology* 8:758–769.

Wagnon, P., Ribstein, P., Francou, B. and Sicart, J.E. (2001). "Anomalous heat and mass budget of Glaciar Zongo, Bolivia during the 1997/98 El Niño year." *Journal of Glaciology*, 47(156): 21–28.

Walther G.R., Post E., Convey P. *et al.* (2002). "Ecological responses to recent climate change." *Nature*, 416:389–395.

Warren, F.J. and Lemmen, D.S., editors (2014). Canada in a Changing Climate: Sector Perspectives on Impacts and Adaptation; Government of Canada, Ottawa, ON, p. 286.

WGMS (World Glacier Monitoring Service) (2016). update to data originally published in: WGMS. 2015. Global glacier change bulletin no. 1 (2012–2013).

Woodworth, P.L. (2005). "Have there been large recent sea level changes in the Maldive Islands?" *Global and Planetary Change*, 49:1–18.

World Meteorological Organization (2005). WMO Statement on the Status of the Global Climate in 2005. http://www.wmo.ch/web/wcp/wcdmp/statement/html/WMO998_E.pdf.

Zemp *et al.* (2008). Global glacier changes: facts and figures. United Nations Environment Programme and World Glacier Monitoring Service.

Zemp M *et al.* (2009). Six decades of glacier mass balance observations — A review of the worldwide monitoring network. Annals of Glaciology 50, doi 10.3189/172756409787769591.

Zemp, M., I. Gärtner-Roer, S.U. Nussbaumer, F. Hüsler, H. Machguth, N. Mölg, F. Paul and M. Hoelzle (eds.). ICSU(WDS)/IUGG(IACS)/UNEP/UNESCO/WMO.Zurich, Switzerland: World Glacier Monitoring Service. http://wgms.ch/downloads/WGMS_GGCB_01.pdf.

27
Biodiversity Conservation

Monowar Alam Khalid

Introduction

"Biodiversity" or Biological Diversity has been defined by International Union for Conservation of Nature as "the variability among living organisms from all sources including terrestrial, marine and other aquatic ecosystems, and the ecological complexes of which are the part; this includes diversity within species, between species, and of ecosystems". It is in fact, the variety of life i.e. different species of plants, animals, microorganisms and ecosystems on earth, which are very important for the upkeep of good health of planet and its inhabitants. Biodiversity is usually observed at three levels, i.e., genetic variability within a species; species variability within the community, and the Ecosystem diversity i.e. organization of species in an area, into distinctive plant and animal communities. Through genetic variability, it influences the characteristics of species in giving various size, shape, colour etc., bringing variety among same species of plants and animals. Loss in genetic diversity may lead to in-breeding amongst species, which may cause its extinction. The species diversity is the variety of animals and plants on this earth causing species richness and healthy ecosystems. The ecosystem variability is distinctive landscapes and ecosystems like deserts, forests, mountains under terrestrial category and lakes, rivers, seas under aquatic category.

Biodiversity is the basis of life and extremely important for the survival of all animals, plants and humans. It has intrinsic value and provides direct and indirect economic, scientific, aesthetic benefits with countless other benefits of providing ecosystem services and raw from ecosystems include domesticated agricu!ture crops, medicines, fibers etc. Nature has traditionally preserved the biodiversity since ages, which is currently under peril due to greed and exploitation of the human population. As righty said by Mahatma Gandhi "Earth provides enough to satisfy every man's needs, but not every man's greed."

Biodiversity in Peril

World over, biodiversity is under threat due to anthropogenic activities arising due to increasing human population, which has escalated crisis of extinction of various species at a faster pace.

Various causes of biodiversity loss are habitat destruction, land use changes and conversion for agriculture and development, climate change, pollution and the spread of invasive species. As per various estimates, we are losing biodiversity hundreds of time faster than natural rate. Nearly 17,291 species out of 47,677 are assessed as threatened with extinction. Coral reefs, which provides protection against storms and floods is threatened as nearly 70 per cent of it is already destroyed. As per IUCN, out of World's 5,490 mammals nearly 79 are extinct in Wild, 188 critically endangered, 449 endangered and 505 vulnerable. Among amphibians, out of total 6285 known amphibians world over, nearly 1895 are in danger of extinction.

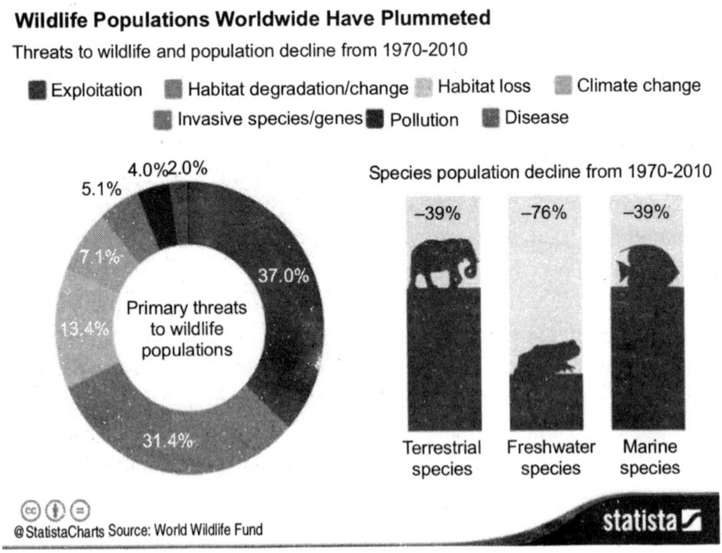

Fig. 27.1: Threats to wildlife.

Source: WWF.

Biodiversity Loss: Matter of Concern

Biodiversity plays an important role in sustenance of life on earth by maintaining healthy ecosystems and providing ecological services like nutrient and water recycling, resistance against invasive species, climate regulation, pollution control, soil formation and retention etc. Floral and faunal biodiversity is richer in tropics but becomes fewer at Polar Regions due to variability of soils, altitude, climate and presence of other species. Also, Climate Change estimates of increase in temperatures of 1.4 – 5.8 degree C (IPCCC) will further affect the species distribution, changes in growing seasons of plants, reproduction changes in animals and increased extinctions. Biodiversity like Amazon Forests and other forest ecosystems help sequester more than 20 per cent of the carbon dioxide emissions. Various factors such as land-use changes, climate change, invasive alien species, overexploitation, deforestation, pollution etc., are contributing to rapidly declining biodiversity. Climate change is expected to further accelerate risk of biodiversity loss through population decline, extinctions, floods, droughts, pests and disease outbreaks etc. Species extinction, although occurring naturally has become 100 times faster due to human activities.

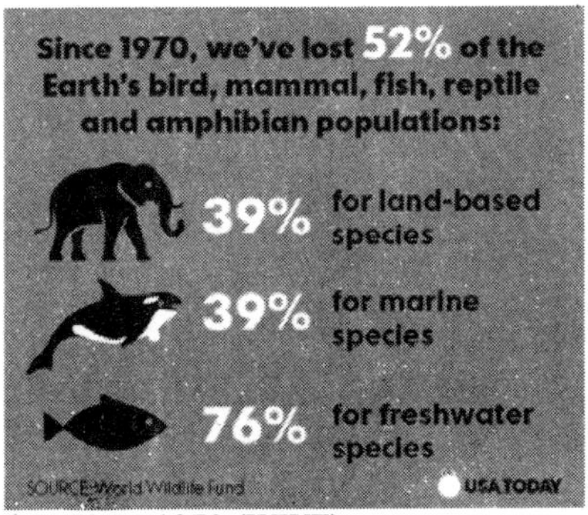

Fig. 27.2: Species loss since 1970 (WWF).

Biodiversity loss will have immense negative impacts on the very existence of humans due to threat to food and energy security, access to clean drinking water, availability of raw material, vulnerability to disasters affecting human health and life of billions. Major reasons for loss of biodiversity are:

- Overexploitation of natural resources
- Population increase
- Poverty
- Habitat destruction

- Developmental activities
- Industrialization
- Urbanization
- Land-use changes
- Introduction of invasive species
- Poor management of resources
- Commercial exploitation of natural resources
- Pesticides and chemical use in agriculture etc.

India is rich in terms of its biodiversity and is among one of the 12 mega-biodiversity countries of the world, having nearly 7.8 per cent of the global recorded species in its 2.5 per cent of the land area globally. India is having 2 among 25 biodiversity hotspots of the world as Eastern Himalaya and Western Ghats along with other biodiversity rich areas in North-east India and Andaman & Nicobar Islands.

Benefits from Biodiversity

Biodiversity is the primary life support system, which sustains life on planet earth and is a must for survival of human beings. Biodiversity provides following benefits directly for humans:

- Food for more than 7 billion humans on earth in the form of grains, fruits, meat, vegetables, fish etc.
- For needs of humans goods like timber, fuel, medicines, papers, fibers etc.
- Pollution and oil spill control through various bacteria, microbes etc.
- Pollination and dispersal through its insects, bees, birds, animals etc.

Other than above benefits for humans, it provides following ecological services:

- Provisioning services: Production of food and water
- Regulating services: Control of climate and diseases, CO_2 level regulation
- Supporting services: Crop pollination, nutrient recycling etc.
- Cultural services: Recreational, aesthetic and spiritual

Biodiversity also provides us lots of other benefits like:

Economic Benefits

Costanza *et al.* (1997) evaluated natural goods and services globally to the tune of about 33 trillion USD per year, whereas for reference The World Factbook (2011) states that in 2010 the GDP of the United States was only 14.66 trillion USD and that of European Union, it was 14.82 trillion USD. A few estimates (TEEB, 2009) put Pharmaceuticals deriving nearly 20-25 per cent from genetic resources valuing at estimated US$ 640 billion.

Commercial Benefits

Various goods obtained from nature are used for commercial purposes to run the industries are timber for fuel, paper and construction, natural fibres for fabrics and other uses, even venoms from animals are used for anti venom medicines, honey and other commercial crops, animal meat and its products etc.

Social Benefits

Social benefits of biodiversity are immense, which cannot be evaluated monetarily. The biggest beneficiary is the nature tourism industry, which earns millions of dollar as people visit natural landscapes to derive pleasure, socialize and for aesthetic benefits. Various ethnic cultures and tribes still exist in preserved areas due to biodiversity.

Wetlands as Repository of Biodiversity

Wetlands are repository of biodiversity and are known as "nurseries of life". Although, they occupy 6.4 per cent of the world's land surface but provide habitat to millions of aquatic and terrestrial plants and animals. They are multi-functional bodies and function as 'kidneys of the landscapes', by maintaining water quality through filtering, recycling and absorbing pollutants. Wetlands are the productive eco-systems of the world and provide a wide array of benefits to mankind as excellent breeding grounds of waterfowl mainly after the Ramsar Convention (1971). Increase in human population and rapid urbanization have put considerable pressure on the wetlands problems for selected aquatic species in particular and ecosystems in general.

Biodiversity Conventions

India through its Ministry of Environment, Forests and Climate Change

(MoEFCC) and state forest departments as custodians takes care of its biodiversity especially the forest resources. There are various conventions in place for conservation of Biodiversity worldwide, a few of them relevant for India are as given below:

Convention on Biological Diversity (CBD) 1992

Convention on Biological Diversity (CBD) 1992, to which India is a Party, recognizes the sovereign rights of States to use their own biological resources and expects the parties to facilitate access to genetic resources by other Parties subject to national legislation and on mutually agreed upon terms under its Article 3 and 15. Convention on Biological Diversity through its Article 8(j) also recognizes contributions of local and indigenous communities to the conservation and sustainable utilization of biological resources through traditional knowledge, practices and innovations and provides for equitable sharing of benefits with such people arising from the utilization of their knowledge, practices and innovations.

Biological Diversity Act, 2002

Indian Government through a consultative process has brought Biological Diversity Act, 2002 with following objectives:

- To regulate access to biological resources of the country with the purpose of securing equitable share in benefits arising out of the use of biological resources and associated knowledge relating to biological resources;
- to conserve and sustainably use biological diversity;
- to respect and protect knowledge of local communities related to biodiversity;
- to secure sharing of benefits with local people as conservers of biological resources and holders of knowledge and information relating to the use of biological resources;
- Conservation and development of areas of importance from the standpoint of biological diversity by declaring them as biological diversity heritage sites;
- Protection and rehabilitation of threatened species; and
- Involvement of institutions of state government in the broad scheme of the implementation of the Biological Diversity Act through constitution of committees.

National Biodiversity Authority (NBA), 2002

India established its National Biodiversity Authority in 2002 as a regulatory body for protecting the country's extensive natural resources and ensuring its economic benefits for the local communities. It also deals with request to access genetic resources of the country by foreigners.

World Biodiversity Day

In recognition to promote importance of biodiversity, UN declared 22 May every year as World Biodiversity Day, which is celebrated by countries all-over the world.

Conclusion

Biodiversity, which is must for survival of human race, needs to be conserved by all means. Overexploitation and destruction of natural resources has already threatened our planet in terms of availability of ecosystem services. If unabated, we may have decline in species populations, lesser ecosystem services, increased droughts and floods, outbreak of diseases due to increased pests etc. It is high time that humanity realizes the importance of biodiversity, which is providing it ecological, social and economic benefits and conserves it for its own survival, livelihood and sustainability.

References

Costanza, R., d'Arge, R., de Groot, R., Farberk, S., Grasso, M., Hannon, B., Van den Belt, M. (1997). "The value of the world's ecosystem services and natural capital." *Nature*.

TEEB (2009). *The Economics of Ecosystems and Biodiversity for National and International Policy Makers,* p. 17.

WWF. 2011a. *The Energy Report*. WWF International, Gland, Switzerland.

WWF. 2011b. *WWF Living Forests Report*. WWF International, Gland, Switzerland.

WWF. 2012. *Living Planet Report 2012*. Biodiversity, biocapacity and better choices. WWF International, Gland, Switzerland.

WWF (2014). *Living Planet Report*, 2014.

28
Environment and Sustainable Development Law

Md. Zafar Mahfooz Nomani

Introduction

Modern technological state sometimes intensifies conflicts between environmental values and developmental needs. Prevailing dichotomy of sustainable development in India is mirrored in underdevelopment, galloping population, mass poverty and a desire for massive industrialization devoid of eco-friendly considerations. The recognition of environmental problems is inseparable from those of human welfare and the process of economic development. These forms of development erode the environmental resources on which human livelihoods and welfare ultimately depend. What is needed is the pursuit of development that meets the needs of the present generation without compromising the ability of future generations to meet their own needs.

The problem lies with economic definitions of sustainable development that focus on optimal resource management for economic development with little safeguard for the services and quality of natural resources. Sustainable development often defined as development that improves health care, education, and social well-being in an ecological context. There is no denying the fact that 'men, women, and children must be the centre of attention with development woven around people, not people around development.' Sustainable development stresses that development be participatory and inclusive of multi stakeholders in decision making. An important component of virtually all definitions of sustainable development is to foster equity encompassing economic, human, environmental, and technological dimensions. The new strategy of sustainable development aims at improving the quality of human life while living within the carrying capacity of supporting ecosystems. The idea of sustainable development reflected in modern environmental legislation encompasses *social properties* so as to keep improving living standards of humanity under the condition of not going beyond the capacity of environment. Sustainable development defined from its *economic properties* stresses that it should aim at making the maximum net profit of economic development on the premise of preserving the qualities of natural resources and not go beyond its service capacity.

International Law and Environment

The doctrinal foundations of international environmental law are based on the doctrine of sovereignty and equality of states. The principle implies that nation states are sovereign and have equal rights and duties as members of the international community. The sources of international environment law are basically treaties and customary international law and "general practice accepted as law" by States. The soft law is comprised of non-binding instruments that lay down guidelines for future action, or through which states commit them politically to meeting certain objectives. Modern international environmental law dates to approximately *United Nations Stockholm Conference on the Human Environment, 1972* and establishment of *United Nations Environment Programme*. Many important legal developments took place in the period surrounding the Conference which include negotiation of the *Convention on International Trade in Endangered Species of Wild Fauna and Flora, Convention on Migratory Species of Wild Animals, Convention on Wetlands, World Heritage Convention, London Ocean Dumping Convention*, and *Convention on Biological Diversity*, and *UNEP Regional Seas Conventions*. Since then, there has been a rapid rise in international legal instruments and new means for coordinating the negotiation and implementation of related agreements, in particular their administrative, monitoring, and financial provisions. The *Stockholm Declaration, 1972* and the *Rio Declaration, 1992* constitute good examples of soft law, although a number of those principles may be said to have crystallized into "harder" obligations representing customary law.

Juridical Framework of Sustainability

The major components of sustainable development which may be considered in legal domain are broadly equity, social justice, economic efficiency and ecological harmony. The sustainability paradigm in law encapsulates sovereignty over natural resources, state obligation to protect the environment, inter-generational equity, good neighbourliness, equitable utilization, obligation to warn and co-operate. A synergistic approach to sustainability is struck at for minimum compliance of law and giving effect to principle that 'every human being has fundamental and equal rights, including the right to access to the resources needed for a decent standard of living.' The protection of human rights and the rights of nature is a worldwide responsibility that transcends all cultural, ideological and geographical boundaries.

The *Brundtland Report, 1987* placed the concept of sustainable development by recognizing development that meets the needs of the present without compromising the ability of future generations to meet their own needs, as foundational priorities of international environmental law. It recognizes the need for inter-generational equity, sustainable and equitable use of resources and the integration of environmental considerations into economic and other development initiatives. This principle is also reflected in Article 3(4) of the *Framework Convention on Climate Change, 1997*. Although specifically recognized as a legal principle in the separate opinion of Judge Weeramantry in *Abcikovo-Nagymaros Case* of the International Court of Justice (ICJ), the very breadth or the concept means that considerable controversy still surrounds this argument none the less it augured in Rio Summit and leaped from human environment to sustainable development. The *Rio Summit, 1992* resulted in formulation of Agenda 21 as an action plan for along with *Declaration on the Environment and Development*, *Framework Convention on Climate Change*, *Convention on Biological Diversity*, and *Non-Legally Binding Authoritative Statement on Forests* in 1992. Thus *Rio Summit, 1992* refined sustainability principle in international environmental law principles as "discrete, discipline-specific" principles.

Development of Environmental Law

The growth of international environmental law is premised on the globalization of environmental problems and concerns, attributable to two crucially interrelated factors such as ecological and economic interdependence. International environmental law being proactive of the *U.N. Framework Convention on Climate Change (UNFCCC), 1997* is a living example of an anticipatory response to the future anthropogenic global climate change. The development of international environmental law can be traced through three main phases from 1972-1992, the *U.N. Conference on the Human Environment* in Stockholm in 1972, *Vienna Convention for the Protection of the Ozone Layer, 1985* and *U.N. Conference on Environment and Development (UNCED), 1992* which resulted in sustainable development and greater environmental compliance.

The Stockholm Conference, 1972 served as a catalyst for several normative environmental principles by ushering a *109-point Environmental Action Plan and Resolution* recommending institutional and financial implementation by the United Nations. The creation of the United Nations Environment Programme established by U.N. General *Assembly Resolution* negotiates global environmental treaties. This phase witnessed *Vienna Convention for the Protection of the Ozone Layer, 1985* to curb depletion of the ozone layer by commercially produced chemicals, principally chlorofluorocarbons (CFCs), *The Vienna Convention, 1985* provided framework convention for general obligations and institutional framework to deal with ozone layer. The *Protocol On Substances That Deplete The Ozone Layer, 1987* after *Montreal Protocol* called for a freeze on the production and consumption of CFCs and halons at 1986 levels, followed by a 50 per cent reduction in CFC use by industrialized countries over a ten-year period. The Protocol was deliberately designed as a flexible and dynamic instrument—countries were allowed to select the most economic mix of reductions, with incentives to reduce the most harmful chemicals. A follow-up to the Stockholm Conference led to *World Charter for Nature, 1982*; *Convention on the Control of Trans-boundary Movements of Hazardous Wastes and their Disposal, 1989* proper waste management and prior informed consent. UNEP also consolidated networking of regional framework conventions protecting the marine environment and sustainable development.

Legal Foundation of Sustainability

The *Rio Declaration*, 1992 heralded new generation of international environmental law such as principles of precaution, polluter-pays, sustainable development, common but differentiated responsibility and environment impact assessment as an integral part of sustainable development. We will examine in some of the basic precepts in lines to follow.

A. Theory of Intergenerational Equity: Sustainable development as "development that meets the needs of the present without compromising the ability of future generations to meet their own needs, as foundational priorities of international environmental law. It recognizes the need for intergenerational equity, sustainable and equitable use of resources and the integration of environmental considerations into economic and other development initiatives. It can best be understood not so much as a principle, but rather as an argument in favour of sustainable economic development and natural resource use.

B. Precautionary Principle: Principle 15 of the *Rio Declaration, 1992* enshrined the precautionary principle which postulates that in cases when serious harm is threatened, positive action to protect the environment should not be delayed until irrefutable scientific proof of harm is available. This principle can be seen to require a reversal of the normal burden of proof, so that a potential actor would need to prove that a proposed activity will not cause harm before it can be sanctioned.

C. Environmental Impact Assessment (EIA) Norms: Agenda 21 calls on countries to access the suitability of infrastructure in human settlements, ensure that relevant decisions are preceded by EIAs, take into account the costs of any ecological consequences and integrate environmental considerations in decision-making at all levels and all ministries. The EIA requirement is also embodied in several international instruments, notably the *1991 U.N. Economic Commission for Europe (ECE), Convention on Environmental Impact Assessment in a Trans-boundary Context, 1991. Biodiversity Convention, 1992*, and the *World Bank Operational Directive 4.01, 1991.*

D. Participation, Access and Environmental Justice: Principle 10 *Rio Declaration, 1992* recognizes environmental issues are best handled with the participation of all citizens. *Aahrus ECE Convention on Access to Information, Public Participation in Decision-Making and Access to Justice in Environmental Matters*, signed in 1998 by 37 countries. *Aahrus Convention* enunciates that "every person has the right to live in an environment adequate to his or her health and well-being, and the duty, ...to protect and improve the environment" and that "citizens must have access to information, be entitled to participate in decision-making and have access to justice in environmental matters." The *Aahrus Convention* obligates signatory states to make environmental information available 'as soon as possible' and 'without an interest having to be stated' by the requester.

E. Common but Differentiated Responsibility: Principle 7 of the *Rio Declaration, 1992* requires states to cooperate in a spirit of global partnership to protect the environment. The principle recognizes that states should have common, but differentiated, responsibilities. Article 4 of the *UNFCCC, 1992* places an obligation on developed countries to take the lead in meeting the required reductions in greenhouse gas emissions. Developing country parties, however, are only obliged to implement these commitments to the extent that developed countries have met their commitments to provide financial resources to transfer technology. The structure of the *UNFCCC Kyoto Protocol, 1997* mirrors the philosophy of common but differentiated responsibility.

F. Polluter-Pays Principle: The *Polluter-Pays Principle* requires that the costs of pollution be borne by the party responsible. The practical implications of this principle lie in its allocation of economic obligations in environmentally damaging activities. This seemingly intuitive principle has not received broad support as precautionary principle. Principle 16 of *Rio Declaration, 1992* supports the "internalization of environmental costs" taking into account the polluter pays principle, but only "with due regard to the public interest and without distorting international trade and investment." The OECD Council recommendation on *Guiding Principles Concerning the International Economic Aspects of Environmental Policies, 1972* endorses the polluter-pays principle to allocate costs of pollution prevention and control measures, so as to encourage rational use of environmental resources.

Compliance and Enforcement of Sustainability

A range of techniques and panoply of international actors are today involved in the enforcement of international environmental law. The enforcement includes a wide array of forms including diffusion of information, monitoring, verification and inspection. In the context of international environment law the general principles of state responsibility and dispute settlement guided at enforcement of international environmental law. As the principal subjects of international law, states assume the obligation to enforce international environmental law. Enforcement by states arises primarily in situations of transboundary environmental harm and involves a determination by an international body, International Court of Justice (ICJ) in The Hague. The ICJ, the principal judicial organ of the United Nations interprets principles of international environmental law. International law agreements mandate implementation, reviews monitoring national compliance with the obligations undertaken under the environmental agreement. Such a review is based primarily on national self-reporting, although some conventions provide for independent means of gathering information. Other conventions may use incentives or disincentives; that are, adopt the "carrot and stick" approach, to obtain participation and ensure compliance.

The classic adjudication during the first part of the century was the *Trail Smelter Arbitration between Canada and the United States*, which affirmed Canada's responsibility for the damage from copper smelter fumes that transgressed the border into the state of Washington. The language of the Arbitral Tribunal has been widely cited as confirming the principle that a state is responsible for environmental damage to foreign countries that is caused by activities within its borders although arbitration is a rare in international environmental adjudication. The recognition of a common interest of States in the global environment may lead to international rules which are considered *erga omnes* applicable to all states and enforceable by all States. The ICJ in the well-known *Barcelona Traction* case, set forth this distinctive category: "(A)n essential distinction should be drawn between the obligations of a State towards the international community as a whole, and those arising *vis-à-vis* another State in the field of diplomatic protection. By their very nature the former are the concern of all States. In view of the importance of the rights involved, all States can be held to have a legal interest in their protection; as a matter of obligations under *erga omnes* doctrine."

Sustainable Development and Human Rights

There is a strong link between sustainable development, human rights and global environmental change. The human rights conventions and principles are relevant to issues of environmental change which include rights of participation, access to information, freedom of speech for the effective management of global environmental change. The problems created by global environmental change raise new issues for those rights already articulated, such as by the creation of environmental refugees and by the potential loss of a way of life by indigenous peoples of the Amazon or of the Arctic. There has been considerable discussion of a right to environment, either as implicitly found in existing human rights instruments or as part of a new articulation of rights. Finally, there is discussion of the rights of future generations in the global environment where intergenerational rights are not linked explicitly to human rights law. The sustainable development and human right synergy can be structurally conceived as having a three pillared, temple-like structure composed of international environmental law, international human rights law and international economic law suggested by Dominic Mc Goldrick.

	Sustainable Development	
	Pillar 2	
International Environmental Law	**International Human**	**International Economics Law**
	Rights Law	

The integrated structure of sustainable development is such that it requires support from each of the pillars. Its central pillar is international environmental law, a discipline of international law that has seen enormous growth in recent decades. The second pillar is international human rights law, that "human beings are at the centre of concern for sustainable development" and that they "are entitled to a healthy and productive life in harmony with nature". Being at the "centre of concern" is not the same as being at the centre of the concept. The third pillar is international economic law, which has similarly seen substantial progress, consensus and rule generation, most notably with the World Trade Organization and its 30 related agreements. The attractiveness of such a simple structure is that it presents sustainable development as integrating and interactive approach. It overarches a broad range of disciplines yet has elements of objective, process and principle.

Sustainable Development and Indian Response

Having roughly 16.6 per cent of the world's population, as well as a large number of the earth's unique ecosystems, India's obligation to the international environmental law is to protect its own environment and to refrain from degrading the global commons. India has traditionally adopted a dualist approach to treaty obligations. Its position on customary international law has been monistic in approach. The theory of parliamentary sovereignty and a quick survey of the Supreme Court rulings on treaty law in India reveal an interesting jurisprudence. There is good record of ratification of the major environmental treaties under judicial ruling and enlightened NGO community. Article 51 and 253 has great impact on the treatment of international law by the legislature as well as courts. The traditional tenets of monism and dualism are perfectly blended in matters of international environmental law. The Indian Courts by giving effects to Article 142 (1) recognized the doctrine of incorporation legal right deriving from customary international law. It would be enforceable by any one of the Supreme Court by order anything 'necessary for doing complete justice.' India blurs the distinction between monism and dualism as evident from the judicial recognition to polluter pays principle in reference to Article 130-R (2) of the *Treaty of Rome, 1957*.

Traditional international law is based on the territorial sovereignty of states, whose legal status is characterized by the three principles of sovereignty, independence, and equality. Thus, as the concept of appropriation — territorial sovereignty — fades out, as states are more and more considered and obliged to act inside the limits of their sustainable development jurisdiction for the interests of mankind. Ever since 1972, the scope of international agreements has expanded significantly: from transboundary pollution agreements to global pollution agreements, from preservation of designated species to conservation of ecosystems; from control of direct emissions into lakes to comprehensive river-basin-system regimes; from agreements that take effect national borders, such as those for world heritages and wetlands. The developments during the last 40 years have been thus to balance needs of the planetary solidarity rights, human rights and environmental justice.

References

A. Qureshi (1996). *The World Trade Organisation.* e.g. the Preamble to the Agreement Establishing the World Trade Organization refers to "allowing for the optimal use of the world's resources in accordance with the objective of sustainable development", GATT: The Results of the Uruguay Round of Multilateral Trade Negotiations (1994).

Ardeti Memeti *et al.*, The Concept of Erga Omnes Obligations In International Law, http://www.newbalkanpolitics.org.mk/item/the-concept-of-erga-omnes-obligations-in-international-law#.WLJ68H_DF_k

Brundtland to Rio (2012). Sustainable Development: Background Paper Prepared by John Drexhage and Deborah Murphy, International Institute for Sustainable Development (IISUSTAINABLE DEVELOPMENT) prepared for consideration by the High Level Panel on Global Sustainability at its first meeting, 19 September 2010 United Nations Headquarters, New York[GSP1-6-Page 7 of 26] *op cit*. An Atlantic article cites it See http://www.theatlantic.com/unbound/polipro/pp9904.htm.

Caccia, Charles (2001). *The Politics of Sustainable Development*, Hammond Lecture Series, Guelph University, 1 November.

Chasek, Pamela (2008). "Sustainable Development in the 21st Century." In Michael Snarr and D. Neil Snarr (eds.), *Introducing Global Issues*, Fourth edition. Boulder: Lynne Rienner.

Gabcikovo - Nagymaros Project (Hungary V. Slovakia) Judgement of 25 September 1997.

Generally: Lynton Keith Caldwell (1991). *International Environmental Policy Emergence and Dimensions*, 22.

Gordon Linsley and Wolfram Tonhauser. *An Expanding International Legal Regime Environmental Protection and Radioactive Waste Management*, https://www.iaea.org/sites/default/files/42304682429.PDF

Gro Harlem Brundtland (1987). *Our Common Future: World Commission on Environmental and Development*, 2-3 OUP, New Delhi.

Hopwood, Bill, Mary Mellor and O'Brien, Geoff. (2005). "Sustainable Development: Mapping Different Approaches." *Sustainable Development*, 13, pp. 38-52.

Inter-governmental Panel on Climate Change (2007). "Summary for Policymakers". In Martin L. Parry, Osvaldo F. Canziani, Jean P. Palutikof, Paul J. van der Linden and Clair E. Hanson (eds.), Climate Change 2007: Impacts, Adaptation and Vulnerability. Contribution of Working Group II to the Fourth Assessment Report of the Intergovernmental Panel on Climate Change. Cambridge: Cambridge University Press, at chapter 12.1.2

International Bank For Reconstruction and Development, World Development Report 1992: Development and Environment, 34 (1992).

Introduction Chapter 1. The Evolution Of International Environmental Law Pages 3-8; http://anthonydamato.law.northwestern.edu/IELA/Intech01-2001-edited.pdf

MacNeill, Jim. (2007). *Our Common Future: Advance or Retreat? Sustainable Development: A New Urgency*. Geneva: Eco Lomics International.

Matthews, Richard A. and Hammill, Anne (2010). "Sustainable Development and Climate Change", *International Affairs* 85(6): 1117-1128 at 1119.

Mc Goldrick, Dominic (1996). "Sustainable Development and Human Rights: An Integrated Conception", 45 *International and Comparative Law Quarterly*, 796.

Najam, Adil (1999). "World Business Council for Sustainable Development: The Greening of Business or a Greenwash?" In Helge Ole Bergesen, Georg Parmann, and Øystein B. Thommessen (eds.), *Yearbook of International Co-operation on Environment and Development 1999/2000*. London: Earthscan Publications, pp. 65–75.

Nicolaas J. Schrijver, (2008). "The Evolution of Sustainable Development", In *International Law: Inception, Meaning and Status*, Brill; Nijhoff.

P. Sands (1944). *International Law in the Field of Sustainable Development:* 65 B.Y.I.L., 303-305, asks which of these sustainable development is.

P. Sands (1995). *Principles of International Environmental Law*, Vol. 1. Achievement of the Millennium Development Goals requires the Conservation and Sustainable Use of Biological Diversity. Montreal,

12 September. Accessed at: http://www.unep.org/greenroom/documents/CBDrelease1209. pdf.

P. Sands (1995). Principles of International Environmental Law, Vol. 1. Birnie and Boyle, *op. cit.* supra n. 1. The Ksentini Report, infra n. 36, at para 24, notes: International environmental law has developed to such an extent that there are some 350 multilateral treaties, 1,000 bilateral treaties and a multitude of instruments of intergovernmental organizations that have been adopted in the form of declarations, programmes of action and resolution.
See also the Stockholm Declaration (1972). Principle 1.

P. Sands, R.G. Tarasofsky and M. Weiss (1995). *Documents in International Environmental Law*, Vol. IIA: 248.

R. Higgins (1995). *Problems and Process — International Law and How We Use It.*

Repetto, Pobert (1998). "Population, Resources, Environment: An Uncertain Future", *Population Bulletin*, Vol. 42, No. 2, 14-34.

Singh, Nagendra (1987). "Right to Environment and Sustainable Development As a Principle of International Law", 29(3) *Journal of the Indian Law Institute*, 292.

Trail Smelter Arbitration (U.S. v. Canada) Arbitral Trib., 3 U.N. Rep. Int'l Arbitral Awards 1905 (1941).

Case Concerning The Barcelona Traction, Light And Power Company, Limited (Second Phase) Judgment of 5th Feb., 1970.

U.N. Economic and Social Affairs (2006). *Trends in Sustainable Development*, New York: United Nations.

United Nations Development Programme, Human Development Report, 1-2 OUP, New York (1991).

United Nations Economic and Social Council (2002). Implementing Agenda 21: Report of the Secretary-General, Second Preparatory Session, 28 January 8 February 2002.

United Nations Secretary-General's High-level Panel on Global Sustainability (2012). *Resilient People, Resilient Planet: A future worth choosing*. New York: United Nations. 66-72

Weiss, Edith Brown (1990). "*Our Rights and Obligations To Future Generations for the Environment*", 84 *The American Journal of International Law*, 199 200.

World Resource Institute, World Resources 1992-93, Oxford Univ. Press: 1 (1992), New York.

29

Population and Sustainable Development

A Case Study of India

Aslam Mahmood

Introduction

Reduction in the human mortality is one of the major impact of Economic development on the human society. Such a reduction can take place either due to greater regularity in food supply (Coale and Hoover, 1958)[1] and/or due to advancement in medical technology or due to both (UN, 1953).[2] Another important demographic factor to show reduction is human fertility. In developing countries, however, the rapid growth of population may make it difficult to accomplish the goals of economic and social changes, which are necessary for fertility reduction (Coale & Hoover, 1953, p. 17). The process continues even today and will be highlighted if we compare the population growth and socio-economic development both in developed and developing countries of today.

Until the beginning of 1880s, the number of human population could reach only one billion (1000 million) and until 1960 it could reach only 3 billion mark. Figure 29.1 shows the movement of World population since the year 1800. As of August 2016, it was estimated at 7.4 billion[3]. The United Nations estimates it will further increase to 11.2 billion in the year 2100[4] (Figure 29.1). Now, roughly the world gains 1 billion people in every 12 years or around 80 million people each year, equivalent to 2,20,000 people a day (Engelman 1997, p. 11)[5].

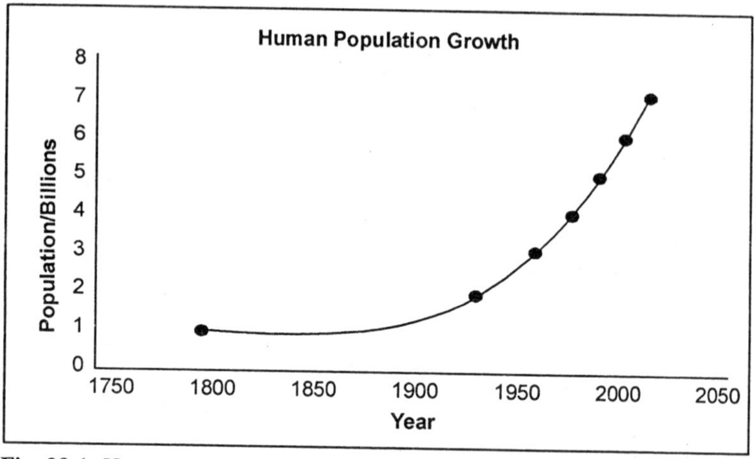

Fig. 29.1: Human Population Growth.

Throughout the history growth of population has been the concern of the human society for reasons depending on the situation. During preindustrial era, due to heavy human mortality; population was considered as an asset due to the requirements of the armed forces, agriculture and administration etc. Later, during the industrial revolution, followed by expansion of imperialism, also population was considered as an economic asset of any society to meet the labour requirement of the industry, management and public administration.

With the expansion of industrial revolution in the West the share of "Labour" and "Capital" in the production also started emerging as the basic issue, which later divided the world into two major camps of the "Capitalist World" and the "Socialist World". This was the period when economist like;[6] Malthus[6-7], (1766-1834) and others (Ed. 1960)[7], Marx[8] (1818-1883) and Ricardo[9] (1772 -1823) etc. devoted serious attention to the discussion on population and resources and reforms to the English Poor Law[10] were suggested.

In the post-industrial era of population explosion in the developing countries, due to reduction in human mortality and continued higher fertility, excessive growth of population was considered as undesirable *vis-à-vis* the infrastructure and the economic and social development among these countries.

Malthus Theory on Population

The consequences of population growing faster than the means of subsistence were initially outlined by Malthus (1959) in his famous essay on population. Thomas Robert Malthus (1766-1834) in his famous essay on population analysed the population growth and food supply in different countries of Europe (An Essay on the Principal of Population 1798) and formulated his world famous theory on population.

Malthus argument is that, given food the basic requirement of human society and passion for sex, growth of human population takes place in geometric progression and growth of resources take place in Arithmetic progression. If this is so no matter wherefrom we start, sooner or later population will surpass the resource limit as shown in Figure 29.2. In the graph dotted line showing the resources remains above the plane line showing the population for most of the time. However after time limit of 9 (in the present case) it fall short of population which over shoots. In such a situation either positive checks or preventive checks will take place to maintain the balance between the population and resources.

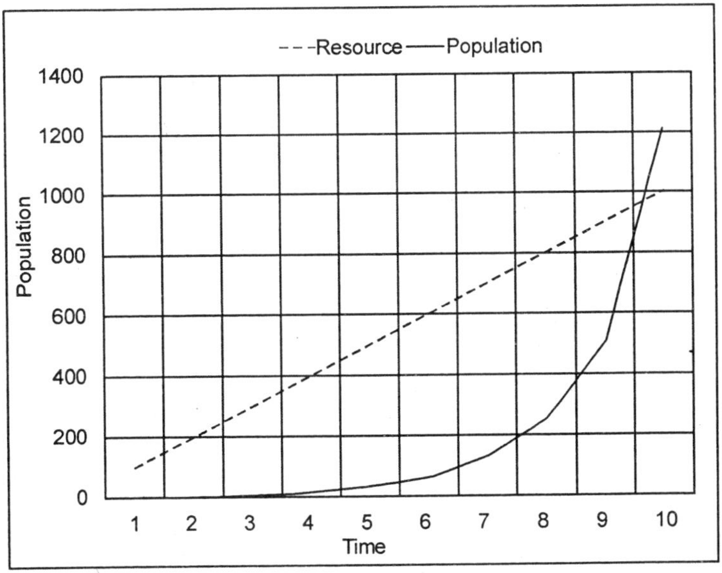

Fig. 29.2: Malthusian Paradigm.

Positive checks will be natural and may involve epidemics, famine, war and many other forms of natural calamities. To prevent positive checks human society can adopt some voluntary checks to control the growth of population such as delayed marriages, lower levels of reproduction rate etc. Malthus a faculty at Cambridge University was also a clergy man, so he did not advocate family planning through abortion. Various methods for preventive checks recommended by him were as given below.

Malthusian Preventive Checks

1. Malthus in his theory argued that in order to escape positive checks human society will have to take necessary preventive checks such as:
2. Abolition of charity through poor laws,
3. Discourage people to have larger size families, by
4. Depriving the labour from the leisure time by increasing working hours,
5. Keeping wages at lower level and make them busy in making both the ends to meet.
6. Reducing the living space, etc.

The whole approach of Malthusian doctrine was to make life difficult for the population specially, for working class, so that they do not find enough time for leisure and multiply.

Malthus has not been criticized for his basic theory as much as for his suggested preventive checks.

Malthus is criticized by economists, sociologists and others on account of not being able to foresee the emergence of modern methods of family planning. However, his main criticism was by the economists like Karl Marx and other socialists as his theory not only provided the basis to abolish the English poor law but was also picked up by the Capitalist to justify the reduction of share of labour in the production.

Karl Marx was of the view that the poor are not responsible for their miseries, it is the system which has not given them fair deal. Capitalists keep the wages at lower level to make labour poor. Through automation a large proportion of labour force is kept unemployed and labour loose its bargaining power. Further means of production of resources should be explored to make it also grow geometrically.

Population Growth and Food Supply

Growth of human population follows a "S" shaped Logistic Curve which almost all the living species also follow. Logistic curve was used by Pearl and Reed (1920) to study the growth of population of U.S.[11]

Logistic curve of growth in the context of the insects with abandoned but fixed supply of food has the following characteristics:

- Slow rate of growth in the beginning.
- As insects become aware of availability of plenty of food supply, they start multiplying faster.
- As more and more insects come to know about food supply the rate of growth become even faster and reaches a maximum when competition starts in getting the food.
- At this point the rate of growth gets a retardation but remains high.
- Further competition make life little difficult, so rate of growth further declines.
- Ultimately the population size stabilises at subsistence level.
- A logistic curve is concave in the beginning and changes its curvature when retardation starts and become convex and ultimately become parallel to X- axis showing zero rate of growth and the value of Y at which it stabilizes.
- The curve is asymptotic to X-axis at the left and to the line of stabilisation on the right.

Logistic Curve and Growth of Human Population

On the long term basis human population too is found to be following the Logistic Law of growth. Whole cycle of Logistic curve may take different time for different societies depending on their level of education and economic developments. When we observe the population growth of a society for a short period of time, we get only a part of the logistic curve it follows. Current population growth curve of many of the developing countries may be the first half of the curve showing exponential growth or a part of it. In the case of industrialised countries it could be the later half of the curve showing the declining growth rate, or stable position. The shape of a hypothetical population following the Logistic Curve is shown in Figure 29.3.

Demographic Transition Theory

Another important theory explaining rapid population growth in developing countries in the context of development is "the Demographic Transition Theory" propounded by Notestein (1945).[12] A good discussion

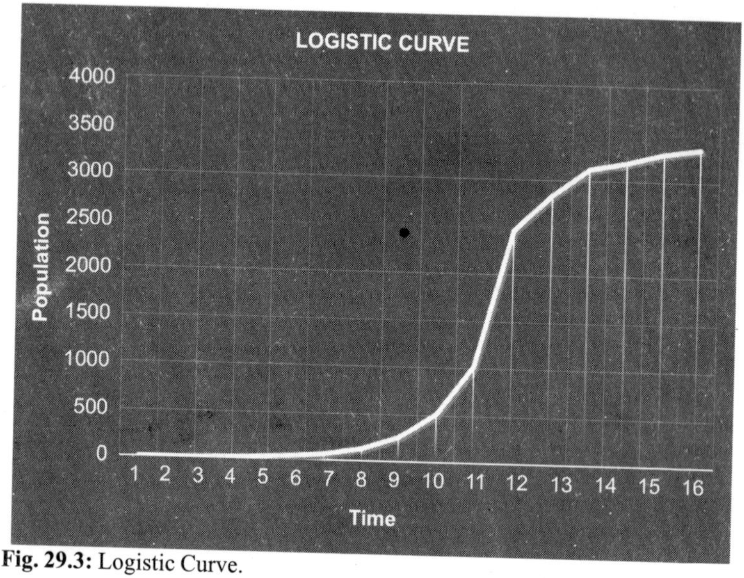

Fig. 29.3: Logistic Curve.

on it can also be found in Dudley Krik (1996).[13] Demographic Transition theory is yet another attempt to explain population growth in relation to the economic development. The theory as propounded by Frank Notestein divides the historical transition of population growth mainly into three main stages. These stages are given as:

Stage I: High fertility, high mortality resulting at a low growth rate of population as was the case in pre-industrial world with rampant influence of killer diseases. Europe 17th century.

Stage II: High fertility and low mortality resulting in higher population growth. Post-industrial revolution era characterized by advances in medical technology reducing mortality. Fertility remains high. Europe 17-18th Century.

Stage III: Low fertility and low mortality, resulting in low growth rate. Later pert of post-industrial revolution era when along with mortality fertility also declined due to higher education and overall social development and better quality of life. Europe 18th century onward.

Stage IV and V relate to stable and declining population, the stage yet not reached by developing countries.

The demographic transition from stage I to stage III is shown graphically in Figure 29.4. Time from 1 to 6 could be first stage of demographic transition characterise as high fertility and high mortality whereas time 7 to 14 could be related to second stage of demographic transition characterised as high fertility and low mortality and time level beyond 14 could be third stage and beyond characterised as low fertility and low mortality.

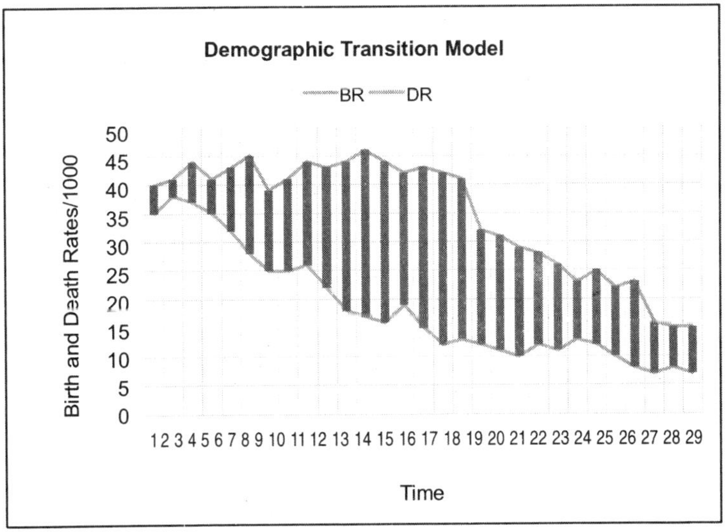

Fig. 29.4: Demographic Transition Model.

In the context of economic growth of western Europe and North America, Kuznet (1966) defined modern economic growth as a sustained increase in population which seldom exceeded 1.0 per cent per annum as compared to the rapid population growth of developing countries during the post-Second World War.

Towards the beginning of the second half of the twentieth century mortality in most of the developing countries started falling down dramatically without any accompanying fall in fertility. As a result, population growth rates in most of the developing countries registered unprecedented increase ranging from 2.0 to 4.0 per cent per annum.

Population Growth in Developed and Developing Countries

Although there is no unanimity among the scientists over the precise impact of population growth on development as tracing the cause and effect in this case is not direct. The cumulative evidence, however, is strong enough to suggest that current rates of population growth pose significant risk to the future of human population. In a short span of time we have noticed that the momentum of growth of human population has become a force and the human society has resolved to counter it by all means.

The growth rate of population in developed and developing countries of the world shown in Table 29.1 since the second half of the last century shows that the population growth rate of more developed regions of world has been consistently lower than the same in the less developed regions.

Table 29.1: Population Growth Rate of Developed and Developing Countries

Region	*Period*			
	1950-55	1990-95	1995-2000	2045-50
More Developed	1.21	0.40	0.26*	–0.23*
Less Developed	2.05	1.77	1.65*	0.55*

Source: World Population Prospects the 1996 version, UN 1998, p. 10.
*Projected.

To understand it in further detail, fertility and mortality the main components of the growth of population are compared for the two regions of the world in the next stage.

Indicators of "Total Fertility Rate" (TFR) and "Crude Death Rate" (CDR) the main components of population growth for "Developed" and "Developing" countries are given in Table 29.2 for the last forty years of the twentieth Century. The Table shows that much of the reduction in the population growth rate of the developed countries is due to a relatively faster decline in TFR as compared to the decline in the death rates which was already very low. Mortality rather has shown a marginal rise in the last decade of the twentieth century due the increasing proportion of population in the older ages. A situation similar to the third stage of demographic transition. In the developing countries, however, due to lack of required socio-economic development, the fertility remains largely unaffected and the decline in the CDR is found to be much faster than the decline in their respective TFR, a situation similar to the second stage of demographic transition showing a rapid population growth. The longer the developing countries remain in the second stage of their demographic transition higher will be the accumulation of population in the younger ages and population explosion will continue.

Table 29.2: Trends of Fertility and Mortality in the World, Developed Countries 1950-95

Period	*World*		*Developed Countries*		*Less Developed Countries*	
	TFR	CDR	TFR	CDR	TFR	CDR
1960-65	5.0	15.6	2.7	9.4	6.0	18.2
1965-70	4.9	13.4	2.4	9.4	6.0	15.0
1970-75	4.5	11.7	2.1	9.4	5.4	12.0
1975-80	3.9	11.0	1.9	9.5	4.7	11.5
1980-85	3.6	11.0	1.8	9.6	4.1	10.5
1985-90	3.4	9.6	1.8	9.6	3.8	9.6
1990-95	3.0	9.3	1.7	10.1	3.3	9.1

Source: World Population Prospects 1996 version UN 1998, p. 20.
TFR = Total Fertility Rates, CDR, = Crude Death Rate (per 1000).

Infant Mortality Rate is another important indicator of population transition. It reflects not only the level of mortality of any society but also indicate the awareness of the society about the population issues. It is a very powerful composite indicator of literacy, health status, population awareness etc. of a society. Table 29.3 gives the IMR for the Developed and the Developing countries of the World for the same period of the last century.

The lack of social infrastructure and its influence on demographic variables can also be seen by taking infant mortality rates (IMR) both for developed and less developed countries as shown in Table 29.3. The Table shows a considerable fall in the IMR in developed countries during the same period of 1960-65 to 1990-95. It fell down to 11 from 33 per thousand during this period — something around 66 per cent decline. In less developed countries also the value of IMR declined but from 135 to 68 per thousand only during the same period — a decline of less than 50 per cent. As IMR is a very sensitive indicator of socio-economic development, the data given in Table 29.3 do indicate a higher socio-economic status of the developed countries. It has been pointed out that right from the beginning of the industrial revolution in Europe, cultural and other developmental factors kept fertility much below the biological maximum (Population Crisis Committee, 1985)

Thus we note that as a result of development in medical technology benefit reach to both the developed countries as well as to less developed countries. However, developing countries due to lacking infrastructure and lower levels of are not in a position to make the advantage of it as much as the developed countries do. As a result there is no parallel fall in the fertility in the developing countries as will be the case in developed countries. Many of the less developed countries, therefore, are likely to continue in the second stage of demographic transition with rapid population growth for quite some time in future. Social development in these countries should not be ignored for long.

Table 29.3: Infant Morality Rate (IMR) for Developed and Less Developed Countries 1960-65 and 1990-95

Year	IMR		
	World	Developed Countries	Less Developed Countries
1960-65	118	33	135
1965-70	102	26	115
1970-75	93	21	104
1975-80	87	18	98
1980-85	78	1	87
1985-90	69	13	76
1990-95	62	11	68

Source: World Population Prospects 1996 version UN 1998, p. 7.

Population Growth and Development in India

Census of India in 2001 recorded the population of India about 1027.02 million as on 1st March 2001 given it the share in the world population of about 16 per cent from 15.2 per cent in 1981.

Table 29.4 gives the population of India (according to present boundaries) and its decadal growth rate for last century. The population of India in 2001 was found to be around three times the population at the time of independence. Another highlight of the table is a consistent increase in the population of the country after 1921. The rate of population growth during 1921-31 was 11.0 per cent, which also kept on increasing until 1971-81 when it reached the maximum of 24.7 per cent per decade. Only during 1981-91 and in 1991-2001, the decadal growth rate of population showed a marginal decline in relation to the previous decades and reached 23.5 per cent per decade and 21.9 respectively. Between 2001-2011, however, the decadal rate of population growth showed a significant decline and registered a growth rate of 17.7 per cent, indicating the positive impact of the sustained government policies of population control.

Table 29.4: Population of India 1901-2001

Year	*Population (in million)*	*Decadal Growth Rate*
1901	238.4	—
1911	252.1	5.7
1921	251.3	–0.3
1931	279.0	11.0
1941	318.7	14.2
1951	361.1	13.3
1961	439.2	21.5
1971	548.2	24.8
1981	683.3	24.7
1991	843.9	23.5
2001	1028.6	21.9
2011	1210.2	17.7

Source: Census of India 2011.

One of the direct consequences of rapid population growth is on the age structure of the population. Percentage distribution of the population of India in three age groups (0-14, 15-59 and 60+) is given in Table 29.5 from1901 to 2011.

The share of 0-14 years has been very large all through the decades.[14] There has been a marginal increase in the aged population 60 years and above age group. The age group of 15-59, however, registered a marginal increase also, due to the increase in the group 60 years and above. The increase in the proportion of the elderly population indicates towards future emphasis on old age care programmes of the country. Population share of the age group (0 – 14) years has shown a consistent decline from 1961 onward and has reached from 41.00 to 30.89 from 1961 to 2011.

Along with developments in science and technology not only the world population has increased but the means of subsistence have also been improved. In the following section, therefore, changes in some of the socio-economic variables having close relationship with population are also discussed.

Table 29.5 provides literacy rates and also total number of illiterates in India after independence.[15] Table shows an overall improvement in the proportions of literates to the total population which has increased from 16.6 per cent in 1951 to 40.7 per cent in 1991. Improvement in the literacy of female however is quite remarkable. It has registered a phenomenal increase from 7.9 per cent in 1951 to 64.46 per cent in 2011. The literacy of male during this period could also increase around four times from 24.9 in 1951 to 82.14 per cent in 2011. Total population of illiterates is gradually declining yet it constitute the major part of the world illiterates.

Table 29.5: Percentage Distribution of Population of India in Different Age Groups 1901-91

Year	*Age Groups*		
	0-14	*15-59*	*60+*
1901	38.60	56.35	5.05
1911	38.45	56.40	5.15
1921	39.20	55.55	5.25
1931	40.00	55.95	4.05
1941	38.25	56.85	4.95
1951	37.50	56.85	5.65
1961	41.00	53.36	5.64
1971	42.02	52.01	5.97
1981	39.54	53.98	6.48
1991	37.25	55.98	6.77
2001	35.44	57.09	7.47
2011	30.89	60.55	8.56

Source: UN 1982 Population of India: Country Monograph series No 10, New York and Census of India 1991, 2001, 2011.

Table 29.6: Literacy Rates of India 1951-2011

Year	*Literacy rates (in per cent)*			*Illiterates (in million)*		
	Total	*Male*	*Female*	*Total*	*Male*	*Female*
1951	16.6	24.9	7.9	—	—	—
1961	28.3	30.9	15.3	333.9	148.5	135.4
1971	29.5	39.5	18.7	386.5	171.9	214.6
1981	26.7	39.5	16.8	424.2	182.6	241.8
1991	40.7	53.6	27.0	491.8	213.3	278.5
2001	65.38	75.85	54.16	450.3	191.3	269.0
2011	74.04	82.14	65.46	282.4	98.0	184.4

Source: M.K. Premi (1991). *India's Population: Heading Towards a Billion,* B.R. Publishing Corp. and Census of India 2001.

Sectoral division of workers as provided by Census of India from 1951 to 2001 is given in Table 29.6. Table shows a slow decline in the share of primary sector and a marginal increase in the secondary sector accompanied by substantial increase in the tertiary sector. Primary sector in the country has declined from 72.3 per cent in 1961 to 57.1 per cent in 2001. Tertiary sector, however, has shown an increase from 16.0 per cent to 25.8 per cent during the same period. Secondary sector which is the core of industrialization, however, has not shown significant increase in this period — although it has also improved from 11.7 per cent to 17.1

per cent during 1961-2001. The Table highlights one of the very important aspects of the population growth on the economy of the developing countries. It indicates clearly that as population grows there is not a matching growth in the formal job market. Most of the people are getting themselves adjusted to informal tertiary sector having low wages and self-employment.

Table 29.7: Sectoral Division of Workers, India 1961-2001

Year	Sector			Total
	Primary	Secondary	Tertiary	
1961	72.3	11.7	16.0	100.0
1971	72.6	10.7	16.7	100.0
1981	69.3	12.9	17.8	100.0
1991	67.4	12.1	20.5	100.0
2001	57.1	17.1	25.8	100.0

Source: M.K. Premi (1991). *India's Population: Heading Towards a Billion*, B.R. Publishing Corp. and Census of India 2001.

Another important area which is seriously influenced by population is land utilization. Percentage of net area sown,[7] and area put to non-agricultural uses is given in Table 29.7 along with area sown more than once from 1951 to 2001.

Table 29.8: Percentage of Net Area Sown, and Area Put to Non-Agricultural Uses and Area Sown More than Once

Year	Total Area (million hectare)	% Area under forest	Percentage of net sown area	Percent uncultivated area	Percent fallow land	Percent of area put to non-agri. uses	Total	Percentage sown more than once
1950-51	284.39	14.23	41.79	17.39	9.88	16.71	100	4.62
1960-61	298.46	18.11	44.63	12.61	7.65	17.00	100	3.21
1970-71	303.76	21.04	46.18	11.54	6.54	14.70	100	8.40
1980-81	304.15	22.18	46.06	10.62	8.11	13.03	100	10.73
1990-91	305.02	22.44	46.26	9.96	7.86	13.48	100	14.31
1991-2001	306.01	22.55	46.16	9.30	8.13	13.86	100	15.43

Source: Central Statistical Organization (2004) Statistical Abstract India, CSO, New Delhi.

The table clearly shows a consistent increase of net sown area as well as area sown more than once as an important consequence of population growth. The table shows a big success story of Indian agriculture which shows that percentage area sown more than once significantly increased from 4.62 per cent of 1950-51 to 15.43 in 2001.

Another important consequence of population growth is on the land put to non-agricultural uses such as urban and industrial purposes. The table also shows a consistent decrease in percentage of uncultivated area from 17.377 in 1951 to 9.30 in 2001.

In the context of the developing countries, the effect of population growth is likely to be more serious on the agricultural production. Table 29.8 shows the total amount of production of cereals and pulses in absolute as well as in per capita terms after independence.

Table 29.9: Absolute and Per Capita Production of Food Grain in India 1950-2001

Year	*Production (million tonnes)*		*Per capita (kg/person)*	
	Cereals	*Pulses*	*Cereals*	*Pulses*
1950-51	42.414	8.41	117.48	23.29
1960-61	69.314	12.70	157.82	28.91
1970-71	96.604	11.82	176.24	21.56
1980-81	118.962	10.63	174.09	15.56
1990-91	162.124	14.26	191.58	16.85
2000-01	188.460	11.08	183.22	10.77

Source: Handbook of Statistics on the Indian Economy, Reserve Bank of India, 2002-03.

The table shows a phenomenal increase in the total production of food grain cereals which was 42.42 million tonnes in1950-51 and increased to 4.4 times in 2000-01 and reached to 188.46 million tonnes. Population of India during the same period could change from 361.09 million to 1028.61 million only, recording a change of less than three times. As a result, the growth of the production of cereals per capita has been found to be continuously increasing during the post-independence period. It was 117.48 kg. In 1950-51 which almost doubled by 1990-91 and reached the level of 191.58 kgs. The last decade, however, has shown a slackness also as the per capita production has gone down from 191.58 to 183.22 kgs. in the decade of 1990-91 to 2000-01.

Another important food grains are pulses, production of which has also increased but only by about one and a half time during this period. It was 8.41 million tonnes in 1950-51 which could rise to 11.08 million tonnes in the year 2000-01. Since the growth of population during 1951 to 1961 is about two and a half times, the per capita production of pulses has gone down drastically from 23.29 kgs. to 10.77 kgs. during the same period.

Unsustainable burden of rapid population growth has its impact on the quality of life of the people also. It is important to note that position of the major countries of the sub-continent of India in terms of 'Human Development Index' prepared by UNDP[17] is not very encouraging. Out of total 174 countries in 1998 report, India ranks 139th much below China which rank 106th. Pakistan in spite of substantial higher per capita real income is only one rank above India due to lower 'Adult Literacy Rate'. Its position is 138th. However, it has climbed 8 notches and in 215 reports its rank was 130 out of 188 countries of the World due to improvement in per capita income and longevity of life etc.

Conclusion

To summarize the above discussion we can say that although population is one of the very important assets of any economy, rapid population growth of less developed countries is likely to create a bottleneck for the development. Developing countries lag far behind to create the required infrastructure matching the need of the growing population. A vicious circle is created. Lack of better quality of life and education do not create a situation conducive for the decline in the fertility. The case study of India shows that although, relatively some of the sectors such as education and food supply etc. may have registered an increase during the post-independence period, it is very unlikely that this increase will be sustainable in future. Performance of the secondary sector is very slow. A large proportion of the growth in the various sectors of the economy is being offset by the growth in population. There are some sectors where per capita value has registered a decline also alongwith the growth of population such as per capita available land (as cultivable land does not increase with the population) and per capita production of pulses etc. such sectors need even more attention.

Unprecedented growth of population accompanied by overall development throughout the globe has been the hallmark of the last century. However, there are regional as well as temporal patterns in this relationship. With increasing burden of population on resources, both developing as well as developed countries have started showing a tendency of reduction in the growth of their population. In their response, however, developing countries lag far behind the developed countries. At regional levels also it is found that different regions and communities have different attitude towards the growth of their population. Any debate on finding motives behind these differentials has generated more controversies than any clarity. In the present study, therefore, an attempt has been made to highlight the relationship between population growth and development in the developed and the developing countries with particular emphasis on India.

The study has used population data from the beginning of the last century and its projections up to the first half of the present century as provided by UN for developed and developing counties of the world. For country study the population data used in the study is as provided by the Census of India in its different reports. The study shows that the differences in the population growth are mainly attributed to fertility differentials across different groups of population. Mortality differentials, in the present context, do not play any significant role. As even after sustained efforts of reduction of fertility its level is still higher in developing countries. Reduction of fertility plays a key role in controlling the growth of population. However, unlike mortality, fertility is found to be more sensitive to the conditions of social and economic development. Co-variation of population growth with several social and infrastructural variables suggest that in India social and economic condition have shown signs of fertility reduction but still have not reached the level to achieve the goals of population control. The chapter emphasizes on the fact that the phenomenal success of India on food production and literacy etc., suggests that if similar efforts are made in social sectors also, population control will not be an unachievable target.

Notes

1. Coale, A.J., and Edger Houver (1958). *Population growth and economic development in low income countries: A case study of India's prospects.* Princeton, N.J.: Princeton University Press, pp. 10-11.
2. UN (1953). *The Determinants and consequences of population trends.* Deptt. of Social Affairs Population Division, Population Studies No. 17, New York, pp. 56-61.
3. "2016 World Population Data Sheet". Population Reference Bureau. Retrieved September 15, 2016.
4. "World Population Prospects—Population Division—United Nations". esa.un.org. Retrieved 2016-09-15.
5. Engelman, R. (1997). *Why Population matters.* Washington: Population Action International, p. 11.

6. Malthus, Thomas Robert (1959). *Population: The First essay.* Am Abor Ann Arbor Paperback.
7. Malthus Thomas (1960). *A Summary view of the principles of population in Three essays on Population* eds., Thomas Malthus, Julian Huxley and F. Osborn, New York,: Mentor Books, pp. 13-59.
8. Karl Marx (1818-1883). *General Law of Capital Accumulation,* Chapter XXV Capital.
9. Ricardo, David. (1919). *Principles of Political Economy and Taxation.*
10. English Poor Laws were a system of relief from 1536 onward and were modified in 1834 to provide workhouses run by poor law Unions.
11. Pearl R. and Reed L.J., (1920). "On the Rate of Growth of the population of United States since 1790 and its mathematical representation, *Proceedings of National Academy of Sciences*, 6, I, Population and Resources.
12. Frank W. Notestein (1945): "Population—The Long View" in Theodore W. Schults (cd.) *Food for the World*, Chicago University Press.
13. Kirk, Dudley (1996). "Demographic transition theory", *Population Studies*, Vol. 50, No. 3, pp. 361-387. Kuznet Simon (1966), *Modern economic growth.* New Haven ct: Yale University Press, p. 20.
14. UN 1982 and 2015. Population of India: Country Monograph series No. 10, New York and Census of India 1991, 2001.
15. Census of India 1961, 1971, 1981 and 1991. M.K. Premi (1991). *India's Population: Heading towards a billion*, B.R. Publishing Corp. and Census of India 2001.
16. Central Statistical Organization (2004). Statistical Abstract India, CSO, New Delhi.
17. United Nations Development Programme (1998). Human Development Report, United Nations Development Programme, New York.

30

Science, Technology and Development

Md. Kalimuddin Ahmad

Introduction

With the advent of cheap microprocessors, computers became affordable tool in our day-to-day life. Why not to use it as an aid in imparting education to students in more effective way? With the availability of internet, the computers can be connected to worldwide treasure of knowledge enabling us to access the information while sitting in a remote place; thus making the concept of global village a reality. Now question arises as how to use this modern hi-tech and continuously evolving technology for spreading education to masses.

In many of the advanced countries, the conventional use of black boards are supplemented with the computer based technology. Our problem is how to address the need of rural India with the changing technological advancement in the urban sector. It is true that a section of India is tuned to the development and adapting to the technology in imparting education to students. But a large section of population is not at all in a position to go side by side with the development—partly because lack of infrastructure and non-availability of well trained teachers.

Lyotard (1984) in his paper has lamented the possible replacement of teachers by computers and other technological devices and mentioned "*If computer can transfer more information to more students in a shortest time span and at lower cost then the efficiency of technology will force teachers out of business*". It is to be mentioned here that computers can never substitute a teacher rather it would assist them in organizing and imparting their lectures in more effective way.

Right now, the adaptation of technology in school education is moving at a snail's pace, while the world outside is speeding at a supersonic rate. The challenge before us is to prepare the children of today *for a world that has yet to be created, for jobs yet to be invented, and for technologies yet un-dreamed.*

Educational Technology: Educationist's View

An adequate knowledge of educational technology and their proper use would enable the teacher to effectively discharge his new role in the educational system in an age of information explosion, knowledge explosion, and population explosion.

Takashi Sakanato (1971) rightly mentioned, *"The educational technology is an applied or practical study which aims at maximizing educational effects by controlling such relevant facts as educational purposes, educational content, teaching materials, educational methods, educational environment, conduct of students, behaviour of instructors and interrelations between students and instructors."*

Therefore, the educational technology not only plays an important role in improving learning through instructional practices but also acts as a catalyst to facilitate change from a more traditional approach to a greater independence for students towards constructive learning. The educational technology needs to be employed in the spread of useful information, the training and retraining of teachers, to improve quality, and to sharpen awareness of art and culture.

Emerging Educational Technologies

Web based education and training programmes are widely offered at educational institutions and companies today. E-learning is defined as the delivery of contents via all electronic media including the internet, intranets, extranets, satellite broadcasts, audio/video tape, interactive TV, and CD-ROM. The web today is used in three different ways by educational institutions:

- Web integration in the class room teaching that works as supplement to the face to face teaching.
- Web used as a mixed mode approach to complement normal

teaching which is normally called blended e-learning.

- Web used independently for teaching and learning as replacement of normal teaching.

Advantages of Educational Technology

Student Achievement: Technology has been proven to help students achieve in reading, writing, and arithmetic. Technology gives educators one more tool to help them reach those goals. Students become engaged and can often facilitate parent involvement at home.

Professional Requirements: Not only does technology benefit students in the education system, it also benefits the educator. There are so many opportunities for teachers to learn and acquire new skills over the internet.

Meeting Special Needs: With the help of Technology, the students with disabilities have been able to achieve remarkable success that would not have been possible otherwise. Technology creates individualized learning environments for students and can play a major role in special needs.

Continuing Education: Technology has also made it possible for those who couldn't finish college or high school to get back into things. Technology brings the learning right to students wherever they may be.

Workforce skills: And last, but certainly not the least, technology has served students well because it has provided them with the skill and knowledge they need to enter the workforce.

Thus, Technology used in the classroom helps students absorb the material. For example, since some people are visual learners, projection screens linked to computers can allow students to see their notes instead of simply listening to a teacher deliver a lecture. Software can be used to supplement class curriculum.

Mathematics: Mother of all Sciences and Technologies

Likewise with the advancement in information technology, there happened to be a definite shift in teaching and research methodology of all subject fields. Mathematics which is the mother of all sciences needs special attention while designing syllabus or developing curricular at different level of education. During last several years, there have been major changes in this subject, both with regard to its significance in other branches and the tools available with us.

Whether it is conditional proposition and syllogisms of Ibn Sina, the work of many other logicians or the work of Nobel Laureate of literature, Bertrand Russell in Mathematical logic, these all lead to modern day fields of artificial intelligence, Computer Science and fuzzy logic; Mathematics has been enriched through this interdisciplinary approach. The Arabs even produced, in Omar Khayyam, a great poet and a great Mathematician who classified equations of the third degree into 25 categories and then attempted to solve them.

The importance of Mathematics can be gauged from the commentary of Proclus, who lived some time in fifth century AD:

> Mathematics arouses our innate knowledge, awakens our intellect, purges our understanding, brings to light the concepts that belong essentially to us, takes away the forgetfulness and ignorance that we have from birth, sets us free from the bonds of unreason; and all this by the favour of the god [Hermes?] who is truly the patron of this science, who brings our intellectual endowments to light, fills everything with divine reason, moves our souls towards Nous [the highest form of knowledge], awakens us as it were from our heavy slumber, through our searching turns us back upon ourselves, through our birth pangs perfects us, and through the discovery of pure Nous leads us to the blessed life. (*Proclus: A Commentary on the First Book of Euclid's Elements*, translated by Glenn R. Morrow, Princeton University Press, 1970, p. 38).

Well, the plight of Mathematics education in our country at the college level has remained quite dismal. The major drawbacks are lack of sufficient number of well-trained teachers and library facilities. This has become one of the major causes of "Math Phobia" among students.

There is an urgent need of improvement of Mathematics teaching in Indian Institutions. The Indian Society of Industrial and Applied Mathematics (ISIAM) right from its inception at Aligarh Muslim University has done yeoman services in this direction. ISIAM has arranged many workshops across the country to train the trainers. However, taking in view of application and wide acceptability of Mathematics in all subject fields much more coordinated efforts are needed.

Several years ago the Nobel Prize Winner from Pakistan Prof. A. Salam, who founded the ICTP in Trieste wrote "*it is a kind of Machiavellism to export technology to the third world without developing science there.*" Neunzert et al. further added, "*it seems to be Machiavellism too, to cultivate pure science without explaining how it can contribute to the industrial development. Teaching and practicing industrial mathematics could be an step away from this Machiavellism.*"

In most of the European universities, the central activity starts from the 2nd semester onwards in the form of modeling seminar. Problems from the real word are presented in a non-mathematical way to groups of 4-5 students; these groups work one semester under a supervisor who plays the role of an industrial client. They transform the problem into a mathematical model, evaluate the model using computer facilities, re-interpret the results in terms of the original problem, and finally present their results. Thus, Mathematics, especially "Industrial/Applied Mathematics", is learnt by doing as Modeling seminars are the opposite of "learning by heart".

Neunzert *et al.* rightly mentioned, *"Only recently the 3rd world began to receive the message of Industrial Mathematics. Therefore, there is an acute shortage of properly educated mathematicians. There are, of course, some excellent pure mathematicians and quite a number of good applied mathematicians in the traditional British sense. But their work is mainly "method driven" ("I do, what I am able to do"), but not problem driven ("I do, what should be done"). Academic careers make this attitude necessary: One has to belong to a scientific family (even if it is very small), one has to publish (even if it is a generalization of a generalization) in order to be promoted. Who dares to work on a modeling problem, when he/she does not know, which kind of mathematics is needed, what the result will be, where it should be published, who (besides may be a company) will be interested in? However: Real career jumps need surprising results, new problems and new ideas — all that could not be expected without taking a risk! Moreover, senior professors do not need a security belt when working on new problems; they could go ahead and give the young scientists a chance and some credit to work on industrial problems. Obviously, the pressure comes from outside: Governments press scientists to contribute to the economic welfare of their countries. Does this really mean a cultural loss? Once more: The very few very best have some right to maintain that — and it is the duty of the many others to protect them, to protect them by proving that their ideas and mathematics as a whole is one of the most useful and valuable technologies."*

What Needs to be done?

- To establish linkage between theory and practice.
- Simulation of well-known models on computer screen (e.g. simulation of casting process etc.).

- To train the trainers.
- To establish centres that could be interdisciplinary in nature.

What does Applied/Applicable/Industrial Mathematics mean?

- To transform Technical, Organizational and Economic problems of Industry (originally posed in non-mathematical language) into mathematical problems. **(Modeling)**
- To solve these problems, by applying modern numerical techniques, with the help of Computers. **(Computation)**
- To interpret the results in terms of original problems. **(Usefulness)**

In short, Industrial Mathematics is basically Modeling and Scientific Computing of Industrial problems and Industrial/Applied Mathematicians are in fact bridge builders from the field of Mathematics to the practical world.

Few Reputed Centres

- ECMI : European Consortium for Mathematics in Industry
- ITWM : Institute of Techno and Business Mathematics, Germany
- OCIAM : Oxford Centre for Industrial and Applied Mathematics
- CSIRO : The Commonwealth Scientific and Industrial Research Organization, Australia
- PIMS : The Pacific Institute for Mathematical Sciences, University of British Columbia, Vancouver, Canada

Many more in USA and other parts of the world.

An Overview of Problems and their Study (undertaken by author's Research Group)

- Analysis of Signals/Images
  (useful in Medical Sciences, Remote Sensing, Stock Exchange, Weather forecasting, Seismic data analysis)
- Image Compression especially for Storage/Transmission)
- Classification of Images helpful in choosing compression techniques)

- Denoising edge detection etc.)
- Defect detection for Car Industry/Furniture Industry)

Analysis of ECG Signals

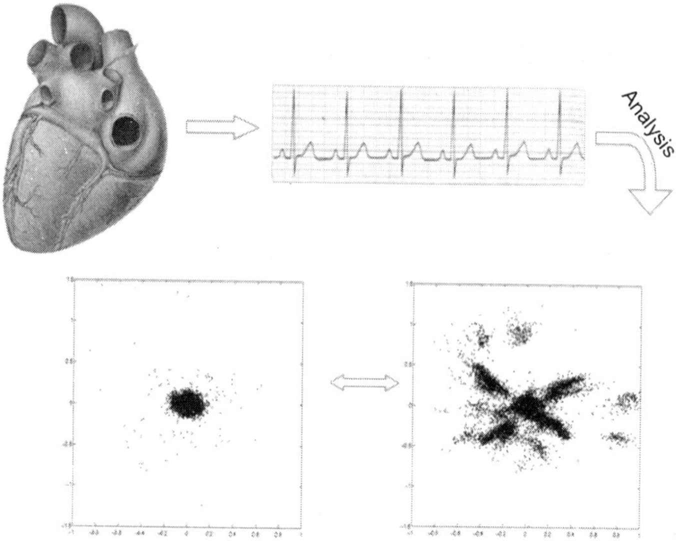

Sampling Theory in Signal and Image Processing (STSIP), 8(2) 2009.
Authors: M.K. Ahmad, H. Knaf and P. Lang.

Image Compression

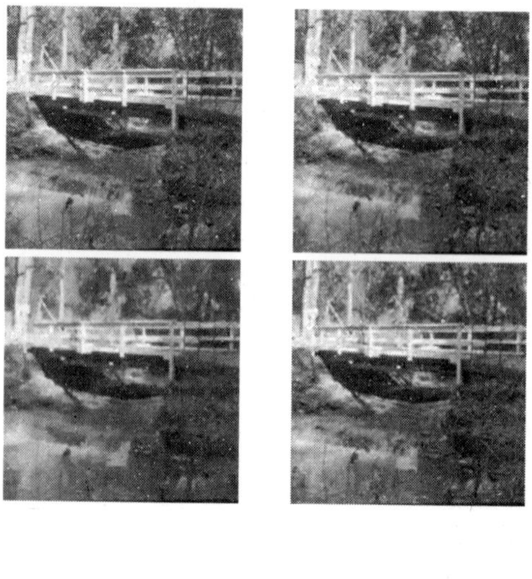

Denoising (PDE based diffusion)

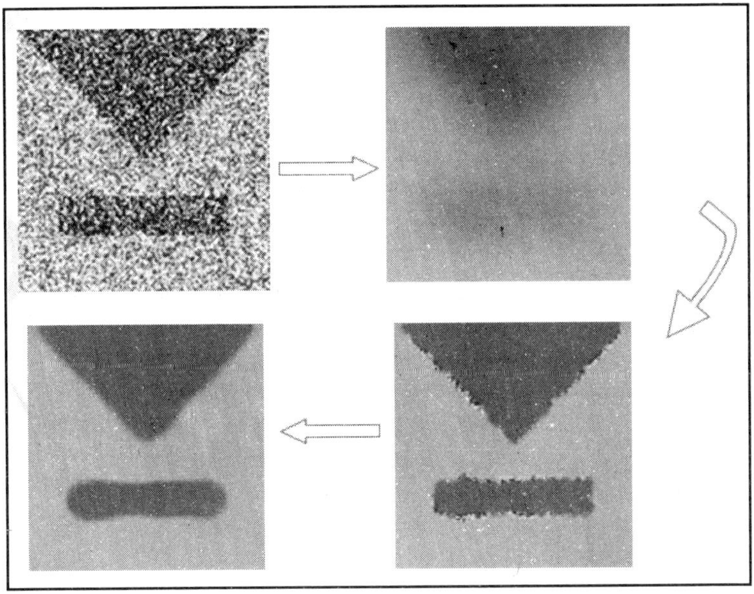

Conclusion and Remarks

The teaching of Mathematics is necessary for the growth and development of a country as it is useful in every domain of life. Thus, properly imparting mathematical values to the masses is the need of the hour. We must take insights from the European methods and implement them in order to accelerate the growth of our nation.

The educational technology goes hand in hand with the scientific development. It is now almost established that students learn more in classes in which they receive computer based instruction and have more positive attitude towards the subject matter being taught. It is also true that the students learn their lessons in less time with computer based instruction.

Therefore, it is imperative to extend such hi-tech facilities in every institution of the country; though this is a difficult task. The government must come-up with a concrete plan so as to address the needs of our future generation. To start with, all the schools in the country must be equipped with a computer lab and at least one modern class room furnished with all sorts of hi-tech appliances; otherwise it would become too late to cope with the fast changing world. Together with infrastructure, equally important is the continuing education programme of teachers.

References

Agarwal, J.C. (2006). *Essentials of Educational Technology: Teaching Learning*, Vikas Publishing House, New Delhi.

Ibn Sina, Abu Ali, al-Shifa: al-Qiyas [ed. by S. Zayed], Cairo 1964, 229-425. *The lithographed edition of al-Shifa*, published in Tehran in 1886 AD includes only the Physics and Metaphysics (in two volumes).

Joseph, G.G. (1994). *The Crest of the Peacock, Non-European roots of Mathematics*, Penguin book.

Klir, George J. and Yuan, Bo (2000). *Fuzzy sets and Fuzzy logics, Theory and Applications*, Prentice-Hall of India, Pvt. Ltd., New Delhi.

Lyotard, J.-F. (1984). *The postmodern condition: A Report on Knowledge*, Minneapolis, University of Minnesota Press.

Muthuchamy, I. and Thiyagu, K. (2009). "U-Learning: The next generation of learning", *University News*, 47(41) Oct. 12-18, 23-26.

Neunzert, H. and Siddiqi, A.H. (1997). *Industrial Mathematics — Ideas and Examples*, Report No. 177, Deptt. of Mathematics, University of Kaiserslautern, Germany.

Shehaby, Nabil (1973). The propositional logic of Avicena, A translation from al-Shifa: al-Qiyas, D. Reidel Publishing Company, Dordrecht-Holland/ Boston-USA.

Talwar, M.S. and Kumar, T. Pradeep (2009). "Podcasting: A new trend of web based technology in education", *University News*, 47(30) July 27-Aug. 02, 13-15.

Ulchida, D. (1996). *Preparing students for the 21st century*, Virginia, American Association of School Administrator.

Zadeh, L.A. (1965). *Fuzzy sets, Information and Control*, 8(3): 338-353.

Zepp, Raymond A. (2005). "Teachers' perceptions on the roles on education technology", *Education Technology and Society*, 8(2): 102-106.

Index